AA

Explorer
Germany

AA Publishing

Front cover
Top: *the modern dome of the Reichstag, Berlin* (Simon McBride); Centre (left to right): (a) *half-timbered houses in Maulbronn* (Max Jourdan); (b) *snowboarding on the Zugspitze* (Max Jourdan); (c) *spring flowers in Munich* (Tony Souter); (d) *the Golden Griffin statue in Potsdam* (Simon McBride); (e) *foaming beer steins at Munich's Oktoberfest* (Tony Souter)
Spine: *drinking a stein of beer in Munich's Hofbrauhaus* (Clive Sawyer)
Back cover
Left: *the Fuggerei houses in Augsburg* (Max Jourdan); Right: *Schloss Sanssouci, Potsdam* (Simon McBride)

All pictures from AA World Travel Library

Busy Marienplatz, Munich (opposite)

Written by John Ardagh, Lindsay Hunt, Michael Ivory, Tim Locke, Michael Kallenbach, Stephen Locke, Colin and Fleur Speakman
Additional writing and research by Tony Evans, Audrey Horne and Robert Tilley
Updated by Teresa Fisher

Published by AA Publishing, a trading name of Automobile Association Developments Limited, whose registered office is Fanum House, Basing View, Basingstoke, Hampshire RG21 4EA. Registered number 1878835.

ISBN: 978-0-7495-4484-3

A CIP catalogue record for this book is available from the British Library.

Colour separation by Fotographics Ltd
Printed and bound in Italy by Printer Trento Srl.

Find out more about AA Publishing and the wide range of travel publications and services the AA provides by visiting our website at www.theAA.com/travel.

Reprinted 2007. Information verified and updated.
First published 1993

Titles in the Explorer series:
Australia • Boston & New England • Britain • Brittany
California • Canada • Caribbean • China • Costa Rica • Crete
Cuba • Cyprus • Egypt • Florence & Tuscany • Florida
France • Germany • Greek Islands • Hawaii • India • Ireland
Italy • Japan • London • Mallorca • Mexico • New York
New Zealand • Paris • Portugal • Provence • Rome
San Francisco • Scotland • South Africa • Spain • Thailand
Tunisia • Turkey • Venice • Vietnam

A02985

How to use this book

ORGANIZATION

Germany Is, Germany Was
Discusses aspects of life and culture in contemporary Germany and explores significant periods in its history.

A–Z
Breaks down the country into regional chapters, and covers places to visit, including walks and drives. Within this section fall the Focus On articles, which consider a variety of subjects in greater detail.

Travel Facts
Contains the strictly practical information vital for a successful trip.

Hotels and Restaurants
Lists recommended establishments throughout Germany, giving a brief summary of their attractions.

ABOUT THE RATINGS
Most places described in this book have been given a separate rating. These are as follows:

▶▶▶ **Do not miss**

▶▶ **Highly recommended**

▶ **Worth seeing**

MAPS
To make each particular location easier to find, every main entry in this book has a map reference to the right of its name. This comprises a number, followed by a letter, followed by another number, such as 176B3. The first number (176) refers to the page on which the map can be found, the letter (B) and the second number (3) pinpoint the square in which the main entry is located. The maps on the inside front cover and inside back cover are referred to as IFC and IBC respectively.

Contents

Robert Tilley has lived in Germany for more than 30 years, where he writes (mostly film-scripts, travel articles, and books) and produces English-language shows for German television. He commutes between homes in Munich, the Bavarian Alps and Mallorca.

My Germany

Visitors may encounter only a few of the facets of this surprisingly diverse country—certainly too few to form a complete picture of present-day Germany and its people. But just a handful would be sufficient to supply a positive picture to add to the collection of snapshots from a holiday tour. First impressions are of course provided by the landscape and the people within it. Germans are uncharacteristically reticent about the often astounding beauty and variety of their country, probably because it would take the lifetime of the average German to discover them all. From the deserted beaches and dunes of the North Sea and Baltic coastlines, the country rises through regions of vast forests and thick woodland, hauntingly romantic river valleys, wild upland and on to the towering Bavarian Alps. Punctuating this map are cities and towns of outstanding beauty and cultural energy and villages where time stands still—each community a living tribute to its people.

And so to the people—the Germans themselves. In general, they are scrupulously correct, friendly and helpful, but that doesn't mean the Germans are unable to relax and just have fun. Only the Spanish can rival the Germans in seizing on any opportunity for a party; it's significant that Spain and Germany have more public holidays than any other European country. And nowhere in Europe is it easier to stock up for a party—the beer is Europe's best and cheapest, and the wine is by no means the worst. A Bavarian lakeside beer bash, a Rhineland wine festival, Berlin's annual "Love Parade", Hamburg's "Dom" festivities, Carnival in Mainz and Cologne, Fasching in Munich—the opportunities for celebration are endless. Other benefits of life in Germany include a public transport system that's the envy of other European countries, moderate prices and a wide range of accessible cultural activities in even the most provincial towns. The only drawback can be the weather!
Robert Tilley

Germany Is
Germany Was

For centuries, Germany consisted of small, independent units. Statehood was achieved only in 1871, when the king of Prussia was crowned Kaiser (Emperor) Wilhelm I. The differences between the peoples were—and still are—very great. Asked to sum up Germany as a country, some foreigners claim that it still doesn't exist. The historical diversity survives in many ways.

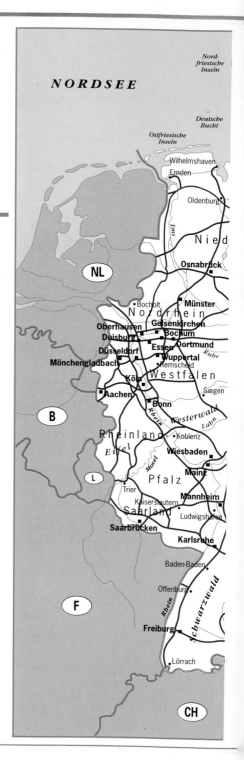

A recent political controversy over government proposals to allow non-German residents to take out dual citizenship threw a new light on a dilemma that caused even the 19th-century German philosopher Friedrich Nietzsche some bother. He said: 'The Germans are characterized by the fact that they never cease asking themselves what is German'.

Germany's former left-wing coalition government of Social Democrats and Greens, led by Chancellor Gerhard Schröder, maintained that the measure would ease the integration of the country's minorities, particularly the Turks. Some have lived in the country for decades and their children were born there. Bavaria's right-wing Christian Social Union, which dominates political life in that *Land* (State), argued that dual citizenship would have the reverse effect, creating a two-nation society.

The major opposition party in parliament at that time, the Christian Democratic Union, headed from 1982 to 1998 by the now disgraced ex-chancellor Helmut Kohl, expanded the Bavarian campaign into a Germany-wide popular plebiscite, with staggering results. Half a million opponents of the proposed dual citizenship legislation signed the petition within its first two weeks.

The dual-citizenship issue today still touches a sensitive German nerve and highlights another central paradox of German nationhood. No other European country can claim to have done more to shelter refugees

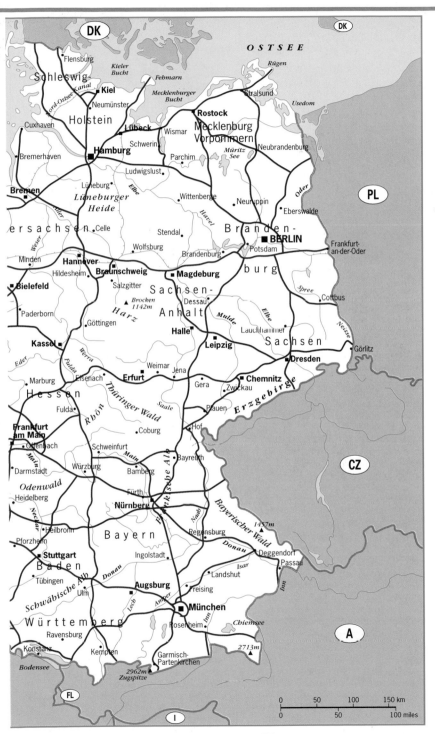

Germany for tourists: an Augsburg café

from the slaughter in former Yugoslavia, while Germany's geographical location also makes the country a natural destination for other migrants from the East. Yet the idea of actually sharing German nationality with these fellow residents is anathema to a large number of Germans. On this central issue, regional, cultural, historical and language differences are forgotten—and a large slice of society, from north to south, west to east, finds unity in the fact of 'being German'. As Nietzsche said 100 years ago, the debate has no end...

Sausage, sauerkraut, beer, coffee and enormous cakes come to mind as typical German fare. And, yes, sausages do come in hundreds of different varieties, while cabbage is consumed quite frequently, along with large quantities of potatoes. These stereotypical images are, as you might expect, only a small part of the picture. The reality is actually much more varied and adventurous.

There are some staple menu items: *Kaffee und Kuchen* (coffee and cake) is a popular afternoon snack, with rich cakes, usually topped with mounds of whipped cream. Beer is found in a variety of forms, from Pilsner to Berlin's *Weisse*, a brew with a sweet syrup added to it, while local wine is a welcome addition to a hearty German meal.

QUALITY AND VARIETY Visitors are often surprised at how well prepared German food is—and at its variety. A visit to the food halls in Berlin's giant KaDeWe department store or the elegant Alois Dallmayr store in Munich will bear this out.

> ❏ In KaDeWe's sixth-floor food hall in Berlin, with its special high-speed elevator that stops nowhere else, there are over a thousand varieties of German sausage—overwhelming to the uninitiated sausage buyer! ❏

German cooking is reputedly heavy, but the country's restaurant scene has been invaded by *neue Deutsche Küche* (*nouvelle cuisine* German style) featuring creative and tasty dishes using traditional German ingredients.

EATING THROUGH THE DAY For most Germans, breakfast may include a boiled egg, cereal and yoghurt, but more probably bread with cheese, jam and/or cold meats.

Lunch, the main meal of the day, could include a juicy *Schnitzel* (cutlet) —usually pork—roasted potatoes and a salad. Dinner is often a cold and lighter meal of bread, a larger variety of meats and cheeses than at breakfast, and, in colder weather, perhaps a soup or stew. A popular dish is a combination of lentils and local varieties of sausage. German desserts are almost always fruit- or cream-based dishes.

The amount of bread consumed by most Germans will astound visitors, and the variety and amount of textured, heavy, dark brown breads in the bakery is amazing. Try them all and decide which you like most.

13

Bread is an important element in the German diet

The homeland of Bach, Beethoven, Brahms, Wagner and Stockhausen, among many other of the world's musical geniuses, Germany has a reputation for nurturing musicians and composers—a centuries-old tradition that survives today. Visitors will find a wealth of musical events, from the historic and classical to modern, up-to-the-minute rock.

Among the joys of a trip to Germany are evenings spent at the Berlin Philharmonic, the Staatsoper of east Berlin, the Hamburg Opera and Munich's National Theatre (home of the Bavarian State Opera), which offer some of the best orchestral sounds and operatic productions to be heard and seen anywhere in the world.

❑ The Berlin Philharmonic—the best orchestra in the country and one of the best in the world—was for many years led by Herbert von Karajan. His successor, Claudio Abbado, came from Italy, while the chief conductor is now Briton Simon Rattle. ❑

Ludwig van Beethoven (above)
The Munich Oktoberfest (top)

A BRIEF HISTORY The German love of music and traditional folk songs can be traced back to pre-Christian tribal times. By the end of the 15th century, with the widespread use of the newly developed organ in churches, national interest and support for classical music had blossomed. In the 16th and 17th centuries, with the Reformation and the flowering of the Lutheran chorale, musical excellence was associated with churches. At this time vocalists, choristers, organists, instrumentalists and their directors worked as professional musicians.

By the 18th century, court patronage was an important source of employment for musicians. German baroque music began to flower in such geniuses as Handel, Telemann and Bach. At the same time, musical theatre was developing in Vienna, and the German *singspiel* became the rage. At the peak of the *singspiel's* popularity, Mozart wrote his last opera, *The*

Magic Flute, and German opera came of age. Beethoven produced his major romantic symphonies and his only opera, *Fidelio*, soon after this time.

Romanticism was in the air in Germany in the 19th century. After Beethoven came Schumann and Mendelssohn, then Brahms, Liszt, and Wagner, who transformed German national folk tales into powerful Romantic operas.

German music suffered a setback in the mid-20th century, under Nazism, when all 'Jewish' music was banned. However, since the war the avant-garde, headed by Karlheinz Stockhausen, has pioneered new musical forms.

THE MUSIC SCENE TODAY The numerous choirs founded earlier in Germany are still the springboard for much of the country's musical talent.

Thanks to the nation's generous tax system, which includes a levy for churches, choirs are found in many small communities. At city, state and national levels, huge subsidies for the performing arts and symphony orchestras help keep standards extremely high, and the cost of tickets for performances exceptionally low. Thus classical music is enjoyed by a greater segment of society in Germany than almost anywhere else, though this has the drawback that tickets are hard to come by.

Visitors are always advised to plan ahead and reserve seats well in advance. However, as in most major cities, the concierge in the bigger hotels invariably has his own excellent contacts and will generally be able to meet your last-minute wishes, encouraged, of course, by a generous tip.

During the 1950s, jazz, officially suppressed by the Third Reich, was effectively a copy of the American scene. By the 1960s foreign jazz musicians had lost their appeal to German youth, and the embryonic rock groups flourishing in Britain, most notably the Beatles, were invited to play in new clubs in Hamburg, Hannover and West Berlin. Their popularity quickly spawned imitators such as the Rattles, who enjoyed great domestic success, but their lack of confidence and rock tradition meant that any songs for foreign markets were sung in English.

Particularly popular was the heavier, more introspective end of the rock spectrum, represented by Amon Duul and Tangerine Dream. The enormous drama of German reunification gave performers such as Udo Lindenberg and the Scorpions ample material for politically rooted numbers, and the Scorpions 'internationalized' the euphoric mood with their hit 'Winds of Change', Germany's own Bruce Springsteen, the rocker Peter Maffei, caught the mood well and kept pace with changes through the 1990s with compositions that pleaded for social harmony in the face of the challenges presented by the painful process of reunification.

Music in all forms flourishes in Germany. Jazz in Hamburg (below); The Berlin Philharmonic Orchestra (top)

15

Health in Germany is a national obsession. Foreigners living in the country remark at how often they are told by Germans that certain foods, certain activities and many prescribed drugs are 'not good for you'. But the German view of health is not usually negative. Good health is seen as an attainable goal, and Germans tend to take a positive, active approach to staying healthy.

Even a dentist will try to talk you out of having an injection of anaesthetic during a filling because of its poisonous content. Germans, it seems, prefer to endure the pain!

With doctors and pharmacists prescribing homeopathic drugs, and people cycling to work on specially designated pathways during the week or enjoying long hikes in the woods and forests during weekends, it is no wonder that the average life expectancy in Germany is one of the highest in Europe.

THE SPA The best place to study this pursuit of good health is at the *Kurort*, or spa town. Spas are dotted all over Germany, from seaside towns to the Bavarian Alps. Usually, they have a giant bathhouse where anyone can take the healing waters.

In most other countries in Europe, spa towns have become relics of the 19th century, but German spas are

❏ Until recently German medical students were required, as part of their qualifying studies, to take a course in *Balneologie*, the science of taking the waters. ❏

kept alive by medical aid schemes that provide for periodic stays of between three and six weeks in spa clinics and hotels. Cuts in government expenditure on health and welfare have trimmed spa benefits considerably in recent years, although anyone with a history of illness can normally spend a few weeks at a spa every three or four years, with most of the cost covered by medical aid. Some of the spas are very luxurious indeed, with 'grand hotel' accommodation and sports facilities ranging from archery, golf and tennis to riding and boating. Many have gambling casinos and glittering nightclubs. Besides the baths, today's modern spa resorts offer such amenities as golf, tennis, horse racing, casinos, boating and skiing—something for every taste. A typical spa treatment might include a mud bath or hydrotherapy, saunas and steam treatments, all followed by a wrap in warm blankets and a compulsory rest.

A trip to some of the large bathing and swimming facilities in spa resorts can be a treat for all family members. Amenities often include wave pools, pools with currents, lap pools and whirlpools. These giant complexes provide enormous fun whatever the weather, as they often have adjoining outdoor bathing areas.

Baden-Baden (below and top) is a popular spa in the southwest

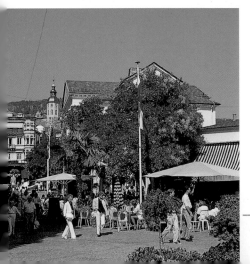

16

THE SPORTING LIFE Nearly half of all Germans between the ages of 10 and 40 engage regularly in active sport, and no less than six million Germans belong to soccer clubs. Soccer is still the national sport. Germany hosted the 2006 World Cup and they reached the semi-finals of the competition. If they are not playing soccer, active Germans ski in the winter and play tennis in the

Snowboarding is becoming popular throughout the country

❏ The German airline Lufthansa tried to ban smoking on domestic flights in the 1990s, but this caused such an angry response from the tobacco industry that the airline quickly caved in and changed its mind. Given that the longest domestic flight lasts less than two hours, this was rather fainthearted of Lufthansa. All European and domestic flights are now non-smoking. ❏

Steffi Graf, victorious at the 1999 French Open Championship

summer. Visitors to Germany will find ample opportunity to enjoy both sports.

Tennis bounced into fashion in the late 1980s with the successes on the international circuit of Steffi Graf, Boris Becker and Michael Stich. While Stich has all but retired from the scene, Becker still enjoys popularity in Germany, which rivals that of racing car driver and seven times Formula One World Champion Michael Schumacher.

THE SMOKING PARADOX Given that Germans are so keen on good health and fitness, it is ironic that many are also smokers.

The no-smoking lobby has no influence, and a campaign to ban smoking in public places has had little effect, even though cigarette advertising has been restricted. However, more and more restaurants now have no-smoking sections and surveys indicate that young people now smoke less than their elders.

The Federal Republic of Germany came into being in 1949 and has proved remarkably durable, being responsible for bringing the West German people from a state of near ruin to their present prosperous condition. It has seen the collapse of the communist system in the former GDR, has absorbed that state, and is now struggling to bring equal prosperity and democracy to the whole of Germany.

The German political structure is based on its constitution—the *Grundgesetz* (basic law), which includes human rights guarantees. It is often used as an excuse for inactivity by politicians, although it has been amended more than 30 times.

THE BUNDESTAG The German parliament has two chambers. The Bundestag, the lower chamber, carries more weight in decision-making. It is directly elected to a four-year term by a system of proportional representation, though the government can call an election earlier after referring to the federal president.

In the 2002 general election, the Social Democratic Party didn't win the most votes but won enough to continue the coalition government with the minority Greens. Chancellor Gerhard Schröder's slim victory was due to the unflattering image of his Bavarian rival Edmund Stoiber and

The Reichstag in Berlin

Schröder's popular refusal to involve Germany in the Iraq war. Steps were taken in 2004 to reform the public health system and reduce the cost of unemployment benefits and social security contributions. Although the necessity of these reforms was accepted by all parties, it provoked strong protests, especially from the trade unions and post-communists. It was no surprise in the 2004 regional elections in eastern Germany that the PDS (successor organization of the communist SED) and the two neo-Nazi parties, DVU and NPD, gained considerable results.

Now all eyes are on the leader of the CDU, Angela Merkel, who became Germany's first woman chancellor in September 2005, and the first 'Ossi' (Easterner) to lead the nation.

It is said she will need all her reputed toughness to hold together the 'grand coalition' with the SPD now.

THE BUNDESRAT The upper house represents all 16 German *Länder* (States). Delegates are chosen by the *Länder* and include state prime ministers. The Bundesrat approves all laws that affect the states. Voting is by a weighted system based on population.

TOP JOBS The German chancellor is not directly elected but usually holds the office as leader of the strongest party in the Bundestag, usually having to rely on coalition partners to gain a majority. The post of federal president is mostly ceremonial; the president is elected for five years.

THE CONSTITUTIONAL COURT Germany's judicial system is led by the *Bundesverfassungsgericht* (constitutional court), which has two chambers, one for individual liberties, the other for political issues. Each court has eight judges, elected by the Bundestag and Bundesrat. In 1994 the court ruled that Germany had the right to use troops abroad, for UN or other Missions, exactly like other NATO members, but in each case parliament had to approve.

EXTREMISTS OUT In Germany, the system of proportional representation allows every voter two votes, one for a constituency candidate and another for a political party. Any political party is excluded from the Bundestag if it polls less than 5 per cent of a party list vote or fails to win at least three constituencies—effectively keeping out the extremist groups.

THE ECONOMIC MIRACLE The rapid economy recovery after near total collapse at the end of World War II— the *Wirtschaftswunder*—transformed West Germany and gave its citizens some of the highest living standards in the European Union (EU). This was despite strong bureaucratic controls that seemed to discourage private enterprise, had minimal emphasis on customer service, and relatively little use of high-tech equipment. Economic success was helped along by American aid programmes. However, it was probably due, above all, to the Germans' hard work, and their desire to forget the past and rebuild their country.

The glass dome on top of the refurbished Reichstag building, home of the Bundestag

SLOWDOWN With the absorption of 17 million people from the former GDR and the world recession in the early 1990s, the miracle began to fade. As the economy stagnated unemployment climbed—particularly in eastern Germany as it moved from a 'command' to a market economy. At the end of the 20th century there were signs that the steadily rising unemployment rate had hit its peak, but there was little hope of a rapid turnaround for the four million jobless.

THE BUNDESBANK Central to the German economy, the bank controlled interest rates, and so inflation. The bank, a semi-independent body, often opposed the economic policies of the federal government. Its national role has now been reduced in the wider European sphere by the dictates of the new European Central Bank, particularly relating to the European monetary unit, the euro.

West Germans have for many years been in the forefront of the environmental or 'Green' movement. 'Green' politics have been much more central to events in Germany than, for example, in Britain where the issues had to be more peripheral. The term 'environmentally friendly' was invented here in the mouthful umweltfreundlich. *An aversion to atomic power provided the motivating force for 10 years of student and youth activism. Habits that have become second nature to environment-conscious people, such as the separation of glass, paper and other waste for recycling, began here.*

NUCLEAR POWER At the height of the German environment debate, the apparently impossible occurred: The Greens entered government in 1998 and a Green activist, Trittin, became environment minister. But Trittin's efforts to introduce radical environmental policies, particularly the abolition of nuclear power, clashed with political realities. Although the Greens' proposal to shut down nuclear power stations became

entangled with legal complications and international commitments, the Red-Green coalition government was able to make a compromise with the energy industries and to phase out nuclear power step by step.

INDUSTRIAL POLLUTION Another central plank of Green policy, a proposed tax on harmful power sources, particularly petroleum, also had to be watered down to meet pragmatic considerations. Nevertheless, some

progress is being made on the environmental front, if not at the speed set out in Green party manifestos. Chancellor Kohl's government inherited industrial pollution of appalling magnitude when the two Germanies were united in 1990. For decades, East German industry placed environmental concerns at the bottom of its list of priorities in meeting Communist-regime targets. The effects of this short-sightedness were visible to anyone going from the West to Berlin: The industrial town of Bitterfeld, on the main line from Bavaria, was constantly swathed in a choking yellow haze, much of it caused by two huge factories producing pesticides, herbicides and paints. The factories have been closed down, but environmentalists say the pollution they caused will live on for decades.

ALTERNATIVE ENERGY Kohl's Environment Ministry tackled the environmental problems of the East with commendable energy, promoting the use of alternative sources of

❑ Germans are particularly avid ecologists: They recycle 59 per cent of their wastepaper and reprocess 71 per cent of their glass bottles and about 70 per cent of their tyres. ❑

power. At least in this area, the Kohl government handed over to the Red-Green coalition an intact plan for the future.

Now, despite the collapse of the Red-Green coalition, Germany is likely to remain in the vanguard of environmental protection in the 21st century as Merkel was formerly Kohl's environment minister.

THE CAR IS KING The traditional German love of the great outdoors, and the almost mystical relationship with the forests that cover a third of the country are important factors that will guarantee Germany's leading role in environmental protection. Nature-loving Germans discuss in hushed tones the statistics showing that almost half the country's trees are terminally ill, victims of 'acid rain' and car-exhaust pollution. But their concern is compromised by the place they reserve in their lives for the very cause of much of the problem: the car.

If anything at all is sacrosanct in changing Germany, it is the motor car. Supported by car manufacturers, motoring organizations and political lobbies, Germans assert their right to drive where and when they please and with no limit on the speed of their vehicles. The same German heart that bleeds to see a tree die pounds with excitement when tearing down the *autobahn* at 200kph (124mph), although many stretches of these roads now have speed limits.

HOPE FOR THE FUTURE Western conservationists have rediscovered a forgotten landscape in the Lower Oder Valley National Park, near the Polish border. The River Oder flows through the middle, with Poland on one bank and Germany on the other. Several projects have been set up to conserve the diverse flora and fauna that have been discovered, including ospreys, sea eagles and beavers.

The German film industry does not operate on the Hollywood scale and has not achieved the same worldwide success. However, things have improved with the international success of Goodbye Lenin *and* Charlotte Link's *Oscar in 2003 for her movie* Nirgendwo in Africa *(Nowhere in Africa).*

Hopes that the German film industry would receive a boost with reunification and the reopening of the old Babelsberg studios in East Berlin failed to materialize in the following 10 years, and most German film-makers entered the 21st century in a cloud of gloom. The golden years of the 1920s and the Fassbinder-led renaissance of the 1970s and 1980s seemed very far away as studios struggled to find a new, financially viable and internationally recognized identity.

THE INDUSTRY'S MALAISE Film-makers watched with frustration as cinemas reported record box-office figures. In 1998, 1.6 billion Deutschmarks were grossed by an ever-growing number of cinemas, yet less than 10 per cent of the films shown were German—most were American. Particularly galling was to see home-grown actors, directors and camera-men on the credits of American-made films, and reports that German public funding had been absorbed by American studios fuelled the frustration even more. Efforts by German studios to break into the American market, or at least to collect an Oscar nomination, were dismissed by the cynics as a naive waste of time. The German film

Jenseits der Stille was shortlisted for the Oscar for best foreign film in 1998, but Germany's 1999 nomination, *Lola rennt*, failed even the nomination test, and German studios were totally shut out of the Oscar awards.

STATE SUPPORT The irony is that the German film industry receives State and central government support that is the envy of other countries. The subsidies are allocated on a regional basis by the country's *Länder* (States), and critics say this is at the heart of the malaise within the film industry. Regional rivalry rules over nationwide cooperation, so that Munich's Bavaria Film Studios is in direct competition with Berlin's Babelsberg Studios, in a contest where neither can win. Twenty years ago, directors such as Ingmar Bergmann and Norman Jewison worked on box-office successes at the Bavaria studios. Now, the studios are engaged mostly in the production of German soaps—and in taking visitors on guided tours of the fading film lots where *Das Boot* and *Cabaret* were produced.

The entrance to the Film Museum on Potsdamer Platz, Berlin

Some aspects of German culture, such as classical music, are internationally known; others are confined within the country's borders. Open any German television magazine, read about the trials and tribulations of the media stars, and marvel—you won't have heard of most of them.

Although Germany has its share of blue-blooded nobility (notably the descendants of the Hohenzollern and Wittelsbach rulers), it is the lives and exploits of foreign 'royals' that make headlines in the popular press.

Famous people in sports (Boris Becker and Michael Schumacher, above) and in politics (Angela Merkel, below)

ROYALTY WATCHING Even in death, Britain's Princess Diana still commands faithful albeit morbid attention, while one member or other of the British royal family is almost daily in the news. The Grimaldis of Monaco are also monitored faithfully by Germany's society reporters, while readers are constantly reminded that they, too, have a European royal—Sweden's Queen, who was a Stuttgart commoner before King Gustav fell under her spell at the Olympic Games in Munich in 1972.

Germany's resident royals keep a low profile, even though the head of the House of Wittelsbach, Prinz Franz von Bayern, as direct descendant of the last of the Stuarts, is Pretender to the throne of Scotland. Germany is more likely to hang royal titles on sports stars than on the princes, counts, viscounts and barons

(and their female equivalents), who are an unobtrusive part of the German social fabric. It is nearly 90 years since Germany had a real Kaiser, yet that is the title bestowed on the country's legendary soccer star, Franz (the 'Kaiser') Beckenbauer, while tennis star Steffi Graf was frequently called the 'princess' of the Centre Court.

23

POLITICAL GIANTS In politics, the departure from the world scene of Germany's heavyweight Chancellor, Helmut Kohl, did not diminish the country's image in the international arena, for he was followed by a leader in the charismatic style of Willy Brandt and Helmut Schmidt—the handsome Gerhard Schröder. Schröder brought more than a whiff of glamour to Bonn and Berlin, for he was accompanied by a young, pretty (and blonde) wife who used to write for *Bild*, the country's leading gossip newspaper.

New chancellor Angela Merkel is now working hard to spruce up her appearance and banish her dowdy image!

The first identifiable permanent settlers in the area that is now Germany were Celtic tribes in the 8th century BC; the Rhineland was a key area of production in their industrial society. But new forces were developing in Europe. The Roman Empire was expanding, and Germanic peoples were on the move from Scandinavia.

Germanic tribes moved to lands east of the Rhine and north of the Black Sea, and their invasions and periodic uprisings created instability within the Roman Empire. Roman attempts to push across the Rhine failed to establish permanent occupation. These ended in AD9; after reaching the Elbe the Romans were pushed back by German tribes under the leadership of Arminius, who destroyed three legions.

Charlemagne's coronation as Holy Roman Emperor marked a new era

RISE OF THE FRANKS By the time of Emperor Constantine, when the empire's capital shifted to Byzantium in the East, Roman rule was beginning to break down. After the introduction of Christianity by Emperor Constantine, the Roman Empire disintegrated and the area that is now Germany was overrun by the Franks. When Charlemagne was crowned Holy Roman Emperor in AD800, Frankish influence stretched across most of Europe.

Civil war followed Charlemagne's death; the Treaty of Verdun in AD843 split the empire into a Latin western section, and a Germanic eastern part led by Ludwig the German. His appointment marked the emergence of a German identity.

THE SAXON ASCENDANCY In the 10th century, the area came under the rule of the Saxons. Otto the Great was faced with invading Magyars from the East and a growing threat from duchies and principalities inside the eastern empire. After defeating the Magyars in AD955, Otto strengthened his ties to the papacy, which led to church dominance over a large part of the country. In AD962, Otto the Great was crowned Holy Roman Emperor.

THE POWER OF THE PRINCES The influence of powerful dynastic German families increased steadily. By the 13th century, the Holy Roman Emperor had little power against feudal princes. Many began to push eastward, conquering Poland and setting up German communities in areas now in Russia and Romania. In 1356, the law regulating the election of an emperor (the Golden Bull) was introduced, based on the votes of four noble and three ecclesiastical electors, excluding the papacy. In the 15th century, the Habsburgs were elected Holy Roman Emperors, and they retained the title until it was abolished some 400 years later.

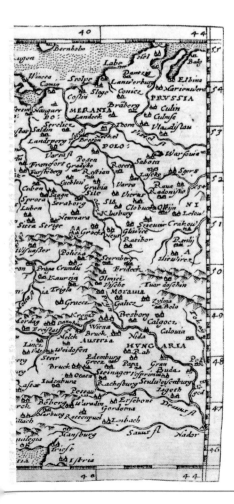

Germany in 1608, from Geographiae Universae tum veteris, tum narae absolutissimum opus *by Giovanni Magini (Köln)*

In the 16th century Germany was suffering under a greedy and powerful aristocracy that appropriated land and held the oppressed peasantry in serfdom. This, alongside an equally grasping and cynical church trading in 'indulgences', led to the religious upheaval of the Reformation later in the same century.

Discontent with the church authorities increased. Martin Luther led accusations over corruption, nailing his '95 theses', an attack against papal abuses, to the door of Wittenberg church in 1517. Luther was excommunicated by the church, but politically powerful German princes were able to protect him from the death sentence.

CENTURY OF CONFLICT After publication of Luther's translation of the Bible, the oppressed in Germany were ready to revolt. The Peasants' Rebellion of 1524–25 brought destruction of church properties but was put down by princely armies.

The period of the Reformation and Counter-Reformation created more than a century of strife between Catholics and Protestants, and by the early 17th century, Europe was embroiled in the Thirty Years' War. Many battles were fought on German lands, bringing about extensive destruction. Negotiations to end the war began in 1643, culminating in the Peace of Westphalia in 1648. The treaty ended the conflict, reduced the status of Holy Roman Emperor and began the decline of the House of Habsburg, while giving power to more than 300 principalities and other territories.

❏ In the 16th century, German mercenaries led the way in high fashion. The style of 'slashing' clothes—cutting slits in the material and pulling the lining through for display—started with battlefield booty used to patch clothes and found its way to the French and English courts. ❏

THE RISE OF BRANDENBURG-PRUSSIA By the end of the 17th century, a power in the area of Brandenburg-Prussia emerged. The Hohenzollern family, who held the Electorate of Brandenburg, defied the laws of the Holy Roman Empire and assumed the title of kings of Prussia. Frederick William, the Great Elector, was the first; the monarchy consolidated itself in the early 18th century. Under Frederick the Great, the third Hohenzollern king, Prussia rose to be one of the dominant European powers in the middle of that century.

Despite liberal laws at home, Frederick asserted Prussia's military authority and, after going to battle with Austria over Silesia, engaged in the Seven Years' War (1756–63). Frederick annexed much of Poland and established Prussia as a counter power to Austria. Prussia's power was tested during the Napoleonic Wars of the early 19th century, but in the Battle of Waterloo in 1815 Napoleon was defeated by the armies of Britain, Hannover and Prussia. The Congress of Vienna, which met that same year and created the Deutscher Bund (German Confederation), established Prussian dominance among some 40 states in the German world, alongside Austria.

GERMAN UNIFICATION Now Germany began to experience the pains of the industrial revolution. Economic reforms and customs unions were introduced to ease the strain caused by the many protective borders in the German region. Also, a wage-earning class as well as a bourgeoisie emerged. Uprisings in 1848 demonstrated how serious the

demands for the dissolution of an older political order in Germany were becoming. In 1862, Prussia's Wilhelm I chose Otto von Bismarck as his chancellor. Within a decade Bismarck united Germany under Prussian leadership. After a war with Denmark over Schleswig-Holstein in 1864, and the Bohemian War with Austria in 1866, all the German states north of the River Main were united.

To gain the support of German southern states (Bavaria, Baden and Württemberg), Bismarck provoked a war with France; after the Franco-Prussian War ended in 1871, Germany was united as the Second Reich, with King Wilhelm of Prussia

The Peasants' Rebellion, 1524–25 (above); Otto von Bismarck (below)

The Rüdesheim Niederwald Monument (below) celebrates German unification in 1871

as kaiser. Bismarck then embarked on a number of liberal and social domestic reforms, as well as creating alliances with Austria and Russia.

WORLD WAR I France sought revenge for 1871 and, together with Russia, feared the strength of the German army. Britain for its part was worried by the threatening expansion of the German navy. These three powers, therefore, stood against the alliance of Germany and Austria in 1914, when World War I broke out over Habsburg claims in the Balkans. Germany's defeat came in 1918, hastened by the entry of the United States into the war the year before.

Germany's defeat in World War I was followed in 1919 by the founding of the Weimar Republic, based on a democratic constitution. The same year, Germany's new leaders were forced to sign the Treaty of Versailles, marking a radical shift in the European balance of power. It called for enormous war reparations as well as the confiscation of, and withdrawal from, territories that belonged to Germany, in some cases, for centuries.

Unemployment and inflation hit Europe after World War I, and in almost every country political movements on the extreme left and right began to gather strength and make themselves heard.

THE RISE OF THE NAZIS During the 1920s, Germany suffered increasing inflation, and at the beginning of the 1930s the worldwide economic crisis brought about a disastrous deflation. Elections in 1930 allowed extremist parties to gain prominence, most noticeably the Nazi Party, led by Adolf Hitler. This attracted the unemployed and destitute, industrialists and other wealthy groups who saw the party's authoritarian policies as a return to the order that the country had known under the last kaiser. Hitler gained more power and was made chancellor by the republic's president, Paul von Hindenburg, in 1933. In February, the Reichstag, the parliament building, was set on fire, an incident orchestrated by the Nazis. Hindenburg declared a state of emergency.

THE ROAD TO WAR The Nazi Party became the only legal party in the country, and Hitler became president as well as chancellor. Democracy was suppressed under Joseph Goebbels's propaganda ministry. Many horrors occurred during Hitler's Third Reich. Jewish people were persecuted and murdered. The government and education systems were perverted. Many of the nation's most talented citizens —often of Jewish origin—emigrated, and gradually the terms of the Treaty

of Versailles were nullified. Hitler's plan for Europe became well understood, but the West was not ready to stand up to him until 1 September 1939, when Germany invaded Poland. Two days later, Britain and France declared war.

WORLD WAR II AND ITS AFTERMATH The war and the vicious activities of Nazis against Jews, Slavs and others are well documented. At first the war went well for the Nazis, but their invasion of Russia in 1941 proved a turning point. Defeats in North Africa and at Stalingrad followed in 1942 and 1943. A German resistance movement developed among the top

Hermann Goering—the Nazi leader responsible for the Luftwaffe

❏ An estimated six million Jews were murdered in the Holocaust, a scheme known as the 'Final Solution'.This was drawn up by Nazi leaders at the Wannsee Conference in suburban Berlin on 20 January 1942. The participants, under the chairmanship of Reinhard Heydrich but acting on Hitler's direct orders, extended Germany's death camps to occupied territories in Eastern Europe, sealing the fate of Jews throughout Europe. The lakeside villa (Haus der Wannsee-Konferenz) is now a memorial and educational centre (*open daily*). ❏

Adolf Hitler entering the Sudetenland at Wildenau in 1938

systems emerged; in May 1949 the territories occupied by the British, Americans and French combined to form the Federal Republic of Germany. Four months later, the Russians created the German Democratic Republic. The two Germanys rivalled each other for more than 40 years, each trying to rebuild a nation out of the ruins and rubble of World War II. They came to represent the cold-war division of Europe, formalized by the erection of the Berlin Wall in 1961.

THE YEARS OF DIVISION Throughout the cold-war period, West Germany's economy became Europe's strongest while East Germany's industriousness made it the most prosperous country in Comecon, the Eastern bloc's economic alliance. By the 1970s, many Germans accepted the division, though they still hoped that Germany would be reunited. Unofficial recognition of the division developed in the Ostpolitik policies of Willy Brandt, when he became chancellor from 1969. Nevertheless, West German political parties, while attempting to work with the leaders of the GDR on some economic and social schemes, still insisted that unification was the ultimate aim.

army leadership and attempts were made on Hitler's life. Germany was totally defeated, and in 1945 Hitler committed suicide. The legacy of the Third Reich and World War II will be a burden to Germany for decades to come. Six million Jewish people murdered in concentration camps cannot, nor should not, be forgotten by the world. Those leaders held responsible were put on trial for war crimes and crimes against humanity.

The victorious Allies divided Germany into four occupied zones under Soviet, US, British and French control. Two separate political

On November 9 1989, the momentous decision to take down the Berlin Wall was made. East Germans had spent many days and nights peacefully demonstrating for political rights. The communist East German regime no longer had the steadfast military support of its closest ally, the former Soviet Union. The government of the GDR finally gave way and opened up points on the wall, allowing its citizens to flood over into West Germany.

Some East Germans had never seen the West in their lifetime, but most had conjured a picture in their minds from television shows that had been beamed across the barbed wire.

ONE GERMANY Within months, a new democratically elected federal government had been set up, with the task of uniting East and West Germany. At first, people thought the process would take several years, but the government moved quickly to merge the two economies, providing East Germans with Deutschmarks on 1 July 1990. East Germany's economy began to deteriorate as a result of the inability of its industries to compete with Western production standards. The Federal Republic's ruling coalition was compelled to move very quickly and absorb the territory of the former East Germany into the republic much faster than had been expected. On 3 October 1990, after more than four decades of division following Germany's defeat in World War II, a dream came true for many Germans when the country was finally reunited.

AFTER EUPHORIA The political leaders in east and west called on the nation to work together and avoid treating the former East Germans as second-class citizens. Sadly, the wall still exists in many people's minds. Those from the east continue to complain that their country was simply annexed by the west, and accuse the West Germans of arrogance, while many West Germans are angry that their taxes have been increased to

pay for reunification (despite repeated assurances by the then chancellor Helmut Kohl that this would not happen).

In the early 1990s, high unemployment, especially in eastern Germany, led to a wave of resentment against immigrants. Many East Germans, unused to other races, reacted with a xenophobia bred of fear and ignorance, and racist incidents grew. This mood was exploited by groups of neo-Nazi thugs both in east and west, who attacked and killed a number of Turks. German politicians were slow to react at first, and in view of Germany's past, fears grew abroad of a revival of Nazism.

But in fact the neo-Nazis are only a tiny minority, and most Germans abhor the violence. The killers of five Turks near Köln in 1993 were finally tried and jailed in 1995. Even so, social unrest seems likely to continue in Germany until the economy becomes stabilized.

RETURN TO BERLIN With unification, the federal government was faced with the important question: Should the seat of government remain in Bonn, the capital of western Germany, or return to Berlin, the historical political heart? Parliament was besieged with concerns about the costs, and fears that a return to Berlin could rekindle old nationalistic attitudes about German leadership in Europe.

Finally, parliament voted narrowly for a return to Berlin, despite the heavy costs. The move was completed in 2000, although some

ministries stayed behind in Bonn to soften the blow to the local economy. In the meantime, infrastructure developments and economic integration of the east have become the main focus of the federal government's policy. Special taxes are being levied to pay for the very costly support scheme.

THE EUROPEAN GOAL Since the Federal Republic of Germany (West Germany) was founded in 1949, national policy has strongly supported European integration. At first through common agricultural and trade policies, and now through economic and political integration, German politicians have used the banner of the European Union as a standard for the next generation.

This priority is sometimes at odds with other European countries, particularly Britain, and some opponents fear German dominance of the Union. Others argue that tight European integration is needed to curb a possible rise of German nationalism. But though most Germans want a politically unified Europe, many remain dubious about the wisdom of relinquishing the historically strong Deutschmark for the common European currency, the euro, which was introduced in Germany and most other members of the European Union from 2002.

Souvenir pieces of the Berlin Wall go on sale (top right)
The Brandenburg Gate in the middle of Berlin (below)

A strong tradition of stories and poetry undoubtedly existed in the German language long before written literature. The one tantalizing glimpse of this was noted down in the Hildebrandslied (The Lay of Hildebrand), *a 9th-century fragment of an alliterative heroic poem. Otherwise, the earliest German manuscripts were of a religious nature, written and preserved as part of the Christian monastic tradition of learning.*

32

By the 12th century, literature had passed from the monasteries to the courts. German versions of French romances, such as the tale of Tristan and Isolde and the Arthurian stories, were written; in about 1200, tales of the hero Siegfried took form in the anonymous *Nibelungenlied.* *Minnesang* (lyrical love songs) also flourished in the 12th century.

THE LITERARY RENAISSANCE
Martin Luther's translation of the Bible (1534) is generally regarded as the first great modern German work of literature, but it was not until the 18th century that German writings, notably those of Johann Wolfgang von Goethe and Friedrich von Schiller, reached a level comparable with that of the Middle Ages. A meeting between Herder and Goethe led to the Sturm und Drang (Storm and Stress) movement. Weimar,

> ❏ Philosopher and mathematician Gottfried von Leibniz (1646–1716) is remembered for the development of differential calculus, for which his notation is still used. His ideas of expressing 'all truth' in terms of simple statements using symbols was a forerunner of modern mathematical logic. ❏

where Goethe and Schiller (above) spent much of their lives, became synonymous with their writings—Schiller's poetry and dramas, and Goethe's dramas (notably *Faust*), novels, poetry and philosophical works.

FROM ROMANTICISM TO NATURALISM
The German Romantic movement started around 1790. It had a profound effect throughout the whole of Europe, and Romantic ideas dominated German literature up to

> ❏ Philosopher Georg Wilhelm Friedrich Hegel (1770–1831) put forward the theory that history, which he called the *Weltgeist* (world spirit), was a developing process of 'consciousness of freedom', from the 'Oriental' through the 'Greek' to the 'Christian– German' period. He saw the process paralleled in three stages of awareness, from 'awareness of objects' through 'awareness of self' to 'awareness of reason.' ❏

GOETHE
1786

❏ The philosopher Immanuel Kant (1724–1804) greatly influenced the 18th-century Weimar literary school with his emphasis on moral duty and aesthetics. ❏

the mid-19th century, with 'folk' poetry and traditional tales (such as those of the Brothers Grimm) being an important element.

TRANSITION The poet and political radical Heinrich Heine marks a transition from Romanticism to realism. Contemporary life became the theme of writers at the end of the 19th century, as in the stories of North Frisian poet and prose writer Theodor Storm, and the plays of Gerhart Hauptmann.

20TH CENTURY At the turn of the 20th century there was a reaction to naturalism in the Nietzsche-inspired poetry of Richard Dehmel and the aestheticism of Stefan George.

❏ The reputation of Friedrich Wilhelm Nietzsche (1844–1900) has suffered as a result of Nazi enthusiasm for his philosophy. His concept of the *Übermensch* (superman) is to blame for this, though it was not connected to the Aryan myth. For Nietzsche the basic motive of human action was the will to have power (he despised Christian morality based on humility). He saw the superman as one who succeeds in overcoming himself.

The greatest German poet of the 20th century was undoubtedly Prague-born Rainer Maria Rilke, whose intense poetic world was spun almost entirely out of his own psyche. Another Prague-born 20th-century giant was Franz Kafka, whose novels and plays shed a grotesque and often absurd light on human experiences. The novelist Thomas Mann explored the contrast between solid bourgeois insensitivity and the fragile world of the artist.

In 1947 Gruppe 47, a group of left-wing writers, was formed. Some members have gained international status, including Heinrich Böll (Nobel Prize winner in 1972) and Günter Grass (Nobel Prize winner in 1999), known for *The Tin Drum*.

Martin Heidegger (1889–1976) espoused a philosophy that was a form of early existentialism. His major work *Sein and Zeit* became one of the most discussed philosophical writings worldwide.

Notable among writers of the former GDR are the innovative dramatist Bertolt Brecht, who died in East Berlin in 1956, and the novelist Christa Wolf.

33

The cover of Hansel and Gretel *by the Brothers Grimm, 1892*

The first architectural style to emerge in medieval Germany—the Romanesque—owed much to the traditions of Rome. The Rhineland has relics of Roman buildings, notably at Trier, where the great Porta Nigra, a gateway in the Roman city walls, still stands. The Roman basilica (meeting hall) inspired many Romanesque churches and cathedrals.

ROMANESQUE AND GOTHIC Fine cathedrals arose during the 11th to 15th centuries: Romanesque Speyer, Mainz, and Worms, then the soaring Gothic wonders of Bamberg, Cologne, Ulm and Freiburg. Sculpture in stone and wood was used to complement architecture. Painting, often done anonymously, can be seen in altarpiece panels and manuscript illuminations.

34

❑ The rococo style, a kind of ultra-baroque, emerged in Germany in the mid-18th century. A French invention, it is characterized by dainty and irregular 'Louis Quinze' motifs. Sanssouci Palace at Potsdam and Cuvilliè's Amalienburg in Munich are examples of the style. ❑

influence. Some of the great names of German art belong to this time, including the Renaissance painter, draughtsman and engraver Albrecht Dürer and the mystical painter Matthias Grünewald. In this period Lucas Cranach the Elder painted the portraits of the leaders of the Reformation, and the two Holbeins, Elder and Younger, were prominent.

The Roman Porta Nigra, Trier

❑ The sculptor Tilman Riemenschneider, the 'Master of Würzburg', bridged the Gothic and Renaissance in Germany. He was one of the first German sculptors not to use gilding or colour in his work. ❑

RENAISSANCE In the late 15th to early 17th centuries, architecture took a back seat as the influence of the church waned and the wealthy middle classes asserted themselves. Many notable buildings show Italian

BAROQUE AND NEO-CLASSICAL The 17th and 18th centuries arguably produced very few distinguished German artists, but saw a brilliant age of baroque architecture by Lukas von Hildebrandt, Balthasar Neumann, Andreas Schlüter and others. During the Age of Enlightenment, Frederick the Great employed Georg Wenzeslaus von Knobelsdorff to help design official buildings for Berlin, and the Prussian capital continued its prominence as an architectural base into the 19th century, as the neo-classicism of Karl Friedrich Schinkel made its mark.

ROMANTICISM As in music and literature, the trend toward Romanticism is seen in art and architecture in the 19th century. Philipp Otto Runge and Caspar David Friedrich, who worked

Rathaus detail, Lemgo

After World War I, the Bauhaus (Building House) movement developed. Its founder in Weimar, Walter Gropius, envisaged cooperation between art and industry, and the name Bauhaus became synonymous with austere functionalism. Nazi hostility led to its dissolution in 1933. Members of the movement settled in other countries, where they continued to have an important influence on architecture and design.

35

THE CONTEMPORARY SCENE
Today, German painters are again prominent figures in the international art world. The current German movement, influenced by the flourishing avant-garde

The Garden Café, *by Ernst Ludwig Kirchner (1880–1938; above)*
People by the Pool, *by August Macke (1887–1914; top)*

in Dresden, were the finest of the German Romantic painters. In architecture, Romanticism is found to an almost absurd degree in castles built for King Ludwig II of Bavaria: the baroque-style Linderhof, the mini-Versailles of Herrenchiemsee and the 'Disneyland' Neuschwanstein.

THE MODERN AGE At the end of the 19th century, many German painters adopted the Impressionist style of France, and painters such as Max Liebermann had strong support from the emerging German bourgeoisie. Jugendstil, the German form of art nouveau, was emerging.

By the beginning of the 20th century, the Expressionist school was in full swing with the founding in Dresden and Munich of Die Brücke (The Bridge) and later Der Blaue Reiter (The Blue Rider) groups. This era inspired many powerful and important works.

interpretations of social and cultural life in a prosperous modern society, has been referred to as neo-expressionism. Postwar Germany's best-known artists include Georg Baselitz and Gerhard Richter, and the late sculptor Joseph Beuys.

Berlin

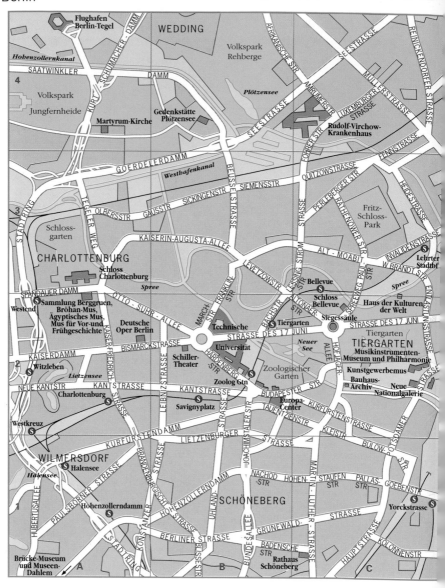

Since the Berlin Wall began to crumble on that extraordinary night in November 1989, the city's two halves have slowly, sometimes painfully, but inevitably fused into something like the fascinating capital city of old. Berlin is now just as interesting for a visitor as it ever was in the middle of the cold war. The minor thrill of crossing Checkpoint Charlie (and wondering if you would ever return) has vanished, and you can now drive unhindered across the Glienicke Bridge (where once only spies set foot), but Berlin remains a compelling city. Now again the capital of a reunited and restrengthened Germany, Berlin is perhaps a litmus test for relations between East and West. Berlin has always been a place on the fringe,

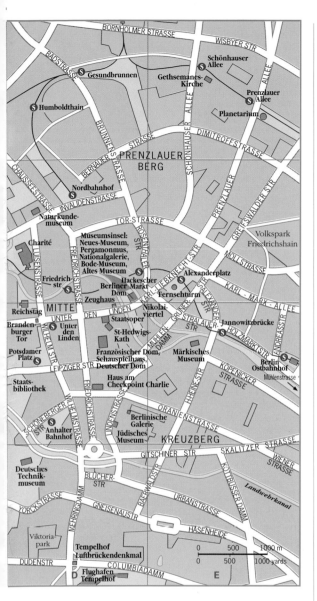

bursting with avant-garde ideas and sometimes subversive culture. Its reputation for decadence, even vice, is not unfounded—mostly a legacy from the Weimar years of the 1920s. It's a city of youth, and a cosmopolitan one. In the late 1960s and 1970s, young people flocked here to study on government grants, or to avoid military service, from which Berliners were exempt. A large number of foreigners have settled here, many of them guest workers. This has enriched Berlin's culture, but has sometimes led to racial tension.

Berlin is a vast city in area—Munich, Frankfurt and Hamburg could all fit within it. Its population is 3.4 million, but huge tracts of the city consist of forests,

TURKISH WORKERS

More Turks live in Berlin than in any other city outside Turkey. Many arrived originally as *Gastarbeiter* (guest workers), to do the jobs that few Berliners wanted to do. Now many of them are second- and third-generation citizens who want their fair share of the city's resources. A high proportion live in the Kreuzberg district. In 1999 they were at the heart of a heated debate over government plans to offer them and other foreign long-time residents of Germany double-citizenship, German and that of their native country. Conservative opposition parties forced the government to retreat and trim the proposed law allowing the children of foreigners to hold dual citizenship until old enough to choose one or the other.

Fabrics at the Turkish market, Maybachufer

villages and lakes, even farmland, contrasting oddly with the intense urbanization of other areas. The west, all but razed by the Allies during Hitler's last stand in 1945, is almost entirely modern. The best of post-war West Berlin is a tour de force, studded with startling examples of art, architecture and design. East Berlin, also badly mauled by the bombs, has been reconstructed in two bizarrely conflicting styles: drab, Stalinist functionalism on one hand and a painstakingly accurate reproduction of grandiose monuments on the other. Two former working-class districts with some intact (or carefully renovated) architecture give a more realistic picture of pre-war Berlin: Kreuzberg in the west and Prenzlauer Berg in the east both display a volatile mixture of bohemian lifestyles and 'alternative' culture.

Berlin gives visitors a sense of double vision. Most cultural venues are duplicated on the other side of the city (two national galleries, two Egyptian museums). Sometimes an extra one is added for good measure (*three* symphony orchestras, universities, and so forth). The city has more than 170 museums, and some are world-class.

The former no man's land astride the wall in the very heart of the city, empty and sinister, was still a hive of construction activity when the German parliament, chancellery, and most government ministries moved there from Bonn in 1999. A huge modern Chancellery has been erected alongside the River Spree next to the Reichstag. Other ministerial offices are nearing completion (at the time of writing) in the new government district near the Brandenburg Gate. The Potsdamer Platz—once a wasteland—now has a massive new complex of offices, stores and housing, while a tunnel for traffic has been carved out beneath the Tiergarten park. However, the mental scars left by the divided city will take longer to heal than the physical ones; attitudes and lifestyle in east and west remain quite different, and suspicions linger.

►► Ägyptisches (Egyptian) Museum   36A2

Altes Museum, Am Lustgarten, Berlin-Mitte
Open: daily 10–6 (until 10 on Thu);
www.aegyptisches-museum-berlin.de
This major collection is housed in the Altes Museum (see page 42). The star exhibit is a bust of Nefertiti; other fine pieces include smiling mummies, a carving of the priest Tenti and his wife holding hands, a flying scarab, and a strange blue hedgehog. The 2,000-year-old Kalabscha Gate was a gift from the Egyptian government in 1973.

►► Alexanderplatz   37E3

Before World War II, 'Alex' was the hub of the Mitte district, the historic core of old Berlin. After the war, many of its buildings were replaced by truly ghastly architecture. The Alexander-Haus and Berolina-Haus are examples of an earlier 'objective' style, dating from the late 1920s. Since the wall came down, the square's antiseptic dreariness has been exchanged for a patina of graffiti and litter, though street musicians and artists add a human touch. One focal point in the square is the Weltzeituhr (world clock) which gives the times in various cities around the world. The high office buildings on the north side are due to be pulled down and replaced by 2013.

TV TOWER
Alexanderplatz's most
unmissable structure is
the 368m-high (1,207ft)
Fernsehturm (TV tower),
like a baseball stuck on
a skewer. The Berliners
call it Telespargel (Tele-
asparagus). An elevator
takes visitors to a view-
ing platform at the top
(40km/25-mile views on
a clear day) and a revolv-
ing restaurant. It was
built by the East German
regime in the 1960s.

*The dome of the
Protestant
cathedral beside
the River Spree*

39

QUEEN NEFERTITI
The famous limestone
bust of Queen Nefertiti in
the Ägyptisches Museum
shows her as a remark-
ably beautiful woman
even by today's Western
standards (best seen in
profile). She was the wife
of the unorthodox
Pharaoh Akhenaton, who
ruled Egypt from 1375 to
1358BC. The first thing
you notice is that she has
only one eye. Some histo-
rians believe Nefertiti
may have suffered from a
cataract, a common com-
plaint in ancient Egypt.
The bust was unearthed
by a German archaeolo-
gist in 1912, during
excavations of
Akhenaton's royal capi-
tal. It was removed from
the Neues Museum on
Museumsinsel toward the
end of World War II to
keep it out of Soviet
hands.

The square has seen revolutionary action several times, including the pro-democracy rallies of 1989. Its history is depicted in eight panels in a pedestrian underpass near the Park Inn Hotel Berlin. East Berlin's television tower, the Fernsehturm, Europe's second highest structure, dominates the square. It totally dwarfs Berlin's second-oldest parish church, the Marienkirche, restored in 1950. Its best feature is a dance of death fresco near the organ.

Southwest of Alexanderplatz is the Rotes Rathaus (Red Town Hall), so named for its bricks, not its politics! A 74m (243ft) tower dominates this neo-Renaissance building, decorated by 36 lively terracotta reliefs depicting Berlin's history. Near its entrance is the bronze Neptunbrunnen (Neptune Fountain).

▶ **Bauhaus-Archiv**   *36C2*

Klingelhöferstrasse 14
Open: Wed–Mon 10–5; www.bauhaus.de
This distinctive building (designed by Walter Gropius) beside the Landwehrkanal holds a variety of exhibits showing how widely the Bauhaus movement influenced 20th-century design, from architecture to typography. Plans and models of Mies van der Rohe's boxlike build-ings, period coffee services and desk lamps, paintings by Kandinsky and Klee, and Marcel Breuer's famously uncomfortable-looking chair are all on display. Computerized information (in English) summarizes the ideas and achievements of the Bauhaus artists. (See also **Dessau**, page 135.)

▶ **Berliner Dom**   *37D3*

Museumsinsel
Open: Mon–Sat 9–7, Sun 12–7; 9–8 (in summer);
www.berliner-dom.de
The Protestant cathedral (Dom) is one of the landmarks of eastern Berlin. Built at the turn of the 20th century in heavy neo-baroque style it is surmounted by an imposing dome. Inside are tombs of the Hohenzollerns and the Imperial Staircase leading to the parish church.

Brandenburger Tor at night

DÖBLIN'S NOVEL
Alfred Döblin drew on his experiences as a doctor in one of Berlin's districts for his novel *Berlin Alexanderplatz*. A pioneer stream-of-consciousness novel, it tells the grim story of an ex-convict released from prison after being wrongly convicted of murdering a prostitute. Trying to build a new life in the Berlin of the 1920s, he winds up in a lunatic asylum, then, eventually, in a bottom-of-the-heap job as a porter.

QUADRIGA CHARIOT
Sculptor Gottfried Schadow's *Quadriga*, the four-horse chariot that crowns the Brandenburger Tor was seized by Napoleon as war booty in one of his Prussian campaigns, but within 10 years the Prussians had recaptured it. Recast in copper after the original was destroyed in World War II, it was vandalized at the end of 1989 as crowds marked the peaceful revolution in East Germany. The *Quadriga* was fit again by August 1991, just in time for the gate's 200th anniversary.

▶▶ **Berlin Wall**   *37E2*

You can still see two sizeable chunks of the old Berlin Wall. The longest section, just over 1km (0.5 mile) long, at Mühlenstrasse, has been declared an historic monument. One year after the fall of the wall, more than 100 artists from all over the world decorated it with their work, and this section is now known as the 'East Side Gallery'. Sadly, the art work is falling victim to decay and graffiti, but it is still worth seeing.

Other sections of the wall, some 180m (590ft) long, are in Stresemannstrasse and nearby Niederkirchnerstrasse, alongside a plot of land where the Berlin branch of the Nazi Gestapo once had its headquarters.

▶ **Berlinische Galerie**   *37D1*

Alte Jakobstrasse 124–128
Open: daily 10–6; www.berlinischegalerie.de
This museum of modern art, photography and architecture (with works by Heckel, Kirchner, Dix and Grosz) focuses on experimental works from 1870 until the present.

▶▶▶ **Brandenburger Tor**   *37D2*

After the erection of the Berlin Wall, the Brandenburg Gate—stranded in no-man's-land—symbolized the division of Germany. It was built in 1788–91 as a triumphal arch for Friedrich Wilhelm II of Prussia by Langhans the Elder. Six tall Doric columns, front and back, form five passages. Under the Prussian Empire, the gate made a spectacular arena for military parades. Draped in swastikas, it also became a symbol of Nazi Germany.

▶▶ **Charlottenburg Museums**   *36A2*

Bröhan Museum (Schlossstrasse 1a. *Open: Tue–Sun 10–6; www.broehan-museum.de*) In this museum you can see a collection of art nouveau and art deco objets d'art: ceramics and glass, silver, paintings and furniture.

Museum für Vor- und Frühgeschichte (Langhans [west] Wing, Schloss Charlottenburg, Spandauer Damm 22. *Open* Tue–Fri 9–5, Sat–Sun 10–5) An excellent collection of material from early palaeolithic cultures through the Bronze and Iron ages. Though depleted after World War

II, the collection of Schliemann's Trojan finds is still remarkable. There are other Trojan finds held in the Bode-Museum (see page 42).

Sammlung Berggruen (Schlossstrasse 1. *Open* Tue–Sun 10–6) The exhibition called 'Picasso and his time' includes more than 100 works by Picasso, as well as pieces by Braque, Klee and Matisse.

▶▶ Checkpoint Charlie   37D2

Friedrichstrasse 43–45
Haus: open daily 9am–10pm; www.mauermuseum.de
Checkpoint Charlie, the former border crossing for foreign visitors, is now mostly a memory. A replica of the sign warning visitors they were leaving the American sector for the Soviet has been erected at the crossing. The original and other memorabilia are found in the nearby Mauer Museum 'Haus am Checkpoint Charlie', which details many of the most dramatic escapes through the heavily guarded crossing, including non-violent struggles for human rights in various countries.

▶▶▶ Gemäldegalerie   36C2

Kulturforum Matthäikirchplatz 4–6
Open: Tue–Sun 10–6, Thu until 10pm
The Gemäldegalerie (Picture Gallery) houses the world-famous royal German art collection: about 2,700 European paintings from the Middle Ages to the end of the 18th century. The German section includes works by Dürer, Altdorfer, Cranach and Holbein the Younger. The Dutch section has works by Rembrandt, Van Eyck, Bruegel, Rubens and Bosch. The museum is next to the Neue Nationalgalerie and the Philharmonic concert hall.

▶ Gendarmenmarkt   37D2

The two churches that frame this lovely square, just south of Unter den Linden, sum up the cosmopolitan openness of Berlin under the rule of Frederick the Great. Both churches, the Französischer Dom (French Cathedral) and the Deutscher Dom (German Cathedral) were built by Protestant Huguenot refugees from France, given refuge by Prussia. A third side of the cobbled square is taken up by Schinkel's neo-classical Schauspielhaus (theatre), now also called Konzerthaus Berlin, which regularly plays host to the Berlin Symphony Orchestra.

▶▶ Jüdisches Museum   37D2

Lindenstrasse 14
Open: Mon 10–10, Tue–Sun 10–8; www.jmberlin.de
This major museum of Jewish history in Berlin opened in October 2001. Its gleaming, labyrinth-like design is the work of the Polish, Berlin-based architect Daniel Libeskind, who also designed the futuristic extension to London's Victoria and Albert Museum.

▶▶▶ Kurfürstendamm   36B2

The famous Kurfürstendamm (Elector's Causeway) dates to the 16th century, when it was a bridleway used by the Prussian kings to reach their hunting lodges in the Grunewald. It became a popular address for Berlin's high society and was remodelled in 1871 by Bismarck, who had been impressed by the Champs Elysées. In World

DIE BRÜCKE ARTISTS
The eight-year association of the artists who called themselves Die Brücke (The Bridge) was unusually coherent. Four young artists, Kirchner, Heckel, Schmidt-Rottluff and Bleyl, founded the group in Dresden in 1905. They wanted to get away from the dull, imitative German art of the 19th century, and painted in a crude style using distortion and clashing colours in order to express emotions rather than verisimilitude. The name of this school of art is expressionism (Brücke-Museum, Bussardsteig 9, *Open* Wed–Mon 11–5; www.bruecke-museum.de).

41

A LOCAL ARTIST
After extensive restoration work, the Liebermann-Villa am Wannsee Museum (*Open* daily Wed–Mon; www.max-liebermann.de) reopened in 2006 at the beautiful lakeside home and garden of the celebrated Berlin Impressionist artist Max Liebermann. The permanent exhibition contains a collection of his garden paintings, pastels and graphic art and shows a documentary about his family and the villa.

TRANSPORT MUSEUM
The Deutsches Technikmuseum (www.dtmb.de), at Trebbinerstrasse 9, Kreuzberg, explains the history of aviation, railroads, cars, shipbuilding, printing, computers and much more. It is housed in market buildings and old workshops of the Anhalter Bahnhof. There is a remarkable Klaus Buscher mural on one external wall (*Open* Tue–Fri 9–5.30, Sat–Sun 10–6).

NIKOLAIVIERTEL
This area southwest of Alexanderplatz and focused on Berlin's oldest recorded building, the 13th-century Nikolaikirche, is a creation of the post-war planners of East Berlin. Destroyed in 1944, it is now a renovated quarter with restaurants and shops, masquerading as medieval Berlin. Some buildings are replicas of originals; others, modern in style, were designed to blend with the surroundings. East Berliners disdainfully referred to the area as Honecker's Disneyland, a reference to the former Communist Party chief, who poured scarce funding into the dubious project.

War II virtually all its great houses were destroyed and it became a long parade of bars and shops. The most striking landmark is the ruined tower of the Kaiser Wilhelm Gedächtniskirche (memorial church), bombed in 1943 but left as a reminder of the war. An exhibition inside refers to cities like Coventry in England that suffered similarly. Don't overlook the box-like modern church next door. It's not much from the outside, but the interior is bathed with the light streaming through rich blue glazing, a gift of reconciliation from France.

The tall, black plate-glass slab, the Europa-Center is nearby (see page 46), surmounted by a whirling Mercedes logo. Be aware, the area at this end of the Ku'damm can be seedy at night, a haunt of the homeless and prostitutes.

▶▶▶ Museen-Dahlem (Dahlem Museums)   36A1
Arnimallee 23–27/Lansstrasse 8
Open: Tue–Sun; www.museum-location.de/dahlem.htm
Dahlem, home of the Free University and a popular residential area, is known for its important group of museums. The **Museum für Indische Kunst** (Museum of Indian Art) has one of Europe's largest collections, with bronzes, wood carving and early Sanskrit manuscripts. The **Ethnologisches Museum** (Ethnographic Museum) has collected half a million objects from around the world, mainly non-European, to illustrate the culture of different societies. The **Museum für Ostasiatische Kunst** (Museum for Far Eastern Art) displays a comprehensive range of art from China, Japan and Korea. The **Museum Europäischer Kulturen** (Museum of European Cultures), set up in 1999, draws on various collections to stimulate greater understanding among European countries.

▶▶▶ Museumsinsel   37D3
Open: Tue–Sun
In 1841 Friedrich Wilhelm IV of Prussia designated Museumsinsel (Museum Island) 'an open space for art and science'. This complex of museums, on an island in the River Spree, is undergoing a 10-year phased renovation that is likely to run until about 2010. Some collections are thus not open to the public at any one time. If you only have time to visit one museum, make it the Pergamon.

The **Altes Museum▶** (*Open* Tue–Sun 10–6) on Lustgarten, was built between 1823 and 1830 by Schinkel. Heavily damaged in World War II and rebuilt in 1966, it shows Greek, Roman and especially Etruscan art. After refurbishment, the **Alte Nationalgalerie** (*Open* Tue–Sun 10–6, Thu until 10pm; www.alte-nationalgalerie.de), which used to be part of it, has opened with its collection of 19th-century paintings and sculptures, including masterpieces by Manet, Monet, Degas, Cezanne and Rodin.

The **Bode-Museum▶▶**, formerly the Kaiser Friedrich Museum, was the final addition to the Museumsinsel. Renamed in 1956 after its founder, the great art-historian Wilhelm von Bode. It contains the Museum für Ur- und Frühgeschichte (Museum of Pre- and Early History); a sculpture collection; the Museum of Byzantine Art and the Münzkabinett, which documents coinage from the 7th century BC to the present.

There are three great wonders of the ancient world in the **Pergamonmuseum▶▶▶** (*Open* Tue–Sun 10–6, Thu

until 10pm), which had to be constructed around them. The colossal Pergamon Altar is a temple of Zeus and Athena from Asia Minor and dates from 180–160BC. Marble steps ascend to a wide colonnade; gods and giants writhe around the plinths. Next are the huge Roman Market Gate and the Orpheus Mosaic, both from Miletus. Third is the most startling exhibit of all—a superb reconstruction of Nebuchadnezzar's Ishtar Gate and Processional Way from Babylon, with lions striding towering walls of azure tiles. Upstairs is the Pergamon's Islamic collection. Don't miss the Mshatta Gate from Jordan and the panelled 17th-century Aleppo Room.

The impressive Babylonian Ishtar Gate in the Pergamonmuseum

▶▶ Neue Nationalgalerie   36C2
Potsdamer Strasse 50 (Kulturforum)
Open: Tue–Wed 9–6, Thu 9–10, Fri–Sun 9–8;
www.neue-nationalgalerie.de
The glass-and-steel New National Gallery was designed by Mies van der Rohe and completed in 1968. The collection of 20th-century paintings, drawings and sculpture includes works by Kokoschka, Klee, Munch and Grosz.

▶ Potsdamer Platz   37D2
For more than 30 years a no-man's-land straddling the Berlin Wall, the Potsdamer Platz is becoming one of the world's showpiece plazas. Two developments, the Sony Center, with its glass tower, and the Daimler Chrysler City mixed ensemble of buildings, dominate the skyline.

▶▶ Reichstag   37D2
Platz der Republik
Open: daily 8am–midnight
Built between 1884 and 1894 for the all-German Parliament, the Reichtstag was burned out in 1933. It was further damaged in World War II, and then nearly forgotten in its corner, close to the Wall, for more than 50 years. Now it has been refurbished and redesigned internally as the home of the German Parliament, the Bundestag. British architect Sir Norman Foster designed the changes, adding to the building a glass dome which serves as a scenic viewing platform.

MUSIC MUSEUM
A bright and cheerful museum, the Musikinstrumenten-Museum (Museum of Musical Instruments; www.mim-berlin.de), in the Kulturforum, Tiergartenstrasse 1, is right next door to the Philharmonie concert hall, home of the famed Berlin Philharmonic Orchestra. It features instruments and their manufacture from the 16th century to the present day, from an ancient set of bagpipes to synthesizers. There are occasional demonstrations of instruments (*Open* Tue–Sun). Both buildings were designed by Hans Scharoun, the prominent post-war architect.

HELL IN SUBURBIA
Sachsenhausen is a former Nazi concentration camp that stands in the middle of an otherwise pleasant Berlin suburb. Now the place is oddly peaceful and birds sing, but during the war thousands of 'undesirables', or *Untermenschen*, were herded here—liberals, pacifists, communists, homosexuals, as well as Jewish people and captured Allies.
Sachsenhausen charts a period of Berlin's history that should never be forgotten.

The head of a dying warrior at the former Zeughaus

▶▶ Sachsenhausen   132 B3

Strasse der Nationen 22, Oranienburg (take S-Bahn to Oranienburg).
Open: Tue–Sun; www.gedenkstaetten-sachsenhausen.de
Sachsenhausen Concentration Camp was opened as a memorial after 45 years in East German hands. First you see the boot-testing track, where prisoners were forced to run on different surfaces carrying heavy weights until they dropped (at which point they would be shot where they lay); then the accommodation blocks, the cell blocks in which prisoners languished in darkness for months until they died; and the 'hospital' where the most horrific experiments were carried out on inmates. The displays consist mostly of photographs and information boards charting the sombre history of the place.

▶▶ Schloss Charlottenburg   36A3

Spandauer Damm 20–24/Luisenplatz
Open: Tue–Sun; www.spsg.de
This vast palace began life in 1695 as a home for Sophie-Charlotte, wife of the future Friedrich I of Prussia. Eventually it became a summer residence for the Prussian kings. The rococo-style Neuer Flügel (New—or Knobelsdorff—Wing) was built for Frederick the Great.
   The gardens, first laid out in 1697 in the French style, were transformed into an English-style garden in the early 19th century. Be sure to see the Schinkel Pavilion, the Mausoleum and the Belvedere, with its fine collection of porcelain (Meissen and Berlin's homegrown KPM, or Königliche Porzellan Manufaktur).

▶▶▶ Unter den Linden   37D2

Berlin's famous thoroughfare—the name means 'under the linden trees'—was once a royal mall. Frederick the Great's bronze equestrian statue, backed by the Brandenburger Tor (Brandenburg Gate), looks down on the swirling traffic from the middle of his great avenue, leading to the River Spree. The French Embassy and the immense embassy of the former Soviet Union (now used by the Russian Federation), dominates the western end of the avenue. It will be joined in 2008 by new American embassy building in an ensemble recapturing the former elegance of this area adjacent to the Brandenburger Tor. The modern British Embassy, designed by Michael Wilford of London, can be found around the corner at its pre-war site in Wilhelmstrasse. It was formally opened by Queen Elizabeth in July 2000.
   If you follow Unter den Linden east you will reach, on the left, the neo-classical palace of the **Humboldt University** building. The restored former **Zeughaus**▶▶ (Arsenal), , which reopened in June 2006, is situated near the eastern end, and houses the Deutsches Historisches Museum (*Open* daily; www.dhm.de). Sculptor Andreas Schlüter designed and cast the 22 heads of dying warriors in the inner courtyard; they are outstanding examples of German monumental sculpture.
   Other buildings worth looking out for are Schinkel's neo-classical **Neue Wache** (New Guardhouse), the restored baroque **Alte Bibliothek**, and the **Deutsche Staatsoper** (opera house), a splendid example of neo-classical architecture.

Excursion

▶▶▶ Potsdam   *132B3*

www.potsdam.de

Public transportation and organized bus tours allow easy access to Potsdam. Its main claim to fame is 18th-century **Schloss Sanssouci**▶▶ (*Open* Tue–Sun; www.spsg.de), summer home of Frederick the Great of Prussia, whose aim was to indulge in cultural pursuits *sans souci*—'without care'. It is widely recognized as the finest example of rococo in Europe. Below it are broad south-facing terraces where Frederick the Great planted vines: Their rows of green-framed protective glass screens are a curious sight.

At the other end of the large park of Sanssouci stands the ostentatious **Neues Palais** (New Palace; *Open* Sat–Thu). Look for the huge Marble Hall and, beneath it, a fine indoor grotto encrusted with shells and minerals. The palace also houses the restored Schlosstheater. Enjoy the fine view from **Belvedere** (*Open* daily. *Closed* Dec–Feb and Nov and Mar Mon–Fri) on the Pfingstberg hill.

Another park, the lakeside Neuer Garten, is the site of **Schloss Cecilienhof**▶ (*Open* Tue–Sun; www.spsg.de) a mock-Tudor residence built for Kaiser Wilhelm II's son one year before the monarchy was toppled in 1918. In 1945 it hosted the Potsdam Conference, when Churchill (then Attlee), Truman and Stalin decided Germany's future.

In the town Try to see the fine Classical **Nikolaikirche** (St. Nicholas Church) by Schinkel and Persius, restored after war damage, and the 18th-century **Holländisches Viertel** (Dutch Quarter). In Babelsberg you can tour the UFA studios (Babelsberg Filmpark. *Open* mid-Apr–Oct daily), where Marlene Dietrich filmed *The Blue Angel*.

ROYAL REBURIAL
Thanks to reunification, Frederick the Great's family was able, in 1991, to carry out the king's wishes and rebury his remains, which had lain at Burg Hohenzollern near Stuttgart, at Sanssouci, next to his 13 greyhounds. Frederick wrote: 'Let me be taken by the light of a single lantern, with no cortege, to Sanssouci, and buried simply on the right-hand side of the terrace'. His wishes were not carried out at the time of his death, since his family was appalled at the prospect of him lying in unconsecrated ground. The evocative reinterment ceremony on the 205th anniversary of Frederick's death, on 18 August, 1991, caused controversy as it was seen by some as a revival of Prussian-style nationalism.

45

Potsdam: Frederick the Great's rococo summer palace is surprisingly small and intimate

Berlin

WEEKEND ITINERARY

SATURDAY

Morning: Board the S-Bahn at the Zoologischer Garten station for Hackescher Markt. Cross the Museumsinsel and devote an hour to the exhibits in the Pergamonmuseum. Take a look in the nearby Berliner Dom (cathedral). Turn down Unter den Linden, take a left opposite the Humboldt University, cross the square (Bebel Platz) where the Nazis burned the books, and then enter one of Europe's most beautiful piazzas, the Gendarmenmarkt. There are several good restaurants here.

Afternoon: Retrace your steps to Unter den Linden, turn left and there before you is the Brandenburger Tor. Take the lift to the viewing platform of the nearby Reichstag, then board bus 200 at nearby Pariserplatz for Potsdamer Platz. Wander down Stresemannstrasse, take a left into Niederkirchnerstrasse, where you'll find a remnant of the Berlin Wall. Continue into Friedrichstrasse and you're at 'Checkpoint Charlie'.

Evening: Try for seats at the Staatsoper Unter den Linden, or at a classical concert at the Konzerthaus or Philharmonie; or tickets for Friedrichstadtpalast, Europe's biggest revue theatre; or for any of the smaller cabarets.

SUNDAY

Take the S-Bahn from Zoologischer Garten station to Potsdam and visit Sanssouci. On return, take in one of the museums at the Kulturforum or stroll around Charlottenburg palace and gardens. Take a meal or refreshment in the late afternoon or evening in one of the many establishments around Savignyplatz.

Shopping

There is only one store that is an absolute must, the famous **KaDeWe** (Kaufhaus des Westens—Store of the West), which claims to be Europe's biggest department store, larger even than London's Harrods and, many shoppers say, with a greater variety of high-class goods. You could spend all day shopping here, but don't miss a

visit to the Feinschmecker Etage (Gourmet Floor), where there are delicacies from all over the world. Not far from the KaDeWe, on Tauentzienstrasse, is the **Europa-Center**. Although it has more than 70 shops and 20 restaurants, there is little of interest to the tourist.

For fashion, visit the Kurfürstendamm and its side streets, particularly Uhlandstrasse and Fasanenstrasse, where exclusive shops sell the latest creations of Berlin's top designers. Fashion of yesteryear is also a Berlin speciality, in the form of stylish second-hand clothing on sale in flea markets and in many other shops in the Kreuzberg, Schöneberg, Charlottenburg and Prenzlauer Berg districts. Around Savignyplatz are a wealth of specialized shops.

Elegant Friedrichstrasse, the premier shopping mecca of the well-heeled, is again developing into an exciting area for shoppers, with new stores opening all the time. The stylishly French Galeries Lafayette is worth a visit just for its amazing interior. The same applies to the revived old heart of Spandau, a select residential suburb. Rather than the inevitable bear, you might choose Berlin porcelain as a souvenir of your visit; attractive, if pricey, it is available from the Ku'damm showroom. If you prefer the 'opposition', try the Meissen showroom on Unter den Linden.

A trendy little precinct has been developed at the refurbished Hackesche Höfe (across from S-Bahn Hackescher Markt). A lively enclosed shopping mall (Arkaden) forms a central part of the reconstructed Potsdamer Platz ensemble between the eastern and western parts of the city.

Markets Local markets abound in Berlin. For bric-à-brac, **Trödelmarkt** in Prenzlauer Berg can produce a bargain, while the lively weekend **Strasse des 17 Juni market** (S-Bahn Tiergarten) offers a wide range of second-hand items. For a taste of the Orient, visit the **Turkish market** on Maybachufer, in Neukölln (Tue and Fri afternoons).

Food and drink

Where to eat German food can be somewhat heavy, but with a degree of Austrian influence and a dash of German creativity, a new generation of chefs have come up with *neue Deutsche Küche*—Germany's version of *nouvelle cuisine* (not cheap).

Highly recommended is **Trio** at Klausenerplatz 14; the **Spree-Athen** in Charlottenburg offers music from old Berlin and six-course meals. If money is no object, the **Bamberger Reiter**, Regensburgerstrasse 7, is your best bet. At the **Opernpalais unter den Linden**, Schinkelklause specializes in a regional dishes.

Die Alte Pumpe, Lützowstrasse 42, with an enormous restored water pump as focal point, is a three-level restaurant with traditional Berlin dishes, and a superb array of sweet and savoury pancakes. Also recommended is its sensational Sunday buffet breakfast.

The eastern part of the city, a culinary desert until reunification, is now able to match the west in range and quality of restaurants, and prices can be significantly lower. The Prenzlauer Berg district is particularly worth exploring, and on Kastanienallee (Nos. 7–9) you'll find one of Berlin's most atmospheric taverns, the **Prater Garten**, which has the city's oldest beer garden.

In the ancient heart of the city, also in the eastern part, is the tavern-restaurant where **Zur Letzten Instanz** (Waisenstrasse 14–16) has hosted Napoleon, Beethoven and, more recently, political leaders Gorbachev, Shröder and Chirac.

Berlin, with its large expanses of lakes and open countryside, has many charming country restaurants within its boundaries: The **Alter Dorfkrug Lübars** in the village of Lübars (Alt Lübars 8) and the **Blockhaus Nikolskoe** in the wooded depths of Glienecker Park are both worth the long journey. **Café Einstein** (Kurfürstenstrasse 58) is a popular (and crowded) re-creation of Viennese coffeehouse culture, with gardens at the back.

The department store **KaDeWe** has a number of counters where you can enjoy a typical Berliner lunch that won't break the bank.

WHERE TRENDIES GO

Yuppies—the Germans call them 'schickie mickies'—are looked down upon. Their habitat is the trendy suburbs, like Grunewald or Dahlem, and they usually shun the tourist spots. You're likely to find creative and arty types in the bars and coffee shops of the Savignyplatz area. But so many students frequent these places, too, that the trendies are not easy to spot. Gainsbourg, at Savignyplatz 5, is the place to be seen on a weekday morning when everyone else is at work. With its leafy terrace, it is an especially popular summer meeting place.

47

WEISSE MIT SCHUSS

A popular summer drink is *Berliner Weisse mit Schuss*—light beer with a shot of raspberry syrup or liqueur, which turns it pink, or extract of the plant woodruff, which makes it green. This 'champagne of the north' was concocted by Huguenots in the 17th century, when they found the local beer too bitter.

Outdoor restaurants and cafés remain popular meeting places

WEEK'S ITINERARY

MONDAY
Morning: Ku'damm and Kaiser Wilhelm Gedächtniskirche; explore side-street shops.
Afternoon: Boat trip on River Spree or tour Potsdamer Platz sights and shops.

TUESDAY
Morning: Dahlem museums, with lunch in museum café.
Afternoon: Finish Dahlem museums or wander around Dahlem village and its small church.

WEDNESDAY
Morning: Neue and Alte Nationalgalerie; Musikinstrumenten-Museum; or Kunst-gewerbemuseum all at Kulturforum.
Afternoon: Take S-Bahn to Potsdam for Sanssouci.

THURSDAY
Morning: Schloss Charlottenburg; walk through the gardens at the back of the castle.
Afternoon: Visit the Bröhan Museum and Sammlung Berggruen, all across from the palace.

FRIDAY
Morning: Tour the Reichstag; Brandenburger Tor; Alexanderplatz; Unter den Linden.
Afternoon: Shopping/leisure or, if stamina allows, Museumsinsel.

SATURDAY
Morning: Visit the open-air market at Winterfeldtplatz, or flea market on Strasse des 17 Juni.
Afternoon: Trip to a suburb such as Lake Tegel, or Wannsee, or Köpenick (Müggelsee).

SUNDAY
Morning: Breakfast at Savignyplatz; visit to an art gallery or museum (such as Bauhaus-Archiv).
Afternoon: Walk around Englischer Garten, part of the grounds of the Schloss Bellevue; or along the River Spree or in the Tiergarten park.

Nightlife

Like New York, Berlin is a city that never sleeps. The nightlife starts in the early hours of the morning, so if you need a good night's rest, you'll probably miss out on the more exciting aspects of the city. Nothing ever gets going before midnight, and while prowling around the discos at 11pm will get you an entrance ticket, you'll find you're alone. Young Germans living in Hamburg or Munich come to Berlin for a weekend of clubbing; there are no laws for closing hours, and many bars and discos stay open until 6am. You might consider the **Friedrichstadt Palast** (Friedrichstrasse 107; www.friedrichstadtpalast.de), highly recommended for all sorts of night shows and revues.

For night bars, discos and cabarets, the liveliest youth scene is in the Scheunenviertel ('barn quarter') in the east, near the New Synagogue; the **Tacheles** (Oranienburger Strasse 54–56) counter-culture centre and the Hackescher Markt area are trendy. If your German is limited choose from one of the international cabaret or revue theatres; they're relatively expensive but have world-class entertainment. Among the best are the **Chamäleon Variete**, (Rosenthaler Strasse 40–1), the **Friedrichstadt Palast** (Friedrichstrasse 107), the **Winter Garten** (Potsdamerstrasse 96) and the **Bar jeder Vernunft**, at Schaperstrasse 24.

The touristy Ku'damm is by day a fashionable shopping street; by night it is the haunt of prostitutes. In Kreuzberg there are a variety of leather bars, discos and strip joints, making up the city's 'alternative' scene.

Cabaret, folk music and dance clubs are scattered throughout the city. For jazz lovers, the **Quasimodo Club** at Kantstrasse 12 is a must. Magazines such as *Berlin-Magazine*, *Tip* and *Zitty* provide details on what's on where. On a different level, there are three opera houses, four symphony orchestras and enough cabaret and theatre to keep you occupied for months on end. In the summer, the **Waldbühne**, the city's open-air arena in the shadow of the Olympic stadium, plays host to classical concerts and performances by international pop stars.

T-shirts for sale

Accommodation

Reunification restored to Berlin some of its finest and most famous hotels, which had been left to decay by the Communist regime. One, the Adlon, Berlin's most historic and best-loved hotel, named after its self-made hotelier owner, was literally stranded for more than 30 years in the no-man's-land at the junction of Unter den Linden and the Brandenburger Tor. Now it has been rebuilt to its former glory. The equally palatial Grand Hotel gleams again in its central location just off Friedrichstrasse, while Berlin's Hilton has made its home in the restored shell of the old Dom Hotel in Mohrenstrasse. The lingering squabbles over property ownership in East Berlin mean that the range of hotel accommodation there is by no means as extensive as in the West and rates are usually higher, although some small pensions, particularly in the Prenzlauer Berg district, offer excellent value for money. Berlin hotels have become very expensive since the wall fell. Increasingly, visitors find themselves using small pensions and bed-and-breakfast accommodation, or staying some distance out of town. Since public transportation is so efficient, the last is quite feasible if you have the time and don't mind quiet evenings or travelling to the centre at night; there are several peaceful hotels in the Grunewald area near the Wannsee. Other options for budget visitors are a number of youth hostels and hotels designed with students in mind. The tourist office provides a free list. Accommodation is basic, possibly without a private bath or shower, but civilized.

If you like more idiosyncratic accommodation, try a pension or small hotel on or just off the Ku'damm in the older houses that escaped bombings. Many are family-run, with characterful rooms, often retaining original art deco or Jugendstil (art nouveau) features. There are several in Wielandstrasse, others in Meinekestrasse. Most hotels lie clustered around the Europa-Center, and are a bit dull. Though generally in good condition, with most facilities and sparklingly clean, they now look quite passé.

If you are a non-smoker it's as well to note that a surprising number of 'health-conscious' Germans smoke (see page 17), and hotel bedrooms may smell of stale tobacco. Ask for non -smoking rooms, if they are available.

Bismarckstrasse, one of the key links in the metropolitan road network

WHERE THE RICH AND FAMOUS GO

The best place to observe the rich and famous is at the Deutsche Opera on Bismarckstrasse—spend the intervals celebrity-spotting in the bars. Between January and March the fashionable world takes to the dance floor in balls, including the Press Ball, usually attended by the chancellor and foreign minister. The most sought-after and elegant ball is organized by the wealthy business community. The top shopping spot is along the western end of the Ku'damm, while top people dine at Facil (Potsdamerstrasse 3); the Adlon; Van (Jagerstrasse 54–55); or trendy Pan Asia (Rosenthalerstrasse 38).

BEDROOMS DEBUGGED

Following the collapse of the Communist regime, many hard-currency hotels were closed for several days so that corridor cameras could be taken out, bedrooms debugged and secret-police rooms converted to hotel use.

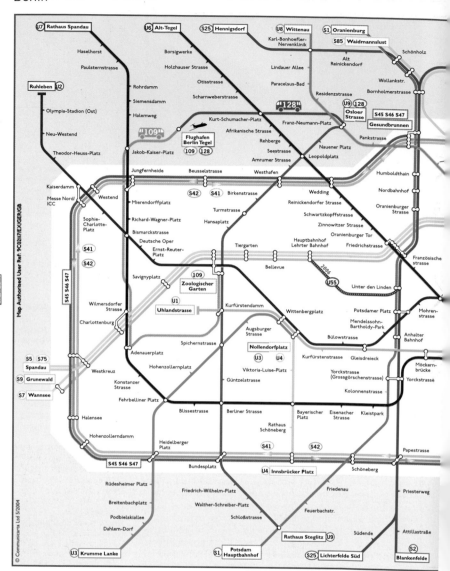

Map Authorised User Ref: 9C0311/IEX/GER/GB

© Communicarta Ltd 5/2004

50

TOURIST OFFICES

The main tourist information office, BERLIN 'inforstores' is situated in the Europa-Center, with its entrance at 45 Budapesterstrasse, near Zoo station and KaDeWe. More tourist information offices can be found next to Brandenburger Tor, Fernsenturm (Alexanderplatz); Neues Kranzler Eck (Kurfürstendammzi).

Transportation

There are few areas in Berlin that you cannot reach by public transportation. Compared with many European cities, traffic congestion is low; buses move at a reasonable speed and keep to timetables. Since reunification the city's twin transport networks (formerly impeded by the wall) have been merged, and the old subway lines and stations reopened. Berlin has an underground rail U-Bahn system (11 lines, excellent for the central areas), an S-Bahn system (10 lines) serving outlying areas, and a conventional rail network for the distant suburbs.

An excellent bus system operates throughout the city, with night services too. There are some ferries, and the

STILE45

Birkenwerder **S8**
Bernau **S2**

(U2)
Pankow

Vinetastrasse

B

(S42)

Schönhauser Allee
Prenzlauer Allee

Greifswalder Strasse

Landsberger Allee

(S41)

Voltastrasse
Eberswalder Strasse

Bernauer Strasse
Rosenthaler Platz
Weinmeister-strasse

Senefelderplatz

Storkower Strasse

A

Rosa-Luxemburg-Platz

Frankfurter Allee

Hackescher Markt

Schillingstrasse Weberwiese Samariterstrasse

Hönow **U5**

(U5) Alexander - platz

Strausberger Platz Frankfurter Tor

Jannowitzbrücke

S42

Klosterstrasse

Ostbahnhof **S3**

Märkisches Museum

Heinrich-Heine-Strasse

S41

Stadtmitte

U1

Spittelmarkt

Warschauer Strasse

Hausvogteiplatz
Kochstrasse

Ostkreuz

Ahrensfeld **S7**

Moritzplatz

Wartenburg **S75**

Strausberg Nord **S5**

Hallesches Tor

Kottbusser Tor

Schlesisches Tor

Görlitzer Bahnhof

Prinzenstrasse

Mehringdamm

Schönleinstrasse

Erkner **S3**

Hermannplatz

Gneisenaustr. Südstern

Rathaus Neukölln

Treptower Park

Platz der Luftbrücke (Flughafen Tempelhof) ✈

Boddinstrasse

Sonnenallee

Paradestrasse

Leinestrasse

Karl-Marx-Strasse

Tempelhof **S41** **S42**

Plänterwald

S45 S46 S47

Hermannstrasse
U8 **S45**

Neukölln

Alt-Tempelhof

Grenzallee

Baumschulenweg

Kaiserin-Augusta-Str.

Blaschkoallee

Ullsteinstraße

Parchimer-Allee

Grünau **S8** **S85**

Zeuthen **S8**

Westphalweg

Britz-Süd

Spindlersfeld **S47**

Flughafen Schönefeld ✈ **S45** **S9**

Alt-Mariendorf **U6**

Rudow **U7**

Königs Wusterhausen **S46**

UDN.6b

51

east has a modernized tram network that has been extended to some western connecting points. Standard fares operate for buses, trams, U-Bahn and S-Bahn (cheaper for short hops, or *Kurzstrecke*, and children). Tickets are valid for two hours and can be used on any system within that time (but not for return or round trips). Before your journey, validate each ticket by punching it into a machine to stamp the time. For visitors planning to explore Berlin extensively, it is worth buying a 'Welcome Card': This gives free travel on public transportation for 48 or 72 hours plus reductions on entry to many museums, theatres and tours.

Ask for details of inclusive or family tickets at any ticket counter.

Official red-starred caps of the old GDR are now collectors' items

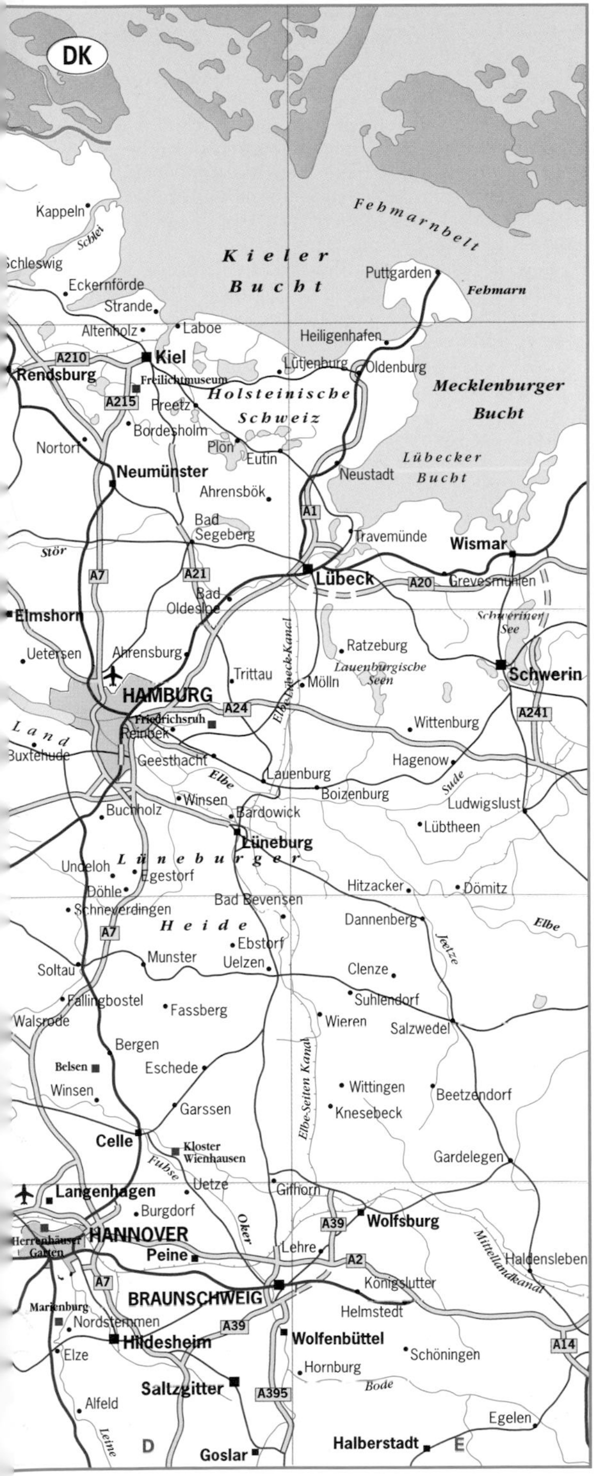

DK

Kappeln
Schleswig
Schlei
Eckernförde
Strande
Altenholz
Laboe
Kiel
A210
Rendsburg
A215 Preetz
Bordesholm
Nortorf
Plön
Neumünster
Eutin
Ahrensbök
Bad Segeberg
Elmshorn
Uetersen
Ahrensburg
Trittau
HAMBURG
Friedrichsruh
Reinbek
Buxtehude
Geesthacht
Buchholz
Winsen
Bardowick
Lüneburg
Undeloh
Döhle
Schneverdingen
Soltau
Fallingbostel
Walsrode
Bergen
Belsen
Winsen
Celle
Kloster Wienhausen
Uetze
Langenhagen
Burgdorf
Herrenhäuser Garten
HANNOVER
Peine
A7
BRAUNSCHWEIG
Marienburg
Nordstemmen
Hildesheim
Elze
Saltzgitter
Alfeld
Leine
D
Goslar

Febmarnbelt
Puttgarden
Febmarn
Heiligenhafen
Lütjenburg Oldenburg
Kieler Bucht
Freilichtmuseum
Holsteinische Schweiz
Lübecker Bucht
Neustadt
Mecklenburger Bucht
Travemünde
Wismar
A1
Lübeck
A20 Grevesmühlen
Ratzeburg
Schweriner See
Lauenburgische Seen
Mölln
Schwerin
Wittenburg
A241
Hagenow
Lauenburg
Boizenburg
Ludwigslust
Lübtheen
Hitzacker
Dömitz
Dannenberg
Elbe
Ebstorf
Clenze
Suhlendorf
Wieren
Salzwedel
Wittingen
Knesebeck
Beetzendorf
Gardelegen
Gifhorn
A39 **Wolfsburg**
Lehre
A2
Haldensleben
Königslutter
Helmstedt
Wolfenbüttel
Schöningen
A14
Hornburg
Bode
Egelen
Halberstadt
E

Stör
A7
A21
Bad Oldesloe
Elbe-Lübeck-Kanal
A24
Elbe
Egestorf
Bad Bevensen
A7
Munster
Uelzen
Fassberg
Eschede
Garssen
Aller
Leine
Oker
A39
A395
Land
Lüneburger Heide
Elbe-Seiten Kanal
Jeetze
Sude
Mittellandkanal

Northwest Germany

Katharinenkirche (St Catherine's Church) in Braunschweig

The northwest includes the two seaports of **Hamburg** and **Bremen**, each an autonomous *Land* (state) on its own, as well as the whole of the *Land* of Schleswig-Holstein and nearly all of Niedersachsen (Lower Saxony). The area lacks the scenic wonders of the south, but it has its own quiet beauties, such as the **Lüneburg Heath**, the windswept North Sea and Baltic beaches and islands and many historic and picturesque towns with buildings of mellow red brick, half-timbers and stepped gables.

Some areas carry on the Hanseatic merchant tradition (see page 75); others are influenced by the great princely houses of the past, such as the Guelphs and Brunswicks. The farms on the rolling plains tend to be large, rich and modern. **Schleswig-Holstein**, long fought over between Germany and Denmark, did not become part of Prussia until 1864, and still has a Danish minority. In 1945 the former dukedoms of Schleswig and Holstein merged to form one *Land* with its capital at **Kiel**. The coastlines of the Baltic and North Sea are very different: The Baltic coast is gently pastoral, cut by low fiords and backed by wooded hills, while the North Sea coast is more flat and stark, buffeted by winds and storms that erode the soil. Major holiday resorts include the offshore island of **Sylt**.

Lower Saxony is misleadingly named, for its Saxon tribes emigrated in the Dark Ages and today it has no connection with true Saxony around Leipzig (see pages 148–149). It has handsome old towns, such as **Celle**, **Lüneburg** and **Stade**, and modern industry, mostly around its capital, **Hannover**. In the coastal area of **Friesland**, which extends up into Schleswig-Holstein, people keep their own culture and language.

▶ Braunschweig (Brunswick)   53D1
A historic city with royal connections: In the 12th century it was the seat of Germany's most powerful ruler, the Guelph prince Henry the Lion. His symbol, a bronze, rampant lion, was erected on the Burgplatz in 1166 and later was adopted as the city's crest. The lion that now stands in the square is a copy; the original, badly corroded by pollution, was removed 20 years ago and is in the **Herzog Anton Ulrich Museum** (*Open* Tue–Sun; www.museum-braunschweig.de), where you will also find works by Rembrandt, Rubens, Vermeer and Cranach. Later (1753–1918) the dukes of Brunswick lived here. The city was heavily bombed and then rebuilt. Today it is mainly industrial (trucks, machinery, and so forth), but fine buildings survive, notably the half-timbered Gothic and Renaissance houses on the Altstadtmarkt, and Henry's Romanesque cathedral. The latter contains his gift of a big seven-branch candelabrum, the splendid Imervard Crucifix (1150), and the tomb of Henry and his English wife, Mathilda.

▶▶ Bremen   52C2
www.bremen-tourism.de
Germany's largest port after Hamburg is a fascinating old Hanseatic city with a quirky, individualist personality. Like its bigger rival, it has a long history of independence. Its people are maritime, outward-looking and liberal-minded. Its port on the River Weser expanded in the 19th century as a base for coffee and cotton imports.

Intense competition from Rotterdam and Antwerp has caused problems for the port. Its shipyards have declined and, despite the arrival of new modern industries (notably aerospace, cars and electronics), many people are out of work. The new university began life in the 1970s, in a blaze of radical leftism. It has now grown milder but remains innovative.

Despite being a northern city, Bremen is full of lively outdoor life—markets, street musicians, festivals. In the **Marktplatz▶** (Market Square) you might find men in sailors' outfits singing sea shanties, or see a man in top hat and tails sweeping rubbish from the cathedral steps (it's a local custom that a man still unwed on his 30th birthday is expected to do this, then marry the first girl who kisses him). The buildings are varied—tall mansions in Weser Renaissance style (see page 119), newer Jugendstil villas with oddly shaped gables, even a windmill on a grassy hill made from part of the old ramparts that enclose the Altstadt (Old Town).

Rebuilt after World War II, much of the Altstadt is traffic-free and best toured on foot. The twin-towered cathedral is a Romanesque/Gothic mix and has a 13th-century bronze font. The arcaded **Rathaus▶▶** (town hall), also Gothic, with some Renaissance, has a noble banqueting hall. Its Ratskeller (cellar restaurant) serves no French wines, only German (a custom kept from Napoleonic days), and has 17th-century cubicles for private parties (a woman and a man dining alone must keep the door open). Outside stand two famous statues. One, built in 1404 as a symbol of independence, is a 10m (33ft) figure of Charlemagne's nephew, Roland. The other is modern: a bronze pyramid of a cock, a cat, a dog and a donkey—the town musicians of Grimm's folktale.

The **Böttcherstrasse▶**, leading off the Marktplatz, is a Jugendstil alleyway designed in the 1920s by the offbeat Worpswede (see page 77) architect Bernhard Hoetger. Its

The statue of the Knight Roland (1404), in stately Marktplatz, bears the sword of justice

55

The Renaissance façade of the majestic Rathaus. Inside is a sumptuous Guildhall

In the North Sea, 90km (60 miles) northwest of Bremerhaven, Helgoland (www. helogland.de) is an unspectacular small sandstone island. Its strategic position, however, commanding the sea-lanes to the North Sea ports, made it a valuable possession. Germany eventually gained ownership in 1890 by swapping it with Britain for the island of Zanzibar.

Celle's crest derives from the mighty Guelph princes who ruled the town from 1378 to 1705

INFORMATION
Celle: Markt 14–16, tel: 05141/12 12

gabled houses form a shopping arcade with stylish boutiques. There are also two small museums (www.pmbm.de), one of medieval art, the Roselius-Haus (*Open* Sat–Thu) and one devoted to Paula Modersohn-Becker and other Worpswede artists (*Open* Tue–Sun). The nearby Schnoor district has narrow streets lined with old fishermen's cottages. It is a popular tourist district, full of crafts stores, cafés and boutiques, but still engaging.

The main museums are outside the Altstadt. The large **Focke Museum►** (*Open* Tue–Sun; www.focke-museum.de) gives a wonderful idea of Bremen's history, with maps, paintings, photos, model ships and much else, set in parkland. The Überseemuseum is one of Germany's leading ethnological museums. The excellent **Kunsthalle's►** varied paintings range from Cranach and Altdorfer via Brueghel and Delacroix to the Worpswede school (*Open* Tue–Sun; www.kunsthalle-bremen.de).

► Bremerhaven   52C3
www.bremerhaven.de
This big workaday port, 60km (37 miles) downstream from Bremen at the mouth of the Weser, was created in 1827 as Bremen's deep-sea port. It is still busy, but the Columbuskaje (quay), where ocean liners used to berth, is now used by ferries and cruise ships. This is also Germany's leading fishing port and has several museums: an aquarium and fishing museum, an outdoor museum with 17th-century peasant houses, and the **Deutsches Schiffahrtsmuseum►** (*Open* Apr–Oct daily; Nov–Mar Tue–Sun; www.dsm.de), a big museum of maritime history with models of old boats and harbours, plus a genuine Hanseatic trading vessel of 1380.

►► Celle   53D2
www.celle.de
This is a stately town, one of north Germany's finest, with a princely history. It has a neat, gridlike Altstadt of 16th- to 18th-century red and white gabled, half-timbered houses, some with upper floors overhanging. Horses are bred in the region and the parade of stallions through the town in early autumn is well worth seeing.

The Lüneburg branch of the Guelph dynasty ruled here from 1378 to 1705. Their handsome white **Schloss►**, enclosed by a swan-filled moat, has a 17th-century theatre that still stages classic plays. The vaulted 15th-century chapel has rich Renaissance decor, while the state rooms are Italian baroque. Nearby, note the biblical quotes on the decorated façade of the Lateinschule (1602), a former college, and the trompe-l'oeil of the old grey Rathaus (1579). Every day at 8.15 (Sun at 9.30) and 5.15 the town's bugler mounts the 235 steps of the Gothic Stadtkirche to blow his horn heavenwards.

Southeast of Celle is a marvel—the 13th-century Cistercian abbey of **Wienhausen**, evocative of medieval times. Since the Reformation it has been a retirement home for lay Protestant women. The stunning medieval tapestries are on display only around Whitsun (late May until late June), but you can see the 14th-century murals in the chapel and the tiny museum containing 15th-century scissors, knives, nailfiles, spectacles and notebooks, all found under the chapel floorboards in 1953.

The harbour at Emden, from the viewing deck of the Rathaus tower

WORKING WINDMILLS
The attractive Grossefehn area near Emden is known for its five hand-some 19th-century windmills. Two have been restored to working order and are again grinding corn. This brings in some money, but the main purpose is to attract tourists. The friendly owner of the Dutch-type mill at Spetzerfehn shows visitors around on weekends and take them up to the gallery to inspect the metal sails. The other restored mill is at Bagband. These are the only working windmills left in the region.

57

▶ **Emden**   *52A3*
www.emden.de
Emden is situated on the Ems estuary and is a herring-fishing base and industrial port for the Ruhr via the Ems-Dortmund canal. The Landesmuseum has displays of weapons and of local history (*Open* Tue–Sun). The new Kunsthalle has a good collection of modern German paintings (*Open* Tue–Sun). The windy Ostfriesland plain is mainly dull, but **Greetsiel** is a pretty fishing village.

▶ **Flensburg**   *52C5*
Set on a fiord by the Danish border, this handsome old port was long part of Denmark and still has a Danish look and ambience. Its fine buildings include the 15th-century Gothic Nikolaikirche and the 16th-century Nordertor (north gate). Flensburg used to be a wealthy merchant town based on Caribbean sugar and rum trade. Its history is documented in the **Schiffahrtsmuseum** (*Open* Tue–Sun) with exhibits that date from the 16th century.

Out on an islet in the fiord to the northeast is majestic, white-walled **Glücksburg Castle▶**, a northern Renaiss-ance jewel. It contains mementoes of its former owners, relatives of the Danish royal family, as well as Gobelin tapestries and a richly decorated banqueting hall (*Open* Apr–Sep daily; Nov–Mar weekends only; Oct closed Mon). The coastal route leads east to the old port of **Kappeln**. From here in the 5th and 6th centuries the Angles, who gave their name to England, went colonizing.

West of Flensburg, near Neukirchen, is the former **home of Emil Nolde▶** (*Open* Mar–Nov daily; *Closed* Dec–Feb), the Expressionist artist (see panel). It is now a museum of his anguished work, with changing exhibitions each season.

EMIL NOLDE
Although he joined the Nazis in 1920, the painter Emil Hansen (called Nolde after his birthplace) was forced into internal exile by the Third Reich. His Expressionistic style of painting was considered to be degenerate by the Nazis. His home, Seebüll, where he painted secretly during the war ('the unpainted pictures') is now a museum.

INFORMATION
Flensburg:
Rathausstrasse 1,
tel: 0461/9 09 09 20;
www.flensburg-tourismus.de

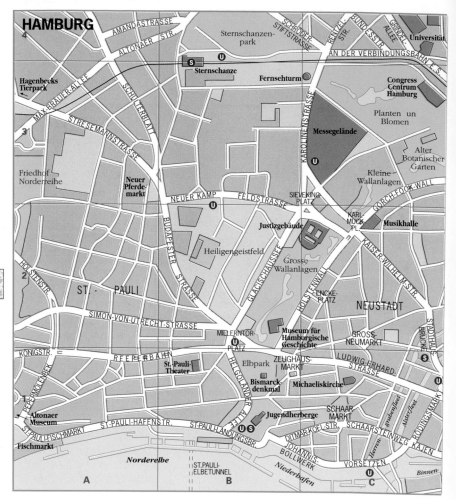

INFORMATION
Hamburg: Steinstrasse 7,
tel: 040/30 05 13 00;
www.hamburg-tourism.de

▶▶▶ Hamburg 53D3

Germany's second-largest city and major port (and Europe's second busiest) is the proud heir of a great merchant-seafaring tradition dating from Hanseatic days. A cultured as well as an industrial city, Hamburg is an unusually spacious and civilized place. For centuries it was a Free Imperial City and today is a *Land* on its own, an autonomous city-state; its most famous son in postwar times is ex-Chancellor Helmut Schmidt, a former city senator, even though Hamburg has traditionally been an SPD city almost without a break since the war.

Set by the broad Elbe some 100km (62 miles) upstream from the sea, it's a town of water—the river, the huge port, the many canals (it has more bridges than any other world city, more than 2,300 against Venice's 400), and the big and beautiful Alster Lake, at its very heart. As it was never a royal or episcopal town but a merchant one, it has few grand or distinguished buildings compared with, say, Munich. Overall, though it is harmonious and after massive wartime destruction has been tastefully rebuilt,

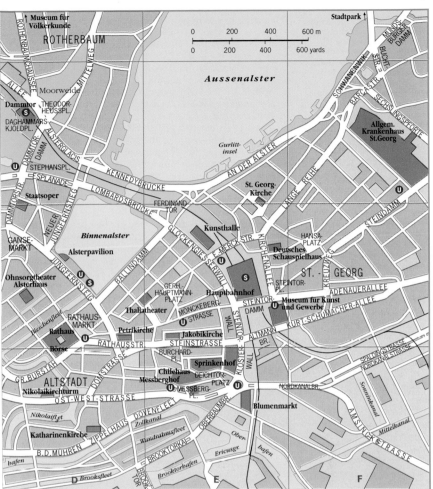

Museum für Völkerkunde
Stadtpark
ROTHERBAUM
MÜNDS-BURGER-DAMM
BUCHT-STR.
SCHWANENWIK
BARCASTR.
SECHSLINGSPFORTE

0 200 400 600 m
0 200 400 600 yards

Aussenalster

Moorweide
Dammtor
THEODOR-HEUSSPL.
DAGHAMMARS-KJÖLDPL.
ALLEE
ROTHENBAUMCHAUSSEE
MITTELWEG
ALSTERGLACIS

Allgem.
Krankenhaus
St.Georg

Gurlitt-insel

STEPHANSPL.
ESPLANADE
DAMMTORSTR.
DAMMTOR-DAMM
KENNEDYBRUCKE
AN DER ALSTER
LANGE REIHE

Staatsoper
LOMBARDSBRUCKE
FERDINAND-TOR
St. Georg-Kirche
STEINDAMM

GANSE-MARKT
Binnenalster
Alsterpavillon
NEUER JUNGFERNSTIEG
BALLINDAMM
GLOCKENGIESSERWALL
E. MERCK-STR.
KIRCHENALLEE
Kunsthalle
HANSA-PLATZ
Deutsches Schauspielhaus
ST. - GEORG

Ohnsorgtheater
Alsterhaus
JUNGFERNSTIEG
GERH.-HAUPTMANN-PLATZ
Hauptbahnhof
STEINTOR-PL.
ADENAUERALLEE
KREUZWEG

Thaliatheater
MONCKEBERG-STRASSE
STEINTOR-DAMM
Museum für Kunst und Gewerbe
KURT-SCHUMACHER-ALLEE

RATHAUS-MARKT
Reichenfleet
Rathaus
Petrikirche
Jakobikirche
STEINSTRASSE
STEINTOR-WALL
ALTMANN-BR.
SPALDINGSTRASSE
NORDKANAL STRASSE

Börse
RATHAUSSTR.
DOMSTRASSE
BURCHARD-PL.
Sprinkenhof
KLOSTER-WALL

GR. BURSTAH
ALTSTADT
Chilehaus
Messberghof
DEICHTOR-PLATZ
NORDKANALBR.
AM SINGE STRASSE

Nikolaikirchturm
OST-WEST-STRASSE
MESSBERG-PL.
Blumenmarkt
Sonninkanal

Nikolaifleet
DOVENFLEET
OBERBAUMBRUCKE
Mittelkanal

Katharinenkirche
ZIPPELHAUS
Zollkanal
Ober
bafen

B.D. MUHREN
BROOKTORKAI
Wandrahmsfleet
Ericusgr.

hafen
BROOKTOR
Brooktorbafen
Brooksfleet
E
F

59

mostly in local redbrick style, avoiding the concrete harshness of so many German towns. There are no skyscrapers to spoil the elegant skyline of green-copper spires by the Alster. In the suburbs are charming Jugendstil wrought-iron balconies, parks and gardens, even old timbered farmsteads and leafy lanes within the city's wide borders. Some streets retain odd names, such as Ole Hoop.

Many North American and British visitors feel instantly at home in Hamburg. Reasons for this include the trim, red brick appearance of its better-off suburbs (reminiscent even of some parts of Boston and certainly of London), the matter-of-fact, reserved character of its people, and the matching coolness of its weather for much of the year. Reserved and even distant they may be, but the people of Hamburg are correct and polite and display that openness to foreigners so typical of port cities. Hamburg is a liberal city —liberal in its politics as well as in its social life. It may lack the exuberance and rough charm of Munich at the other end of the country with which it is so often compared, but it is no less appealing for that.

MEDIA CAPITAL

Since World War II, Hamburg has been the press and media capital of Germany. The First Channel television news shows are edited here, as are some of the big weekly magazines, such as *Der Spiegel* and *Stern*. The national newspaper *Die Welt*, launched in Hamburg after the war, has moved to Berlin, but the city is still home to the weekly *Die Zeit*, intellectual symbol of the city's liberal, free-thinking tradition.

FERRY-HOUSE CEREMONY

Hamburg-bound ships are greeted at the entrance to the harbour with a brief ceremony enacted at the Schulauer Fährhaus (ferry-house) in Wedel. During daylight hours every ship over 500 BRT is welcomed with the formal raising of the flag of its registered country and the respective national anthem. Captains and crews of arriving ships are also hailed with a welcome message in their own language (or farewell to departing ships). You can experience the ceremony from the terrace of the ferry-house, which also has a café and restaurant. In the cellar is a large collection of ships in bottles.

Hamburg has long been a major commercial hub. First established as a port at the beginning of the ninth century, then a leader of the Hanseatic League (see page 75), it created Germany's first stock exchange in 1558 and was a Free Imperial City from 1618. Wrecked by a fire in 1842, it was rebuilt on a spacious scale. Its growth came in the late 1800s due to sea trade with America. Later, this free-thinking town was less welcoming to Hitler than other towns were, and the Nazis never held major rallies here, but it was to suffer from British RAF fire raids in 1943.

Although it has shared in the post-war economic miracle, Hamburg is no longer Germany's richest city, overtaken by others as industry shifted south. This huge port suffered as a result of Rotterdam's better situation for the Atlantic trade. Although modern industry has arrived, notably in electronics and aerospace, unemployment remains high. After 1945 Hamburg was cut off from its natural markets in the GDR and Poland, but today it is reclaiming them, and its prospects have improved.

Despite the decline of the old merchant firms, there is still much wealth in Hamburg. With its musical tradition —it's the hometown of Mendelssohn, Brahms, and the first German opera house opened here in 1678—there's a wealth of culture here as well. Since World War II Hamburg opera and ballet have been as good as any in Germany, the former under the great Rolf Liebermann, the latter under John Neumeier. Theatre has shone under Jürgen Flimm, Peter Zadek and Michael Bogdanov. Since

The city of Hamburg, viewed from the harbour

its merchant rulers were less concerned with collecting art treasures than were the aristocrats of south Germany, Hamburg has few major art museums. But it is a key focus for classical and popular music: Big record companies are based here. The Beatles played here regularly before going on to fame in Britain and the United States. Placido Domingo began his career at the Hamburg opera house.

THE FREE PORT

Hamburg's wealth is based on trade and commerce. One important source of earnings is the *Freihafen* (free port), which is a customs-exempt area where goods can be stored in transit or processed for re-export without incurring duty. It is also the biggest market for Oriental carpets in the world.

The port and central Hamburg With annual traffic of some 85 million metric tons, this is Europe's fourth-biggest port, taking vessels of up to 110,000 tons. Its terminals can load or unload rapidly, using few workers. This has put many dockers out of work, but it suits the owners of the containers, as port dues are high. A good way to start a city visit is a guided **boat tour of the port►** (starting from the Landungsbrücken in the suburb of St. Pauli). You'll be shown the 68km (42 miles) of quays, the 4km (2.5-mile) Köhlbrand bridge (1975), and the protective walls built after the 1962 floods that caused 350 deaths. Near the eastern side of the port, Speicherstadt is an impressive group

A boat tour around the harbour at Hamburg offers interesting views

of high gabled brick warehouses by canals. Built in the 1880s, they are still used for storage but the area is being developed for offices and homes.

Nearby is what remains of the Altstadt after the 1842 and 1943 fires. Here is Gothic Katharinen Kirche (St. Catherine's Church), with a baroque tower; Nikolaikirche (St. Nicholas's), with its slim spire, has been left partly in ruins as a war memorial. Attractive gabled warehouses line the Nikolaifleet canal, and many of the 17th-century merchants' houses off the narrow Deichstrasse are now atmospheric restaurants. To the west, the baroque church of Michaeliskirche (St. Michael), the finest in northern Germany, has a famous tall green tower (with a good view from its platform). The nearby **Krameramtswohnungen▶**, an alley of 17th-century almshouses, is a most picturesque surviving corner of old Hamburg.

Glance at the high-pedestalled statue of an arrogant Bismarck with sword in hand, in a park by St. Pauli. Move onto the Hamburg history museum, which has photos and models of city and port, and a large model railway (*Open* Tue–Sun; www.hamburgmuseum.de). Farther along the broad inner ringway you'll come to the rebuilt Opera House, then to an area of shopping arcades, wonderfully stylish and luxurious, with startling window displays—Hanse Viertel and Galleria are the best. The massive Rathaus, with its heavy, lavish interiors built in 1897 in the neo-Renaissance style seems symbolic of the city's proud heyday. The broad square and the canal beside it are attractive with smart restaurants and cafés beneath the arcades. Nearby are Jakobikirche (St. Jacob's) late Gothic hall-church, and Petrikirche (St. Peter's) with its high 14th-century tower. Beyond the ringway looms

Hamburg's massive neo-Renaissance Rathaus is still the seat of the city's government, the Senate

LOCAL BEER
Hamburg beer is known for being cold, with a good head (like its citizens, some would say), and it's also strong. A popular drink of the harbour district is *Lütt un Lütt*, beer fortified with schnapps—not a drink for the fainthearted.

62

Flowers bloom in the Planten und Blomen flower park

the glass-vaulted roof of the Hauptbahnhof (station), next to the **Museum für Kunst und Gewerbe▶** (arts and crafts; *Open* Tue–Sun; www.hamburger-kunsthalle.de), which has Renaissance furniture, Jugendstil ornaments, and authentic Japanese tea ceremonies in a real tea house (*Open* Tue–Sun). The **Kunsthalle▶▶**, the city's main art museum, offers a huge collection of paintings, from north German primitives via European masters to the Romantic Caspar David Friedrich, Dix and Klee. A separate gallery for contemporary art was added in 1997.

Alster and the north side The **Aussenalster▶**, the larger outer lake, is a focus of the city's life used for recreation. Against a setting of spires, handsome villas and weeping willows, sails glide and Hamburgers stride the shore paths with their dogs. There are outdoor cafés for summer; in winter the lake sometimes freezes so hard that, despite police warnings, stalls selling *Glühwein* (mulled wine) are set up on the ice.

The trendy residential district of Harvestehude, on the lake's west side, contains the charming village of Pöseldorf, with bistros and bars frequented by media folk and the smart set. At the **Museum für Völkerkunde▶** (ethnology; *Open* Tue–Sun) do not miss the Javanese shadow puppets among the displays of Developing World folk art brought to Hamburg by past explorers. Nearby is the university, founded in 1919; farther on are the attractive Planten und Blomen flower park, the Botanical Garden (illuminated fountains on summer nights), and the TV tower (with a fine view from its top). To the north, the Hagenbeck Zoo pioneered the civilized trend of letting zoo animals live outdoors in some freedom (*Open* daily).

St. Pauli and Altona The suburb of St. Pauli, a former fishing village, is best known for its garish main street, the notorious **Reeperbahn▶**, which has changed its tone three times. It began in the 19th century as a fairly respectable amusement district for the new transatlantic passenger trade, full of terrace cafés with live orchestras; the sailors' brothels were in side alleys. After the war, as the liner age waned, it slid downmarket into sex and voyeurism for tourists and businessmen. Today, due in part to AIDS, the Reeperbahn is moving back to 'decency'—the biggest brothel has closed, and hotels and chic restaurants are opening—but if you wish you can still spot the women in the pink-lit windows of the Herbertstrasse. St. Pauli also has a new Museum of Erotic Art (*Open* daily), with some 500 works on show. The Star Club, where the Beatles first won fame, is no more.

On the quayside below, the traditional St. Pauli Fischmarkt (fish market) is held early every Sunday morning. It is now mainly a flea market, with food stalls, but does sell some fish. Go afterwards to the exuberant Fischerhaus restaurant for a Hamburg breakfast of eel-and-plum soup, herring and beer.

The big suburb of Altona, Danish until 1864, still feels like a separate town. It has white patrician houses and fine views of the river. Its **Altonaer Museum▶** (*Open* Tue–Sun), rebuilt after a fire, is Hamburg's nicest museum, with splendid old ships' figureheads and fishing boats, local costumes, rural interiors and paintings of Schleswig-Holstein scenes. Beyond Altona, you can stroll under trees by the river at idyllic Övelgönne, where some old boats now form a 'museum harbour' (*Open* daily). Visit the neo-classical Villa Jenisch (with superbly furnished interiors) and the Ernst-Barlach Haus (works by the sculptor), both in a pretty park (*Open* Tue–Sun; www.baralach-haus.de). Finally you reach the former fishing village of Blankenese, with its steep alleys lined with old houses clinging to the slopes.

63

Some girlie 'live-shows' still survive along the once-so-garish Reeperbahn

INFORMATION
Hannover: Ernst-August-
Platz 8, tel: 0511/12
34 51 11;
www.hannover.de

ROYAL CULTURE
Hannover's golden age
began in the mid-17th
century when a branch of
the House of Brunswick
built a royal palace.
Under the ambitious
Elector Ernst August and
his cultured wife,
Princess Sophie, the city
saw a flowering of the
arts. Handel gave con-
certs and the philosopher
Gottfried Leibniz was
court librarian for 40
years.

*The ornate Herren-
hausen gardens contain
a fountain with Europe's
highest jet and are per-
haps the finest baroque
gardens in Germany*

►► Hannover 53D1

Hannover is Germany's major trade fair city alongside Frankfurt and was a natural choice of venue for the huge international fair Expo 2000. It is a place of great historic importance, with much worth seeing. It was the princely seat of the House of Brunswick from the 17th century, and the House of Hanover inherited the British throne in 1714 through a Stuart connection. Hannover became a kingdom itself until its absorption by Prussia in 1866. Its people, with a reputation for being reserved, speak the most precise and purest German.

The modern central area, around the broad Kröpcke square and the opera house, is affluent and spacious. From here you can stroll through the rebuilt, picturesque Altstadt, full of interest; the half-timbered Ballhof (1650), now a theatre; the historical museum, with old maps and state coaches; the taverns of the narrow Krämerstrasse; the high gabled façade of the15th-century Altes Rathaus; and the Gothic Marktkirche with its superb stained glass. On the banks of the little River Leine, opposite the neo-classical Leineschloss (now housing the Landtag), are three insouciant pop-art sculptures, the 'Nanas' ('wench' in French), by the French artist Niki de St-Phalle. The Gothic Aegidienkirche with its blue tower has been remained half-ruined after wartime bombing, as a memorial.

The grandiose neo-Gothic Neues Rathaus (1913), across the ringway, has models of the city before the bombing. The adjacent **Kestner Museum**► (*Open* Tue–Sun), covered in an odd honeycomb of concrete, contains Greco-Roman antiquities and much medieval art. Farther on, close to the Maschsee, an artificial lake used for water sports, are two other major museums: the **Landesmuseum**► (*Open* Tue–Sun; www.nlmh.de), with paintings of many periods, notably German late 19th century, and the **Sprengel Museum**► (*Open* Tue–Sun; www.sprengel-museum.de), good for 20th-century art (Klee, Picasso, Beckmann and

the Hannover-born surrealist Kurt Schwitters).

In the western suburbs you can see the masterly baroque **Herrenhausen►►** (gardens open daily, museum closed Mon), the former royal gardens of the Brunswicks. The main one, Grosser Garten is formal and French with a maze, statues and fountains which are sometimes lit up (one jet rises 82m/269ft). This is a wonderful setting for the concerts and plays performed here in summer. The Georgengarten contains a museum devoted to the hugely popular cartoonist and poet Wilhelm Busch (1832–1908). The smaller botanical Berggarten has a wealth of interesting tropical plants and flowers. The royal palace of the House of Hanover was destroyed in the war, but the royal mausoleum, with the tomb of George I, survives. An addition is the Regenwaldhaus (Rainforest House), a huge subterranean greenhouse filled with 7,000 exotic plants and topped by a stunning glass roof (*Open* daily).

THE BRITISH THRONE
The Hanoverian King George III watched helplessly from his throne in London as Britain lost its American colonies in the War of Independence. He encouraged friendly German states to send troops to help the British forces in North America, but to no avail. Many American families trace their ancestry to these German mercenaries.

The Michaeliskirche, one of Hildesheim's two restored Romanesque churches, dates from the 11th century

►► Hildesheim   *53D1*

Apart from the 14th-century Tempelhaus, few of the many old buildings of this distinguished town survived the war. Some have been well restored, notably the Gothic Rathaus and two Romanesque churches: the Michaeliskirche and the **cathedral►**, where there is an 11th-century carved bronze column, with biblical scenes. A rose bush in the cathedral's finely arched and columned cloisters plays a central role in Hildesheim history. The bush is said to be more than 1,000 years old and appeared to have been destroyed in an air-raid in early 1945. But when peace came in May, 1945, it revived and bloomed—confirming a centuries-old belief that Hildesheim will live as long as its celebrated rose bush!

INFORMATION
Hildesheim:
Rathausstrasse 18–20,
tel: 05121/1 79 80;
www.hildesheim.de

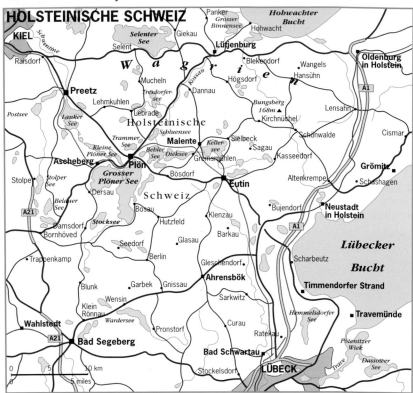

NORDSTRAND ISLAND
The island of Nordstrand, connected to the mainland near Husum by a man-made isthmus, provides a stark reminder of the threat posed to this stretch of coast by the North Sea. Nordstrand is part of a much larger island that was torn apart by disastrous sea-flooding in 1362 and 1634. One large piece of the former island, Pellworm, is now a 8km (5-mile) ferry-ride away, while other islets, called the Halligen, are distributed along the coast of Nordfriesland, like the front line of a defence wall in face of the unpredictable North Sea.

INFORMATION
Husum: Grossstrasse 27, tel: 04841/8 98 70; www.husum.de

► **Holsteinische Schweiz**   *53D4*

This is a gentle region of woods and low hills that are good for walking, and lakes for sailing and swimming. Its local nickname, Holstein Switzerland, was given to it in the last century to attract tourism. Its a misnomer, for none of the hills are higher than 168m (550ft). You can tour the lakes by excursion boat from Plön, an old town with a big white baroque hilltop castle that formerly housed a Prussian army college.

At Eutin, a pleasant town of 18th-century brick buildings, there's another baroque castle, with a moat and bronze cupola. In summer, its pink courtyard hosts the operas of Carl Maria von Weber (1786–1826), born in Eutin. Nearby Malente is a little lakeside resort where water galas are held. Grömitz is the best of the nearby Baltic seaside resorts.

► **Husum**   *52C5*

This graceful old North Sea fishing port and market town is close to a region of polders. The history of these reclaimed tracts of land and the age-old battle against sea and storm is well recorded in the Nordfriesisches Museum (visit www.nissenhaus.de, for opening times). Another museum is in the home of Theodor Storm (1817–88), a suitably named poet and novelist whose work movingly evokes the life of this strange, flat, melancholy region (*Open* Apr–Oct daily; Nov–Mar Tue, Thu, Sat pm only). Friedrichstadt, to the south, was built in the 17th century by Dutch Protestant refugees. It's a picturesque little Dutch-looking town of stepped gables, canals and cobbled streets. St. Peter Ording, a resort with good sandy beaches, known for its sulphur cures, is on the long peninsula to the west.

▶ Jever   52B3

This brewery town is known for its pilsner beer and for its pink hunting **Schloss▶** set in a moated park. This once belonged to the Russian czars, hence the portraits of Catherine the Great, alongside local costumes, toys and furniture in its museum.

On the wall of the café by its gates is an old Glockenspiel (musical clock) where figurines of Catherine and others do an hourly dance. In the Marktplatz, note the Renaissance sarcophagus with marble statues, situated in the belfry next to a modern church.

▶ Kiel   53D4

At the head of a broad fiord, always lively with shipping, stands Schleswig-Holstein's capital, formerly the leading German naval base. Heavily bombed in World War II, it has been gracelessly rebuilt and has few notable buildings except for the restored Jugendstil Rathaus (1911). Shipping

The Olympiahafen (harbour) at Kiel

67

is still a major activity. The 100km (62-mile) **Kiel Canal**, which links the Baltic with the North Sea, is the world's busiest, with 50,000 ships a year—ahead of Panama or Suez.

There's a bracing sea walk along the Hindenburgufer (quay) to the Holtenau locks, where the passage of ships between canal and sound is an impressive sight. At **Laboe**, the high brick tower shaped like a ship's stern is Germany's main naval war memorial. Its museum includes a model of the 1916 Battle of Jutland and a restored World War II U-Boot submarine (*Open* daily).

The Schleswig-Holsteinisches **Freilichtmuseum▶** (*Open* mid-Mar–Oct daily; Nov–mid-Mar Sun only) at Molfsee is one of the best of the outdoor museums of rural life. About 60 old buildings, half-timbered and redbrick in the regional style, including three windmills, a watermill, a 16th-century vicarage, and an 18th-century manor (note its 1817 school timetable), are set in a pleasant park; bakers, carvers and potters work here and sell their products.

INFORMATION
Lübeck: Holstentorplatz
1, tel: 01805/88 22 33;
www.lubeck-tourismus.de

THOMAS MANN
Thomas Mann's family
left Lübeck for Munich in
1891, when Thomas was
16 years old. He recorded
his youth in his masterly
novel *Buddenbrooks*
(1901), which first made
him famous. It gives a
vividly detailed picture of
the city's upper-crust
society and is a poignant
study of human frailty. Its
central characters were
based on real people and
this did not please
Lübeck. Mann won the
Nobel Prize for Literature
in 1929.

*Lübeck's Altstadt (old
town) is famous for its
decorative brickwork and
façade decoration*

►►► Lübeck   *53E4*

This Baltic river port and one-time leader of the Hanseatic
League (see page 75) is a stately old city with tremendous
local pride and a lovely relaxed, civilized ambience.
Although the city was heavily bombed and then rebuilt, its
main streets still evoke its wealthy merchant heyday. Here
you will see those high zigzag gabled façades often mistak-
enly thought of as Dutch. In fact the old builders of Lübeck
invented this style, which the Dutch later copied. Some old
houses also have the unusual Lübeck brickwork which uses
alternating strips of red unglazed and black glazed brick.

In the Middle Ages this 'Queen of the Hanse' was the
main business base of northern Europe, and Germany's
largest town after Köln (Cologne). Later it lost ground to
Bremen and Hamburg, but it still handles a great volume
of cargo, and has some big industries. Its position on the
old GDR border was once a handicap, but today it is
reforging links with its natural Mecklenburg hinterland.

Some of the old merchant families still flourish today.
One leading family, the Manns, wealthy grain dealers,
produced two great writers, Thomas (see panel) and
Heinrich. One of the family's old houses, at Mengstrasse 4,
was the stage for the dramatic scenes of Thomas Mann's
novel *Buddenbrooks*. It has been rebuilt since World War II
bombing and now houses a museum of the Manns' life
and work (*Open* daily; www.buddenbrookhaus.de).

Lübeck's medieval heart lies between two arms of
the River Trave and is best visited on foot. The grander
quarter, with fine old houses, is west of the central Breite

Strasse; the artisan quarter is to the east. To make a circular tour, enter by the **Holstentor►**, an imposing red
twin-towered gateway housing a museum of local
history. Here there are some 16th- to 17th-century
gabled warehouses by the river, used to store salt in
transit from the Lüneburg mines to Sweden.

Cross the river and you can visit the Gothic Petrikirche
and the beautiful Music Academy, converted from
22 merchant homes (concerts are occasionally held
here). In the narrow street called simply Kolk, the
marionette theatre and puppet museum have a splendid
and intriguing collection of exotic oriental puppets
(*Open* daily).

The Marktplatz at Lübeck, with the impressive Marienkirche in the background

RATZEBURG AND MÖLLN
South of Lübeck are two charming old towns. Ratzeburg, on a lake, has a tall redbrick Romanesque cathedral on its outskirts. Mölln, with its 14th-century Rathaus, is where the folk jester Till Eulenspiegel is said to have died of the plague in 1350. Touching the thumb of his statue (in the market) is supposed to bring good luck. Before reunification Ratzeburg was the archetypal frontier town. Until recently the eastern shore of the lake near the town (which is built on an island) was fenced off, forming the border between West and East Germany.

69

To the southeast, the double-towered cathedral (1173) is Romanesque with a Gothic chancel; the nearby **St. Annen Museum▶** (*Open* Tue–Sun) contains relics of old Lübeck. Just to the north, in an area of mewslike alleys, are two 17th-century almshouses, Füchtingshof and Glandorpshof, built for the widows of merchants and craftsmen and still used as homes for the elderly. On the 14th-century façade of the Katharinenkirche (now a museum; O*pen* Apr–Sep Tue–Sun) are fine modern statues, three of them by Barlach. The nearby Behnhaus and Drägerhaus are elegant houses, now small museums showing Mann souvenirs and paintings by Munch (*Open* Tue–Sun).

The **Heiligen-Geist-Hospital▶** (*Open* Tue–Sun), built in the 13th century as an old peoples' home, has a superb vaulted Gothic chapel with old frescoes. In the Gothic Jakobkirche are 17th-century organ lofts. Just opposite, the tall step-gabled Sciffergesellschaft, a Renaissance mansion built for the Seamen's Guild, today serves as a tavern, very popular with tourists. The lofty Marienkirche, with the highest brick nave in the world, was the main church of the merchant rulers. Badly bombed, it has been skillfully restored to its original style. The composer Dietrich Buxtehude (1637–1707) was its organist for nearly 40 years.

The handsome Gothic/Renaissance **Rathaus▶** should be seen for its council chamber and the memorial to eight citizens shot for their resistance to the Nazis.

Lübeck is famous for its marzipan, the rich almond paste that Germans love. The famous Niederegger store sells marzipan in all kinds of shapes (including realistic-looking oranges, apples and a selection of other fruits).

TRAVEMÜNDE
Officially a district of Lübeck, Travemünde is Germany's oldest seaside resort. Bathing huts appeared on its long sandy beach as early as 1802, and the health fad of seawater dips and sea-air inhalation cures attracted not only the Lübeck bourgeoisie (captured in Thomas Mann's *Buddenbrooks*) but also titled visitors from much farther afield. Today's Travemünde has lost much of its former glitter, although it has a casino and a couple of fine old hotels.

INFORMATION
Lüneburg: Rathaus am
Markt, tel: 04131/2 07
66 20;
www.lueneburg.de

*Lüneburg's large and
elegant Rathaus has a
sumptuous interior. In
the council chamber
are delicate wood
sculptures by Albert
Von Soest (1566)*

►► Lüneburg   53D3

This is a distinguished old town on the edge of the heath
that bears its name, the Lüneburger Heide. In the Middle
Ages it grew prosperous from its salt deposits, which were
sold to Scandinavia and the Baltic towns; there is a salt
museum in the former saltworks (*Open* daily). Tall houses
with oddly shaped stepped gables line the broad street
called Am Sande; some still have the iron bars near the
roof used for pulling furniture up from the street.

The big yellowish **Rathaus►** (13th to 18th century) has a
superbly ornate interior: a Renaissance council chamber
with detailed wood carvings, and a Gothic Fürstensaal
(princes' chamber) with lamps made from stags' antlers.
Close by is the highly picturesque **Wasserviertel►**, the old
river port, with a gabled Renaissance brewery, a half-timbered millhouse by the water and an 18th-century crane.

At **Ebstorf**, to the south, little remains of its 14th-century
Benedictine abbey save a Gothic gallery and cloister. Its
main attraction is a copy of a 13th-century map of the
world: The original was destroyed in the war.

►► Lüneburger Heide (Lüneburg Heath)   53D3

The gently undulating Lüneburger Heide is a large and subtly beautiful area stretching from the Elbe down to the River Aller, near Celle. Although best visited in August or September, when the juniper shrubs are in leaf and the vast tracts of heather are in bloom, this varied landscape is well worth visiting at any time. You'll find low valleys, marshy ponds, pastures full of sheep and forests rich in game.

In the three big nature reserves cars must stay on the main road, but you can rent a horse and cart, horse or bicycle and go meandering down quiet, clearly signposted paths. In some places, cross-country skiing is possible when snow falls in winter. The sheep, known as *Heidschnucken*, that browse on the juniper and heather yield a delicious fragrant mutton which is found on the menus of many local restaurants. About a dozen herds still roam in the area.

The main nature reserve is just west of the Hannover–Hamburg autobahn and has several entry points. Among them are Undeloh to the north and Döhle to the east, two pretty villages reachable by car. From either you can hike or ride to the Wilseder Berg, a 169m (554ft) hill that offers a wide view of the heath. The rolling heathland is covered with oaks, pines, birches, red-berried junipers and, above all, with heather. There is heather everywhere. The villages have stalls selling heather bouquets (in season) and kitschy heather ornaments of all kinds.

At Egestorf, a picturesque village east of Undeloh, heather is used to decorate the altar of the Protestant Heidekirche, an unusual half-timbered structure that—from the outside —looks less like a church than a dwelling. Several churches in the area have curious-looking wooden belfries. Wildpark Lüneburger Heide at Nindorf, near Egestorf, keeps more than a thousand different animals (*Open* daily).

BELSEN CAMP
One of Nazi Germany's most notorious concentration camps, Bergen-Belsen, on the southern edge of the Lüneburger Heide, was burnt to the ground after British forces liberated it in 1945, but today there is a memorial to the 50,000 prisoners who died there and a small museum documenting their suffering. The cruelty inflicted on the Bergen-Belsen prisoners, most of them Jewish, was particularly hideous, and the camp's bestial commander, Josef Kramer, and 10 guards, including three women, were hanged for their crimes. The memorial and the museum, accessible by bus from Bergen and Belsen, are open daily.

71

The poet Hermann Löns sentimentally extolled the glories of the Heide. His memorial tomb stands alone in an area of cairns and ancient chamber tombs near Fallingbostel, southwest of Soltau. Farther west is the huge **Vogelpark Walsrode►** (*Open* daily), a bird sanctuary where parrots, flamingos, cranes and ostriches are among the rich variety of species of birds from the world over that live and fly freely here. There's a playground for children at the sanctuary. A larger, well-known amusement venue, popular with young people, can be found at Heidepark, a theme park near Soltau (*Open* daily Apr–Oct).

*The huge Lüneburg Heath has wide expanses of birch and pine trees, as well as its famous heather (*Heide*) and juniper bushes*

Northwest Germany

In the 1960s the island of Sylt became 'the St. Tropez of the north', a much publicized haunt of German film stars and wealthy playboys, many of whom flew in regularly in private planes for weekend beach parties. In the 1990s Sylt lost some of its glamour as Germany's jet set rediscovered the Mediterranean island of Mallorca, although the big mansions behind the North Sea dunes still often resound to the noise of parties.

Oldenburg: Kleine Kirchenstrasse 10, tel: 01805/93 83 33; www.oldenburg-tourist.de

▶ **Minden** 52C1

This busy junction town on the Weser has a huge *Schachtschleuse* (lock), 85m (279ft) long, that links the river with the Mittelland canal; a small museum describes the lock's workings and the Weser area. The cathedral has a Romanesque façade and a striking 11th-century crucifix. At the Porta Westfalica, a scenic spot to the south, the River Weser has forced its way between two wooded hills. On each stands an unlovely memorial: a tower dedicated to Wilhelm I and a statue of Bismarck.

▶▶ **Nordfriesische Inseln (North Friesian Islands)** 52B5

This low-lying archipelago off the west coast of Schleswig-Holstein is popular with holidaymakers. There are hotels on Amrum and Föhr, islands served by ferry, but the biggest and by far the best-known island is Sylt▶▶, a long strip of land linked to the mainland by a causeway that bears a railway but no road. Cars must board the train shuttle at Niebüll, and fares are high.

Sylt is a legend in Germany for showy jet-set tourism. Its windy but bracing climate has made it a fashionable resort since the 19th century; Thomas Mann and Marlene Dietrich used to vacation here. Today its heyday is past, but Sylt remains a haunt of tycoons, politicians, editors and others seeking privacy. Sylt's history far predates tourism: Witness the 12th-century church at Keitum, and the Altfriesisches Haus, an old farmhouse that is now a museum of local lore and history.

The remorseless wind from the North Sea whips the clouds into odd shapes, causing shifting patterns of light, and this lends Sylt a special beauty. The North Sea coast has high dunes in the form of reddish cliffs, above a long and broad sandy beach. Coastal erosion is a serious problem, but Sylt is a paradise for bathing and surfing, as well as for cycling, riding and jogging. It attracts huge numbers of sport lovers and health-conscious people from all social classes, almost all of them Germans. Sylt has nine separate resorts. Westerland is the biggest, but not the most fashionable. Of the others, Keitum is the prettiest, a showpiece full of boutiques, galleries and thatched cottages. The trendiest is Kampen, where bars and nightclubs try to keep alive the glory of the 1960s. One short street, Strönwai, is known as Whisky Strasse, its neat modern thatched villas bizarrely constructed into bistros and boutiques. Kupferkanne, a former wartime bunker on the cliffs, is a popular garden café.

▶ **Oldenburg** 52B3

A modern, spacious town with a new university and a river port linked to the North Sea by a tributary of the Weser, Oldenburg is also the market base of a rich farming region noted for horse and cattle breeding. In the small Altstadt, agreeably closed to traffic, some handsome older buildings remain, notably the Gothic Lambertikirche and the 15th-century Lappan tower. The nearby Schlossgarten has splendid ancient oaks and beeches. Of the three museums, the Augusteum has paintings from the Worpswede colony (*Open* Tue–Sun); the Landesmuseum, in the former ducal palace, contains works by Tischbein (1751–1829) and reconstructed farmhouse interiors (*Open* Tue–Sun);

and the natural history museum (*Open* Tue–Sun) has displays of 2,400-year-old corpses that were preserved over the centuries in nearby peat bogs.

Bad Zwischenahn►, to the west, is one of the most fashionable of North German spas and a large summer resort, beside a big lake much used for water sports. The Johanniskirche is an exceptionally lovely church, with charming paintings on its wooden gallery, 16th-century frescoes on its wooden ceiling, and a fine painted altar. The well-kept lakeside gardens contain an outdoor rural museum, the **Ammerländer Bauernhaus►** (*Open* Mar–Oct daily. *Closed* Nov–Feb) with a real windmill, old cottages and a superbly restored 17th-century redbrick farmhouse from the plain nearby: Humans and animals used to live together in its one huge room. At Ocholt village, to the west, is the picturesque old Howieko water mill.

► Osnabrück   52B1
Today heavily industrial, producing paper, textiles and metalwork, this town of 164,000 people is also strongly historical, having been a bishopric since 785. Here, and in Münster, the 1648 Peace of Westphalia was negotiated—in a room in the Rathaus that is now called the Friedenssaal (peace hall). The room bears portraits of the signatories of the peace treaty. The town has three fine old churches but the rest of the buildings are mostly modern. A new museum designed by Daniel Libeskind is devoted to the painter Felix Nussbaum, born in Osnabrück in 1904 and murdered at Auschwitz in 1944 (*Open* Tue–Sun).

Beside this modern fountain in Osnabrück is a satirical sculpture (of bishop and townsfolk), in a style common in German towns today

73

THE FRIESIANS

The Friesians first settled in the Netherlands and on Germany's west coast in prehistoric times, driving out their Celtic predecessors. They were eventually conquered and converted to Christianity by Charlemagne. The distinct Friesian language is still spoken by a tiny and dwindling minority along the coast.

OPEN-AIR MUSEUMS

Northwest Germany, like other areas, has a number of open-air museums (*Freilichtmuseen*) of rural life. Old farmhouses and other buildings have been collected and reassembled, complete with old furniture and farm implements. It is a key aspect of modern Germany's new concern with tradition and ecology.

INFORMATION

Schleswig:
Plessenstrasse 7,
tel: 04621/85 00 50;
www.schleswig.de

In the Schleswig region, many cottages are white-washed, in contrast to the red-brick and half-timbering so common in north Germany

▶ Ostfriesische Inseln (East Friesian Islands)   52A4

This is the eastern half of a long string of offshore islands that extends into Holland. Not surprisingly, this part of Friesland is quite like Holland, with windmills, dikes and black-and-white Friesian cows.

The seven German islands, all inhabited and reachable by ferry, are popular for summer holidays, thanks to their bracing climate and broad sandy beaches backed by high dunes. Langeoog has an important bird sanctuary; the old church on Spiekeroog has mementoes of the Spanish Armada; and Borkum and Juist are lively family resorts, good for horseback riding and sailing. The most populous island and biggest resort is Norderney, 12km (7.5 miles) long. It is reached by regular ferries from Norddeich, which will take cars. To discourage motorists, car fares are high and so for a short stay it might be best to park at Norddeich and travel by foot or taxi on the island.

Norderney is not a fashionable resort, but it has an elegant-looking casino and lots of amenities. The little Fischerhaus museum gives details of the history and folklore of the island, a resort since 1797. The town and hotels are at its western end and the rest is rolling dune, much of it covered with wild grass. The interior seems like desolate moorland, with the sea out of sight behind the dunes, but the long sandy beaches are excellent. The insistent wind is a problem, as in other North Sea resorts; the beaches are neatly dotted with big hooded wicker chairs that give protection. As on Sylt, coastal erosion is a menace, and breakwaters are being built to check it.

▶▶ Schleswig   52C5

Starting life as a Viking trade base, this attractive old seaport stands at the head of the Schlei, a long, low fiord filled with small boats. Just to the south is an interesting museum of Viking culture and history, the **Haithabu** (*Open* Apr–Oct daily; Nov–Mar closed Mon). The town's towering redbrick Gothic cathedral contains the beautiful Bordesholm Altar (1521). In the nearby Holm district you'll find little streets of old fishermen's cottages that are a bit too neatly restored.
Continued on page 76.

At a time when Germany had yet to become a single political unit, its cities and merchant groups, benefiting from lively international trade, formed a wealthy and influential sector of medieval society. When these groups joined they became an impressive force. The Hanseatic League was a union of 150 mainly north German towns, and the most powerful economic and political power of the region.

Having started in the mid-14th century as a loose association for the protection of German tradesmen, the league created a single market that covered all trade between the North and Baltic seas, a market that it fully controlled under the leadership of the town of Lübeck.

One of the league's ships (top)
Merchant ships unloading their cargo at Danzig in the 16th century (above)

Member cities followed the decisions of the Hansetag, the league's representative assembly. Any breaches of these decisions by a city would bring on the process of *Verhansung*, the boycott of the city by all others. No trade would take place with the boycotted city, nor could it use the league's common facilities abroad

until it was brought back into line. By using such measures, the league managed to influence the economic and political development of each city as it wished. But this defect in the system—a loss of individual sovereignty—was compensated for by the enormous advantages of membership: no customs duties, common protection against competition, harmonized units of measurement, and so forth. The parallels with the modern European Union and its Single Market, together with the common euro currency, are remarkable.

By 1370 the league was so strong it waged war against Denmark in order to gain free access to the Baltic Sea. However, with the development in the 16th century of nation-states such as Sweden and Russia, the influence of the Hanseatic League began to wane and by the time of the Thirty Years' War (1618–48), its useful life had ended.

Lübeck (above) and Danzig were both chief cities within the league

VIKING SETTLEMENT
Close to Schleswig, the
8th- to 9th-century Viking
settlement of Haithabu
was a major commercial
base. Trade in
Scandinavian furs and
marine ivory and slaves
from east of the Baltic
passed through the
settlement on the way to
Western Europe and
Arab territories.

Continued from page 74.

Schleswig's main glory is the moated white **Schloss Gottorf►►** (16th to 18th century), former home of the Holstein-Gottorf family, who acceded to the Russian throne in 1762. It is full of riches—an ornate Gothic hall with a painted ceiling, a Renaissance chapel with a carved ducal gallery and a Schleswig regional museum (*Open* daily; Nov–Mar Tue–Sun; www.schloss-gottdorf.de). Next door is the **Nydam Boat►►**, one of the world's oldest surviving vessels, dating from the 4th century. This elegant 23m (75ft) oaken craft, built to be manned by 36 oarsmen, was found well preserved in the Danish marshes in 1863. In another room are the gruesome and unforgettable 'moor corpses', skeletons of those who, 2,000 years ago, were tied up, blindfolded and left to die on the marshes, perhaps as a punishment for crimes.

INFORMATION
Stade: Hansestrasse 16,
tel: 04141/40 91 70;
www.stade-tourismus.de

► Stade   52C3

This is a restored old Hanseatic port near the Elbe west of Hamburg. An unusual wooden crane, formerly used for unloading grain, stands by the narrow curving harbour. It is bordered with handsome old houses—best of these is the white-and-pink Renaissance one, No. 23. Upstream is the Altes Land, a picturesque district of cherry and apple orchards, best seen at blossom time. The old brick farmhouses, many thatched and timbered, are also attractive.

ELM WINDMILL
Windmills played a major
role in the economic life
of this breezy part of
northern Germany before
the arrival of gas and
electricity. One of the
last windmills to serve
Hamburg was dismantled
a century ago and re-
erected in the village of
Elm, southwest of Stade.
It is a handsome 18th-
century Dutch model,
thatched with specially
prepared reeds.

► Visbek   52B2

Down a woodland path near this village south of Oldenburg are some strange megaliths that Stone Age man created from granite boulders left by the Ice Age. One long double line of stones, forming a burial chamber with adjacent sacrificial table, is known as the Visbeker Bräutigam (bridegroom). Similar but smaller is the Visbeker Braut (bride). To the west, at Cloppenburg, the **Niedersächsisches Freilichtmuseum►** (*Open* daily; www.museumsdorf.de) is an excellent example of the many museums of traditional rural life that are so popular in Germany today. In a big park, farmhouses and other old buildings from all over the *Land* have been rebuilt and arranged to look like an old village. There's a tiny school, church, manor, ducks and sheep in a pen, plus an old pub.

INFORMATION
Wolfenbüttel: Stadtmarkt
7, tel: 05531/862 80

►► Wolfenbüttel   53D1

A dignified old town which, for three centuries, was the residence of the dukes of Brunswick. Chief relic of that time is the great white Schloss, with its fine Renaissance tower and baroque additions. Handsome old half-timbered houses line the Stadtmarkt and Holzmarkt.
   The **Herzog-August-Bibliothek►** (*Open* Tue–Sun) was Europe's leading library in the 17th century; among its six million volumes are precious medieval illuminated manuscripts. The playwright Gotthold Ephraim Lessing was its librarian from 1770 to 1781; his home next door is now a museum of his life and work (*Open* Tue–Sun).

► Wolfsburg   53E1

The principal factory of the Volkswagen car company is located here, founded by Hitler in 1938 to produce the 'people's car', better known as the 'Beetle'. The plant pioneered industrial robots and you can go on a guided tour to watch these orange mechanical creatures perform precise balletic steps as they assemble the latest models.

►► Worpswede   52C3

In the 1880s Worpswede was colonized by a group of gifted young artists and writers from Berlin and Munich, who were drawn by the melancholy beauty of the moorlands. When they left, the odd houses they built began to crumble; these have now been restored, and several contain private galleries of pictures painted by the Worpswede colony. The most interesting is in the former home of one of the colony's most talented founder-artists, Otto Modersohn, the **Museum am Modersohn-Haus►** (*Open* daily). It has works by the Worpswede artists, whose ideas were close to the Pre-Raphaelites: Fritz Mackensen, Otto Modersohn, Paula Modersohn-Becker and the eccentric Romantic Heinrich Vogeler are represented. The architect Bernhard Hoetger has left several offbeat buildings and sculptures.

The picturesque old harbour of Stade is no longer in use. A museum in the Schwedenspeicher tells the story of the town's remarkable history

77

The Rhineland

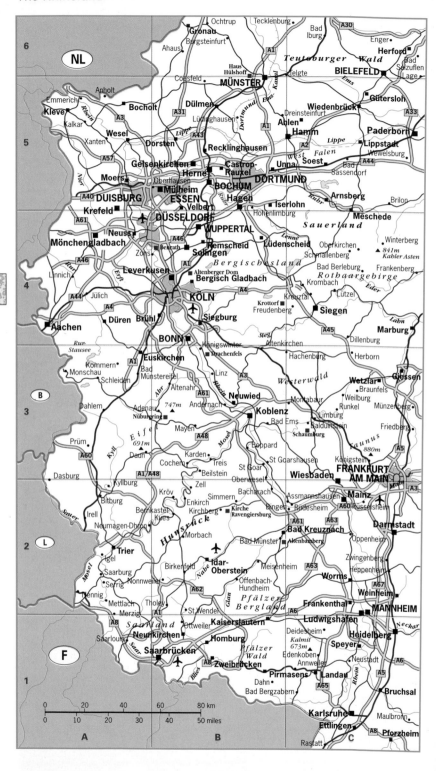

This westernmost part of Germany focuses on the mighty Rhine and its tributaries, some of them scenic rivers in their own right—the Mosel, Lahn and Ahr. Other tributaries—the Saar and above all the Ruhr—have given their name to great industrial conurbations.

This is a region of contrasts. The Ruhr cities, comparatively new, have their own identity and high cultural status, but none compares with the richness of 2,000-year-old Köln (Cologne), one of the great cities of Europe. Düsseldorf is the capital of the *Land* of Nordrhein-Westfalen, relaxed Mainz of the *Land* of Rheinland-Pfalz, while Bonn has now lost its role as Germany's capital, though some government departments remain.

To the west, the Eifel and the Hunsrück have some of Germany's loneliest and most rugged landscapes. To the southeast, the Palatinate wears a kindlier air, perhaps due to the warm red sandstone from which many of its buildings are made. Beyond the deep trench of the Rhine Gorge are further uplands, of which the most extensive is the Sauerland, its rivers and woods a haven for the crowded populations of nearby cities.

To the north, the hills give way to the rich agricultural countryside of the North German Plain, where riverside poplars take the place of beech and spruce forests.

The region's vineyards are the world's northernmost, with delightful wine villages and cheerful cellars and taverns. Life is taken less seriously here than in other parts of Germany, particularly in the Catholic cities of Köln (Cologne) and Mainz, where exuberance knows no bounds during the pre-Lenten carnival.

This was the most Romanized part of Germany, with the Rhine forming the frontier of the empire for centuries. Potent reminders of the Roman presence exist in Trier, with the greatest concentration of Roman monuments north of the Alps. French influence has been felt constantly, as successive kings, revolutionaries, emperors and republican governments all sought to push France's frontier eastwards.

Today, no other part of Germany is so intimately tied to its neighbours across the unguarded frontiers, in links aptly symbolized by joint administration of nature parks that lie along the Belgian and Luxembourg borders and by a park that straddles the Franco-German border near Saarbrücken, the Deutsch-Französischer Garten.

Bingen seen across the Rhine from the Niederwald Monument above Rüdesheim

The Rhineland

INFORMATION
Aachen: Friedrich-Wilhelm-
Platz, tel: 0241/1 80
29 60; www.aachen.de

HOTTEST SPA
The spa in Aachen's suburb of Burtscheid, with a water temperature of 76°C (169°F), is the hottest in Central Europe. Most of the hotels in Burtscheid offer health treatments using the hot water, which has a high concentration of therapeutic minerals.

Aachen's splendid Rathaus is built on the site of Charlemagne's palace, of which two towers survive

▶▶ **Aachen**   78A4

Germany's westernmost city, the country's gateway to many visitors from Great Britain and Belgium, Aachen deserves more than passing attention.

The city limits extend to the frontiers of both Belgium and the Netherlands; a popular excursion is to the Dreiländereck, the wooded hills where the three countries meet. In the late 9th century Aachen's location attracted Charlemagne (Karl der Grosse, or Charles the Great) who built a fine palace here from which to rule the Frankish Empire, which extended over most of Western Europe. Aachen's hot springs may have influenced the emperor's choice: He was a notable bather. Though Aachen is still a spa town, with a good reputation in the treatment of rheumatism and similar afflictions, empire and palace have long since crumbled away, save for the Imperial Chapel. But what a fantastic chapel!

Forming the focal point of the city's **Dom** (cathedral), **Charlemagne's** octagonal **chapel**▶ ▶ ▶ is one of the key monuments of early Christian Europe. It has a two-floor arcaded gallery and is embellished with marble brought from Italy. The huge 12th-century chandelier hanging from its dome is one of the many treasures that make the cathedral such a storehouse of ecclesiastical art. In the light and airy 14th-century Gothic chancel is the Ambo, an extraordinarily ornate pulpit, as well as the gorgeous altar front known as the Pala d'Oro and the golden shrine containing Charlemagne's mortal remains. In the gallery is the imposing stone throne on which some 30 German kings were crowned. An incomparable array of precious objects—crucifixes, chasubles and reliquaries—fills the **Schatzkammer**▶ ▶ (cathedral treasury; *Open* daily).

The first German city to be taken by the Americans in late 1944, Aachen sustained severe damage, but enough of the Altstadt remains to remind us that this is an ancient and lived-in place. Appropriately for a spa town, water features prominently in the townscape; the lighthearted Puppenbrunnen (Dolls' Fountain) has figures with movable limbs, while the thermal springs themselves are housed in neo-classical pavilions designed by the great Prussian architect Schinkel.

Dominating the marketplace is the fortress-like Rathaus; its splendid Kaisersaal (Emperor's Hall) is decorated with 19th-century paintings of episodes in Charlemagne's career and also houses reproductions of the crown jewels (the Habsburgs having made off with the originals to Vienna).

Museums The Suermondt-Ludwig-Museum (*Open* Tue–Sun) has old masters as well as medieval sculpture, while the Ludwig Forum (*Open* Tue–Sun) specializes in postmodern work. The Couven Museum (*Open* Tue–Sun) has well-appointed interiors showing how the comfortable classes lived in the 18th and 19th century. More unusual is the Internationales Zeitungsmuseum (International Press Museum; *Open* Tue–Fri), commemorating Paul Julius Reuter's early days, when his news service depended on carrier pigeons flying between Brussels and Aachen; the intriguing displays reveal how the news has been reported, or misreported, over the years.

▶ **Bocholt** 78A5

This cotton town close to the Dutch border is graced by two architectural landmarks. Dedicated to St. George, the late Gothic hall church has a spectacular west window and a high altar with a fine 15th-century depiction of the Crucifixion by a Cologne master. The gabled and arcaded Renaissance Rathaus is one of the best preserved of its kind in the country.

Wasserburg Anholt stands right on the frontier with Holland, 16km (10 miles) west of the town. The origins of this moated stronghold go back to the 13th century, when the squat tower known as the Dicker Turm was built. The castle now houses the local museum (*Open* May–Sep Tue–Sun; Oct–Apr Sun afternoon only).

▶▶ **Bonn** 78B4

For centuries, Bonn languished in pleasant provincial obscurity on the west bank of the Rhine at the point where the great river flows past the Seven Mountains into the flatlands around Cologne. In 1949, the committee assembled here to draft the constitution of the new West German state decided that the city should be made the seat of government of the Federal Republic. Far from the East German border and with no metropolitan pretensions of its own that might upset more obvious candidates, such as Frankfurt, Bonn had the advantage of being a short ferry ride across the Rhine from the Rhöndorf home of Konrad Adenauer, the elderly but immensely shrewd chancellor of the newborn state.

Express trains were persuaded to stop in Bonn, rather than steaming straight through, and an influx of civil servants and diplomats helped double the population. The notion that one day Berlin would resume its rightful place as the nation's capital inhibited grandiloquent government building; parliament was housed in a teach-

Aachen's little squares are full of outdoor cafés and statue fountains— one fountain is made of bronze dolls

INFORMATION

Bonn: Windeckstrasse 1, tel: 0228/77 50 00; www.bonn.de

▶▶▶ REGION HIGHLIGHTS

82

BEETHOVEN'S BONN
Bonn's most famous son, Ludwig van Beethoven (1770–1827), left the place at the age of 22 for Vienna, never to return. He is commemorated in Bonn by a statue, the Beethovenhalle (a modern concert hall) and an annual international festival. His birthplace contains an exemplary display of memorabilia, including, most poignantly, the ear trumpets that failed to breach the barrier of the composer's advancing deafness (*Open* daily).

INFORMATION
Düsseldorf:
Hauptbahnhof,
Immermannstrasse 65b,
tel: 0211/17 20 20;
www.duesseldorf-tourismus.de

ers' college, the president in the 19th-century Villa Hammerschmidt and the chancellor in the next-door Palais Schaumburg. By the 1970s, hopes for reunification were fading, and lumpy modern 'official' buildings began to transform the townscape. By the year 2000 the German parliament, president, the chancellery and most ministries moved to Berlin. There was no shortage of tenants for the vacated buildings, and several ministries and government agencies remained in Bonn. Nevertheless, the Rhineside area that once hummed with government activity has lost its old 'buzz'.

Look for the spectacular complexes housing the Kunstmuseum (City Art Museum; *Open* Tue–Sun) with its August Macke collection and the National Art and Exhibition Centre (*Open* Tue–Sun; www/kah-bonn.de), the latter's 16 rusty columns symbolizing the German *Länder*. Much damaged in the last war, Bonn's old core still contains plenty of evidence of its long past. Prehistoric, Roman and Frankish remains are in the Rheinisches Landesmuseum, where the star exhibit is the skull of a Neanderthal man, found near Düsseldorf in 1856 (see panel opposite).

The late Romanesque/early Gothic *Münster* (minster), with its tall central tower, airy interior and splendid cloisters, is one of the finest of many such churches in the Rhineland. The prince-bishops of Cologne preferred to reside in backwater Bonn rather than among the more rowdy citizens of their cathedral city; their contributions to the urban scene include the pink rococo Rathaus, as well as the Residenz and the Poppelsdorfer Schloss, both part of the university.

One of Bonn's great assets is its setting (its humid climate less so). The vast Rheinauen Park links the city to the river and gives fine views of Drachenfels peak and the Seven Mountains (see page 100). Southwards lies the old spa of Bad Godesberg, with a pleasant riverside promenade, while the terrace of the Godesburg, the ruined castle above the town, offers a fine panorama.

▶ Düsseldorf 78B4
Capital of Nordrhein-Westfalen, Germany's most populous *Land*, money-conscious Düsseldorf is the showcase in which the country's wealth is dazzlingly displayed. The city's skyline is dominated less by its numerous old churches than by such monuments of modern commerce as the coldly elegant Thyssen skyscraper. As well as the headquarters of many of the great Ruhr industrial concerns, Düsseldorf has also attracted numerous Japanese firms, which have made it the base of their overseas operations; the city's Japanese community is now the largest in continental Europe, though still much smaller than London's.

Private affluence is balanced by a strong sense of civic pride dating back to the city's rule by its electors, the most notable of whom was Johann Wilhelm (1679–1716). Known affectionately as Jan Wellem, he laid out the spacious new districts beyond the Altstadt and attracted artists to the city; he is commemorated by a statue in front of the Renaissance Rathaus. Modern Düsseldorf is well endowed with parks, gardens and landscaped pedestrian areas, so that strolling is traffic-free.

Theatre, music, opera and cabaret thrive here, and the city's galleries are outstanding; the collection of Paul Klee paintings in the **K20** or **Kunstsammlung Nordrhein-Westfalen**▶▶ (*Open* Tue–Sun) is the biggest in Germany.

Excursions

Schloss Benrath (*Open* Tue–Sun), a sumptuous rococo palace in a fine park, is a popular local outing. It was built in the mid-18th century by a French architect for one of Jan Wellem's successors.

The **River Wupper** snakes through a steep-sided valley to the east of Düsseldorf. Wuppertal is a string of industrial towns that forms a linear city. Birthplace of Friedrich Engels in 1820, the city has an outstanding collection of 19th- and 20th-century German and French art in the **Von der Heydt Museum**▶ (*Open* Tue–Sun), and is the home of Germany's leading modern dance company, created and run by the great Pina Bausch.

Wuppertal is also known for its Schwebebahn, the overhead railway that has stitched its disparate communities together since 1901. The railway harmed its reputation as Germany's safest and most reliable transport system in 1999 when one of the cars jumped off the line and plunged into a shallow river, killing five passengers. Downstream, the valley is crossed by a more conventional railway line, carried 107m (350ft) above the river on the Müngstenerbrücke, Germany's highest railway bridge. This links the town of Remscheid with Solingen, a traditional hub of steel production where the Klingenmuseum (*Open* Tue–Sun) displays every possible kind of cutlery. Farther downstream still, high above the river, is the spectacularly sited castle (*Open* Jan–Feb, Nov–Dec Tue–Sun; Mar–Oct daily) of Burg an der Wupper, which houses the local history museum.

▶▶ The Eifel   78A3

Bounded by the Rhine, the Mosel and the country's border with Belgium and Luxembourg, the rugged Eifel is the northwesternmost of Germany's upland massifs. In

BRAHMS TO BEUYS
Writers, artists and musicians have been associated with Düsseldorf. The poet Heine was born here. Brahms, Mendelssohn and Schumann all found the atmosphere congenial, as did the ex-Messerschmitt pilot and postwar *enfant terrible* Josef Beuys (*d.*1986), whose felt-and-fat sculptures won international attention, if not always complete approval.

LIVELY ALTSTADT
Düsseldorf brews an unusual beer, 'Alt', not unlike a pale ale, consumed in large quantities in the Altstadt (Old Town). Echoes of the days when the city was no more than a riverside fishing village can still be picked up among the many bars, pubs, restaurants and discos, which pack Germany's most crowded restaurant and bar scene, an Altstadt zone just 1sq km (0.3sq mile) in area.

NEANDERTHAL MAN
The valley of the little Düssel River was a popular retreat of the poet Joachim Neander (1650–80), who gave it his name. The site of the cave where the skeletal remains of a Neanderthal man were found in 1856 is marked by a plaque. The skull is now in the Rheinisches Landesmuseum (*Open* Tue–Sun) in Bonn, but there is a small museum at the cave with displays on life 60,000 years ago.

Düsseldorf's Königsallee, known as the 'Kö', is lined with some of Europe's most stylish cafés and shops

The Rhineland

The Ahr Valley, home of some of Germany's best red wines

BAD NEUENAHR

While ancient Ahrweiler has kept its town wall, with towers and gates, the spa town of Bad Neuenahr is a 19th-century creation, dating from the discovery of medicinal springs here in 1852. Parks and gardens provide a manicured setting for visitors taking their cure. Below the Silberberg hill, the remains of a patrician Roman villa now form the Museum Römervilla (*Open* Apr–mid-Nov Tue–Sun).

OPEN-AIR MUSEUM

In a wooded setting on the edge of Mechernich-Kommern, the Rheinisches Freilichtmuseum (Rhineland Open-Air Museum) is an extensive collection of carefully re-erected traditional buildings of the countryside, including wind and water mills and workshops, as well as cottages and farmsteads (*Open* daily).

spite of its proximity to great areas of population, its sweeping heights, vast forests and deep valleys offer endless opportunities for escaping the crowds.

The area's core is formed by the Hohe Eifel, composed of ancient volcanoes. Its highest point is the Hohe Acht, a basalt peak of 747m (2,405ft). The hills are pitted with strange circular lakes known as *Maare*, formed by violent volcanic explosions that also left other curiosities in the shape of 'bombs', like the one near the little spa town of Daun. Perhaps the loneliest part of the Eifel is the Schnee-Eifel, to the west, where cross-border nature parks merge with the Belgian and Luxembourg Ardennes. To the north is a 'Lake District', formed by the damming of the Rur and Erft rivers, and very popular with holidaymakers from across the Dutch and Belgian borders. More popular still is the valley of the River Ahr, descending eastwards through a series of picturesque wine villages to the Rhine.

Monschau▶ Overlooked by its medieval castle, and generally agreed to be the prettiest place in the Eifel, Monschau winds along the steep-sided valley of the River Rur. Among its black-and-white houses stands the grand redbrick residence known as Rotes Haus (*Open* Easter–Nov Tue–Sun); its interior is evocative of the comfortable lifestyle of its 18th-century proprietor, a dealer in the cloth for which the town was famous.

Bad Münstereifel With its walls still enclosing an intricate web of cobbled streets and alleyways, this is one of Germany's best-preserved medieval small towns. The River Erft chatters alongside the main street, while the castle stands guard over one side of the valley, the buildings of the town's renowned spa on the other. The best townscape is to be seen in the Orchheimer Strasse, where the high-gabled and intriguingly carved Windeckhaus forms a perfect composition with its neighbours. On the lonely plateau to the east of the town is a great surprise, the utterly unmedieval structure of the Eifelsberg radio telescope, the largest in the world. The country road to the east drops down into the romantic valley of the River Ahr.

Altenahr A pretty little place, dominated by its castle ruin and with many inviting wine cellars where you can taste the local wines, Altenahr marks the western end of Germany's northernmost wine-growing area. Sheltered by the Hohe Eifel, the slatey slopes rising precipitously from the twisting river provide excellent growing conditions for vines. The local Spätburgunder, 'a velvety, noble wine', is considered by many connoisseurs to be easily the best of the country's otherwise rather undistinguished reds.

Maria Laach► This splendid Benedictine abbey (*Open* daily) stands in what was once a remote setting beside the largest of all the volcanic lakes in the Eifel, the Laacher. Founded in 1093, the great six-towered abbey church is one of the grandest and most harmonious Romanesque buildings in Germany. After the dissolution of the country's monasteries in 1802, the abbey's numerous art treasures disappeared, leaving the interior looking rather bare but still very dignified.

SCHLOSS BÜRRESHEIM
The castle, southwest of Maria Laach, owes its exceptionally picturesque appearance to successive waves of building and rebuilding from the 12th to the 19th century. The interior, unusually for Germany, is well furnished, and there is an attractive formal garden with high hedges (*Open* Jan–Nov daily. *Closed* Dec. Guided tours only).

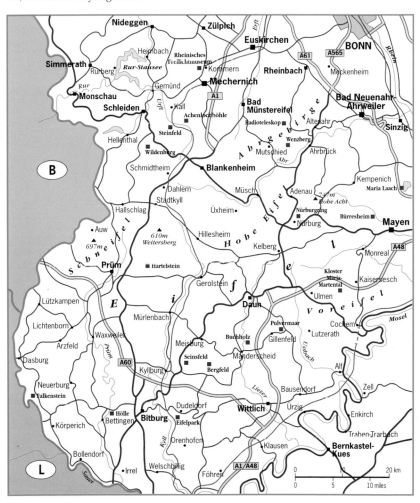

ANNE OF CLEVES

Daughter of one of Kleve's dukes, Anne of Cleves (1515–57) became Henry VIII's fourth wife in 1539. Their marriage was intended to consolidate an alliance of Protestant rulers, but Henry took a dislike to the meek and unprepossessing 'Mare of Flanders' and had their unconsummated union annulled after just six months.

INFORMATION

Köln: Unter Fettenhennen 19, tel: 0221/304 00; www.stadt-koeln.de

CRAZY CARNIVAL

Of German pre-Lenten carnivals, the biggest and most boisterous is Cologne's and it fits well with the city's spirit of fun-loving whimsy. First a Carnival Prince is elected along with his two henchmen, the Peasant and the Virgin (she has always been a man, save under the Nazis who hated transvestism). They 'rule' the city during the *Tolle Tage* (Crazy Days). On Thursday vengeful women may cut off the tie of any male (very Freudian). Sunday is devoted to satiric floats, and on Monday a million people line the route for the main parade, full of pirouetting majorettes. Discover more at the new Kölner Karnevalsmuseum (*Open* Thu, Sat–Sun; Tue, Wed and Fri by appointment; www.kk-museum.de).

► Kleve (Cleves)   78A5

The last substantial place on the west bank of the Rhine before the Dutch border, Kleve is an ancient ducal residence whose *Oberstadt* (upper town) is built on the low hills rising over the floodplain of the great river. To the southwest of Kleve is the vast forest tract known as the Reichswald, the scene of bitter fighting as the Allied armies prepared to cross the Rhine early in 1945. To the northeast stretch watery flatlands where the Rhine once wandered at will before being confined behind its present high embankments.

The medieval counts of Kleve eventually rose to the rank of duke, though their bid for even more enhanced status by marrying into the English royal family came to nothing (see panel). Though virtually destroyed in World War II, the town still has their castle, the Schwanenburg, and by the fine parks and gardens they laid out.

Excursions

Emmerich, 8km (5 miles) east, is reached from Kleve by the country's longest suspension bridge. The brick-built port of Emmerich makes its living from the river, and celebrates this long-standing connection in its Rheinmuseum (*Open* Sun–Fri).

Kalkar, 12km (7.5 miles) southeast, was famous in the late Middle Ages for its talented woodcarvers. This small town boasts a brick church with an astonishing array of fine altarpieces, as well as a number of houses with stepped gables and a 15th-century Rathaus.

Xanten, 27km (17 miles) southeast, was rebuilt after its near-destruction in early 1945. This is a neat little town which has conserved stretches of medieval fortifications (including the picturesque Kleve Gate) and a cathedral crammed with splendid artwork. The town lies between two Roman settlements, civilian *Colonia Ulpia Traiana* to the north and military *Castra Vetera* to the south. The civilian town is now an archaeological park, with thorough reconstructions of fortifications and buildings that attempt to bring the days of Roman occupation back to life (*Open* daily).

►►► Köln (Cologne)   78B4

With the twin spires of its glorious cathedral visible far away across the surrounding plain, this is one of Germany's great metropolitan cities, a focus of culture and learning as well as industry and commerce.

First founded by the Romans in 33BC, *Colonia Agrippina* achieved city status under Emperor Claudius in AD40. Its importance at this time is reflected in the superb Dionysus Mosaic forming the focus of the modern **Römisch-Germanisches Museum►►** (*Open* Tue–Sun) in the city's heart. By the Middle Ages, Cologne had become the largest city in Germany, with no fewer than 150 churches. The Altstadt is consequently huge, extending to the semicircular Ring, a boulevard laid out along the line of fortifications demolished in the 19th century but still punctuated at intervals by the surviving city gates (Eigelstein Tor, Hahnentor, St. Severin's Tor).

The city suffered the first Allied 1,000-bomber raid in 1942, and in the course of the war 90 per cent of the buildings in the middle of town were destroyed. Their replacements may not always be of the highest architectural quality, but planners' retention of the ancient street pattern has helped maintain something of the spirit of the city's 2,000 years of history. Konrad Adenauer, later to be West German chancellor, was the city's mayor between 1917 and 1933. Another distinguished son of Cologne in this century was the novelist Heinrich Böll, who spent most of his life and set many of his books here. His satirical wit and Catholic humorism are typical of the character of the Rhineland.

Cologne's atmosphere is that of a city-state, its strong local patriotism expressed in its own impenetrable *Kölsch* (dialect). Kölsch also happens to be the name of Cologne's

EAU DE COLOGNE
In the 18th century an Italian resident distilled an astringent liquid from flower blossoms. Intended originally as an aphrodisiac, the famous Kölnisch Wasser (Cologne water, or eau de Cologne) is more commonly used as toilet water (eau de toilette).

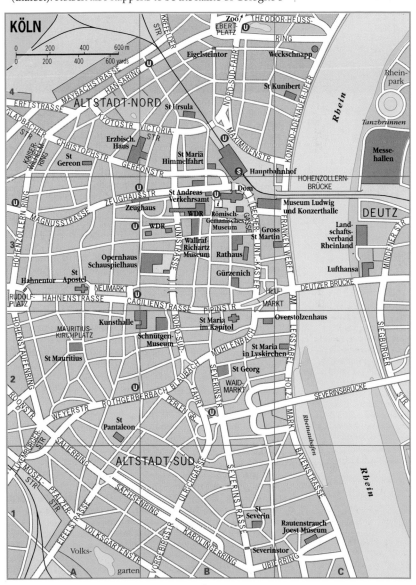

KÖLN

The towers and spires of Köln cathedral (right) and the Romanesque Gross St. Martin dominate the city's riverside landscape

ST. URSULA
Daughter of a 4th-century British king, the virginal St. Ursula is reputed to have been murdered in Cologne by rampaging Huns, along with 11,000 other Christian maidens. This spectacular end led to her beatification and commemoration in the city's coat of arms, as well as in the church that bears her name.

excellent beer, served in small glasses, which have been known to prompt revolt among Bavarian visitors used to seeing it served in litre mugs. The number and variety of Cologne breweries rivals even Munich's, and the Rhinelanders claim their beers are stronger and better than anything brewed in Bavaria. Cologne's beer taverns also rival Bavaria's, and Cologne waiters have an almost Gallic charm that contrasts with the brusqueness of the buxom Munich beerhall waitresses. The Rhinelander is probably the friendliest, most hospitable and amusing German you'll meet, and nowhere is this friendliness more evident than in Cologne.

Most visitors probably get their first glimpse of Cologne from the hall of the main train station, whose high windows frame the clifflike side of the cathedral. Walk out along the railway bridge (Hohenzollernbrücke) to enjoy the city's silhouette rising over the bustle of traffic on and alongside the Rhine.

The **Dom**▶▶▶ (cathedral) is one of the world's great Gothic structures. Begun in the 13th century, it was completed only in the 19th, still in faithful accord with the intentions of its medieval architects, whose original drawings had miraculously survived. Externally its sheer mass is relieved by the lacelike delicacy of its masonry, while the vast interior contains such incomparable works of art as the majestic golden shrine of the Magi, the 9th-century Gero Crucifix, the glorious 15th-century Cologne School altarpiece painted by Stefan Lochner, and superb stained glass. If you make the stiff climb up the south tower you will be rewarded by a fine panorama over the city.

The well-designed pedestrian spaces, characteristic of so many German cities, invite exploration. Next to the Dom is the **Römisch-Germanisches Museum**▶▶ (*Open* Tue–Sun), with its wonderful collection of Roman art found locally (notably the Dionysus Mosaic) as well as items such as toys and clothes that illustrate daily Roman life. Towards the Rhine is a modern complex housing the Philharmonie, the central concert hall, as well as the **Museum Ludwig**▶▶ (*Open* Tue–Sun), with its major collection of German and international art of the 20th century, including works by such masters as Dix, Beckmann, Kirchner and Barlach. This is also the place to see samples from post-war pop artists Roy Lichtenstein and Andy Warhol. Not to be missed are the exquisite late medieval paintings of the Cologne School and other treasures from earlier centuries on display in the new building of the **Wallraf-Richartz-Museum**► ► (*Open* Tue–Sun).

Leading southwards from the Dom is the narrow Hohe Strasse, a downmarket tourist shopping street. Other streets and passageways penetrate the core of the Altstadt, focused on the Alter Market and the 14th-century Gothic Rathaus, with its Renaissance loggia. Before the completion of the Dom, the distinctive four-turreted tower of the Romanesque church of Gross St. Martin dominated the skyline; completed in 1172, this is one of the city's several **pre-Gothic churches**► (a grouping unique in Europe), each with its own special features. St. Pantaleon, from the 10th century, is the oldest; St. Gereon is the most spectacular, with a superb delicately ribbed, 10-sided tower, the Decagon; while St. Maria im Kapitol is richly furnished, with remarkable 11th-century carved doors. The best place to see religious art and furnishings is in the deconsecrated church housing the **Schnütgen Museum**► (*Open* Tue–Sun); the squeamish should avoid the exquisitely carved *memento mori* (corpses in the last stages of decay).

Many striking places of worship were built in the 20th century, notably St. Gertrud, north of the Ring, or Neu St. Alban, to the west, with a dimly lit, highly atmospheric interior. Nearby is the Fernmeldeturm (telecommunications tower), 243m (794ft) high, offering a vast panorama. The large Imhoff-Stollwerck Museum (*Open* Tue–Sun), devoted entirely to the history of the production of chocolate, stands on an island in the Rhine.

Excursion

Altenberger Dom is about 16km (10 miles) northeast of Cologne among the woodlands of the hilly countryside known as the Bergisches Land. This is no cathedral but a former Cistercian monastery, one of the finest examples of Gothic architecture in Germany, restored in the last century. Both Catholics and Protestants worship here.

NIGHT TRAIN
'The Express feels its way and pushes the darkness along.... Then suddenly the ground roars like a sea: we are flying, suspended, royally through air seized from the night, high above the current...Rushing like torches.' – Ernst Stadler, *Journey over the Rhine Bridge at Cologne by Night.*

89

SCHLOSS AUGUSTUSBURG
Brühl, 15km (9 miles) southwest of Cologne, has Germany's largest theme park, Phantasialand (*Open* Apr–Oct), as well as the pleasure gardens from an earlier time that surround Schloss Augustusburg, the sumptuous rococo palace of the archbishops of Cologne (*Open* Tue–Sun. *Closed* Dec and Jan). This echo of Bavarian light-heartedness has an ornate staircase by the great south German architect Balthasar Neumann.

Cafés in Cologne

GOETHE'S LOVE
Goethe came to Wetzlar as a young man and fell for a local girl, Charlotte Buff, who was already betrothed to another man. The experience was distilled by Goethe into *The Sorrows of Young Werther*, a key work of German *Sturm und Drang* (Storm and Stress). Charlotte's house (Lottehaus) is now a museum devoted to the sad affair (*Open* Tue–Sun).

Bad Ems (above)
Limburg (below)

▶ Lahn Valley   78C4

Rising in the Rothaargebirge nature park (see page 102) and flowing for much of its length through a wooded gorge, the River Lahn winds past picturesquely sited castles, ruined like Balduinstein or romantically rebuilt like Schaumburg and Braunfels, before joining the Rhine near Koblenz. The valley can be explored by car, but also along riverside foot and cycle paths, by pleasure-boat, canoe and raft or by railway, which often hugs the river more closely than the road.

Each of the Lahn towns has a highly individual character. The classic spa town of **Bad Ems** was popular with Kaiser Wilhelm I; his statue stands in the immaculate riverside gardens. As well as haughty hotels, aristocratic Ems has a casino, an onion-domed Russian Orthodox church, and a cable-hauled railway to hoist health seekers up to the modern spa installations on the heights above the narrow valley. Both **Nassau** and **Diez**, the latter with a high-walled castle, are associated with the Orange-Nassau dynasty which was involved in European national rivalries and royal intrigues in the 17th and 18th centuries.

Limburg ▶, in a more open part of the valley, has won a number of prizes for its careful conservation work, and the results can be enjoyed among the picturesque timber-framed houses of the medieval heart. Alleyways lead up to Limburg's **cathedral ▶**, on a rocky spur overlooking the river. With its exterior repainted in the red-and-white livery of medieval times, the cathedral is a fine example of the transition from Romanesque to Gothic. The cool interior has unique 12th-century paintings, while the Diocesan Museum and Treasury house ecclesiastical art objects (*Closed* Mon and mid-Nov to mid-Mar).

The medieval Burg at **Runkel** was once the biggest castle along the Lahn; its rugged walls still rise imposingly over the old village with its bridge and weir.

The stronghold at **Weilburg** (*Open* Tue–Sun) is different altogether, an elegant Renaissance residence built by the counts of Nassau. Ornate interiors are complemented by terraced gardens stepping down to the river, which almost encircles the spur on which the castle and its dependent little baroque town are built. Boat traffic can take a shortcut through the promontory via a 235m (770ft) tunnel, the longest of its kind in Germany.

Wetzlar's industries make a variety of products, of which Leica cameras may be the most famous. But this is a historic town, too, for over 100 years the seat of the law courts of the Holy Roman Empire. Towering over the old houses that step down to the seven-arched bridge over the Lahn is the unfinished cathedral, a strange amalgam of Romanesque and Gothic.

▶ Mainz   78C2

Seat of the government of Rheinland-Pfalz, 2,000-year-old Mainz is endowed with most of the good things to be expected of a lively provincial capital: a cathedral, an archbishop's palace, an ancient university, museums and an attractive Altstadt. Its position on the banks of the Rhine and its exceptionally mild climate may explain the cheerful atmosphere; its great pre-Lenten Karneval is second only to Cologne's for high spirits, and there are more jollifications, such as Johannisnacht in March and a big wine festival in August/September.

The great red sandstone cathedral, with its six towers, looms over the largely pedestrianized central area. Essentially Romanesque, though with many later additions, it has a spacious interior containing the splendid tombs of its powerful prince-bishops. The Diocesan Dom-Museum off the Gothic cloisters (*Open* Tue–Sun) houses some of the wonderfully sensitive sculpture of the mysterious medieval mason, the Master of Naumburg.

A short walk from the cathedral, the banks of the Rhine hold a medley of public buildings ancient and modern, including the exuberant Renaissance-baroque Schloss housing the Römisch-Germanisches Zentralmuseum (*Open* Tue–Sun). There are more spectacular Roman artefacts in the Landesmuseum nearby (*Open* Tue–Sun).

Start a stroll 'inland' through the Altstadt with its half-timbered houses and wine taverns, at the Marktbrunnen, the delightful Renaissance fountain. Perhaps the outstanding work of modern art in Mainz is to be found in the Gothic Stefanskirche; the church's **stained glass▶**, which glows with visionary intensity, is the work of the great Russian artist Marc Chagall, who took as his theme 'Reconciliation'.

▶▶ Marburg   78C4

With half-timbered houses clustering around the castle high above the River Lahn, a great **church▶** dedicated to St. Elisabeth, and a venerable university, Marburg seems to represent the essence of medieval Germany.

The focal point of Marburg's Altstadt, particularly in university terms, is the Marktplatz, with its late-Gothic Rathaus and St. George fountain. In this part of town, the steep streets are supplemented by stairways. One leads up to the Schloss, the residence of Elisabeth's descendants, the Landgraves. Built from about 1260 on, it has a three-floor Rittersaal (Knights' Hall) and houses part of the outstanding collections of the Universitätsmuseum (University Museum; *Open* Tue–Sun).

A window by Chagall in Stefanskirche, Mainz

91

INFORMATION
Mainz: Brückenturm am Rathaus, tel: 06131/28 62 10
Marburg: Pilgrimstein 26, tel: 06421/9 91 224

GUTENBERG, PRINTER
Johannes Gutenberg, a native of Mainz, revolutionized communications by elaborating the idea of printing using movable metal type, rendering the painstaking work of the medieval scribe obsolete. Between 1452 and 1455 he printed some 200 bibles, one of which can be seen in the Gutenberg Museum. Housed in the Renaissance mansion known as the Römischer Kaiser, the museum includes a replica of his original workshop with an operating press. Hounded by a grasping partner, Gutenberg made no money from his extraordinary achievements, though in later life he was elevated to the petty nobility and given a pension by the elector of Nassau. Mainz celebrated the 600th anniversary of Gutenberg's birth in the year 2000 by expanding and renovating the museum (*Open* Tue–Sun).

The Rhineland

BOAT TRIPS

While it's possible to drive the whole length of the signposted Mosel-weinstrasse, it's more fun to do at least part of the trip by steamer. Various permutations of car, boat and even train travel are possible and can be investigated locally (a good one is the train from Cochem to Traben-Trarbach and return by steamer). You can also choose to walk up to the viewpoints offered by the many castles—intact or in ruins—along the route. Though extremely popular, the Mosel is less commercialized than its counterpart, the Rhine Gorge. River traffic is less intense, and the railway runs along only one bank, often wandering off altogether. You can always get away from the crowds by taking to the footpaths or coming out of season; vineyards in winter have a special charm.

INFORMATION

Cochem: Enderplatz 1, tel: 02671/6 00 40

Münster: Heinrich Brüning Strasse 9, tel: 0251/4 92 27 10

The River Mosel at Zell, a charming wine town whose round tower was part of its defences in medieval times

Opposite page: Cochem, with its romantic castle overlooking the Mosel River

THE MOSEL

The 514km (319-mile) Mosel River rises in eastern France. For 34km (21 miles) it forms the border between Luxembourg and Germany; it then travels 242km (150 miles) in Germany, ending in the Rhine at Koblenz.

►►► Mosel (Moselle) Valley 78B3

Rising high up in France's Vosges Mountains, the Mosel forms the boundary between Germany and Luxembourg before reaching the ancient city of Trier. From here to its confluence with the Rhine at Koblenz, the river cuts through the Hunsrück and Eifel uplands in a series of extraordinary loops and bends lined by vineyards that produce the famous Mosel wines. Every square metre of steep slope able to catch the sun is completely covered with a forest of poles to hold the vines steady in the rather slatey soil. The white wines that are yielded range from crisp, young vintages to sweeter, late-harvested ones, all of them sold in distinctive slim green bottles.

It was the Romans who brought the vine to this north-eastern extremity of their empire. A replica of the famous Roman Wine Ship (the original is in the Landesmuseum in Trier) stands in the Peterskapelle in Neumagen, the town where it was found. Downstream is the charming double town of **Bernkastel-Kues►**, renowned for its Doktor vineyard. Interesting Renaissance houses line the sloping market square with its fountain, while the odd-shaped Spitzgiebelhaus ('the house of the pointed gables') nearby comes straight out of a picture book. Among the vines above the town stand the ruins of Landshut castle. On the far bank, Kues has a Gothic almshouse still serving its original purpose; in the chapel is a fine 15th-century altarpiece.

Another double town spanning the river is the resort of **Traben-Trarbach**, not particularly attractive, but a useful base for touring the area. In the square at **Zell** is a curious statue of a black grimacing cat, subject of a local legend (*Schwarze Katz* is one local wine). Fortified **Beilstein** is dominated by the massive ruined castle once owned by Metternich. **Cochem's** picturesque setting, with its romantically rebuilt castle crowning a vine-clad knoll, has inevitably made it one of the most-visited places along the river. Equally popular is **Burg Eltz►**, a short distance up a deeply wooded side valley. This is one of Germany's dream castles (built between the 13th and 16th centuries), its sheer walls rising spectacularly

through the trees and capped by steep-pitched slate roofs and an array of turrets. The interior is relatively intimate, a succession of small courtyards with half-timbered façades. A tour includes the hall of banners, the 'treasure chamber' and a fascinating collection of old weapons. The castle is open only from April through October (daily), but even in the winter months the walk up to its ramparts is captivating.

More castles follow, one at **Thurant** and two at **Kobern-Gondorf**, before the river makes the last of its sinuous turns at **Winningen**, a charming vineyard village with Germany's oldest (1320) half-timbered house, at Kirchstrasse 1, and then flows beneath the great autobahn bridge that marks the approach to Koblenz and the river's junction with the Rhine.

▶ **Münster**   *78B5*

The historic capital of Westphalia, Münster is a prosperous university city, proud of its Catholic identity in a largely Protestant province. Its varied architectural heritage suffered badly in World War II, but local pride has expressed itself in loving restoration and reconstruction.

The bustle on the Domplatz (Cathedral Square) is presided over by the handsome, twin-towered **cathedral▶**, built in the early 13th century in the transitional style between Romanesque and Gothic. The interior is richly endowed with statuary, tombs and altars, and has a remarkable astronomical clock of 1540, with automata that come to life daily at noon for the benefit of the assembled crowds. The foundations of the present building's 8th-century predecessor can be seen in the cloisters; beyond is the treasury, which has an 11th-century jewel-studded reliquary of St. Paul.

As well as the cathedral, Münster has other remarkable churches, including the 14th-century Überwasserkirche, with an elaborately decorated tower, and the Gothic Lambertikirche. The three cages hanging from the latter's tower once held the corpses of leading Anabaptists, Protestant extremists, who in the 16th century unwisely overthrew church rule and proclaimed the millennium. This rash act precipitated the massacre of the townsfolk and the Anabaptists' own execution by mercenaries in the

**PFÄLZER WALD
(PALATINATE FOREST)**
The splendid stretches of forest of this upland country, much of it protected as a nature park, form the most extensive area of continuous woodland in the whole of Germany. To the east rises the Haardt, a high ridge that then falls steeply to the vineyards lining the Weinstrasse (see page 107). To the south, linking with the Vosges Mountains in Alsace, are the sandstone hills of the Wasgau, weirdly weathered into castle-crowned cones, cliffs and spikes.

With its timber-framed houses and millstream, the little town of **Annweiler** is a good base for exploring the southern part of the forest. Within easy reach is a clutch of castles. Overlooking the town itself is 11th-century Trifels, where Richard the Lionheart was imprisoned in 1193. Splendid views from the chapel tower include the lesser castles of Anebos and Scharfenberg. To the southwest is Berwartstein, typifying the 19th-century Romantic view of what a crag-top castle should look like. Nearby Drachenfels, now a ruin, had no need of walls, so sheer were its natural defences. Dahn is the best place to investigate the effects of wind and weather on the soft local sandstone. Eroded into strange shapes, it formed the building material for Dahn's three castles, all of them erected within the same perimeter wall.

pay of the bishop. From the Lambertikirche, the city's main thoroughfare, the Prinzipalmarkt, is lined with the arcaded and gabled Renaissance town houses (mostly rebuilt) of prosperous merchants. At the far end is the superb Rathaus, with a wonderful panelled chamber (*Open* daily, Sun am only)—the Friedenssaal (Hall of Peace); this is where the Peace of Westphalia was signed in 1648, bringing to an end the Thirty Years' War.

Less flamboyant than its south German equivalent, the baroque style evolved by the local architect Johann Schlaun resulted in a number of notable buildings, such as the aristocratic mansion called the Erbdrostenhof, the unusual circular Clemenskirche and, above all, the huge palace of the prince-bishops (1767–73), now the main building of the university.

The new Graphikmuseum Pablo Picasso has a unique collection of nearly 800 lithographs by the Spanish artist (*Open* Tue–Sun). Medieval sculpture and old masters feature in the Landesmuseum (*Open* Tue–Sun). Rural Westphalia has been re-created on the banks of the Aasee, the city's big recreational lake, at the Mühlenhof open-air museum, with a fascinating collection of old buildings, water mills, windmills and timber-framed farmsteads (*Open* daily; www.muehlenhof-muenster.de).

The agriculturally rich and rather damp area around Münster—the **Münsterland▶**—is famous for its country houses, most of them moated. Ranging from the grandiose 'Westphalian Versailles' at Nordkirchen to the more homely Haus Rüschhaus just outside Münster, these delightful *Wasserburgen* (water castles) could hold your interest for days. Start at the 700-year-old Burg Vischering (near Lüdinghausen), which conveniently houses an informative Münsterland museum (*Open* Tue–Sun). Rüschhaus was from 1826 to 1846 the home of the great poetess Annette von Droste-Hülshoff, who was born nearby at the lovely **Hülshoff water-castle▶**. Its Renaissance and neo-Gothic buildings are on two tiny islands, within a moat where swans glide (*Open* daily Mar–Dec; www.burg-huelshoff.de).

Nahe Valley and the Hunsrück   78B2
The idyllic valley of the River Nahe runs northeastwards through a series of gorges to join the Rhine at **Bingen**. The picturesque vineyards along its course are among Germany's smallest wine-producing areas, but the Nahe white wine is highly prized among connoisseurs. It has a fresh yet full taste that approaches the best of the Rheingau wines. Farther north is the rugged Hunsrück, a high plateau of upland farms and extensive forests of beech and spruce. Quaint old houses stand on the bridge at **Bad Kreuznach**, a good starting point for a tour of the Nahe. This pleasant spa town comes complete with strange timber structures known as 'salinas' in which brine is vaporized for the benefit of health seekers.

Bad Münster is another spa, south of Bad Kreuznach on the B48. It is overlooked by the lofty castle called the Ebernburg. To the west of Bad Münster on the riverside road, and shouldering the river aside, is the mighty cliff known as the **Rotenfels**. Vines flourish in the narrow strip of soil at its base, as they do on the slopes around the villages that succeed one another upstream.

At **Odernheim** the valley of the River Glan leads to medieval **Meisenheim**, which has an array of picturesque old houses and a fine stone church. The road along the Nahe valley can then be rejoined near the abbey ruins at Disibodenberg.

Beyond the health resort of **Sobernheim**, the village of **Monzingen** has particularly fine half-timbered houses, among them the Altes Haus of 1589. Off the main valley to the north the castle ruin of **Dhaun** affords a splendid panoramic viewpoint, while **Kirn** is dominated by another ruin, the **Kyrburg**.

The steep rock face at the town of **Idar-Oberstein** is also crowned with fragments of old fortress, but the real curiosity here is the Gothic church set into the cliff itself and reached via 214 steep steps from the town's market square. Much is made of the history of mining, cutting and polishing precious stones at the Museum Idar-Oberstein and the **Edelsteinmuseum▶** (Museum of Precious Stones), with 9,500 gems on display (both open daily); and the Steinkaulenberg mine (*Open* May–Oct daily; Nov–Apr Tue–Sun. *Closed* Tue).

A half-hour drive north from Idar-Oberstein will bring you onto the Hunsrück Höhenstrasse. This fine highway was built in the inter-war period to relieve unemployment and help open up this inhospitable area, then one of Germany's poorest and most isolated regions. More prosperous today, the Hunsrück is still a lonely place.

The Nahe River flows along the southern side of the Hunsrück plateau. Here Edgar Reitz, born nearby, at Morbach, set and filmed his masterly 15-hour epic Heimat *(1984), the saga of a local family from 1919 until 1982*

95

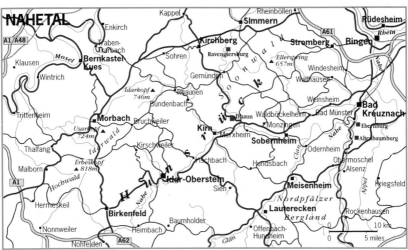

From the Niederwald memorial high above the Rhine, a chairlift (top) descends to Rüdesheim, where the tourist-filled Drosselgasse (above) is lined with picturesque 18th-century taverns

►►► Rheintal (The Rhine Valley) 78C1

The Rhine invariably conjures up a string of clichés: a rocky gorge with a robber baron's castle clinging to each crag; vineyards growing precariously on the steep slopes; passengers waving at each other from the decks of white steamers; unbridled merriment in the cobbled streets of cheerful wine villages. Accurate enough, like all clichés, yet really only applicable to the Rhine Gorge, the relatively short Bingen–Koblenz stretch of the 1,320km (820-mile) river. A mountain torrent near its source in the Swiss Alps, and still pretty untamed at the great falls near Schaffhausen, the Rhine is for most of its length the watery equivalent of a many-laned highway, a traffic artery tying together the canal and river systems of most of Europe. Below Lake Constance the river largely forms the boundary between Germany and Switzerland, turning north at Basel to flow across the broad plain between the French Vosges Mountains and the Black Forest. Its erratic past, when it wandered freely over its floodplain, means that cities are built on one bank only, or even a fair distance away, like Strasbourg and Karlsruhe. Fed from the east by its tributaries the Main and Neckar, the Rhine near Mainz is up to 800m (2,625ft) wide, a dimension it attains again only well below its gorge. Downstream from Bonn the river matures, carrying the heavy traffic of the industrial Ruhr region across the flatlands linking north-west Germany and the Netherlands to its ocean outlet at Rotterdam's Europoort.

Places of interest along the river (L = left bank, looking downstream; R = right bank) are described from south to north (ie downstream), from Wiesbaden to Bonn.

Between Wiesbaden and Mainz the vines of the **Rheingau** (R) extend to the very top of the high south-facing slopes. Sheltered from the north by the wooded Taunus hills, this is one of Germany's most renowned wine regions. It has its own scenic highway, the Rheingau-Riesling-Route, which hops up and down among the slopes taking in such pretty places as Kiedrich, with a Gothic church full of fine furnishings. Eberbach Abbey has a splendid collection of winepresses and provided the setting for the film *The Name of the Rose* (1986). Johannisberg Castle has a panoramic view.

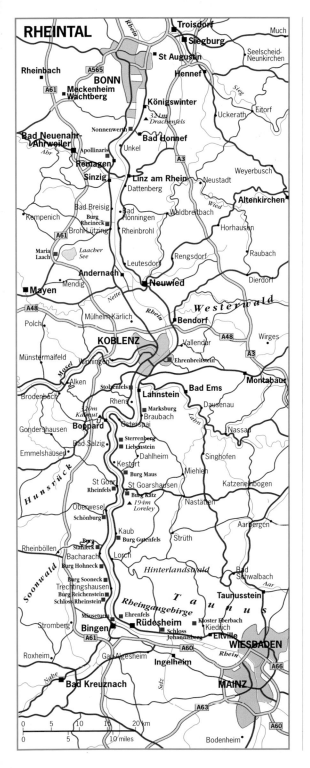

TRAVEL OPTIONS

There are many ways of getting acquainted with the Rhine Valley's spectacular landscape. Even the hurried visitor should consider leaving the autobahn and driving along one of the riverside roads. There are railway lines along both banks of the river, offering two choices of landscape—and speed. Those in a hurry should opt for the western route, used by InterCity and EuroCity expresses connecting Köln, Bonn, Koblenz, Bingen and Mainz. The eastern route is served by the slower, regional trains which stop at all of the resorts on that side of the river. For the best views of the Lorelei rock take the western route. Drivers with time to spare can try the sign-posted scenic routes on either bank (Rheingoldstrasse on the left bank, Lorelei-Burgenstrasse on the right), which link minor roads together to give some of the best views down into the gorge. There's a high-level route for ramblers, too—the Rheinhöhenweg—while cyclists can ride along sections of the old towpath. Remember that there are no bridges between Koblenz and Mainz, though there are plenty of ferries (some for foot passengers only). Perhaps the most relaxing and time-efficient mode of transportation is to go one way by boat (possibly downstream) and return by train (combined tickets available; see the helpful leaflet in English published by German Rhine Line).

The Rhineland

LORELEI ROCK
A particularly rugged section of the gorge leads to the high Lorelei rock, around which the river makes one of its more tortured twists. This legendary haunt of troglodytic dwarfs may be the place where the treasure of the Nibelungs is buried, but it is known above all as the place from which a flaxen-haired temptress (the Lorelei) lured sailors to a watery grave with her seductive song (definitive version by the Romantic poet Heine). The danger to shipping is real enough: The river is forced by the rock to squeeze itself through a gap only a third of its normal width, and here it reaches its greatest depth of 20m (65ft).

The Rheingau's 'capital' is Rüdesheim; the tavern-lined Drosselgasse alleyway does its best to contain the high tide of tourists washing up from the landing stage. Genuine picturesqueness fights it out with the tackiness of fast-food places and souvenir shops. High above the town stands the Niederwald memorial. Its massive figure of Germania celebrating the German unification after victory over the French in 1871 is in better shape than the crumbling remains of Ehrenfeld castle nearby.

At the railway town of **Bingen** (L) the Rhine narrows and turns north to enter the gorge. This turbulent section is known as the Binger Loch (Bingen Hole) and still presents some difficulties to navigation, though the reefs of hard quartzite that once gave rise to dangerous rapids have long since been blown up.

This is followed by a succession of strongholds (L): Rheinstein, Reichenstein and Sooneck. Tiny fiefdoms, good defensive sites and the chance of extorting tolls from traffic on the river help explain the building of numerous castles. Many now stand in ruins, while most of the others were overzealously restored in the 19th-century rush to re-create a more than medieval Middle Ages, a mania that went to the lengths of embellishing railway tunnels with turrets and battlements.

Boppard, a large and very lively resort, especially at wine-festival time, has outdoor dancing in many of its Rhineside cafés

MOUSE TOWER
Standing guard in the stream at Bingen is the 13th-century Mäuseturm (Mouse Tower). Legend has it that this is where Bishop Hatto of Mainz was eaten alive by mice in just retribution for a variety of misdeeds (hoarding grain in time of famine, burning bands of beggars to death...to name a few).

Attractive, slate-roofed **Bacharach** (L) has its fortress, too, Burg Stahleck, now a youth hostel. Towers and ramparts still protect this attractive little town; its main enemy is now the railway trains roaring past on its embankment. It's touristy, to be sure, but there's lots to see along its cobbled streets and around the pretty marketplace.

Kaub (R) is overlooked by Gutenfels Castle, where the lords continued to exact tribute from passing traffic until well into the 19th century. Their instrument for doing so was the 14th-century Pfalz, the extraordinary white toll-castle standing shiplike amid the stream. **Oberwesel** (L) is dominated by verticals—the Ochsenturm near the waterfront, the red tower and slate steeple of the Liebfrauenkirche (Church of Our Lady), and the keeps and ramparts of Burg Schönburg high above.

St. Goar (L) is overlooked by **Rheinfels►**, a city-sized castle that French revolutionaries did their best to demolish, without quite succeeding. Burg Katz (Cat Castle) above **St. Goarshausen** (R) can't match Rheinfels for size; it was built in the late 14th century by the count of Katzenelnbogen to outface his territorial rival, the bishop

of Trier, whose fortress downstream the count disdain-fully nicknamed Burg Maus (Mouse Castle). Beyond are two more castles, Sterrenberg and Liebenstein (R), named 'the Warring Brothers' after a 14th-century family feud.

As befits its origins—it was founded by the Romans—**Boppard** (L) is the most substantial place along the gorge, with two fine churches, remains of Roman and medieval defences, and a Heimatmuseum in the Archbishop's Castle (*Closed* Mon and Nov–early Apr). The town turns an attractive face to the Rhine and its long promenade dates from the 19th century, when it first became popular as a place of retirement and refined tourism. Hotels abound, together with taverns dispensing the produce of the big Bopparder Hamm vineyard. Boppard is a good starting point for river trips and for excursions inland as well; a branch railway winds up through the woods to the rugged Hunsrück region (see page 95), or there is a chairlift up to the famous Vierseenblick viewpoint (*Open* Apr–Oct).

Old-fashioned **Rhens** (L) and **Braubach** (R) are both worth a visit. High above the latter is the imposing sil-houette of **Marksburg▶**, the only medieval castle to have escaped ruin or wholesale restoration, and consequently able to give a truly authentic feel of life along the medieval Rhine. **Stolzenfels** (L), opposite Marksburg, is one of the more thoroughgoing efforts at making a ruined castle better than new.

The city of **Koblenz▶** has made the most of its position at the confluence of the Rhine and Mosel since Roman times. Four-fifths flattened in World War II, the town is still worth a stroll, starting perhaps at the Deutsches Eck, the promontory between the rivers. A massive masonry plinth bears a statue of Kaiser Wilhelm I, a controversial symbol of German nationhood. The original statue was blown up by American forces in the last days of World War II, but a replacement was erected on the site after

Burg Stahleck, a typical Rhine castle, stands above the quaint old wine town of Bacharach, its narrow streets lined with wine bars and craft shops in half-timbered houses

INFORMATION
Boppard: Altes Rathaus, Marktplatz, tel: 06742/ 38 88; www.boppard.de

Koblenz: Bahnhofplatz 17, tel: 0261/3 13 04

The Rhineland

100

REMAGEN BRIDGE
In early 1945, the Ludendorff railway bridge at Remagen was the only bridge to survive defenders' attempts to blow up all the Rhine crossings. Secured by a company of infantry from the American 9th Armoured Division, the bridge resisted bombing, shelling and attack by V2 rockets and frogmen for 10 days before falling into the river. By this time it had enabled several Allied divisions to establish a bridgehead on the far bank of Germany's last natural barrier to invasion. It has not been rebuilt, but the abutment on the left bank houses a small Peace Museum.

DRACHENFELS
Legend has it that Siegfried, hero of the Ring Saga (*Nibelungenlied*), killed a dragon that lived on the Drachenfels rock, and bathed in its blood. This made him invincible, except for an area between his shoulders where a leaf had fallen while he bathed.

Koblenz where the River Rhine and the River Mosel meet—note their different colours at the confluence

German reunification. The riverside promenades enfold the old town, with its two fine twin-towered churches, Romanesque St. Kastor and the Liebfrauenkirche. On the heights on the far side of the Rhine is the vast fortress of Ehrenbreitstein, an impressive setting for the August fireworks extravaganza 'The Rhine in Flames'.

Between Koblenz and Bonn the riverside scenery remains varied and interesting. Attractive towns include **Andernach** (L), Roman and medieval; and **Linz** (R), whose Schloss contains two unusual museums, one of musical instruments, the other of medieval torture instruments. **Sinzig** (L), has a perfect example of a Rhineland Romanesque church. High above **Remagen** (famous for its bridge; see panel) stands a virtual scale model of Cologne Cathedral, the pilgrimage church dedicated to St. Apollinaris.

Downstream, the river divides to flow past Nonnenwerth (Nuns Island), overlooked by the ruins of **Rolandsbogen** (L), supposedly built by the paladin Roland to give him an occasional glimpse of his fiancée, who became a nun on the (false) news of his death. It commands a fine panorama of the old volcanic hills on the far bank, collectively called the Siebengebirge (Seven Mountains). These myth-encrusted heights have long furnished the stuff of fairy-tales and legends, the most potent story (see panel) being that of the dragon that met its end at the hands of Siegfried on the 'castled crag of **Drachenfels**'▶ (Byron), today Europe's most popular summit, climbed by three million visitors every year.

Walkers can try to escape the crowds among the lovely woodlands of these miniature mountains with their 30-odd (not seven) peaks, many of them topped by castle ruins. At their base lie the riverside resorts of **Bad Honnef** and **Königswinter**, with the **Konrad Adenauer Gedenkstätte**▶ (*Open* Tue–Sun) in Rhöndorf between them. This is housed in the former residence of federal Germany's first and perhaps greatest chancellor, whose liking for his home ground seems to have influenced the choice of Bonn, just downstream, as the country's provisional capital.

Germany's 11 main wine-growing areas follow the valleys of the Rhine and its tributaries the Mosel, Main, Nahe and Neckar; the former GDR has some little-known vineyards around Naumburg and Dresden. The mild climate and 2,000 years' expertise (the Romans introduced the vine to these parts) mean that these vineyards—farther north than any other major vineyard—yield some of the world's greatest (and most expensive) wines.

Most German wine is light, largely from the white-wine-producing Riesling, Müller-Thurgau and Silvaner grapes, but about one-eighth of the total production is red, little known abroad but much appreciated at home. Wine production has created spectacular landscapes. The need to capture as much sunshine as possible explains the remarkable terracing on the steep sides of the valleys, where even the most inaccessible south- or west-facing slope is cultivated. Wines are best tasted where they are made, but nowhere more so than in Germany.

New tastes German wines are traditionally sweet, but the recent hankering after a more 'sophisticated' taste has encouraged a range of *trocken* (dry) or *halb-trocken* (medium-dry) wines. Categorization and labelling are strictly regulated, producing useful information about the area of origin and standard of a particular bottle. A *Deutscher Tafelwein* (German table wine) is a pleasant, unpretentious product from one of five main areas. A *Qualitätswein* (quality wine), of a higher standard, must be characteristic of both grape type and one of the 11 main regions. A *Qualitätswein mit Prädikat* (quality wine with distinctive features) has special attributes: The grapes must be fully mature and the wine have a certain percentage of alcohol without added sugar. All wines within this category (beginning with those designated *Kabinett*) come from one district. The very best wines are those made with ripe and overripe grapes, selected specially, either in the vineyard (*Spätlese, Auslese*) or in the vat room (*Beerenauslese, Trockenbeerenauslese*). Trockenberrenauslese is the summit of German wine culture, made from raisinlike grapes affected by the mould known as 'noble rot' and picked as autumn expires.

Even as the first winter frosts take hold in the vineyards the vintners are still busy, producing the country's great rarity: Eiswein. This is made from specially selected grapes left to mature still further on the vine and deliberately allowed to freeze. The wine from these frozen grapes is an aromatic delicacy, so rare and expensive that it's normally only obtainable in half-bottles.

Germany's sparkling wines, known as Sekt, are not in the champagne league, but many brands—produced by the champagne method—are of very high quality, and one producer takes great pride in supplying at least one (anonymous) royal house.

Only a fraction of Germany's wines are produced from red grapes (below)

101

SAUERLAND AND ROTHAARGEBIRGE

Little known abroad, these green hills make a wonderful playground for the cities of the Rhine and Ruhr. Consisting of forested ridges broken by occasional gorgelike valleys, the area is an important water-gathering ground, with many reservoirs providing opportunities for watersports. Outdoor life isn't confined to one season: The chief resort, Winterberg, has probably the best winter-sports facilities north of the Alps.

The hills are attractive rather than spectacular, with more or less continuous forest cover. The most comprehensive view is from the bare summit of the Kahler Asten (841m/2,759ft) in the Rothaargebirge (Redhair Heights), the easternmost of the four nature parks making up the area. With abundant ores and minerals beneath the surface, wood for fuel and rushing streams for power, the valleys attracted metalworkers long before the Ruhr was industrialized. Some spots have the dismal air of a place past its prime, but elsewhere the industrial tradition has been used to advantage, with good examples of industrial archaeology. The building tradition is a distinctive one, with many fine old timber-framed and whitewashed houses under steep slate roofs making a harmonious picture against the invariably green background. There are sturdy upland villages around the Kahler Asten (Nordenau, Oberkirchen, Grafschaft...), and most of the towns have some features of interest, such as Altena, dominated by its castle.

INFORMATION

Essen: Hauptbahnhof 2, tel: 0201/8 87 20 41; www.essen.de

▶ The Ruhr   78C5

Named after the river running along its southern boundary to join the Rhine near Duisburg, Germany's 'Kohlenpott', or Black Country, is still Europe's greatest industrial agglomeration, though coal and steel are no longer as important as they once were. Population, though still an impressive 5.5 million, has declined, spread over a combination of varied settlements ranging from such great cities as **Essen** and **Dortmund** to picturesque riverside places such as **Kettwig** and **Herdecke**.

The Ruhr was never a continuously urbanized area, and sensible planning has ensured that the whole conurbation is now interspersed with green spaces threaded by footpaths and cycleways that connect central city areas with splendid new parks (like Essen's Grugapark) and with the open countryside. Ruhr tourist authorities have mapped out four new routes for holidaymakers. One of them takes visitors back into the early industrial age, incorporating a series of preserved pitheads and technological curiosities.

It is still industry that characterizes the scene, and most visitors are here for business rather than pleasure. Urban pleasures are plentiful, however. Each city proclaims its own identity and boasts an enviable array of cultural facilities. Galleries abound, foremost among them the **Museum Folkwang▶** in Essen, with superb collections of 19th- and 20th-century painting (*Open* Tue–Sun), and the Ruhrland Museum with its dour souvenirs of the life of 19th-century miners and steelworkers (*Open* Tue–Sun). **Recklinghausen** has a rarity, a museum devoted almost entirely to icons (*Open* Tue–Sun). **Bochum**'s modern Städtisches Schauspielhaus (City Theater) enjoys an international reputation for its classical and avant-garde productions. Oberhausen has been revitalized by a huge shopping mall with 200 stores built on the site of a former steel plant. At Hagen is a remarkable open-air museum, the Westfälisches Freilichtmuseum, devoted not to rural life but to the early technology of the region (*Open* Apr–end Oct Tue–Sun).

Bochum's **Bergbaumuseum▶** (Mining Museum), with its excellent displays and underground galleries, is outstanding (*Open* Tue–Sun), and the city also has an Eisenbahnmuseum (Railway Museum; *Open* Mar–mid-Nov Tue–Fri and Sun). Industrial history can be enjoyed in the open air, too, notably in the Muttental, near **Witten**, where the Bergbauhistorischer Rundwanderweg (Mining Heritage Trail) features horse-operated pithead gear and the chapel where the miners gathered to pray and be counted before descending.

With the digging of coal went the drinking of beer, and brews evolved to quench the miners' thirst taste just as good today, with a more distinctive character than their Bavarian counterparts.

▶ Saarland   78A1

Like the Mosel, the Saar rises in the Vosges Mountains in France, joining the larger river just above **Trier**. It has given its name to Germany's third smallest *Land*. Long disputed between Germany and France, and still with a Gallic air about it, the Saarland and its capital, **Saarbrücken**, look to the future rather than back to their grimy past of rust-belt industries based on coal and steel.

Thus, while Saarbrücken makes the most of its definitely limited architectural heritage (18th-century Schloss and Rathaus), it promotes itself as a business and cultural base, and cultivates a 'green' image.

Industry extends downriver to **Saarlouis**, founded by Louis XIV as one of the fortresses consolidating his hold on France's eastern frontier and the town's market square still has the air of a parade ground.

Below **Merzig** the valley narrows and begins to run through a wild, spectacular defile. **Mettlach** is an important base of the ceramics industry, and here is based Germany's leading commercial ceramics manufacturer, Villeroy-Boch, with headquarters in an 18th-century Benedictine abbey. The Keramikmuseum in the nearby Schloss Ziegelberg, formerly the palatial home of the Boch family, contains an interesting history of German ceramics, spanning more than two centuries (*Open* Apr–Oct daily; Nov–Mar Mon–Sat). The viewpoint at **Cloef** overlooks the great loop in the river—the Saarschleife.

Downstream from **Serrig**, scrub and woodland give way to vines, and from here the valley takes on an attractive Mosel-like character. At the heart of this region is 1,000-year-old **Saarburg**, with a castle and a stream dropping precipitously past houses and vineyards.

The countryside between the Saar and the Mosel was popular with the Romans. Among the 50 or so villas that have been excavated, the one at **Nennig** has the largest mosaic floor north of the Alps, with scenes of the hunt and of gladiators. Other Roman remains, with reconstructions of original buildings, can be seen in the **Römermuseum Schwarzenacker**, an open-air museum near Homburg east of Saarbrücken (*Open* daily Mar–Oct; Nov–Feb Sat–Sun). To the north, **Ottweiler** has a carefully conserved Altstadt and St. Wendel, a three-towered church, while near **Nonnweiler** is the Hunnenring, the spectacular remains of a Celtic fortified settlement.

Modern industrial Saarbrücken, by the French border, has not only a Franco-German Park but a bilingual Franco-German Lycée/Gymnasium, a practical example of the new entente

INFORMATION
Saarland: Franz-Josef-Röder-Strasse 17,
tel: 0681/92 72 00;
www.
tourismus.saarland.de

THE RURAL RUHR
The Ruhr is not only industrial but idyllically rural too, at least on its southern side. Here disused mineheads and steel-works have been cleared away, to give the river valley back to nature. Close to Bochum's factories you'll find winding country lanes, glens where deer graze and the romantic castle of Blankenstein. There are new pleasure marinas and old villages with quaint cobbled paths and streams.

Drive

Route north from steelmaking Siegen to medieval Soest

The old core of Siegen, with its Schloss, overlooks the River Sieg. Rubens was born here, and there are several of his paintings in the castle's Siegerland museum.

To the northwest Freudenberg's black-and-white houses step harmoniously up the hill. Beyond Olpe is the largest of the region's lakes, the Biggesee. The landscape varies from rocky (at Attendorn) to industrial (around Rönkhausen) to grandiose (in the Lenne Mountains).

To the west of the Sorpe dam is the Luisenhütte. Arnsberg, an ancient administrative base, rises in tiers over the River Ruhr. Like the Sorpe and Eder dams, the Möhne dam was attacked by Britain's Royal Air Force in 1943. After five attempts, the masonry wall of the dam, 34m (112ft) thick at its base, was breached, flooding a vast area and disrupting water supplies to the armament industries of the Ruhr. Long since repaired, the dam holds back a 10km (6-mile) lake used by water-sports enthusiasts (north shore) and birds (south shore).

Soest is approached from the south across the Kassel–Ruhr autobahn

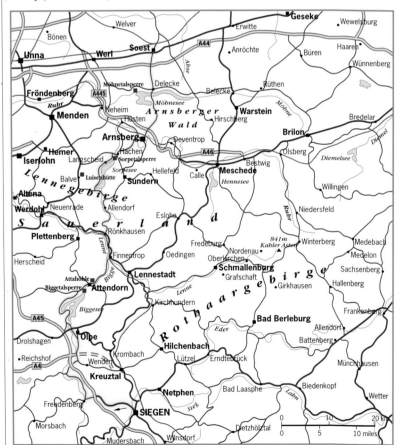

INFORMATION
Soest:
Teichsmühlengasse 3,
tel: 02921/6 63 00
500–50; www.soest.de

In Soest, many red-roofed and half-timbered houses line the streets within the ramparts

▶▶ Soest   78C5

In the Middle Ages Soest was the most important city in Westphalia, making good use of its position on the Hellweg (the ancient highway running right across northern Germany) to trade with Novgorod and Milan, Bruges and London. Having escaped the industrialization that befell Dortmund, its old rival, Soest still wears an attractive medieval air.

Near the baroque Rathaus stands a sturdy pair of Romanesque churches, each with an impressive west-work, topped, in the case of the St. Patrokli-Münster, by a formidable tower. The Petrikirche has frescoes attributed to a local master of medieval times, Konrad von Soest, who also painted the altar in the nearby chapel dedicated to St. Nicholas.

Reflected in the waters of the pretty little lake, the Grosser Teich, are the twin spires of the Gothic Wiesenkirche (Our Lady of the Meadows). The stained glass of the splendidly light interior includes a depiction of the Last Supper with typical Westphalian refreshments on the table—ham, beer and pumpernickel, along with some Steinhäger, the local schnapps. On rising ground nearby is St. Maria zur Höhe (Our Lady of the Heights), with original Romanesque paintings.

Soest's attractive ambience has drawn artists; works by two local men, Heinrich Aldegrever (a follower of Dürer) and Wilhelm Morgner (a contemporary of the Expressionist Emil Nolde), are shown in the modern Wilhelm-Morgner Haus (*Open* Tue–Sun). The municipal museum is in the 16th-century Burghof, next to a town house dating back to the 12th century (*Open* Tue–Sun).

To the south, the River Möhne, a tributary of the Ruhr, has been broadened to form the Möhnesee, whose dam is famous: In 1943 a squadron of Lancaster bombers of Britain's Royal Air Force—the 'Dambusters'—success-fully bombed it, and 125 factories were wrecked by the the subsequent flooding.

BERTELSMANN
In decentralized Germany, many institutions are scat-tered in various cities. Thus the world's largest publishing firm, Bertelsmann, has its head-quarters in modest Gütersloh, a true company town, swarming with edi-tors and printers. The Bertelsmann world empire embraces other publishing giants such as Doubleday, Random House, Bantam Books, commercial televi-sion, a Berlin daily newspaper, a leading mag-azine group and a book club with 4.5 million mem-bers in Germany, 29 million worldwide.

The Rhineland

INFORMATION
Trier: An der Porta Nigra,
tel: 0651/97 80 80;
www.tit.de

ROMAN CITY
First established by the
Celtic Treveri peoples,
Trier was called *Augusta
Treverorum* in 15BC,
becoming one of the
most important Roman
cities north of the Alps.
With a population of
80,000—close to today's
total—it flourished as an
imperial residence and
capital of the western
part of the empire.
Emperor Constantine
made it Germany's first
bishopric. By the Middle
Ages, Trier's prince-bishops were powerful rulers.
But the city's most influential son was Karl Marx:
The house where he was
born in 1818 is now a
fascinating museum of
his life and work (*Open*
daily. *Closed* Mon am
Nov–Mar).

*Modern Trier, once
the Roman Empire's
northern capital*

►►► Trier   78A2

Trier, among the vineyards of the Mosel Valley, is probably the oldest city in Germany. Its heritage of buildings
spanning two millennia makes it irresistible for visitors.

Start by exploring Trier's compact heart at the massive
Porta Nigra►►, the biggest and best-preserved Roman
gateway in Europe, so named for the blackened appearance of the huge blocks of limestone from which it is
made. In the Middle Ages it was converted into a church
in memory of St. Simeon; the nearby monastery bearing
his name has a fine courtyard with two-floor cloisters.

The traffic-free Simeonsstrasse leads to the Hauptmarkt,
with its ornate Renaissance fountain. On the rise to the
east is the huge **cathedral►**, begun by Constantine but
predominantly Romanesque with a baroque interior,
filled with valuable medieval artefacts.

Part of Constantine's great imperial palace, the brick
Konstantinsbasilika►► survives as a Protestant church;
apart from the Pantheon in Rome, it is the biggest
enclosed space to survive from the days of antiquity. Next
door, in total contrast, is the lighthearted strawberry-and-
vanilla façade of the rococo Prince-Bishop's Palace; its
formal garden extends south to Trier's third great Roman
monument, the **Kaiserthermen►** (Imperial Baths). The
excavated remains of the baths can be visited daily. Other
Roman remains and artefacts are on show in the
Rheinisches Landesmuseum►. This is Germany's largest
collection of Roman antiquities, with a 3rd-century stone
relief of a Roman wine ship as its world-famous highlight
(*Open* daily; *closed* Mon Nov–Apr).

Trier's further delights include a 20,000-seat Roman
amphitheatre, the piers of a bridge over the Mosel, the
Bischöfliches (Episcopal) **Museum►** (*Open* daily; closed
Mon Nov–Mar), the medieval interior of St. Matthias
Church, St. Paulin Church by Balthasar Neumann, and
modern Karl Marx Haus.

> *At the foot of the Haardt Mountains, forming*
> *the eastern rim of the vast Palatinate Forest,*
> *lies a cheerful, sun-drenched countryside that*
> *produced fine wines for the Romans. Today the*
> *delightful wine towns and villages of the*
> *Rheinpfalz are linked by one of Germany's*
> *best-known touring routes, the Deutsche*
> *Weinstrasse or Wine Road. Some 80km (50*
> *miles) long, it links Bockenheim in the north to*
> *the border with Alsace in the south.*

Pfalz wines are made from a variety of grapes; the whites span the whole quality range from everyday table wines to the most exquisite Trockenbeerenauslese. Reds account for only 10 per cent of total production. No one should miss tasting the wines offered in traditional vintners' houses opening off cobbled village streets. Every place has something special: half-timbered or mellow red sandstone houses; the remains of medieval fortifications; a ruined castle on a hill... The landscape gives continual pleasure, too, with ever-changing views of hills and broad plains. The benevolent climate means that not only vines but other southern plants thrive, such as fig, almond and chestnut trees, tobacco and maize. Kallstadt is proud of its local delicacy, *Saumagen* literally 'sow's belly', but actually a delicately spiced and delicious meatloaf-type dish—former Chancellor Helmut Kohl always served it to his state guests.

Bad Dürkheim celebrates the vintage with Germany's biggest wine festival, the Wurstmarkt. Deidesheim has one of the best arrays of restaurants and inns, including the oldest tavern in the Palatinate. Medieval Neustadt, with its viticultural institute, is the region's miniature metropolis, while nearby Hambach Castle is where Germany's black-red-gold flag was raised by patriots for the first time in 1832. There are stunning panoramas from the Kalmit summit (673m/2,208ft), a short way into the hills, or from Bavarian King Ludwig I's summer residence, Schloss Ludwigshöhe. The fantastic turrets and ramparts of another castle, Madenburg, loom over Eschbach. Beyond the resort of Bad Bergzabern, the route's terminus is marked by the huge Weintor gateway.

107

Weinstrasse vineyards

Central Germany

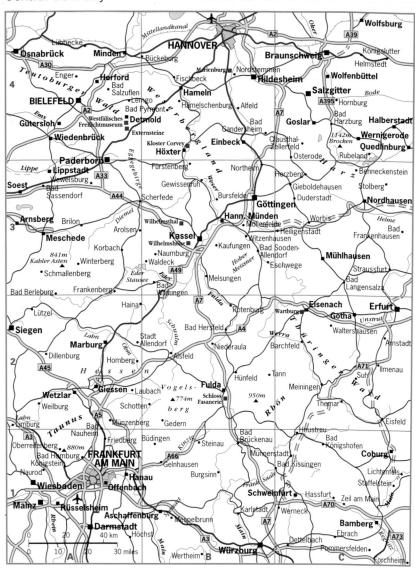

The Germans tend to keep the charms of Central Germany to themselves. Only a handful of towns, such as **Hameln** (Hamelin), with its Pied Piper fable and spectacular Weser Renaissance houses (see page 119), are on the international tourist circuit. Although it has none of the drama of the Alps, it can be rewarding making your own discoveries in the numerous attractive small towns and rolling, forested uplands. The state of **Hessen** (Hesse) is crossed by the River Main and **Frankfurt** is its chief city. Frankfurt was used by the Americans as an administrative base after World War II and is very much the heart of Germany. It did, however, exist long before the Americans arrived, although fragmented along geographic and religious lines. In 1866 Hesse was incorporated in the kingdom of

Prussia, and five years later became part of the Greater
German Reich. While Frankfurt, the banking capital of
Germany and seat of the European Central Bank, remains
the heart of the country's economic wealth, other towns,
notably **Kassel** in north Hesse, generate income from
industrial output. Not far away from the urban
landscapes of the 20th century are reminders of slower-
moving times in such old towns as **Marburg** and **Alsfeld**.

For lovers of the countryside, the **Vogelsberg**, a plateau
created by a volcanic eruption approximately 30 million
years ago, is a little-developed area of hills and forests.
The unspoiled rural landscape embraces sleepy medieval
towns studded with romantic castles and evokes the tales
of the Brothers Grimm, who lived and worked in the area.
The region stretches from **Göttingen** up into the
Weserbergland, whose green hills (which rise to 500m/
1,640ft) flank the Weser, one of the loveliest rivers in
Germany. Attractive little towns with entire streets of
half-timbered buildings flank this sinuous river and have
given rise to their own recognized class of architecture:
Weser Renaissance. Today it's literally fairy-tale country,
traversed by one of Germany's most enchanting holiday
routes, the Deutsche Märchenstrasse (German Fairy Tale
Road). The path into the traditional fairy-tale past begins
in Hanau, an unlovely town famous in this context only
because it is the birthplace of the Grimm brothers. The
route winds lazily on, through the little hilltop town of
Steinau an der Strasse, where the two Grimms grew up,
crossing half the length of Germany before ending at the
coast, at Bremerhaven. The **Harz Mountains**, which comprise the highest ground in the region, once were divided
by the East–West German border. Now they offer opportunities for discovering the lesser-known Germany.

*Alsfeld's town square,
with the Rathaus in
the background*

This door is typical of the ornate architecture of Alsfeld, a key focus of folk tradition

INFORMATION
Darmstadt: Luisenfeld 5,
tel: 06151 9515013;
www.darmstadt.de

JUGENDSTIL
Darmstadt was a focus of the Jugendstil—German art nouveau. The style began as quite floral and naturalistic, but after the 1900s it took on an increasingly abstract form. The architect Peter Behrens, who built a house for himself on the Mathildenhöhe, was an enthusiastic exponent of the late Jugendstil.

▶▶ Alsfeld   108B2
Set amid the rolling, wooded Vogelsberg hills on the pretty Schwalm River, Alsfeld is a picturesque old town with some fine half-timbered Renaissance buildings. The folk traditions here inspired the Grimm brothers and at summer festivals the girls still wear the local red folk costumes. Outside the Walpurgiskirche is a fountain with a figure of a goose girl in the style of costume worn by Little Red Riding Hood.

In the Marktplatz the tiny, quaint 1516 Rathaus (town hall) stands above arcades where markets were once held. Opposite is the Renaissance-style Hochzeithaus, built for weddings, as its name implies. Fine examples of baroque architecture can be seen in the Rittergasse, notably the Neurath Haus at No. 3 and the Minnigerode Haus at No. 5. In Hersfelderstrasse, Nos. 10 and 12 are among Germany's oldest half-timbered buildings.

▶ Bielefeld   108A4
This big industrial town has manufactured linen since the 16th century. Today it is also a base for engineering, electronics and food-processing. It has an interesting art gallery, the Kunsthalle (*Open* Tue–Sun), which has some German Expressionist works (including several by Beckmann), and sculptures by Rodin, Moore and others.

Herford, an old Hanseatic town nearby, has a late Romanesque Münster and a number of Gothic churches; of these, the Johanniskirche has notable 17th-century woodwork and stained-glass windows.

▶ Darmstadt   108A1
This otherwise dullish industrial town is best known as the heartland of the Jugendstil (art nouveau) movement of the early 1900s. An artists' colony was established on the low hill of Mathildenhöhe, and their **Jugendstil buildings▶** still stand there (see panel): the Ernst-Ludwig-Haus with its Adam and Eve figures on the portal, the Behrens Haus and the Hochzeitturm (wedding tower), designed for the wedding of Grand Duke Ernst Ludwig in 1905. The spectacular Russian Orthodox chapel with its gilded domes dates from the 1890s. A collection of Jugendstil objects is displayed in the Landesmuseum near the reconstructed 18th-century Schloss (*Open* Tue–Sun). The Schlossmuseum (*Open* Sat–Thu) contains *The Madonna of Jakob Meyer*, a masterpiece by Hans Holbein the Younger.

▶ Detmold   108A4
Until 1918 this town was capital of the principality of Lippe, and it still has a strong sense of its own identity. Its noble 16th-century castle (Residenzschloss) has Brussels tapestries and souvenirs of the family of Prince Bernhard of the Netherlands, whose seat was here. There are British Army barracks in the town, nicknamed 'Little London'.

To the south is the Teutoburger Wald, a long, narrow range of wooded hills with two interesting sights on its crest. One is the Hermannsdenkmal, a 26m (85ft) green-copper statue of Arminius, the local chieftain who in about AD9 rallied the Germanic tribes to oppose Rome's rule and defeated its legions close by. Erected under Bismarck, the memorial became a focus for German nationalism since the Nazis sometimes held rallies here.

*Duderstadt, a small
town right beside the
former GDR border, has
over 500 half-timbered
buildings. This one is
the town hall*

111

The **Externsteine▶** nearby is a cluster of high rocks in strange, toothy shapes, which were once used as a place of worship by pagan tribes, and later by Christians. Carved on one rock is a 12th-century bas-relief depicting the Descent from the Cross. Also hewn from the rock are a tomb and a pulpit. The summer solstice used to be celebrated here, as the sun rose between the rocks.

If you want to take a closer view, you can climb up the new stairways carved into the rock. On the plain below there is a large ornithological park, as well as the Westfälisches Freilichtmuseum, an open-air museum that has a display of nearly 100 reassembled farm buildings from the region (*Open* Apr–Oct Tue–Sun).

▶ Duderstadt   *108C3*

Only 21km (13 miles) east of the university town of Göttingen, Duderstadt has a successful blend of Renaissance and Gothic architecture, which can be seen both on Hinterstrasse and in the Rathaus. The Westertorturm (gate tower) is notable for its twisted narrow roof. The town contains two worthwhile churches: the Gothic St. Cyriakuskirche, decorated in ostentatious baroque style, and St. Servatiuskirche, refurbished in the art nouveau manner after a fire in 1915.

▶ Einbeck   *108B4*

A small town with a population of almost 29,000, Einbeck was known in the Middle Ages for its beer. There were no fewer than 700 breweries at that time, but only one of them survives, producing a well-known strong beer, the Einbecker Bockbier. Guided tours of the brewery can be arranged by appointment with Einbecker Brauhaus.

Around the cobbled Marktplatz and in the Tidexer-strasse are half-timbered Gothic and Renaissance houses. The oldest choir stall in Germany (1288) is in the Stiftskirche St. Alexandri.

▶▶▶ REGION HIGHLIGHTS

Alsfeld *page 110*
Frankfurt-am-Main
pages 112–115
Fulda *page 116*
**Goslar (and
Huldigungssaal)**
page 117
Hameln *page 119*
Hannoversch Münden
pages 125–126
Harz Mountains
pages 122–123
**Kassel (for Schloss
Wilhelmshöhe and park)**
page 124
Lemgo *page 125*
Weserbergland
pages 130–131

Central Germany

A PROUD HISTORY

Barbarossa and other early German emperors were elected in Frankfurt, and from 1562–1806 the Holy Roman Emperors were crowned here. Goethe, born in the city, called it 'Germany's secret capital', and the first pan-German parliament met here in 1848–1849. The city began to mint its own money in the 16th century; then in the 19th century local financiers, such as Rothschild, made it into a key world focus of banking. After 1945 it was proposed as the new federal capital, but Adenauer insisted on Bonn—a pity, very many people think. Today, together with Hannover, it is Germany's major trade-fair venue, and it has the country's leading international airport. Industry includes machine tools and chemicals.

Frankfurt's financial district as seen from the River Main

►► Frankfurt-am-Main   108A1

Urban American visitors smile indulgently at the name Germans sometimes give to Frankfurt-am-Main—'Mainhattan', a word-play incorporating the name of the river on which it stands and the cluster of skyscrapers that form its downtown skyline, unique in Germany. Compared to Manhattan itself Frankfurt is small town stuff. Yet by German standards its assembly of tall office buildings is impressive; The 'Wolkenkratzer' (literally 'cloud-scrapers') include mainland Europe's largest office building, the 299m (981ft) Commerzbank tower, designed by Britain's Sir Norman Foster, and the new European Central Bank headquarters. Frankfurt is also the home of the still-powerful German Central Bank, the Bundesbank, and has branches of nearly 400 world banks. The German Stock Exchange is also based here. Despite its position as the German—and now European—financial capital, Frankfurt is by no means just a money-spinning metropolis. Visitors arriving at its huge international airport are well advised to spend a day or two getting to know Frankfurt's other face.

There's a great deal for the tourist to see, including some of Germany's best museums. Because the city is rich, it has the money to spend on culture, such as high-class opera, and at its annual Book Fair—the world's largest—literature and commerce join hands. Many other international trade fairs are also held here.

Frankfurt has a metropolitan, outward-looking ambience, largely due to all the high-profile international activity. It is also a city of tensions, with relatively high levels of crime and drug abuse and one of Europe's largest immigrant populations. Politically, it has a history

of left-wing activism, possibly because of its visible symbols of capitalism. By 1999, however, the right-wing Christian Democrats had become the major party in the city council, forming a 'Platform' (an informal coalition) with the Social Democrats. A Christian Democrat Lady Mayoress led the city.

One local hotbed of leftism has been the famous university (35,000 students), where radical philosophers such as Habermas and Adorno once expounded new ideas. This city of money is also a lively focus of the alternative avant-garde, with many fringe theatres and a big jazz scene. The controversial film director Rainer Werner Fassbinder once worked here.

The main sights are central, and many can be toured on foot. Near the Messegelände (exhibition centre) and the central station is the financial district, where the 24-floor Deutsche Bank twin towers are the most graceful of the city's skyscrapers (the Bundesbank itself is out in the suburbs). Much of this central area was gracelessly rebuilt after wartime bombing, but some older buildings have been well restored, notably the big neo-classical opera house (though operas are now staged elsewhere). The 15th-century Eschenheimer Turm is one of the 42 towers that used to encircle the city. The Börse (stock exchange) is nearby and the 18th-century **Hauptwache** (guard room). The **Goethehaus▶▶** (*Open* daily), an adjacent museum opened in 1997, is the family home where the poet was brought up. It has been well restored.

Before the bombing, Frankfurt had the biggest medieval Altstadt in Germany. Little now survives save for a carefully restored sector around the cathedral and the Römerberg, a cobbled square lined with fine half-timbered houses. The **Römer▶**, a group of 15th-century houses that once formed the Rathaus, has a Renaissance stairway leading to the stately Kaisersaal. Across the square is the tiny Gothic Nikolaikirche and the History Museum. Just to the east is a fascinating zone where new modernistic buildings have purposely been put up next to ancient ones. The new glass-walled Shirn Kunsthalle, an arts centre, overlooks the ruins of a Carolingian palace and a Roman bath (around AD100) beside

THE ROTHSCHILDS
The name of this great banking family comes from the words *rother Schild* (red shield), after the shield that hung on the family's house in the ghetto in Frankfurt-am-Main. Born in 1743 in Frankfurt, Mayer Amschel Rothschild was the founder in 1766 of the Rothschild bank. It handled the fortunes of Europe's royalty and played a large part in financing the Napoleonic wars. Mayer Amschel's elder son, Nathan Mayer, founded the British branch of the family bank in Manchester in 1800, and the second son, James Mayer, developed the French side of the family's business in Paris.

113

The opera house (left), built in the 1880s, is now used for conventions, while operas are staged in the city theatre. The high Gothic cathedral (below) is a local landmark, even if dwarfed by some of the skyscrapers

Once the setting for royal ceremonies: Frankfurt's cobbled square, Römerberg

INFORMATION
Frankfurt: Hauptbahnhof, tel: 069/21 23 88 49; www.frankfurt-tourismus.de

GOETHE THE GREAT
Born in Frankfurt-am-Main in 1749, Goethe is undoubtedly Germany's greatest literary figure, and a lifelong lover of women. The young Johann reluctantly studied law in Leipzig, where he met his first love, Käthchen Schönkopf. He continued his law studies in Strasbourg, where he had another love affair and met the German writer and thinker Herder. With Herder's help, Goethe became part of the Sturm und Drang (Storm and Stress) movement. In 1771 he returned to Frankfurt to write and practise law before moving to Weimar in 1775.

St. Bartholomew's Cathedral►, with its lofty Gothic tower. The emperors were crowned in this austere reddish church, which has medieval murals and choir stalls. In the adjacent Wahlkapelle the Holy Roman Empire's seven electors chose their king, and the cathedral's little museum displays the adornments they wore (*Open* Tue–Sun). The nearby 15th-century St. Leonard's Church has impressive examples of stained glass.

Frankfurt prides itself on its impressive collection of museums, most of them grouped together in conveniently accessible form along the Main River. Berlin has its 'museum island', Frankfurt its 'museum river bank', a riverside complex of no fewer than seven museums (*all closed* Mon). From west to east they are: (1) the **Liebieghaus museum of sculpture►**, ranging from ancient Egypt to the baroque; (2) the important **Städel Museum of Art►►**, with a collection of works by Holbein, Cranach, Tintoretto, Rembrandt, Renoir, Monet and a rich array of German painting, including Tischbein's portrait of Goethe sitting pensively near Rome, and works by Liebermann, Thoma, Beckmann, Kirchner and Nolde; (3) the Communications Museum, with details of stamps, mail coaches and telephones; (4) the Deutsches-Architektur-Museum, offering a tour of world architecture in a house constructed within a house; (5) the Film Museum, mostly technical and scientific; (6) the Museum of Ethnography, with objects from native tribes; (7) the Museum of Applied Art, with a collection of glass, porcelain, Jugendstil furniture, a good Asian and Islamic section and more, all in a lovely new building.

On the other river bank is Germany's most interesting museum of Jewish history, the **Jüdisches Museum►** (Jewish Museum; *Open* Tue–Sun), housed in the former Rothschild palace. The museum is divided into two sections: One illustrates the Jewish contribution to Frankfurt's cultural life, the other documents the history of Frankfurt's Jewish community, from the Middle Ages to the present day.

Frankfurt's reputation as a cultural and financial city leaves first-time visitors unprepared for the bohemian charm of its Sachsenhausen quarter, south of the river, a leafy, residential district, with some old city mansions and cider taverns unique to Germany. They serve up cider comparable to the best of France or Britain (see panel).

If zoos are your thing, Frankfurt has one of Germany's best, with a spectacular aquarium of rare fish and a special section on nocturnal creatures. Dead or extinct animals, such as dinosaurs, can be studied in the Senckenberg natural history museum, which is near the university and the large Grüneburg Park, containing botanical and tropical gardens.

Two towns near Frankfurt are well worth a visit. **Offenbach**, Germany's chief leather-making town, has a big museum devoted to the subject (*Open* daily). **Höchst**, home of the giant Hoechst chemicals firm (now called Aventis), has a charming undamaged Altstadt and several fine old buildings. One is the Justiniuskirche of Carolingian origin; another is the baroque Bolongaro palace, former home of Italian snuff makers. Höchst was a famous porcelain-producing base in the 18th century.

POWERFUL CIDER
Frankfurters cross the river to let their hair down in the cider houses of Sachsenhausen. *Apfelwein* (*Appelwoi* or *Ebbelwei*) is the local brew, but if you're not used to this cider the first quaff could take your breath away—it's dry, almost vinegary, and very strong.

115

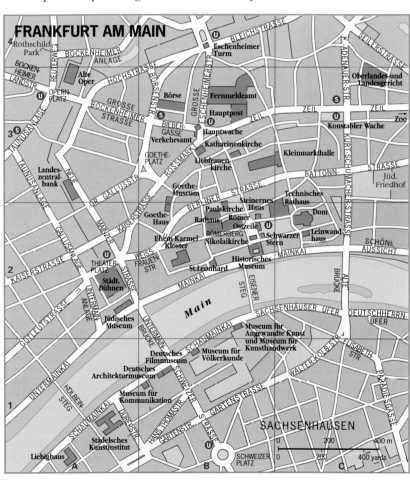

FRANKFURT AM MAIN

Main

SACHSENHAUSEN

SCHLOSS FASANERIE
If you haven't yet had your fill of baroque, visit Schloss Fasanerie (guided tours Apr–Oct; *Open* Tue–Sun), built for the 18th-century prince-bishops of Fulda. Its sumptuous décor and size are almost over-powering, but the park offers a relaxing respite. (You get there on bus 3 or 4 from Fulda.) Near the town is the Kirche auf dem Petersberg (Petersberg Church), built on a 400m-high (1,312ft) rock and visible from afar.

INFORMATION
Fulda: Bonifatiusplatz 1, tel: 0661/1 02 18 14; www.tourismus-fulda.de

116

The tall 14th-century Adolfsturm overlooks the old streets of the 'dual' town of Friedberg

► **Friedberg**   *108A1*

Few Jewish bathhouses remain in Germany but Friedberg has one of them. The Judenbad here is a particularly fine example of this type of ritual bathing place. Built in the 13th century, it descends 25m (82ft) below ground level, reached by 74 steps. The Burg (Imperial Town) was built by the Emperor Frederick Barbarossa in 1180 and today remains a district community, as in medieval times. The separation of church and state is apparent, with the other main part of town being focused on the Stadtkirche, dating from the 13th and 14th centuries.

►► **Fulda**   *108B2*

Since the 8th century, Fulda has been one of Germany's most important bases for Catholic religious instruction. It all began when a Benedictine abbey was founded here by St. Boniface, an English missionary to the pagan Germanic tribes. The abbey became a famous focus for culture and learning throughout the Christian world.

Today the town contains a variety of architectural styles. Above all there is a wealth of baroque, a style that extends to the huge palace (now a museum; *Open* daily) and even the former police station. The main **Dom** (cathedral) was rebuilt by Johann Dientzenhofer (one of a noted family of architects) at the beginning of the 18th century, having been inspired by Italian baroque architecture; in fact, he worked from a model copy of St. Peter's in Rome. The Michaelskirche (*Open* daily) is one of the oldest churches in Germany, with a crypt dating from AD822.

The Hanauisches Amtshaus at **Steinau**, about 24km (15 miles) southwest of Fulda, was the boyhood home of the Brothers Grimm and today a puppet theatre re-enacts their fairy-tales. The much-fortified Schloss contains a museum that is devoted to the Grimm brothers (*Open* daily pm mid-Jan to mid-Dec).

► **Gelnhausen**   *108B1*

This town of Gelnhausen is said to have been founded by Emperor Frederick Barbarossa in 1170 (it is sometimes called Barbarossa Stadt). It stands on a slope of the Kinzig Valley (close to the Naturpark Hessischer Spessart, which is good walking country with its forested hills). The town was built as a military foundation and is still partly sur-rounded by fortifications.

The Marienkirche (St. Mary's) is a multi-towered Romanesque church that looks over Gelnhausen from above. The chancel is the best feature of the interior, with its high altar and a shrine depicting the Madonna with four saints. The unusual choir stalls are ornately deco-rated, and there are two well-preserved tapestries. Barbarossa's castle, the Kaiserpfalz, stands on an island in the River Kinzig, but now only ruins remain of the former stronghold (*Open* Tue–Sun).

Büdingen, about 10km (6 miles) north of Gelnhausen, possesses an intact town wall that dates from the 15th and 16th centuries and is distinguished by squat towers and pierced by elaborate Gothic gateways. You can take guided tours (minimum of four people) of the Schloss (tel: 0642/9 64 70. *Open* Mid-Apr to mid-Oct Sat and Sun at 2, 3, 4, 5; winter by appointment) over a still-inhabited 12th- to 17th-century building ranged around a courtyard.

Many of the older houses in Goslar are half-timbered, like these lining a stream in the heart of town

►► Goslar 108C4

One of the loveliest towns in north Germany, Goslar is also a winter-sports resort that is very popular with Berliners. It was a seat of the Salian Emperors in the 11th century, then a Free Imperial City. In the Middle Ages it became a centre of silver and lead mining. Merchants began to pour in, lead and silver were increasingly mined and refined, and this led to a building boom around the 16th century, the peak of Goslar's prosperity. This explains its legacy of fine buildings from different epochs—Gothic, Renaissance, baroque. Many are half-timbered or of stone, rather than the usual north German red brick. The mines, in the hills south of the town, ultimately went bankrupt and the last one closed in 1992. By the 19th century, Goslar was prospering again under Prussian domination.

The Altstadt is full of interest for the visitor. The traffic-free, cobbled Marktplatz, surrounded by dignified stone and half-timbered houses with elaborate slate roofs, has a quaint chiming clock (modern) on the treasurer's building, which performs four times a day—at 9am, noon, 3pm and 6pm—with scenes outlining the mining history of the town dating back to the Middle Ages.

In the old arcaded Rathaus, a fine Gothic building, the **Huldigungssaal►►** (*Open* daily) is covered from floor to ceiling with splendid frescoes from around 1500; it also holds the Goslar Gospel (1230). Across the square, the 15th-century Kaiserworth, once a guildhouse, is now a hotel: On the left-hand-side corner gable is an impudent statue of a boy ejecting a coin from his backside (symbolic of Goslar's former right to mint coins). The square also has a fountain with two large bronze basins surmounted by an imperial eagle. Many of the houses in the streets off the square are half-timbered (*Fachwerkhäuser*).

The Siemenshaus (*Open* Tue and Thu am) was built in 1693 by Hans Siemens, an ancestor of the Berlin industrialist who created the Siemens electrical empire. The Goslarer Museum (*Open* Tue–Sun) contains a detailed outline of the artistic and cultural history of the Harz region, as well as models of the town. The Mönchehaus (*Open* Tue–Sun) contains a modest collection of modern art. The terrace by the statue of Bismarck near the station offers a good view of the town that includes its encircling hills.

INFORMATION
Goslar: Markt 7,
tel: 05321/7 80 60;
www.goslar.de

117

FRANKFURT FURORE
The ongoing Left/Right feud in Frankfurt came to a head in 1981, when work began on a new runway for the airport, Germany's largest. Greens, anarchists and others staged sit-ins, to protest that farms and forests would be damaged and the runway would benefit only the US Air Force. There were violent clashes with the police, some of whom over-reacted brutally. Local opinion was polarized and everyone took sides. Finally the runway *was* completed—the environmentalists had lost. The airport authorities are currently looking at further expansion to meet rapidly growing air traffic demands.

FRIEDLAND CAMP
At Friedland, near the former GDR border south of Göttingen, there used to be a large transit camp for political refugees arriving not from the GDR but from other east European countries. Here they stayed while their papers were processed, before moving on to a new life in some West German town. The camp now welcomes *Aussiedler*, East Europeans with German family roots who wish to settle in Germany.

INFORMATION
Göttingen: Altes Rathaus, Markt 9, tel: 0551/49 98 00; www.goettingen-

The Gänselieselbrunnen at Göttingen (top right) and the door of the city's 16th-century pharmacy (below)

▶ Göttingen   *108B3*

Göttingen is first and foremost a university town. The university, named after its founder, the elector of Hanover, who was also George II, king of Great Britain and Ireland, has given the town a hallowed reputation as a leading place of learning. The university has produced several Nobel Prize winners, and is the headquarters of the Max Planck-Institut, which groups some 50 high-level scientific research bodies all over Germany. Max Planck, creator of the quantum theory in physics, spent his final years in the town and is buried here.

The 30,000 university students and 2,500 teachers and professors bring added life to the town, which prides itself on its Gothic churches and neo-classical buildings, such as the Aula, or Great Hall, scattered about the campus. The students have made the town hall area and its Ratskeller the hub of activity. Even during vacations you will find throngs of young people milling about, and nightlife is always interesting. A famous music festival devoted to Handel is held in June. There is a tradition for students to visit the *Gänselieselbrunnen* ('Goose Lizzie's fountain') in the middle of town in front of the Rathaus, once they've completed their examinations, and to kiss the bronze statue of a graceful young girl.

The Vierkirchenblick (viewpoint of four churches) is a particularly memorable sight. Stand at the southeast corner of the Markt and you will see, to the east, the 15th-century St. Albanus; to the south, St. Michael; to the west, the two octagonal towers of the Johanniskirche; and to the north, St. Jakobi, the tallest, which stands at 72m (236ft). There are half-timbered houses in the old quarter of the town—one dating from 1563, northeast of the Markt, houses the old pharmacy and is also elaborately and attractively decorated.

►► Hamelin (Hamelin) 108B4

There is more to Hameln than just the legend of a man in a strange costume, and a plague of rats. There are many attractive half-timbered buildings left, despite severe damage during the 1618–48 Thirty Years' War (World War II fortunately had less impact).

The town is a treasure house of immaculately restored buildings in the so-called Weser Renaissance style of the 16th and 17th centuries. Typically this makes use of scroll decorations and pinnacles on gables, carved-stone banding and large bay windows. The **Rattenfängerhaus**► (Rat Catcher's House), at Osterstrasse 28, dates back to 1603 and is a good example. Its carved stonework is embellished with busts and heads, and there is an inscription about the Pied Piper on the side—the house was actually built for a councillor.

The Hochzeitshaus (Wedding House), at Osterstrasse 2, was built between 1610 and 1617 and was used for burghers' weddings. On the side facing the Marktplatz, the Pied Piper clock features mechanical figures, which appear daily at 1.05, 3.35 and 5.35pm precisely.

A stroll through the streets will reveal other beautiful old buildings. Two in Osterstrasse house the Museum Hameln (*Open* Tue–Sun), with a collection of religious art, local history and Pied Piper lore.

Excursion

Hämelschenburg, about 16km (10 miles) south of Hameln, is a magnificent example of the Weser Renaissance style. The castle (guided tours Mar to mid-Oct; *Open* Tue–Sun) was built between 1588 and 1618 in a horseshoe shape. Farther down the Deutsche Märchenstrasse is Bad Pyrmont, a popular traditional spa.

North of Hameln is **Fischbeck** (8km/5 miles), where there is a convent dating from the 10th century. The church is 12th-century and has a fine Romanesque crypt.

INFORMATION
Hameln: Deisterallee 1, tel: 05151/95 78 23; www.hameln.com/tourism

WARTIME SORROW
The poet Max Herrmann Neisse used the story of the Pied Piper to express the sorrow of the wartime evacuation of children: 'So dead are squares and gardens now like Hameln after the rat catcher's revenge: the children have all left us, a mother's heart is trembling under every roof.'

'Rat pastries'

PIED PIPER PLAY
Thanks to the Pied Piper legend, immortalized by Goethe and then in verse by the English poet Robert Browning, Hameln has become famous far beyond Germany. Every Sunday afternoon from mid-May to mid-September, between noon and 12.30, a Pied Piper play is performed on the terrace of the Hochzeitshaus.

Local children play the part of rats, lured away by the Piper's music

THE BROTHERS GRIMM

Northern Hessen, around Kassel, is the heartland of the folk tales collected by Jacob and Wilhelm Grimm. Born near Frankfurt, they spent their early careers (1805–30) as court librarians at Kassel, where they conceived a passion for folklore and spent many years collecting their material orally from country people. Jacob was the scholar, Wilhelm the poet who put the tales into readable form. After their death, other writers tried to make the tales less frightening to children.

HARZ WITCHES

The Harz is famed for its witch legends. The eve of 1 May is believed to be the Walpurgisnacht, the night of the witches' sabbath on the Brocken (1,142m/3,747ft), the highest mountain in the region; this occasion is an episode in Goethe's famous play, *Faust*.

There is a strange mixture of the comic and the tragic in German folklore—the piper of Hameln who charmed the rats away, then, because he was not properly paid, took the children with him, too, and Tannhäuser, the knight who abandoned his vows and went into a strange mountain to spend the rest of his days in the company of Venus. The most celebrated mountain in Germany is the Kyffhäuser, east of Göttingen, where the Emperor Frederick Barbarossa slumbers in a hidden cavern, radiant with gold and jewels. His great red beard has grown almost three times around the stone table at which he sits. A shepherd once strayed into the cavern and spoke to the emperor, who told him that he must remain there until the ravens cease to fly around the peak outside.

Traditionally, the 16th-century Dr. Johann Faust, a mountebank who toured throughout Germany but who is particularly associated with the city of Erfurt, sold his soul to the devil in return for knowledge of science and alchemy, and died with his neck being wrung by an archdemon. The devil was, however, outwitted at Cologne, for the great cathedral was built there supposedly according to a plan drafted by him as a lure to gain the soul of the architect. The clever architect came to a rendezvous carrying a crucifix, which kept the devil at bay while he snatched the document.

In many parts of the country there are traditions of the *Wilde Jagd* (wild hunt), a ghostly cavalry crashing through the forests to the accompaniment of trumpets and shouts. This is a survival of the cult of the great Teutonic deity Odin.

The transfer from paganism to Christianity, too, is represented in various legends, such as that of the Drachenfels, a mountain near Bonn, where it is said that a wicked fire-breathing dragon tried to seize a beautiful Christian maiden but was hurled by the girl's prayers into the river below.

The Rhine is the most venerable of European rivers. According to legend, a treasure trove lies hidden in it and the secret was known only to the last two Nibelung heroes, who refused to divulge it despite torture and death. When the sun shines on the Rhine, the reflection of this treasure can be seen, but none of it can be found. Old lore also tells of Charlemagne, who was espe-

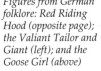

Figures from German folklore: Red Riding Hood (opposite page); the Valiant Tailor and Giant (left); and the Goose Girl (above)

cially partial to a castle that he had at Ingelheim. When he noticed that the snow melted quickly on the hills of Rüdesheim, west of Mainz, he established fine vineyards there, and now his spirit can be seen on spring nights, blessing the vines. A predilection for wine was also shown by the 14th-century Emperor Wenzel, who once feasted in a beautiful meadow at Rhens, south of Koblenz, and was so impressed with a cask of fiery wine from Bacharach that he sold his realm for it.

At Bingen, in the 10th century, lived Hatto, a bishop who was so rapacious that in time of famine he refused food to the starving multitude. By divine punishment his palace was infested with mice. To escape the pests, he retired to a tower in the Rhine, but he was pursued there by the mice and devoured by them. More fortunate was a prisoner in Frankfurt long ago, who was offered his freedom if he could hit a weathercock on a wall tower with nine consecutive shots from his musket. He succeeded, leaving holes in the weathercock in the perfect shape of the figure nine.

At Darmstadt, a story is told of a poor and inept knight stopping to pray at a roadside statue of the Virgin Mary. He fell into a faint, and while he remained there, the Virgin took on his appearance and won the laurels at a great tournament.

A fine deed was performed by the women of Weisberg, north of Stuttgart, whose town was besieged during the civil wars of the 12th century. They begged to be allowed to depart in safety with whatever they could carry with them. This request was granted, and they walked unmol-ested through the enemy lines, each lady carrying her husband on her back.

BROCKEN SORCERY
Goethe in *Faust* describes the sorcery associated with the Brocken in folklore: 'And when we sail around the top, first skim the ground, then fill it up, that all the Brocken height may be smothered in swarms of witchery.'

HARZ

Langelsheim
GOSLAR
Seesen
Lautenthal
Bockswiese
Wildemann
Bad Grund
Clausthal-Zellerfeld
Riefenbeek
Osterode
Sankt Andreasberg
Sieber
Herzberg
Gieboldehausen
Bad Lauterberg
Bad Sachsa
Duderstadt

Oker
Vienenburg
Bad Harzburg
Ilsenburg
Hahnenklee
Torfhaus
Brocken 1142m
Altenau
Oderteich
Schierke
Hohegeiss
Zorge
Walkenried
Ellrich

Osterwieck
Heudeber
Derenburg
Wernigerode
Elbingerode
Elend
Rappbode-Stausee
Tanne
Benneckenstein
Stiege

Badersleben
Halberstadt
Harsleben
Blankenburg
Thale
Bad Suderode
Hasselfelde
Friedrichsbrunn
Güntersberge
Stolberg
Rottleberode

Gröningen
Wegeleben
Gernrode
Quedlinburg
Ballenstedt
Selke
Harzgerode
Unterharz
600m
Morungen
Wippra
Wippra

Nordhausen
Sangerhausen

SILVER LINING

The Harz region has a strong mining tradition associated with gold and silver, and for this reason the mountains were once known as the 'Treasury of the Emperors'. Clausthal-Zellerfeld was a busy mining town until the last mine closed in 1931. Its Oberharzer Bergwerksmuseum (Mining Museum of the Upper Harz; *Open* daily) has displays of tools and explanations of some unusual local mining methods. The local church was built of wood in the 17th century. Amazingly, since its interior furnishings are also all wooden, it has escaped destruction by fire. At St. Andreasberg, the Silberbergwerk (silver mine) known as Grube Samson (the Samson pit) offers daily guided tours. The mine was in operation from 1521 to 1910 and reopened in 1951 as a museum (*Open* daily).

The neat spa town of Bad Harzburg at the foot of the Harz Mountains

▶▶ Harz   108C3

Straddling the old East–West German border, the Harz Mountains, the highest land in northern and central Germany, are a rewarding area for exploration. Summits rise to over 1,000m (3,281ft) and although the 'Little Switzerland' nickname may be an exaggeration, it contrasts strikingly with the surrounding plains.

On the west side, hotels are efficiently run, restaurants and cafés plentiful, buildings well restored and neat pine forests crossed by well-signposted paths and skiing routes. In the east, everything is catching up fast, and now there is virtually little difference between the two.

The Harz region comprises two distinct areas—the **Oberharz** (Upper Harz) in the west, containing vast areas of delightful forests and valleys suitable for long refreshing walks, and the **Unterharz** (Lower Harz) in the east, which has more open land scattered with beech forests. The Brocken was situated just east of the boundary between the former German Democratic Republic and the Federal Republic. It is still possible to spot the old border posts but difficult to discern where the border once was.

Because it is relatively easy to get to the Harz from several German cities, it has become a popular tourist destination, in both summer and winter. An unpredictable climate, often damp and cold, does not deter the visitors who come for the walking, skiing and spas. They follow in the footsteps of 19th-century Romantics, who saw the Harz Mountains as the epitome of poetic landscape.

Since reunification, you can visit this area without constraint. **Wernigerode▶**, a well-preserved 14th-century town with its very beautiful Rathaus and other half-timbered houses with ornate façades, is packed every weekend, even when the weather is not good. In nearby historic **Halberstadt** the Gothic cathedral (Dom St. Stephanus) dates back to the 13th century. **Stolberg** also has some fine streets of half-timbered houses. **Quedlinburg▶** with its UNESCO World Heritage status has a superb collection of timber-framed buildings. The spa and health resort of **Bad Harzburg**, a short drive from Goslar, is a good base from which to explore the Harz region.

The highest point of the Harz, the **Brocken▶** (1,142m/3,747ft), was in the old forbidden zone close to the border, but now it can be visited again, either on foot or by Brockenbahn to the scene that features in Goethe's *Faust*. You can go up by cable-car to the Hexentanzplatz in the lovely **Bode** Valley south of Thale, or visit the giant caves at **Rübeland** with their stalagmites and stalactites, which are also worth exploring.

The Romkerhalle waterfall, in the Harz, lies close to the high rocky cliffs of the Bode gorge

123

Walk

Goslar to Hahnenklee (11km/ 7 miles)

Hahnenklee is a leading ski resort.

Start at the parking area at the Forst-haus Königsberg, on the western edge of Goslar. Follow the blue circle marked route, passing the Glockenberg on the right and then the Hohekehl on the left. Follow the Alte Harzstrasse to the Auerhahn. Scale the final 300m (984ft) to the Bocksberg (726m/2,381ft) or follow the path to Hahnenklee, from where a bus will take you back to Goslar.

Walk

Bad Harzburg to the Brocken (about 16km/10 miles)

The Brocken (1,142m/3,747ft) is the highest point of the Harz region, not quite Alpine standard, but still a demanding hike. Make sure that you are wearing good walking shoes or boots, and take a change of clothing,

a snack and a drink in a knapsack. Set out from the tourist information office at the Haus der Natur on the southern edge of Bad Harzburg (where you can pick up a hikers' map). Just up on the left (opposite a car park) head off on the upwards trail marked by a blue cross, following it to the Ecker-stausee dam. Below the dam, take the trail marked by a blue line on a white background, which will lead you to the Brocken. It is a long, upwards slog, but you can relax on the journey home by taking the mountain railway down the valley and a bus back to Bad Harzburg.

WILHELMSHÖHE PARK
From the rear of Schloss Wilhelmshöhe there's a fine view over the Wilhelmshöhe Schlosspark, as splendid a 'Romantic' landscape park as any in Europe, begun soon after 1700. It is crowned by a vast Hercules statue (copy of the Farnese Hercules in Naples) atop a towering 70m (230ft) grey granite monument. Below it are waterfalls and fountains (activated in mid-afternoon Wed, Sun and public holidays mid-May to early Oct) and some 18th-century follies—Pluto's Grotto, Devil's Bridge, baroque temples and the startling grey-pinnacled castle of Löwenburg, which may look medieval but is pure romantic fake.

SCHLOSS WILHELMSTHAL
Just north of Kassel, the pretty rococo Schloss Wilhelmsthal is worth a visit: its ornate interior, designed by Cuvilliés, contains Tischbein portraits of ladies (*Open* Tue–Sun).

Hessisches Landesmuseum in Kassel

► **Kassel**   *108B3*
Badly bombed in 1943 and rebuilt in a dull style, the principal city of north Hesse is today an industrial base for engineering and chemicals, and has little charm (its Altstadt has vanished). But its setting amid wooded hills is pleasant, and it is worth visiting for famous Schloss Wilhelmshöhe and its park as well as for its excellent museums—the city has the largest number of leading museums in Central Germany.

The *Landgraves* (counts) of Hesse developed Kassel in the 17th and 18th centuries, creating the great Wilhelmshöhe park and encouraging industry. They were avid art collectors, a tradition kept alive today with the famous avant-garde and multimedia Documenta exhibition, held every five years since 1955 (next in 2007). One of its patrons was the late Joseph Beuys, who planted 7,000 oak trees in Kassel as an action sculpture. In central Kassel is the Documenta's main venue, the opera house and the curiously shaped Ottoneum, Germany's oldest theatre (1606).

Best of the nearby museums is the Hessisches Landesmuseum (*Open* Tue–Sun) with its early astronomical and scientific instruments, prehistory and an unusual display of wallpapers dating from the 16th century. A small museum nearby (*Open* daily) is devoted to the Brothers Grimm, who lived and worked in Kassel. The Neue Galerie (*Open* Tue–Sun) has 19th- and 20th-century paintings, few of them notable, but there are some attractive canvases by Tischbein, who was born near Kassel.

In the western suburbs is the pink granite **Schloss Wilhelmshöhe**, where the Westphalian King Jerome Bonaparte, younger brother of Napoleon, held lavish court (1807–13). The castle has a Schlossmuseum and also houses the large and excellent **Galerie Alter Meister►►** (*Open* Tue–Sun), notable less for its antiquities than for its excellent paintings, especially Italian, Flemish and Dutch (note Teniers's *Peasants' Dance*).

▶▶ Lemgo   108A4

One of the best-preserved towns in northern and central Germany and formerly a member of the Hanseatic League (see page 75), Lemgo was once known as the Leipzig of Westphalia because of its printing presses (Leipzig was the publishing capital of Germany). In the 15th and 16th centuries trade with Flanders and England brought wealth to Lemgo. Today signs of this early prosperity are much in evidence, particularly as the town escaped damage in World War II. The unusual old **Rathaus▶** consists of eight adjacent buildings dating from different periods. You'll find many half-timbered houses with a rich variety of façades in Breitestrasse, the town's main street. At No. 19 there is the **Hexenbürger-meisterhaus▶** (House of the Witches' Mayor), completed in 1568, a famous example of the Weser Renaissance style with characteristic oriel windows. The house gets its name from Hermann Cothmann, who sentenced 90 women to death for witchcraft when he was mayor of Lemgo, from 1666 to 1681. It houses a Heimatmuseum (local history museum) with a macabre display of instruments of torture (*Open* Tue–Sun).

The Marienkirche is a Gothic hall church with a Renaissance organ still in excellent shape, both in sound and appearance. Take advantage of any concert being performed in the church. The 13th-century Nicolaikirche, with its two dissimilar towers, shows both Romanesque and Gothic work.

▶ Hannoversch (or Hann.) Münden   108B3

A delightful old town of narrow streets and black-and-white half-timbered houses, Hann. Münden stands, in the words of a well-known poem, 'where Werra and Fulda kiss each other', for these rivers meet here, and the Weserstein, a monumental stone, marks the spot. The bridge over the Werra behind the Schloss dates

INFORMATION
Lemgo: Kramerstrasse 1,
tel: 05261/9 88 70;
www.lemgo.de

FINE REMBRANDTS
The Staatliche Museen Kassel collection of Old Masters has an outstanding assembly of 12 paintings by Rembrandt. One masterpiece is *Jacob Blessing the Sons of Joseph*, a late work of remarkable tenderness.

DR. EISENBART
Hann. Münden's most
famous son, Johann
Andreas Eisenbart, was
an 18th-century doctor
with allegedly miraculous
powers. A costume play
commemorating his life
is performed outdoors on
Sundays from mid-May to
the end of August.

*Scrollwork, pyramids
and statues adorn Hann.
Münden's Rathaus
(right), in a town rich in
old half-timbered houses*

from no later than the 14th century. In the Marktplatz
there are buildings in Weser Renaissance style, including the very handsome gabled Rathaus. The St.
Blasiuskirche is a Gothic hall church with a late 14th-
century bronze font.

▶ **Münzenberg**   *108A2*
You can visit medieval Burg Münzenberg, about 30km
(19 miles) north of Frankfurt-am-Main, all year round
(*Open* daily). You will be able to see the grounds, the fortifications and living quarters. The latter are heavily
decorated in the Romanesque style, especially apparent in
the rounded arches of the windows and the gallery. There
is a keep at each end of the complex. The well-maintained
grounds are pleasant for a leisurely stroll, and there is a
magnificent view from the top of the east tower, which
takes in the low-lying Wetterau, a region between two
upland massifs, the Taunus and the Vogelsberg. The
entire area, with its extensive forests and quiet villages,
attracts people from Frankfurt when they wish to escape
from their noisy and polluted city.

▶ Paderborn 108A3

This ancient Westphalian town is an active commercial and industrial base. It entered history in AD799, when Charlemagne had an important meeting here with Pope Leo III, reaching an agreement that led the following year to the creation of the Holy Roman Empire. The site of the palace where the meeting took place came to light during the rebuilding of the city after World War II. Paderborn's main landmark is its **cathedral▶**, which dates mainly from the 13th century: Its Romanesque tower has become the city's emblem. The Bartolomäuskapelle (St. Bartholomew's Chapel), a separate structure north of the cathedral, was Germany's first hall church (11th century). On the exterior of the cathedral, note the Paradiesportal, a 13th-century porch on the south side. Another porch, the Brautportal, bears sculpted scenes from the life of Christ. Just below the church of the Abdinghof monastery are more than 200 warm springs, the source of the little River Pader. The German computer pioneer Heinz Nixdorf is commemorated by a computer museum at his factory (*Open* Tue–Sun).

▶ Taunus 108A1

The rolling hills of the Taunus, densely clothed in forests, are Germany's richest region of mineral springs, which have resulted in opening up several famous spas. The region's proximity to Wiesbaden, Mainz and Frankfurt-am-Main has helped in its development. There are several good roads giving easy access to the peaks—the highest is the **Grosser Feldberg**, an important telecommunications base at 880m (2,887ft). You can drive near the summit, then climb the tower on top (167 steps) for a grand view.

The little town of **Königstein im Taunus** is situated high up, well away from the main slope. Its most interesting feature is Burg Königstein, a mighty ruined castle with 16th-century bastions and 17th-century projecting defences. Built around 1200, the castle was finally destroyed in 1796.

Bad Homburg▶, in the foothills of the Taunus, used to be one of Europe's most fashionable spas, visited by Kaiser Wilhelm II, the Prince of Wales, and other prominent guests (Dostoevsky set *The Gambler* here). Today it has moved somewhat downmarket, but the big Kurpark is still attractive, with a Russian chapel and a Thai temple, gifts from royal visitors from those lands. In the middle are the medicinal springs and lawns and walks. The stately white high-towered 17th-century Schloss was the residence of the Landgraves of Hesse-Homburg and subsequently summer palace of the kings of Prussia. Concerts take place in the Schlosskirche.

North of Bad Homburg, amid pleasant forests, is the *in situ* reconstruction of **Saalburg Römerkastell Roman Camp▶** (*Open* Mar–Oct daily; Nov–Feb Tue–Sun; www.saalburgmuseum.de), originally guarding the adjacent Limes fortifications, marking the northern extent of Roman occupation (still visible, to varying degrees).

Just outside the village of Neu Anspach is the **Freilichtmuseum Hessenpark** (www.hessenpark.de) with reconstructed Hessian buildings, including a functioning bakery and workshops that produce crafts. (Museum *Open* Mar–Oct daily.)

Paderborn's massive 13th-century cathedral exemplifies, in its interior, the transition from Romanesque to Gothic

FIRST CASINO
Bad Homburg claims a number of 'firsts'—the Spiel Casino, the first casino and inspiration for Monte Carlo; the first flush toilet in Germany; and the famous homburg hat.

▶ Waldeck

Thanks largely to the spa resort of Bad Wildungen, the Waldeck region, just southwest of Kassel, has become one of the most popular tourist areas of central Germany. The countryside is attractive, with dense forests and gentle hills cut through by the course of the River Eder. The most spectacular feature of the locality is the great lake formed behind the Edertalsperre (Eder Dam).

The waters of **Bad Wildungen** are used mainly to treat kidney and gall-bladder complaints, as well as problems of hypertension and metabolism. Peaceful walks cross the Kurpark to the Georg Viktor spring. The Evangelische Stadtkirche (Protestant church), which is famed for its altarpiece of 1403 by Konrad von Soest, has a 14th-century tower that overlooks the rest of the town. Farther east, the fortified town of **Fritzlar** occupies a site above the River Eder. Dom St. Petri, founded by St. Boniface in 724, is

Burg Waldeck has a Witches' Tower, with three prison cells. It stands above the Eder Dam, which was blown up by a 4-ton RAF bomb in 1943, causing severe flooding (right and below)

essentially late Romanesque with baroque additions. Huge crypts are the main feature of the cathedral and pre-date its reconstruction in 1180. The Marktplatz is also interesting, containing an appealing range of half-timbered buildings.

In the town of **Waldeck** itself, part of the castle of the Waldeck princes (Burg Waldeck) is now a hotel, and there is a museum in the vaults that relates the history of the House of Waldeck (*Open* Easter–Oct daily). One of Germany's largest feudal castles, **Burg Waldeck▶** was built in the late 12th century and much added to in subsequent centuries. It was abandoned by the House of Waldeck in the 17th century. The view from the castle terrace is particularly impressive. Spread out below the castle you can see the Eder Dam with its artificial lake, surrounded by wooded shores.

About an hour's drive away is **Korbach**, with its many old timber houses. The town was formed after two fortified settlements, Altstadt and Neustadt (Old Town and New Town), amalgamated.

North of Korbach is **Arolsen**, its regular plan very much the creation of the Waldeck princes who lived here. Their baroque-styled Schloss, which hosts concerts and theatre evenings, is at the eastern end of the main street. Built between 1714 and 1724, the palace was inspired by Versailles; but some of the rooms were not decorated until almost a hundred years later, in 1811.

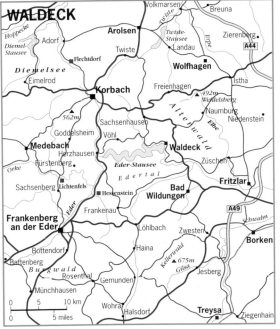

A view from Waldeck's castle towards Eder Dam

Weserbergland

▶▶ Weserbergland   108B4

The Weserbergland is a region of green hills lining both banks of the River Weser. This is one of Germany's most picturesque river valleys, and it is well worth taking four or five days to follow the river's course north. You can take either the passenger boats that glide downstream, or drive along one of two roads. Take the Wesertalstrasse (Weser Valley Road) or, on the other side of the river, the B80, part of the Deutsche Märchenstrasse (Fairy Tale Road) route the Brothers Grimm took when they gathered their famous fairy-tales. The towns and villages along the way are characterized by the Weser Renaissance style of architecture.

A good route starts at the old town of **Hann. Münden** (see pages 125–126), founded in 1170 by Henry the Lion. From there, go through the beautiful Kaufunger Wald, a forest south of Hann. Münden, part of which is a nature park. Now go north to the romantic 14th-century **Schloss Sababurg**, where the Brothers Grimm used to attend hunting parties. It is said to be the model for the castle in *The Sleeping Beauty*, and is now a hotel. The nearby zoo, with bears and penguins, is Germany's oldest (1571).

Further on, **Bad Karlshafen** is a beautiful Weser-harbour town, founded in 1699 for French Huguenot settlers, while **Höxter**▶ has a townscape of elaborately painted and carved façades, and a magnificent Renaissance alabaster pulpit in the twin-towered Kilianikirche. The Dechanei (Deanery) and Rathaus are two of the most eye-catching buildings, and busy Westerbachstrasse is perhaps the finest street. Nearby, at **Corvey**, you can see the Imperial Abbey (AD822), with a rare example of an original Carolingian west end (*Open* Apr–Oct daily). The poet Hoffmann von Fallersleben, author of the German national anthem, worked in the abbey (now converted to secular use) as court librarian. The library has an extensive collection of Romantic literature.

Continuing north, the Rathaus at **Bodenwerder**▶ was once the home of Baron Münchhausen, famous for tall stories about his unbelievable feats (he did actually live, but his true exploits were somewhat tamer than the tales). The building houses a small museum that commemorates the baron and his exploits. At **Hämelschenburg**, you can visit the splendid Weser Renaissance castle (1588–1610) (see page 119), while the nearby town of **Hameln** is famous for its story of the Pied Piper (see page 119). At the Porta Westfalica, the Weser breaks through the mountains into the north German lowlands and continues north through Bremen and Bremerhaven (see pages 54–56) before flowing into the North Sea.

▶ Wiesbaden   108A1

The capital of Hesse and an important spa, Wiesbaden lies between the Rheingau wine region and the Taunus Mountains. The Romans first used its healing waters and built a forum; one arch now survives from their time. The spa's 26 hot springs have long attracted visitors; today it is popular with the rich and famous, artists and business-people. Many thermal baths are inside hotels, but two can be visited without an overnight stay: the Kaiser Friedrich Bad in Langgasse and the Thermalbad in Leibnizstrasse (both *Open* daily).

There are countless literary and musical associations. Goethe came here, as did the Russian writers Turgenev and Dostoevsky. Robert and Clara Schumann, Brahms, and Wagner were also visitors. Wiesbaden hosts a series of annual events, ranging from horseback-riding competitions to wine tastings. In May an important festival attracts top foreign theatrical companies.

The Griechische Kapelle (Greek chapel), built in 1845 as a mausoleum on top of the Neroberg (245m/803ft), overlooks the town. Other sights include the Stadtschloss, which became a royal castle in 1866 and is used today as the seat of the Hesse state parliament. There is an old town hall and the Städtisches Museum (town museum; *Open* Tue–Sun). It contains many important paintings including works by the Expressionist artist Alexei von Jawlensky, who worked with the Russian artist Kandinsky in Munich and later settled in Wiesbaden, where he died in 1941.

TAKING THE CURE

Wiesbaden's neo-classical Kurhaus was built in 1906. It houses the Spielbank casino (note the portico with six Ionic columns).

Be warned that saunas in Germany are often unisex, so if you are not used to this, check with the facility beforehand. Make an appointment for a massage in advance if possible, as the masseurs tend to be booked up.

INVORMATION

Wiesbaden: Marktstrasse 6, tel: 0611/1 72 90; www.wiesbaden.de

131

Wiesbaden's stately Kurhaus, today housing a concert hall, casino and congress centre, has an amazing interior dating from 1907—a mix of neo-Byzantine, neo-classical, neo-baroque and art nouveau

In the days when it was the German Democratic Republic (GDR), visitors to eastern Germany were hedged about with visas and customs checks, and controlled on where they could go. But all that has changed totally since the Berlin Wall fell. The east, now fully part of Germany, can be toured freely and is mostly well equipped for tourism.

It richly rewards a visit. There is the great city of Dresden, heavily bombed but still full of culture and history, and its rival, Leipzig, is equally interesting. There are many fine historic smaller towns, such as Schwerin and Stralsund, Quedlinburg and Erfurt. Weimar, home of Goethe, Schiller and Herder, is a major world literary base, at the heart of Germany and in 1999 was Europe's 'Cultural City'. The region has many superb museums and fine old palaces and castles, notably the Wartburg at Eisenach, where Martin Luther translated the Bible. In fact, the east produced many of Germany's leading writers, painters, thinkers and musicians, such as Hauptmann, Lessing, Bach, Handel and Wagner.

In the south there is some beautiful scenery, hilly and wooded—the Thüringer Wald, the Harz mountains and the Erzgebirge. The north is flat, but not without charm, such as the great woods, lakes and rivers of the Spreewald and Mecklenburg, and the wide beaches of the Baltic.

In many ways the east now looks much like the west, yet below the surface lie differences. Many people are poorer than in the west and unemployment (more than 20 per cent in some areas) is far higher than the national average; many towns have been renovated, but some suburbs are still derelict and neglected. Nearly all the roads are now up to western standards, and new fuel stations are plentiful. There are many new modern ones, or well-renovated older ones, in the more expensive brackets. Good medium-priced hotels are less frequent but family pensions are appearing. And you can always find rooms in private homes at low prices; these can be booked through a tourist office. Restaurants of all kinds are now plentiful, but food is seldom as good as in the west. Lots of lively bars and cabarets have sprung up in the towns.

The worrying rise in racially motivated crime all over Germany, but particularly in pockets of the east, has attracted a lot of media attention in recent years, not least because many Germans themselves are very concerned about a possible revival of fascism. In fact, this is a Europe-wide phenomenon, but tourists are seldom targeted, and visitors to east Germany are not particularly more at risk here than elsewhere. Simply take the precautions you would in any town, such as avoiding travelling alone on public transport at night. Most East Germans are very hospitable, welcoming visitors with a warmth often found lacking in the more prosperous West. A whole generation grew up with Russian as their first foreign language, but English is now increasingly spoken.

Woodlands of Vogtland
(see page 166)

Eastern Germany

134

INFORMATION

Brandenburg:
Steinstrasse 66–67,
tel: 03381/20 87 69;
www.stadt-
brandenburg.de

Colditz: Johann-David-
Köhler-Haus, Ander
Kirche 1, tel: 034381/4
35 19; www.
fremdenverkehrsamt-
colditz.de

Dessau: Zerbster Strasse
2c, tel: 0340/2 04 14
42; www.dessau.de

*Bernburg, which lies
south of Magdeburg, has
an imposing Renaissance
castle surrounded by
15th-century ramparts*

▶ Bernburg
132B2

Bernburg is interesting mainly for its huge Renaissance castle (*Open* Tue–Sun), with buildings of different styles and ages grouped around a large irregular courtyard. On one side, steep wooded slopes extend down to the River Saale and the lower town. Bernburg also boasts, in both the lower and upper towns, well-kept town walls and streets of 16th- to 18th-century town houses. The outskirts, though, are rundown and industrial.

There is another Renaissance palace situated at **Köthen**, 20km (12.5 miles) to the east, where Bach worked for six years as court *Kapellmeister* before moving to his final post in Leipzig. A small museum is dedicated to him here (*Open* Tue–Sun). There are also some particularly fine aristocratic houses dotted around central Bernburg.

In the other direction, 19km (12 miles) west of Bernburg, **Aschersleben** clusters below the 80m (262ft) tower of St. Stephen's, a fine 15th-century Gothic hall church. There are several attractive burghers' houses in the heart of the ancient town.

▶▶ Brandenburg
132B3

Brandenburg is surrounded by numerous lakes along and around the River Havel, an area popular for excursions. Known as Havelland, it is famous for its birdlife—reed warblers, marsh harriers, bitterns, storks, herons and cranes can be observed in abundance.

Both town and *Land* take their name from the castle known as the Brandenburg, first mentioned in AD948. It took 200 years before this seemingly impregnable fortress was finally overcome by a warrior prince with the delightful name of Albrecht the Bear. Both old and new towns remained separate members of the Hanseatic League until 1518, and only joined together in 1715.

Brandenburg's cathedral took seven centuries to complete. It has a 13th-century Saxon crucifix, a 14th-century Bohemian altar and countless valuable manuscripts. The town hall (1480) has a 5m (16ft) figure of Roland, a symbol of civic rights, dating from 1474.

▶ Colditz
132B1

The old town of Colditz, on the River Mulde in central Saxony, has a picturesque central area with an attractive

town hall, marketplace and 13th-century parish church. The old castle on a hill overlooking the town achieved notoriety during World War II as a formidable prisoner-of-war camp, from where a number of British officers made escapes. After the war the castle was used as a hospital but has now been transformed into a museum and a restaurant. Mementoes of escapees are kept in the town museum, including some false German uniforms, photographic material and a printing press (*Open* daily).

►► Dessau   *132B2*

Dessau is world-famous among architects and designers as the home of the Bauhaus movement (see panel). The building from which it gets its name was built by Walter Gropius in 1925–26 and still stands—restored in 1977 to something like its former glory—in a suburban avenue 2km (1.2 miles) northwest of central Dessau (*Open* daily). There are also examples of Bauhaus architecture on the outskirts, including a 300-dwelling housing project at Dessau-Törten, where No. 38 Mittering has been fully restored to the original design. The house shared by Paul

Klee and Wassily Kandinsky has also been restored and is used for exhibitions, while Lyonel Feininger's house has become a memorial centre for composer Kurt Weill, born in Dessau in 1900 (both *Open* Tue–Sun).

Much of central Dessau, also famous as the site of the Junkers aircraft factory, was destroyed in the war and has been rebuilt in modern style. Fortunately, the city has three estates that provide relief from the general drabness of its post-Bauhaus architecture. Within the city limits is the neo-classical Schloss Georgium (1790), set in a fine park, and just outside Dessau are two fascinating estates. The nearest, Schloss Mosigkau, 9km (5.5 miles) southwest, was commissioned by Prince Leopold of Anhalt-Dessau for one of his daughters, Anna Wilhelmine. She lived there as a recluse and left the splendid property to an order of nuns. The palace has one of Germany's few baroque picture galleries and an impressive collection of furniture (*Open* Mar–Nov Tue–Sun). East of Dessau is **Wörlitzer Park►**, beautifully landscaped gardens based on the 18th-century English style, with lakes, canals and decorative pavilions.

The exterior of the Martin Gropius Meisterhaus, Dessau (above)
Colditz castle (top right)

THE BAUHAUS
The Bauhaus movement was founded by Walter Gropius in Weimar in 1919. His school of art became an experimental laboratory for architects, engineers, painters, sculptors and designers. The aim was to bring together aesthetics with the needs of an industrial civilization. Thus the courses at the Bauhaus school were directed at the creation of forms suitable for mass production.

Semper Opera House, Dresden

INFORMATION
Dresden: tel: 0351/
49 19 20;
www.dresden-tourist.de

1945 AIR RAID
On 13–14 February, 1945, in the most intensive air raid of the war in Europe, over 2,000 Allied bombers attacked Dresden in three giant waves. The city was packed with refugees from the advancing Red Army, and thousands of virtually unprotected families were among the 35,000 people who died in the raids and the resulting fire-storm, compared by some historians with the horrors of Hiroshima and Nagasaki. Sixty per cent of Dresden was destroyed. The aim was to break morale. But many critics, even among the Allies, have since argued that so cruel a raid, so near the war's end, on a town of little strategic value, was simply not justified. Among the older generation of Dresden, memories are still painful and some bitterness is still evident.

▶▶▶ **Dresden**   *132C1*

Dresden used to be one of the loveliest cities of central Europe—'Florence on the Elbe', it was called. It never quite recovered from the great air raid of 1945 (see panel) and many of its fine baroque buildings still wear a stunned, blackened look (exacerbated by decades of neglect and industrial pollution). In the 1950s and '60s, much of the city was rebuilt in a blocky, Stalinist style, impressive in its scale and self-confidence, but not much fun to explore. Even today, some of the outlying areas are still grimy and derelict.

For all this, Dresden is not to be missed. Enough of its enormous cultural heritage remains, providing plenty of worthwhile sights and famous works of art. Most of them date back to the city's heyday as capital of Saxony, especially to the reign of the aptly named Augustus the Strong in the late 17th and early 18th centuries. Even at the height of the cold war, considerable efforts were made by the East German authorities to restore the most important of those monuments that were not smashed to pieces. Since unification, this process has accelerated. Encouraged by Dresden's revived status as capital of the state of Saxony, western investors have poured money into building projects, which have begun to transform the central area and give the city a renewed claim to its old reputation for culture, commerce and gracious living. Germany's second-largest bank, the Dresdner, is again proudly present in the city where it was born in 1872.

What to see The **Brühlsche Terrasse**, a gracious, elevated terrace on the south bank of the Elbe, and once known as 'Europe's balcony', lies at the heart of the historic part of Dresden, surrounded by gaunt, dignified buildings in a range of styles. Immediatley behind it, the 18th-century Stadtschloss has undergone major renovation work and the sumptuous collection of the Wettin electors is returning to its historic home in the Dresden Royal Palace, having been on exhibit in the Albertinum for 30 years. The Grünes Gewölbe (Green Vault) reopened in 2004, and in September 2006 the Historisches Grünes Gewölbe (Historical Green Vault)–a dazzling treasury meseum and the epitome of baroque decoration—reopened on the ground floor of the west wing, to coincide with the 800th anniversary of the city of Dresden. Itcontains the royal collection of silver, gold and jewellery (including a unique collection of 18th-century ceremonial jewellery), as well as the star of the show, *The Court of Delhi on the Birthday of the Great Mogul*, a set of 132 gold, enamel and bejewelled painted figures.

By the Bruühlsche Terrace stands one of Dresden's most important galleries, the Albertinum▶▶▶, a 16th-century building that once served as an arsenal and which currently contains one of the world's most impressive art collections (*Closed* from January 2006 for refurbishment).

The nearby **Frauenkirche** (Church of Our Lady)▶ is Germany's largest baroque and Protestant church. Ever

HELLERAU GARDEN CITY
A short tram ride into the Dresdner Heide, north of the city, brings you to Hellerau, site of Europe's first 'garden city', built along lines pioneered by Britain's Ebenezer Howard. The beautiful little settlement grew from a community of artisans, housed in idyllic surroundings, into a cultural citadel. World War I interrupted Hellerau's development and the Third Reich killed it completely. Restoration is nearly finished, but even idealists admit Hellerau will never recapture its earlier glory.

137

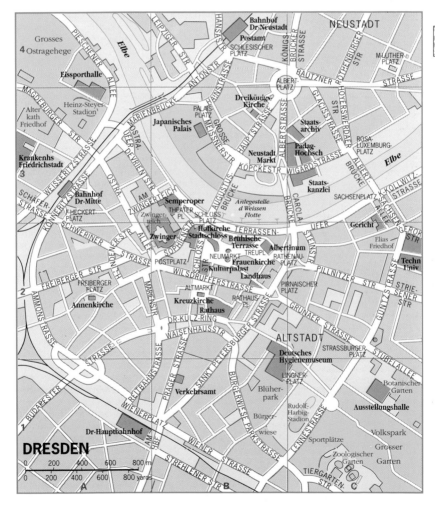

DRESDEN

Meissen
Döbritz
Elbe
Coswig
Radebeul
Schloss Moritzburg
Dresdener Heide
Radeberg
Arnsdorf
Bischofswerda
Neukirch
Lausitzer Bergland
A4
Nossen
Wilsdruff
Siebenlehn
Mohorn
Tharandt
Kurort Hartha
Klingenberg
Freiberger Mulde
DRESDEN
Schloss Pillnitz
Freital
Dohna
Heidenau
Sächsisch
305m Basthei
Hohnstein
Stolpen
Neustadt
CZ
Sebnitz
Kreischa
Pirna
Stadt Wehlen
416m Lilienstein
Schweiz
Bad Schandau
Hinterhermsdorf
FREIBERG
Dippoldiswalde
Reinhardtsgrimma
Berggiesshübel
Liebstadt
Glashütte
Bad Gottleuba
393m
Königstein
Krippen
Elbsandsteingebirge
522m
Schmilka
Rosenthal
Branderbisdorf
0   10 km
0   5 miles

Detail from the Zwinger

PROUD SAXONY
One of Germany's main industrial regions, Saxony has an intense local patriotism, like Bavaria. It even retained its own king until 1918, within a united Germany. The centralized GDR then removed its separate identity. Today Saxony is again an autonomous *Land*, under its prime minister from the west, Georg Milbradt. There is strong rivalry between Dresden, the historic capital, and the other big Saxon city, Leipzig.

since 1944 it was kept as a ruin, in memory of the horrors of the bombing of World War II, but now at last it has been expensively rebuilt in its old style, to be completed by 2006. The **Hofkirche** (royal cathedral), which was built between 1739 and 1755 in Italian baroque style contains a fine mid-18th-century organ by Silbermann.

Facing the cathedral across the square stands the celebrated **Semper Opera House**▶▶ (guided tours available), built by Gottfried Semper in 1838–41 and subject to a huge restoration schedule by the German Democratic Republic. It was eventually reopened in 1985, to reveal a very high standard of comfort and facilities as well as painstaking attention to period detail.

A few steps away is Dresden's most famous sight, the **Zwinger**▶▶▶ (keep), a complex of baroque-style pavilions grouped around a graceful, relaxed courtyard. It gets its name from the ancient fortifications that occupied the site: The buildings themselves date from 1711 to 1728 but have been added to and altered. They contain a treasure house of museums (*Open* daily), including a world-famous porcelain collection and a science museum. Now that restoration work has been completed, the Gemälde-galerie Alter Meister (Gallery of Old Masters) has returned to the Semperbau at the Zwinger. The collection includes Raphael's *Sistine Madonna*, Giorgione's *Sleeping Venus*, and works by Canaletto (many of them scenes painted on his visits to Dresden), Rembrandt, Vermeer and Titian.

Behind the Zwinger you will find the **Langer Gang** (long passage), a 16th-century arcade with Italian-style white pillars. Outside it bears a huge 19th-century porcelain frieze depicting Saxon princes. Nearby are two more museums, of zoology (*Open* Wed–Mon) and transport (*Open* daily).

Farther away from the river, the scene becomes bleaker, marked by big blocks and wide open spaces. One of these, the **Altmarkt** (old market), was the bustling heart of a great city before it was razed in 1945; it has now recovered some of its bustle, but the charm will be harder to restore. In its southeast corner stands the **Kreuzkirche** (Church of the Holy Cross), which dates back to 1764–92 and is the oldest church within the boundary of the former city walls. It is home to Dresden's famous choir, the Kreuzchor, which performs here most Saturday afternoons. To the south of the Altmarkt, you can continue along modern, pedestrianized **Prager Strasse**, on which

The River Elbe at Dresden, heavily polluted in GDR days, has now been cleaned up

stand the city's larger restaurants and hotels. There's a little more of the feel of pre-war Dresden across the Elbe in **Dresden-Neustadt**, which has many imposing 19th-century buildings and is based around a car-free main boulevard, the Hauptstrasse.

Excursions The best bet is to take a paddle steamer (the **Weisse Flotte** boats leave from the landing platforms by Terrassenufer) along the Elbe to some of the worthwhile destinations just outside Dresden. One option is the old town of **Meissen** (see page 152).

A very pleasant alternative is to go upstream to **Schloss Pillnitz►** (10km/6 miles southeast), a charmingly relaxed grouping of summer palaces built in Chinese style and dating from 1723; it's set in a beautiful wooded section of the Elbe Valley and is surrounded by a small park. Farther upstream is **Pirna** (20km/12.5 miles from Dresden), an old market town that straddles the river. Its market square has fine medieval houses, and the Marienkirche (St. Mary's Church) is one of the finest late Gothic hall churches in Saxony. **Pirna** is known as the gateway to Saxon Switzerland (Sächsische Schweiz; see page 155).

The **Dresdener Heide** (Dresden Heath) starts on the northeastern edge of town and is easily reached by public transportation. It's a relaxed area of open woodland, crossed with well-marked paths.

►► Eisenach   132A1

Despite its small size, this city nestling in wooded hills at the northwest end of the Thüringer Wald has an enormous importance in the history of German civilization. This is because of its position at the foot of the

INFORMATION
Eisenach: Markt 9,
tel: 03691/7 92 30;
www.eisenach-tourist.de

THE GROSSER GARTEN
The Grosser Garten (or Volkspark), a large 17th-century park about 1.6km (1 mile) southeast of central Dresden, includes a baroque pleasure palace and the city's zoo. The Parkeisenbahn, an enormous model railway with five stations and 6km (4 miles) of track, runs through the park. The Deutsches Hygiene Museum, built for the 2nd International Hygiene Exhibition (held in Dresden in 1930), is best known for its glass models of a woman, a cow, and a horse (*Open* Tue–Sun).

PROPERTY CLAIMS
Eisenach's big department store, Schwager, is back in the hands of its Schwager family owners. It was expropriated by the GDR in 1950, and the family fled west: Now they have reclaimed it, and business is booming in its modern premises. But of the east's million or so property claims, few have been solved so easily: some are by Jewish former owners, dating from Nazi times. This huge and complex property problem has deterred investors and hampered renovation. If, in a street of neatly restored houses, one remains decrepit, it may be that the lawyers can't decide who owns it.

Wartburg▶▶, a spectacular hilltop castle (*Open* daily) dating back to the 11th century. It became an early focus for music and poetry, hosting the traditional *Sängerkrieg*, a competition for singer-poets, in the early 13th century, subsequently immortalized by Richard Wagner in his opera *Tannhäuser*. Two centuries later the fortress achieved a place in world history when it sheltered Martin Luther, who had been outlawed by the Roman Catholic Church for his 'heretical' views. During the year Luther spent here (1521–22) he worked on his German translation of the Bible.

It is a half-hour uphill slog to the castle, but the footpath winds pleasantly through thick woods of ash, beech and elder. You can also drive to a parking area just below the castle, from where youngsters can hire a donkey for the last few hundred metres to the castle courtyard. Within the castle walls you will find a very romantic hotel, with snug bedrooms, deep-cushioned comforts, open fireplaces and a baronial dining room. A tour of the castle takes in Luther's study, the castle's art collection and various halls, including the enormous Festsaal (banqueting hall) which was decorated with murals by Moritz von Schwind in the 19th century.

Back down in the town, a major point of interest is the J. S. Bach house (*Open* daily), commemorating the birthplace of Eisenach's most famous son. As well as a collection of music and instruments, and a very pretty garden, the museum offers short recitals on some of the keyboard instruments. Nearby is the 15th-century house, prettily restored, where Luther stayed as a student: it too is now a museum (*Open* daily), with details of his translation of the Bible. The composer Richard Wagner often visited Eisenach while staying with the Liszts in nearby Weimar. He is commemorated with the most comprehensive exhibition on his life and work outside Bayreuth, the Reuter-Wagner-Museum (*Open* Tue–Sun). Eisenach also has a small automobile museum (*Open* Tue–Sun) that contains examples of Wartburg cars, produced at Eisenach in GDR days in a huge factory with 8,000 workers. It is now run by Opel.

One of Eisenach's attractions is its big squares surrounded by graceful houses: In the middle of the largest (the Markt) stands St. George's Church, which has an unusual galleried interior decorated with murals.

Old Wartburg models in Eisenach's car museum: GDR citizens sometimes had to wait 10 years to buy one

An old street of medieval Erfurt, neatly restored under the new regime

CITY OF FLOWERS AND TOWERS

Erfurt is known as the 'city of flowers and towers' because of its horticulture and its profusion of churches. The city is Europe's largest producer of seeds, and one of its most famous sons, the botanist Christian Reichart, pioneered seed research. Every summer the city hosts a horticulture, garden and landscaping exhibition.

▶▶ Erfurt   132A1

The capital and largest town of Thuringia, Erfurt has distinct charm despite some less attractive development. But at its core lies an extensive and, for the most part, well-preserved medieval town, crowned by its imposing cathedral and the nearby Gothic church of St. Severin. The church's pointed spires loom over the large, irregularly shaped Domplatz (cathedral square), which is used for funfairs and markets of all sorts.

The **cathedral▶▶**, reached up a flight of 70 steps from the square, dates back to the mid-12th century and was built in the form of a Romanesque basilica, though it gained a Gothic choir in the mid-14th century. It contains some fine works of art, including a Romanesque altar, carved wooden stalls and 14th- to 15th-century stained glass. The largest bell in eastern Germany, the 'Gloriosa', hangs in the middle tower. The 14th-century St. Severin's boasts some of Germany's finest early Gothic architecture and an extraordinary 15th-century font.

Down in the town, there's a wealth of fine buildings and streets to see. Some of the ancient houses are still in poor shape, but many others have now been renovated, especially around the two pedestrianized main squares, the Anger and the Fischmarkt. Close by is the fascinating **Krämerbrücke▶** (Merchants' bridge), spanning the wide and shallow River Gera. Lined with tall, narrow half-timbered houses, it is the only bridge of its kind north of the Alps. Nowadays, humbler trades in the narrow cobbled

INFORMATION

Erfurt: Benediktplatz 1, tel: 0361/6 64 00; www.erfurt.de

141

Many antiques shops fill the St. Andreas quarter of old Erfurt

LIGNITE POLLUTION
Lignite used to provide 83 per cent of the GDR's electricity, and much of the open-cast mining of this 'brown coal' was done in the Lausitz region around Görlitz, where millions of tons of dust were scattered and the giant craters resembled a bomb site. Many of the mines have now been closed, and the blighted landscape is being replanted with grass and trees.

street that passes between the houses have given way to antiques shops. A few streets away you can see the restored 13th-century Augustiner church and monastery which once included Martin Luther among its novices (*Open* daily; guided tours only to the monastery).

A couple of kilometres southwest of central Erfurt, the 15th-century (but much altered) Cyriaksburg castle stands in leafy grounds, part of which are given over to a large permanent museum and exhibition devoted to all forms of gardening and horticulture, a long-established Thuringian local industry (*Open* daily).

▶ Erzgebirge   132C1

The Erzgebirge is a range of mountains stretching for 140km (87 miles) along the Czech frontier from the Vogtland (see page 166) to Saxon Switzerland (see pages 155–156). It includes the highest point in eastern Germany, the Fichtelberg (1,214m/3,983ft). The western part of the range is characterized by steep-sided valleys and thick forests, dotted with villages and small industrial towns; the eastern part, to the east of the River Flöha, consists mainly of high plateaus and is more open in appearance.

The whole area gets its name (*Erz* means ore) from the mineral ores that have been mined here since the 12th century, starting with silver and tin. The area was one of the main holiday resorts of the old GDR, and visitors from farther afield are now coming here for the good skiing, hiking and walking.

As the mines became exhausted, people started a variety of crafts, and the area is well known for its toy-making industry. Look for the crafted and painted wooden Easter eggs; you will find them only in the Erzgebirge. Bright wooden nutcrackers are another special craft.

Annaberg-Buchholz is the largest town in the area and has a spectacular hall church, the biggest in Saxony, dating from 1499 to 1525, with a fine main portal and several beautiful altars. The town of **Frohnau** (2km/1.2 miles west) has an unusual industrial museum, Frohnauer Hammer (*Open* daily), originally (1436) a corn mill, but which was then converted to a silver and iron forge in 1621. To the south, **Ober-Wiesenthal** is a winter-sports resort at the foot of the Fichtelberg; the 1,214m (3,983ft) summit can be reached by cable car for a fine view.

In the eastern part of the Erzgebirge, **Seiffen**▶ has been the heart of the Saxon toy industry since the 18th century. This remains active today, turning out hand-carved Christmas decorations, wooden nutcracker figures in local costume, and much else. You can watch the craftsmen at work, and see details of the industry and exhibits detailing its significance to social history, in the large Spielzeugmuseum (Toy Museum; *Open* daily) which shows many of the traditional items made in the area. The Freilichtmuseum, on the Deutscheinsiedel road out of town, shows furniture and exhibits on the folk history of the region (*Open* daily).

SCHWARZBIER
Small East German breweries experienced a welcome renaissance following reunification, and some are making inroads into areas previously dominated by the big West German companies. An East German speciality is *Schwarzbier*, literally 'black beer', in reality a smooth, dark, stout-like brew. It is brewed according to the centuries-old German 'purity laws', with additional roasting of the barley malt giving the beer its rich colour. Try Eisenach's *Schwarzer Drachen* (Black Dragon) or the *Köstritzer Schwarzbier*—both are quite delicious.

143

▶▶ Görlitz 132C2

Görlitz is a large and extremely ancient city that once spread across both banks of the River Neisse but, following World War II, found itself straddling the German-Polish border.

The German part of town contains most of the old heart, which has many crooked, narrow streets rich in medieval buildings, both secular and religious. The most interesting examples are grouped around the part-arcaded Untermarkt (lower market square), which has a fine collection of Renaissance and baroque town houses. Keep a lookout particularly for the house at No. 22, which has an unusual portal.

In nearby Neissestrasse, look out for house No. 29 (the 'Biblische-Haus') which dates from 1570 and bears bas-relief scenes from the Old and New Testaments. The Rathaus (town hall) has an unusual mixture of styles, dating mostly from the 14th and 16th centuries.

Görlitz on the Polish border, known for its mechanical industry, has a fortified 14th-century gateway close to its upper marketplace

INFORMATION
Görlitz: Brüderstrasse 1, tel: 03581/4 75 70; www.goerlitz.de

The town hall clock in Görlitz

INFORMATION
Gotha: Hauptmarkt 2,
tel: 03621/22 21 38;
www.gotha.de

▶ **Gotha**   *132A1*

Gotha, which traces its beginnings back to the year AD775, acquired European-wide significance when it became the residence of the princely house of Sachsen-Gotha-Altenburg. Later it shared with Coburg the title of 'residence city' of the historic house of Sachsen-Coburg und Gotha, often described as the 'stud farm' of the royal houses of Europe. Germany's version of the *Debrett* guide to the nobility, the *Almanach de Gotha*, was first published here. The middle of Gotha is dominated by the 360-room 17th-century baroque **Schloss Friedenstein▶**, which stands on a hill above the main square. Ranged around a large, square courtyard, the massive white-painted, arcaded buildings incorporate a museum of local history and cartography (*Open* Tue–Sun), a theatre and a library. Another highlight is the long, narrow Hauptmarkt (market square), which stretches down the hill. At the top of the square is a group of restored Renaissance buildings, and the neo-Renaissance red-and-white town hall.

Excursion
Friedrichroda is a small, relaxed resort on the edge of the Thuringian Forest: A 16km (10-mile) ride on the narrow-gauge Waldbahn (tram route 4) takes you through the fields and backyards of this pretty and unspoiled area.

▶ Greifswald and Usedom   *132B4*

Greifswald lies on the eastern side of Mecklenburg-Vorpommern, not far from the Greifswalder Bodden, a shallow, virtually tideless bay of the Baltic. In the 13th century monks founded this settlement near their coastal monastery of Eldena. In 1278 the town became part of the Hanseatic League (see page 75). In 1648, after the Thirty Years' War, Greifswald was granted to Sweden, only to return to Germany in 1815 under Prussian rule.

Greifswald has fine buildings, notably an originally Gothic town hall (rebuilt in the 18th century after a fire), the 13th-century Marienkirche, half-timbered St. 'Spiritus Hospital, and town houses with elegant gabled façades. The painter Caspar David Friedrich was born in Greifswald in 1774 and spent much of his life here. His evocative paintings of coastal seascapes and the ruins of Eldena Monastery provide a record of the landscape as it was early in the last century. Some of his best work can be seen in the Charlottenburg Palace in Berlin.

Usedom Not far from Greifswald, across the straits of the Peene Strom, lies Usedom, a strangely shaped island that straddles the Polish–German border. Wollin, the eastern part of the island, is Polish territory. There are excellent beaches, with small seaside resorts at Bansin, Heringsdorf, Ahlbeck and Zinnowitz (the last overlooked by a castle) and inland lakes such as the Gothensee and the Schmollensee.

Eighty-five per cent of the surface area of Usedom, mostly meadowland, woods, bays and dunes, is protected landscape, much of it nature reserve. The area is peaceful and tranquil. In clear weather you can see the southeast tip of Rügen island, while the border crossing at Ahlbeck brings nearby Poland's Swinemünde within easy access.

PEENEMÜNDE
Peenemünde, on the northern extremity of Usedom, was the unlikely place where, during World War II, the physicist Wernher von Braun and other German scientists developed and tested the notorious V1 and V2 rockets. This high technology was put to better use in post-war times when von Braun joined the US space research team and helped to develop rockets for the US space programme and the successful first flight to the moon.

145

Greifswald is a handsome old university town on a flat plain close to the Baltic

Halle's Rathaus, itself no beauty, presides over an old town of fine buildings with a great musical and intellectual tradition

INFORMATION
Halle: Leipzigerstrasse 105–6, tel: 0345/122 99 84; www.halle.de

▶ **Halle**   *132B2*

Now a major industrial and cultural base, Halle is one of eastern Germany's oldest cities and was the birthplace of the composer Handel (see opposite). A more recent son of Halle is the former German Foreign Minister, Hans Dietrich Genscher, who did much in 1990 to persuade the Russians to accept German unification. Halle's wealth came originally from the mining of salt. The city's Technisches Halloren-und Saline Museum brings much of that past to life (*Open* Sun–Tue). Halle's most striking landmark is the four-towered, 16th-century church of Unser Lieben Frauen in the market square.

The nearby Roter Turm (Red Tower) became a symbol to the people of Halle of their struggle against feudal domination. The Moritzburg, the city's art gallery (*Open* Tue–Sun), is a late 15th-century Gothic fortress, built as a stronghold for the powerful archbishops of Magdeburg. In the Alter Markt don't miss the fountain of a boy with a donkey, the town's historic symbol.

▶ **Heiligenstadt**   *132A2*

A small, quiet resort on the River Leine, Heiligenstadt boasts a long, partly pedestrianized main street dominated by the parish church of St. Martin. The middle of town was partly destroyed by fire in 1759, but several half-timbered and Renaissance houses survive from earlier times, among them the 15th-century Mainzer house and the baroque Rathaus.

Set at the heart of the hilly and part-forested Eichsfeld region, Heiligenstadt has long been popular as a place for rest and recuperation.

Georg Friedrich Handel was born in 1685 (the same year as J. S. Bach) in the city of Halle, where his statue now surveys the market square. His complete mastery of composition is evident from the fact that he wrote 46 operas, over 30 oratorios and a large number of cantatas, concerti grossi, pieces of sacred music and other instrumental and vocal works.

Against the wishes of his father, a noted barber-surgeon, Handel became organist at Halle Cathedral at the age of 17, while studying law. In 1706 he left for four years in Italy, where he became known as a virtuoso harpsichordist and violinist, earning himself the title of *il caro Sassone* ('the dear Saxon'). He also wrote his first operas—including *Almira* – in the Italian style.

On his return from Italy in 1710, Handel was appointed Kapellmeister (orchestra and choir conductor) at the court of the Elector of Hannover. Handel followed his master when the elector succeeded Queen Anne to the English throne as George I in 1714.

The *Water Music* may even have been written to appease his patron. If this was the composer's aim, he was certainly successful, since, on his succession to the monarchy, George I doubled Handel's pension.

In London Handel busied himself in the composition of more operas, but with mixed fortunes. This patchy operatic success caused him to experiment with a new musical form, the oratorio. In this new area of composition success was immediate and undoubted: Handel conducted no fewer than 15 separate oratorio concerts in 1735 alone.

In 1737 Handel suffered a stroke; nevertheless, the next five years saw him complete many of his finest works, including *Saul* (1739), *Israel in Egypt* (1739) and *Messiah* (1742). However, his health continued to deteriorate and in 1759 he died.

Georg Friedrich Handel is buried in Poet's Corner in London's Westminster Abbey.

147

The Halle house (above) where Handel was born, now a museum (Open daily)

Georg Friedrich Handel, master of the oratorio (right)

Old and new architecture in Jena

MUSEUMS AND MEMORIALS
There's a lot to see in Leipzig. The former Imperial Court of Justice, where Hitler set the phoney Reichstag fire trial, is being returned to judicial use after serving as an art gallery. The Museum der Bildenden Künste, Katharinen-strasse 10 (*Closed* Mon), was built as a new home for the city's collection, noted for its Dutch and German paintings (Cranach, Friedrich). You can see the farmhouse, now a museum, where Schiller wrote his *Ode to Joy* (*Open* Tue–Sun). Or inspect the huge, hideous Battle of Nations Monument, completed in 1913 to mark the 1813 battle at Leipzig where the Prussians and allies defeated Napoleon, and 100,000 perished.

► **Jena** 132B1

The vast modern housing complex of Lobeda, which marches along the valley connecting the middle of Jena with the highway, makes a sad introduction to this ancient university town, famous also for its optical industry started by Carl Zeiss in the mid-19th century. Zeiss's name and work are commemorated in the planetarium (the world's oldest working one), which is in the botanic garden just north of central Jura. There is also an optical museum (*Open* Tue–Sun).

Jena has illustrious associations with some of the greatest figures in German culture: Hegel and Schiller taught at the university, and Goethe was a frequent visitor.

One end of the enormous market square, lined by the 14th-century town hall and Gothic St. Michael's Church, has some charm, but with most of the rest of the middle rebuilt in monumental modern style, topped by a 26-floor cylindrical university building, the city depends heavily on its past glories.

►►► **Leipzig** 132B2

Founded by Slavic settlers in the 7th and 8th centuries, Leipzig had become an important German stronghold by the 10th century and a flourishing base where the great east–west and north–south trade routes intersected on the Thüringian-Saxon plain. Its name derives from Urbs Lizi, or 'the town of the lime trees'.

Today Leipzig is Saxony's largest city, a major industrial, shopping, cultural and administrative base with 550,000 inhabitants, renowned for its long associations with trade, science, humanism, music and publishing, as well as for its twice-yearly trade fair.

Leipzig's university was founded in 1409. Martin Luther preached here many times and disputed passionately with his opponents. Books were printed for the first time in Leipzig in 1481, laying the foundations for the city's long publishing tradition. Music was first printed in Leipzig in 1754. Bach worked as cantor and director of music at the **Thomaskirche►** for the last 27 years of his life until his death in the city in 1750. A bronze plaque in the church marks his grave. Richard Wagner was born in the city in 1813, but later had to flee for his life for supporting radical

Instant art: a street artist produces a portrait to order in Leipzig, where there are long-established links with many branches of the arts

Looking towards Leipzig's Marktplatz and Altes Rathaus

THE NIKOLAIKIRCHE
Protest against the 40-year-long Communist dictatorship in East Germany came to a head in the late 1980s in Leipzig in regular prayers for peace at the Nikolaikirche, led by Neues Forum, an alliance of Christian and liberal-democratic protesters. Candles were lit and carried by thousands of people of the city as a potent symbol of peaceful protest, which helped to bring about the downfall of the hated Honecker regime. Prominent among dissidents was the cele-brated Leipzig conductor Kurt Masur. The Nikolaikirche, built between the 13th and 16th centuries, has an inspiring 18th-century interior that symbolizes hope—elegant white columns soaring upwards and bursting into delicate green palm fronds at their apex, crowned by a ceiling in shades of pink and green, complemented by stately white pews.

views. The world-famous Leipzig Gewandhaus orchestra, for many years headed by conductor Kurt Masur, is based at the Neues Gewandhaus concert hall.

Much of central Leipzig is now traffic-free, with fine old squares, gardens, courtyards and shopping arcades opening out of the main pedestrianized areas. Despite some brutal rebuilding of office blocks, apartments and the university in modern concrete, many superb buildings remain. The richly decorated railway station is one of the most impressive in Germany.

The **Old Town Hall▶** houses the Alte Börse, the old Stock Exchange, built between 1678 and 1687 and is one of the city's loveliest baroque buildings. You can see many other fine baroque façades in the heart of the city, for example in the Katherinenstrasse.

INFORMATION
Jena: Johannisstrasse 23, tel: 03641/80 80 50; www.jena.de

Leipzig: Richard-Wagner-Strasse 1, tel: 0341/7 10 42 65; www.leipzig.de

GOETHE IN LEIPZIG
Goethe studied law in Leipzig as a young man, and set a scene of *Faust* in Auerbach's Cellar, still to be found in the Mädlerpassage, where Mephistopheles is made to ride out on a barrel of wine.

Modern sculptures adorn Leipzig's trendy new shopping area

The medieval monastery of Our Lady in Magdeburg, a harmonious Romanesque ensemble

INFORMATION
Magdeburg: Ernst-Reuter-Alle 12, tel: 0391/1 94 33; www.magdeburg-tourist.de

THE MAGDEBURG HEMISPHERES
A 17th-century experiment by Magdeburg's scientific mayor, the physicist Otto von Guericke (1602–86), who wanted to prove the great strength of atmospheric pressure (the force exerted by the air around us), has ensured that Magdeburg's fame has spread worldwide. Von Guericke put together two metal hemispheres and removed the air from inside them, to form a vacuum. When 16 horses (eight tied to each hemisphere) failed to pull them apart, he conclusively proved his thesis.

► Magdeburg   *132B2*

As early as AD968, this archbishop's seat was the heart of the church's mission to Christianize the Slavic population. The city's original constitution of the same date became known as the Magdeburg Laws, and was used as a model for the establishment of numerous other towns in eastern Germany.

Magdeburg's 13th-century **cathedral**►► (*Open* daily) is the oldest great Gothic religious building in Germany, and its scale is a testimony to the power and influence of the city in the Middle Ages. Superb statues of the Wise and Foolish Virgins stand by the Paradise Doorway on the north side. Inside are remarkable seated statues (13th century) of Otto I and his wife Edith.

Though around 90 per cent of Magdeburg, including part of the cathedral itself, was destroyed by Allied bombing in World War II, its central areas have been rebuilt and elegantly laid out with boulevards and shops, and many of the historic buildings have been carefully reconstructed or restored.

The Monastery of Our Lady, north of the Domplatz, now houses a collection of medieval wood sculptures and also the national collection of contemporary small-scale sculptures (*Open* Tue–Sun). A wine cellar in the Buttergasse dates from 1200 and was discovered only by chance during rebuilding operations.

In the old market square, which used to be the heart of the old city, there is a baroque town hall and the Eulenspiegel Fountain, a modern tribute to the medieval prankster Till Eulenspiegel. The baroque composer Georg Philipp Telemann (1681–1767) was born in Magdeburg, and the concert hall bears his name.

Germany's biennial international garden and horticultural show was held in Magdeburg in 1999, and the Elbauenpark, created for the event, has being integrated into the urban landscape. The show's focal point, an extraordinary leaning tower, built at a greater angle than Pisa's famous campanile, has been kept as an unusual tourist attraction (*Open* park: daily in the summer; tower: Tue–Sun).

►► Mecklenburgische Seenplatte and Müritz National Park   *132B4*

The Mecklenburgische Seenplatte (Mecklenburg Lake District) consists of over a thousand lakes. These are a residue from the last Ice Age, when retreating glaciers left great moraines—banks of sand and pebblelike detritus. The moving ice also carved out channels and basins through which the escaping water formed rivulets and waterfalls. Storms carried loose sand into hilly dunes, which, as the climate warmed, became carpeted with woodland to create an undulating landscape patterned with small lakes.

The 322sq-km (124sq-mile) Müritz National Park was founded in October 1990 from Germany's largest nature reserve. It extends from Waren to beyond Neustrelitz and from the Müritzsee's eastern shore to the source of the Havel. Sixty-five per cent of the area is forest, 25 per cent moorland and water, 6 per cent meadow and grazing land and around 4 per cent is under cultivation. About 200 years ago the River Elbe was widened and deepened, causing the water level of the Müritzsee to sink by 2m (6.5ft), so that the low-lying eastern banks of the lake dried out, with consequent changes to the natural flora.

The Müritzsee, or Morcze (small sea) as it was known by the Slavs, is one of more than 100 lakes in the national park. It is 6m (20ft) deep and 27km (17 miles) long and is Germany's second-largest lake. Conditions in the lake area can be severe, particularly during February, when blocks of floating ice are common; heavy thunderstorms and impenetrable mist can also be a hazard at other times of the year. Carpets of beautiful white water lilies cover stretches of water in the summer months.

RELICS OF THE PAST
Archaeological remains indicate that the Mecklenburgische Seenplatte was already settled by mesolithic (Middle Stone Age) times. Neolithic stone graves, pottery and flint axes, Bronze Age jewellery, a Roman import of a richly decorated silver bowl in Iron Age times, and 7th-century evidence of Slavic settlement bear witness to the area's complex history of settlement and resettlement. Among especially attractive townships in the area, many of them of Slav origin, are Neustrelitz, Feldberg, Mirow and Wesenberg.

INFORMATION
Nationalparkamt-Müritz, Schlossplatz 3, Hohenzieritz, tel: 039824/25 20; www.nationalpark-meuritz.de

NEUBRANDENBURG
This ancient fortified town is on the eastern edge of the lake district. Its Altstadt (Old Town) was largely destroyed in the war, but the 13th-century ramparts survive, with their four quaint brick Gothic gateways, nicely restored. One of these, the Treptower I or, now houses a local history museum (*Open* daily). And tiny half-timbered houses are built into the ramparts at some points—one of them is now a bookshop.

The sculpted doorway of the Monastery of Our Lady, founded in 1015 by Augustinian monks. The cloister is superb

CHEMNITZ AND MARX
This big industrial city and working-class bastion was called Karl-Marx-Stadt by the GDR regime, but has now reverted to its true name. In its main square in 1971, the GDR placed a titanic 12m-high (39ft) Soviet-made bust of the bearded Marx himself, with his slogan, 'Workers of the world, unite!'. Attempts to remove this anachronistic monument —one of the few surviving official memorabilia from the Communist era—have foundered on stiff opposition by a left-wing lobby in the local council. Ironically, Marx had no links with the city during his lifetime.

The lake boasts 700 varieties of plants and grasses, 800 varieties of butterfly, and countless species of insects. It is noted particularly for its orchids, gentians, sundew and rare grasses, especially in the area known as the Spukloch (the Ghost's Hole). Only Scandinavian Fjallrinder (white unhorned cattle), sheep and horses are allowed to graze in this particularly vulnerable area. Rare birds such as cranes, white-tailed eagles and black storks enjoy the strictly protected habitat. The shore woodland consists of alder, birch, oak, beech and fir. Wild deer that roam in the forest can at times cause problems by overgrazing.

Despite the emphasis on nature protection, there are plenty of well-marked paths for walkers, riders and cyclists to enjoy. The lake is used for boating and sailing, though parts of the lake and its shore are restricted to exclude boats so that the breeding of the most vulnerable bird species is not disturbed.

At Meissen's porcelain factory, visitors taking the guided tour can watch skilled craftsmen and women at work

INFORMATION
Meissen: Markt 3, tel: 03521/4 19 40; www.touristinfo-meissen.de

MEISSEN WINE
Vineyards on the banks of the Elbe River around Meissen are among the northernmost in Europe and produce an excellent white wine. In the days of the old East German Communist regime Meissen wine was a rare and coveted drink, served at State banquets and other official occasions. The vineyard output is not high, so the wine is still relatively difficult to find and also quite expensive, but it is well worth hunting out.

▶▶ Meissen   *132C1*

Meissen's castle, the Albrechtsburg, which stands on a rock rising above the broad River Elbe, was the birthplace in 1710 of the European porcelain industry, using local china clay deposits. Ever since, the town's name has been closely linked with the finest decorative tableware. The **Staatliche Porzellan-Manufaktur** factory offers a demonstration of work (*Open* daily), but the main attractions are on and around the **Albrechtsburg ▶**.

The castle itself (*Open* daily except 10–31 Jan) dates back to AD929 and is a showpiece of late Gothic architecture. The rooms inside have richly decorated ceilings and vaulting. The nearby Dom (cathedral), which shares the triangular hilltop site, is older still, dating from the mid-12th century, though its soaring twin spires, which dominate the whole area, are early 20th century.

Down in the middle of town, around the picturesque market square, you'll find numerous medieval town houses and a Renaissance brewery.

About 16km (10 miles) east, in pleasant parkland, is **Moritzburg Castle ▶** (*Open* Apr–Oct daily; Nov–Dec, Feb–Mar Tue–Sun; Jan weekends only), a well-preserved 16th-century hunting lodge containing a collection of baroque furniture and exhibits on the history of hunting. Two rooms are devoted to the radical artist Käthe Kollwitz, who came here to escape the Nazis in 1944–45.

▶ **Mühlhausen**   *132A2*

Mühlhausen's old town is quiet and remarkably well preserved, encircled by town walls that you can still walk around. They are punctuated by towers and gateways leading to murky cobbled streets lined with ancient houses. In the middle are several impressive churches, including the enormous hall church of St. Marien (the second largest in Thuringia, after Erfurt Cathedral), as well as Renaissance mansions. The part-Gothic town hall has an attractive inner courtyard and incorporates a 16th-century church.

The town is associated with Thomas Müntzer, a leader of the Peasants' Revolt that was organized from here in 1524–25; he was seen by the former East German regime as an early revolutionary (though Martin Luther warned against him). The town has several monuments and memorials, including one to Müntzer himself in the St. Marien church and one to the Peasants' Revolt in the former monastery church, Kornmarktkirche (*Open* Tue–Sun).

Scholtheim (16km/10 miles east) has half-timbered houses, a baroque castle and a Romanesque church.

▶ **Nordhausen**   *132A2*

Nordhausen lies on a sloping site above the River Helme and forms the southern terminus of the narrow-gauge railway crossing the Harz (the Harzquerbahn), which is partly operated by steam trains. Dating back over 1,000 years, the middle of town is still partly encircled by walls. The pleasant, irregularly shaped market square is lined with half-timbered houses and overlooked by the twin towers of St. Basil's parish church, an imposing and spacious late 15th-century Gothic building. A few blocks away, the modest Dom zum Heiligen Kreuz (Cathedral of the Holy Cross) dates back to the 13th century, with a Romanesque crypt and a 14th-century nave lined with massive octagonal pillars.

Heavy air strikes late in World War II damaged parts of central Nordhausen, but numerous half-timbered houses survive, notably along the Barfüsser Strasse, at the top of which stands the Flohburg, a large black-and-white structure dating back to 1500. The large stone Renaissance town hall bears a figure of the knight Roland, a long-established symbol of the town.

To the southeast of Nordhausen (about 20km/12.5 miles) lies the **Kyffhäuser Nature Park**, an area of modest but very striking wooded hills rising to 477m (1,565ft) on the Kulpenberg, topped with a TV transmitter. The Kyffhäuser (453m/1,486ft) bears an 80m (262ft) monument to Kaiser Wilhelm I (*Open* daily). Legend has it that one of his predecessors, Friedrich I, dreamed of German unity on this site and would sleep until the day it came, but there have so far been no reports of him waking up. On the western edge of Kyffhäuser, there's bathing at the Kelbra reservoir and the ruins of nearby Rothenburg castle lie in a secluded woodland setting. To the south is the small town of **Bad Frankenhausen**, with mineral springs, a spectacularly leaning church (more precarious than the Leaning Tower of Pisa) and a gigantic **mural**▶ completed in 1987 by the Leipzig artist Werner Tübke. Measuring 123m by 14m (403ft by 46ft), it depicts the decisive battle of the Peasants' Revolt in 1525.

INFORMATION
Mühlhausen: Ratsstrasse 20, tel: 03601/40 47 70; www.muehlhausen.de

153

DORA-MITTELBAU
Thousands of slave workers assembled V1 and V2 rockets in underground bunkers at the Dora-Mittelbau concentration camp outside Nordhausen during World War II. Twenty thousand died or were executed for not fulfilling work norms, or for the slightest lapses in discipline. The camp's crematorium still stands and has been made into a memorial for the Dora-Mittelbau victims.

RECYCLING
Rostock has found a novel way of recycling the rusty old ships that made up much of the merchant fleet of Communist-run East Germany. One decommissioned 40-year-old freighter has been converted into a youth hostel, with 85 beds. The 'Traditionsschiff', tied up in the Rostock harbour suburb of Schmarl, has cabins for two or four people, ideal for budget-minded couples or families. Although it's officially a youth hostel, there is no age limit on guests.

WARNEMÜNDE
This old fishing-port-cum-resort near Rostock has much appeal. The huge ex-GDR hotel on its broad sandy beach is not attractive, but at the east end of the promenade there is a lively old quarter of fishermen's cottages, now full of cafés. Fishing boats line the quay and car ferries arrive from Denmark, Finland and Sweden.

▶▶ Rostock   132B4

The city of Rostock has a long history. Originally a Slavonic coastal fortress, after being sacked in 1161 by King Waldemar of Denmark, it was settled and developed in the 13th century by German merchants and soon became a prosperous port, part of the famous Hanseatic trading league (see page 75). In 1419 one of the first universities in northern Europe was founded in Rostock, and the city became a focus for learning and culture, though from the 17th century onwards its economic importance declined compared with the rapidly growing rival ports of Hamburg and Kiel.

Much of the older part of this strategically situated Baltic port was destroyed in World War II—only four of the 22 former ancient city gateways remain, but these include the handsome 54m (177ft) Kröpeliner Tor, dating from the 13th century. Several of the city's medieval churches have been restored, and there are some attractive gabled merchants' houses.

The city grew rapidly in importance during the postwar years, being developed into a major Eastern-block shipbuilding and industrial base and becoming East Germany's main seaport. The port was particularly significant in terms of trade to and from the former Soviet Union. While this traffic has almost vanished, business with Nordic countries is growing. There are impressive museums of shipbuilding and shipping, and a large zoological garden and botanic gardens (*Open* daily).

Excursions

Rostock is a conveniently situated base from which to visit a number of small but attractive seaside resorts along the Baltic coast. It's worth making the trip to the graceful old spa town of **Bad Doberan**, with its celebrated 14th-century Cistercian monastery, if only to take the narrow-gauge steam railway with the charming nickname of 'Molli'. This links Bad Doberan with **Ostseebad Heiligendamm**, Germany's oldest Baltic seaside resort, founded in 1793. It is celebrated for its charming period cottages, which resulted in it being known as 'the white town by the sea'. There is a lovely neo-classical spa building, or Kurhaus, in the middle of town, and nearby is the Conventer See Nature Reserve, a wildlife sanctuary.

Kühlungsborn, also linked to Bad Doberan by 'Molli', is a far newer seaside resort, developed from three villages which fused during the 1930s. As well as a heated sea-water bathing pool, the town has a 4km (2.5-mile) sandy beach. Notable features are an early Gothic church with a wooden tower, and a 19th-century windmill.

▶▶ Rudolstadt   132A1

Rudolstadt nestles in the valley of the River Saale, on the eastern fringes of the Thuringian Forest. Its wide, pleasant main square, flanked on one side by an imposing medieval town hall and clock tower, is bypassed by the traffic that thunders through this town; from here it's a short, steep climb up to Schloss Heidecksburg, a graceful baroque hilltop palace ranged around three sides of a courtyard. It houses collections of furniture, painting and weapons, and in the summer plays host to a number of music concerts.

PRIVATIZED HOTELS

In the old GDR, the state-run hotels were decent but dreary. New small privately run hotels of character, like those in the West, are now at last emerging in tourist areas such as Sächsische Schweiz. Many of them offer good Saxon cooking and a really friendly atmosphere. In the cities, the former giant state-run hotels have mostly been taken over by western chains such as Hilton and Maritim. In Dresden, one 18th-century baroque mansion is now a small luxury hotel. Another, medium price, is run by the Lutheran churches. There are several of these church-run hotels in East Germany, and they invariably offer excellent value for money.

155

Further cultural attractions are provided by the small Thüringer Landestheater (provincial theatre), which was founded by Goethe, a frequent visitor to the town (as was Schiller, who met his wife, Charlotte, here).

Across the river from the castle and historic base is the Thuringian Farm Museum (Volkskundemuseum), where two fine half-timbered farmhouses stand in an attractive parkland setting (*Open* Mar–Oct Wed–Sun).

Excursions

About 8km (5 miles) to the northeast of Rudolstadt lies Grosskochberg, home of **Kochberg** castle, owned by the von Stein family, whom Goethe often visited. Many of its rooms have been restored to how they were in Goethe's time. **Paulinzella** (23km/14 miles west) has romantic 12th-century monastic ruins in a wooded setting.

▶ Sächsische Schweiz

Some of Germany's most dramatic scenery lies only a short way upstream along the Elbe, between the outskirts of Dresden and Czech border. Called the Saxon Switzerland National Park, it is also known as the Elbe Sandstone District.

High sandstone cliffs and crags form a deep gorge through which the River Elbe flows. They have been exposed, weathered and worn over millennia by frost, wind and rain into a series of fantastic sculptured shapes—pillars, towers, arches and stacks towering nearly 300m (984ft) above the river. In places they are exposed as bleak, bare crags, a kind of Central European Grand Canyon. In other parts trees and shrubs twist out of cracks, cling to crevices, crowd onto summits and form the kind of fantastic landscape that inspired such painters as the great 19th-century Romantic Caspar David Friedrich. Ancient woodlands—pine, beech, oak, maple,

INFORMATION

Sächsische Schweiz: Bahnhofstrasse 21, Pirna, tel: 03501/470147; www.saechsische-schweiz.de

NAPOLEON'S DOWNFALL

The Festung Königstein, one of Germany's largest and most impressive fortresses (*Open* daily), played a major role in the ultimate downfall of Napoleon. In a heroic defensive action in August 1813, about 14,000 German and Russian troops garrisoned in the fortress turned back an offensive by 40,000 soldiers of Napoleon's élite Garde Française. The French were trying to block a retreat to Bohemia by Austrian forces after their defeat in the Battle of Dresden. The holding action by the German and Russian forces saved the Austrians from total decimation and strengthened the military alliance that was later to defeat Napoleon at Waterloo.

Schwerin lies on a lake that stretches to the gardens of its great castle

fir—flourish around and between the craggy rocks, forming a dense green backdrop to the sculptured formations.

Between the crags wind deep, narrow gorges, some of them barely a couple of metres wide—cool and shady on even the hottest summer day. Many of them are penetrated by winding footpaths that suddenly emerge into full daylight at thrilling viewpoints. Narrow tributary valleys of the Elbe, especially the Polenz, the Sebnitz and the Kirnitz, also create dramatic features within this unique area of natural beauty.

At **Bastei►** (road access and car parking), a footbridge was built from stone in the 1850s, 194m (636ft) above the Elbe, creating a remarkable viewpoint. It is linked to a series of pedestrian walkways across the crag summits, all with safety rails.

Across the river at Königstein, a massive crag has been used as the base of a great medieval fortress dating back to the 14th century. The Festung Königstein was strategically placed to defend the valley. Later the fortress played a major role in the ultimate downfall of Napoleon at Waterloo (see panel).

Although the area is now strictly protected as a national park and nature reserve, access is easy from Dresden by road along the B172 and by rail.

A series of ferries cross the river to such small riverside resorts as Stadt Wehlen, Kurort Rathen, Schmilka and Bad Schandau. In the summer months, the Weisse Flotte boats operate regular passenger trips along the river from Dresden, which thus serves as a convenient base for visiting this area.

Across a bridge from the castle, Schwerin's state theatre lies in an old town that is now grace- fully restored

WISMAR AND GÜSTROW
The old Hanseatic sea- port of Wismar belonged to Sweden from 1648 to 1803 and retains traces of that influence. The finest of the old buildings around the market square is the 14th- century Alter Schwede (Old Swede), with a strik- ing stepped-gable façade. To the east lies the ornate Gothic cathedral. In Güstrow there is a superb Renaissance palace (Rathaus), while works by the modern sculptor Ernst Barlach (1870–1938) are displayed at his former studio and the Gertrudenkapelle (both *open* Tue–Sun).

▶▶ Schwerin   *132A4*

The old city of Schwerin in Mecklenburg has some lovely half-timbered houses at its heart, and an imposing cathe- dral, founded in 1171. The town hall in the market square has a medieval core, though with a neo-Gothic façade of 1835. The early 18th-century Nikolaikirche, also called the Schelfkirche, is the finest of Mecklenburg's baroque churches. The imposing Kollegiengebäude in Schloss Strasse is the administrative headquarters of the state gov- ernment. Boat trips operate from the middle of town across the Schweriner See to Zippendorf, where the 138m (453ft) television tower provides splendid panoramic views of lake, city and countryside.

Schwerin's spectacular **castle▶** is set on an island, joined to the mainland by twin bridges. Reminiscent of a Loire château, it was built for the dukes of Mecklenburg in the 1840s as a mix of mock-Gothic and mock- Renaissance; one of the architects, Gottfried Semper, designed Dresden's Semper Opera House. The castle now houses the Mecklenburg-Vorpommern State Parliament. You can visit the restored throne room and other dark-panelled state rooms (*Open* Tue–Sun). In the north wing there is a beautiful church. To the south of the castle are baroque pleasure gardens, with canals, groves and paths in formal geometric patterning. To the north- west, in the former castle garden, is the state theatre and the art gallery, with a collection of Dutch and Flemish masters (*Open* mid-Apr to mid-Oct fdaily; mid-Oct to mid-Apr Tue–Sun). Muess, near Schwerin, has a Freilichtmuseum in the form of a reconstructed village.

INFORMATION

Lübbenau: Ehm-Welk-
Strasse 15,
tel: 03452/36 68;
www.spreewald-online.de

THE SORBS

The Sorbs are a Slavic people who have kept their own language and culture in two regions of Germany: in Lower Lusatia, around the Spreewald, and in Upper Lusatia, in the southeast of Saxony east of Dresden. Signposts and official notices in both areas are in two languages—German and Sorbian—and Catholic churches use the Sorbian language in their liturgy. There is also a Sorbian publishing house, a regular newspaper, a school and a Sorbian-German folk theatre. Many Sorbian customs are preserved, such as Easter Riding, a mixture of pagan and Christian. During Lent young people go from house to house playing bagpipes and fiddles, asking for eggs and bacon, and money. Straw brooms are burned like the witches of old, and Easter eggs are decorated with beautiful, intricate designs. Sorbian national costume is extremely vibrant with intricate embroidery, now generally worn only for festivals and holidays.

►►► The Spreewald   132C2

The River Spree southeast of Berlin, between Berlin and Cottbus, flows through an area of low-lying countryside, splitting into countless minor tributaries and creating the complex area of lakes, ponds, marsh, wetland and riverine woodland known as the Spreewald. There are also areas of low-lying farmland that are drained by a network of small canals and dikes.

This area has a unique beauty, due to the effects of light both in early spring, when the birch trees lining its water channels are reflected in the water, and again in late summer and fall, when the luxurious vegetation turns the shortest excursion into an adventure. Much of the area is now a Biosphere Reserve, reflecting both the natural beauty and wildlife interest of the area and its rich cultural associations, particularly with the Sorbian settlements in the area. Ortenburg, a castle in the 1,000-year-old town of **Bautzen**, is said to be the place where the Sorbs tribal fortress used to stand.

Today Bautzen, with its baroque- and Renaissance-style buildings, is the focus of Sorbian culture and tradition, and the seat of the Sorbian national organization, the Domowina.

The region is divided into the **Unterspreewald**, north of Lübben, and the larger and better-known **Oberspreewald**, north of Lübbenau. The whole of the Spreewald teems with game, such as wild boar, deer, partridges and pheasants. Here, too, are white storks and herons in abundance.

The area also has its own highly characteristic form of local transportation—narrow barges or punts that carry both people and goods along the myriad channels between villages and outlying farms in the forest. A popular summer activity for visitors is to be punted along

canals, canalized rivers and streams, though motors have replaced muscle power in most instances.

The Lower Spreewald, around the Lübben area, is a large enclosed forest region with alder, birch and beech interspersed with areas of open, low-lying meadowland and water meadows. This provides an ideal habitat for numerous plants and animals and biotopes for amphibians, water-loving insects, rare dragonflies, kingfishers and cranes.

The attractive Sorbian township of **Lübben**, which was founded in 1150, has a history going back as far as the Middle Stone Age. Its castle, with richly decorated rooms, was built in the latter stages of the Renaissance and later became the seat and capital of the Lower Lusatian government. The town is the gateway to both the Upper and Lower areas of the Spreewald, with motorized punt services into the forest. From **Lübbenau**, a small tourist resort, there are splendid walks into the Oberspreewald along well-signposted paths over old canal-side dikes that go deep into the forest. In nearby **Lehde**, a fascinating open-air museum has traditional Sorbian farmhouses with their own distinctive waterside architecture—a kind of miniature Venice in the forest. In the summer months motorized barges link Lübbenau with Lehde. The soil for the pleasure grounds of Lübbenau's early 19th-century castle was brought by barge. Inside, look out for the old locomotive and carriage of the narrow-gauge train the Spreewaldguste, which ran for the last time in 1970.

The historic town of **Burg** is the eastern gateway of the Oberspreewald. There is another Biosphere Reserve here, of eels, pike and flounder in abundance; woodruff (used to tint the Berlin Weissbier bright green) also flourishes. Labyrinths of water channels are crossed by high wooden bridges, at least 300 of them around the town of Burg and its satellite parishes alone. Water lilies bloom along quieter stretches of water and the whole area, with several nature reserves, is a naturalist's paradise. The town of **Cottbus**, near the Polish border, has a fine altarpiece of Jonah and the Whale in the Oberkirche.

A popular summer outing for Berliners is punting along the Spreewald canals (above and left)

159

SPREEWALD PRODUCE
Market gardens in the area provide produce for nearby Berlin and Spreewald pickles are a much-prized delicacy. Plant extracts are also produced and used in a variety of homeopathic remedies.

Eastern Germany

MARITIME GLORY
The sleepy little Baltic port of Barth was a busy shipbuilding base just over a century ago, rivalling Rostock and even the North Sea cities of Bremen and Bremerhaven. In 1877, according to local records, Barth had no less than four shipbuilding yards and 18 shipping companies. Nearly 200 merchant sailing ships were registered in town. But then came the age of steam, and Barth was badly equipped to keep pace with the rapid changes. Today, only a museum (*Open Tue–Sun*) reminds visitors of its short-lived maritime glory.

160

Stralsund is nearly completely surrounded by water and is an ideal base from which to explore the Baltic coast

►► Stralsund   132B4

Stralsund occupies a defensive position on a small hillock between the Strelasund, the narrow strait that divides the Isle of Rügen from the mainland, and two attractive small lakes, the Knieperteiche and Frankenteiche.

Like Rostock, this was a Hanseatic town, but between 1648 and 1815 it became part of Sweden before it was reclaimed by Prussia. The old town and small harbour have particularly fine architecture, including impressive merchants' houses. There is a remarkable reddish-brick town hall in the Alter Markt dating from the 13th century, with a high elegant façade. The Marienkirche dates from 1298, and two surviving towers are both 15th century in origin. The middle of town has an attractive pedestrianized market area, and scheduled passenger boats from the harbour link the mainland with the island of Hiddensee and the Darss peninsula. The rail and road bridge linking Stralsund with the Isle of Rügen was built only in 1936.

Stralsund is a good base from which to explore the **Vorpommersche Boddenlandschaft National Park**—a national park consisting of a long, mainly wooded coastline along the Baltic, close to such small fishing villages and quiet seaside resorts as **Prerow**, **Zingst** and **Wieck**. This is an area of sand dunes, winding sandbanks, mudflats, and shallow seas, rich in birdlife, including many waders and coastal birds, and for that reason strictly protected. The area is a sanctuary for thousands of migratory birds, including some of the largest colonies of marine birds in northern Europe. The coastal region itself is famous for its ancient woodlands, including rare shrubs and grasses.

Rügen► The whole of the Isle of Rügen is worth exploring. **Putbus** is a sleepy little inland resort deliberately planned by a local prince early last century to be like an English spa town, with elegant houses around a green 'circus' in the style of Bath. There is a fine neo-classical theatre, while the former Kurhaus in 'English' parkland is

There are fine stretches
of virtually tideless beach
with clean sand around
the small Stralsund
resorts. Many attractive
thatched cottages and
farmhouses lie along the
Darss peninsula and in
many of the villages, that
give the area an 'English
feel', though the style is
markedly different. The
coastal road from
Stralsund via Barth to
Ribnitz Damgarten is a
particularly attractive
drive (there is also a bus
service from Barth sta-
tion). It follows the
narrow peninsula
between Darss and
Fischland; the peninsula
encloses areas of quiet
inland sea and saltwater
marsh known as Bodden,
with their spectacular
birdlife. There are well-
signposted bicycle paths
and walkways along the
coast, especially along
the raised defensive
embankments, partially
enclosed by woodland.

the parish church. A narrow-gauge steam railway, known
as 'Rasender Roland' (Rushing Roland), links Putbus with
the seaside resort of Göhren. It puffs its way through an
idyllic landscape of old meadows, scattered woodlands,
small lakes and storks' nests to the seaside resorts of Binz
and Göhren, with their fine sandy beaches.

The narrow peninsula to the south, which is known as
Mönchgut, is protected as a Biosphere Reserve and is safe-
guarded as much for its cultural qualities as for its
landscape. There are old farmhouses and thatched fishermen's cottages, ancient meadows crowded with brilliant
wildflowers, many of them rare, and low coastal cliffs and
pebbly beaches overlooking a distant coastline stretching
to Usedom and the Polish border. In the little museum in
Göhren you'll find some examples of 19th-century
Staffordshire ware, traded and brought back from
England by sailors.

Sassnitz is an old port and ferry terminal on Rügen,
where train and car ferries leave for Trelleborg in Sweden.
Originally it was a small fishing port and quarry town,
but it later became a holiday resort, and there are still
some handsome 19th-century villas to be seen around the
older part of the town. Immediately to the north of
Sassnitz lies Jasmund National Park, which has some of
the most impressive coastal scenery in Germany. High
chalk cliffs crowned by dense beechwoods overlook the
quiet Baltic Sea.

Though thousands of visitors crowd the Kaiserstuhl,
a tall chalk cliff and fine viewpoint, a few hundred metres
away along the coastal path all is quiet, with equally
impressive views. At Wissower Klinken, weather-carved
chalk cliffs provide a dramatic feature that became the
subject of one of the most famous of Caspar David
Friedrich's Romantic paintings. The beech woods, as well
as the meadows and the heathland, provide a habitat for a
rich flora, especially orchids. Fauna includes small rep-
tiles and rare butterflies.

▶▶ Thüringer Wald (Thuringian Forest)   132A1

The Thüringer Wald covers an area of ancient hills stretching for about 100km (62 miles) southeastwards from Eisenach, and averaging about 30km (18.5 miles) wide. By German standards, the hills are not especially high—the highest point is the Grosser Beerberg at 982m (3,222ft)—but the area is crossed by numerous narrow valleys and is densely settled with old-fashioned villages and small industrial towns. The area is heavily forested, mostly with fir and beech trees, but the woodlands are interspersed with meadows and orchards, and there's plenty of variety from one square kilometre to the next.

Because of its small scale and varied scenery, the Thüringer Wald is excellent walking country, and has long been popular for quiet country vacations and excursions, as well as for cross-country skiing in winter. A long-distance path, the Rennsteig, runs southeastwards from the Wartburg for 160km (100 miles) within the Thüringer Wald. Even for those not inclined to tackle its full length, it offers lots of opportunities to get into the countryside. Like many of the shorter paths that criss-cross the area, it's well marked ('R' symbols on trees and signposts) and easy to follow.

Today the Thüringer Wald offers a reasonably good variety of accommodation. Proximity to western Germany has encouraged many local people to try their hand at catering for visitors, and you'll find plenty of

MODERN TROUBLES
Despite the Thüringer Wald's many charms, it also has its sad side. Emissions from nearby open-cast brown-coal mines have caused dreadful air pollution in many parts, and a survey in 1989 showed that more than half the trees were affected. A massive post-reunification clean-up has slowed down the rate at which trees are falling prey to pollution, but it's still a worrying problem as Germany begins the 21st century. It's not an exclusively East German problem, either; surveys of pine forests in southern Germany have produced alarming results, but here the major cause appears to be heavy motor traffic.

MEININGEN'S THEATRE
This little town in southern Thüringia is the home of one of Germany's grandest theatres, built in 1908 in the style of a Greek temple. Meiningen was the capital of a duchy in 1680–1918, and Duke Georg II, married to a famous actress, created its theatre, which subsequently helped reform the international stage with its approach. It continues to flourish in spite of financial constraints. Brahms conducted the first performance of his Fourth Symphony here. Richard Strauss and Max Reger also worked in Meiningen.

small pensions and *Zimmer frei* (rooms to let) signs even in the villages, together with family-run restaurants and bars. There's plenty of Thüringer *bratwurst* to go around, often purchased from roadside barbecues. Thuringia has many of its own folk songs and folk dances. These were discouraged under the centralized GDR regime, but are now being revived.

What to see The best of the forest scenery in the Thüringer Wald lies along a line fairly close to the Rennsteig, and you will have to come off the main roads to see it (see page 165 for a suggested route).

Of the smaller places towards the heart of the forest, it's worth making for **Schmalkalden** for its fine half-timbered houses grouped around an imposing irregular market square. Nearby Schloss Wilhelmsburg dates back to the 1580s and is one of Thuringia's most important Renaissance buildings (*Open* Apr–Oct daily; Nov–Mar Tue–Sun). **Bad Liebenstein** has dignified spa buildings lining its leafy avenues and there are extensive views from the ruins of medieval Liebenstein castle, while nearby 18th-century Schloss Altenstein is in an English-style park. **Wasungen**, set in the wooded Upper Werra Valley, has numerous half-timbered buildings (including a fine three-floor town hall dating from 1533) in its specially protected central area. **Friedrichroda** (see also page 144) is a relaxed forest resort with parks, an open-air

163

In the Thüringer Wald, the well-tended villages have red roofs and grey slate façades. In some parts there is skiing

Tanks used to patrol the Thüringer Wald, close to the old border with West Germany

swimming pool, a lake and a large early 19th-century castle, Reinhardsbrunn, now a hotel. The nearby Marienglashöhle caves (*Open* daily) have unusual gypsum crystal formations.

Oberhof is an important local winter-sports base, dominated by the strikingly modern Hotel Panorama, built in the form of two ski jumps. A botanical garden, the Rennsteig Garten, contains 4,000 specimens collected from all over the world including many rare alpine plants (*Open* mid-Apr to early Nov).

A number of larger towns of historical and architectural interest ring the edge of the main forest area. **Suhl** was the capital of the whole region when this was part of the GDR, and gained high-rises and an egg-box-style shopping precinct. Famous since medieval times as a home of gun making, the town also has a weapons museum (*Open* Tue–Sun) in the 17th-century malthouse building. The nearby old main street, the Steinweg, has been pedestrianized and has several fine 18th-century houses.

Ilmenau, a glass- and porcelain-making town, was a popular retreat of Goethe's and has several places associated with him: the Amtshaus (official's house), the Gabelbach hunting lodge, and the Goethe hut and Kickelhahn, all linked by a footpath called Auf Goethes Spuren (in Goethe's footsteps).

Arnstadt gave J. S. Bach his first job as an organist, in the baroque church that now bears his name, and a jaunty statue of the great man watches over the small market square of this very well preserved small town. The baroque Neues Palais (*Open* Tue–Sun) has a remarkable collection of 400 dolls made locally in the 18th century. The surrounding landscape of lush, gentle hills is exceptionally pretty and is known for its botanical rarities, including German gentians. **Lauscha**, to the south, has long been a glassblowing town; it invented Christmas tree decorations in 1848 and still produces them.

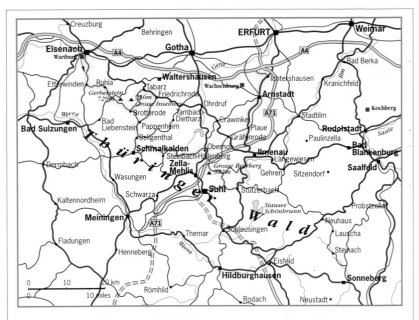

Drive

Thüringer Wald

This 187km (116-mile) tour starts from Eisenach.

Go out of Eisenach for 12km (7.5 miles) on the B19 Meiningen road, turn left at Etterwinden on an unmarked road to Ruhla and Brotterode. Turn left towards Tabarz. After 4km (2.5 miles) there is a park-ing area on the right, then climb the Grosser Inselberg (about half an hour each way, on an easy path) for the mountaintop café and a great view.

Continue to Tabarz, then right on the B88 road to Friedrichroda; leave by a minor road to Schmalkalden, then take minor roads to Steinbach-Hallenberg and Oberhof.

Turn right onto the B247; drive 1km (0.5 mile) south, then turn left on a minor road. This follows the Rennsteig and passes the Grosser Beerberg.

Continue to the main B4 road, turn left and return through Ilmenau and Arnstadt, to take the E40 highway back to Eisenach.

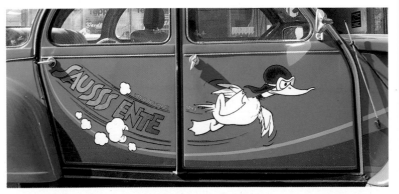

CITY OF CULTURE
Weimar was Europe's 'City of Culture' in 1999, and the year was celebrated with the reopening of a major German art gallery, the Neues Museum (New Museum). This imposing neo-Renaissance city palace, built in 1868, was plundered by the Nazis, who banished most of its modern works. It was then left to decay by the East German Communists. A West German gallery owner, Paul Maenz, breathed fresh life into the historic building by donating much of his private collection. Among the treasures of modern art, all dating from 1960, are works by the American minimalists Dan Flavin, Donald Judd, Carl Andre and Sol Lewitt. (*Open* Tue–Sun *Modest admission charge.*)

The rich wheat fields of Vogtland. Many state collective farms have now become cooperatives

▶ **Vogtland** *132B1*

This hilly region of forests, steep-sided valleys, isolated rocks, lakes and dams extends along the southern frontier of the former GDR, to the Erzgebirge on the Czech border (see pages 142–143). The area is dotted with small industrial towns, some of which are famous for making musical instruments, and with modest spas based on mineral-rich springs. The area's relaxed character and varied scenery make it a good choice for simple, open-air pursuits, notably walking on the many well-marked paths. There's some sailing on the lakes and reservoirs, too.

Some of the best scenery is around **Klingenthal**, a straggling semi-industrial village situated right up against the Czech frontier and famous for its manufacture of harmonicas. Five kilometres (3 miles) to the north of Klingenthal lies **Schneckenstein**, the only place in Europe where topaz can be found—there are still some isolated rock formations in the area.

Schoeneck, 12km (7.5 miles) northwest, marks the southern end of the dramatic, deeply cut valley of the Steinicht River. About 20km (12.5 miles) north of the town, around Schnarrtanne and Beerheide, you'll find some of the Vogtland's prettiest woodland scenery.

The biggest of the reservoirs is **Stausee Poehl**, near the region's main town, Plauen, but there are many attractive small lakes in the area stretching south from here to Markneukirchen and Bad Elster.

Markneukirchen, Germany's leading musical instrument producing town since the early 19th century, has a small baroque castle, the Paulusschloessel. A collection of 3,000 musical instruments is housed in the Musikinstrumentenmuseum (*Open* Tue–Sun).

Bad Elster, in a quiet wooded valley off the main road, has spa buildings dating from the mid-19th century. At **Landwüst**, 6km (4 miles) to the east, there's a small open-air folk museum with farm implements and local history collections (*Open* Tue–Sun). It is easy to make day excursions to the famous Czech spa towns of Karlovy Vary (Karlsbad) and Mariánské Lázn (Marienbad).

▶▶▶ **Weimar** *132A1*

Although only a modest-sized town, Weimar is one of Germany's greatest cultural treasures. With public buildings, parks, squares and boulevards, it feels like a small capital city, which indeed it was, of Sachsen-Weimar from 1547 to 1870. Following a meeting of the German parliament in the city in 1919, it gave its name to the ill-fated democratic republic that preceded the Hitler years, and was capital of Thuringia from 1919 to 1949. The city was lucky enough to be spared wartime destruction, and for 40 years after World War II it escaped the effects of mass international tourism. Now it is catching up fast, and has acquired a Hilton hotel and a wide choice of bars and restaurants. Many of the fine buildings have been expensively restored.

Weimar's list of cultural connections is almost endless: Goethe spent most of his working life here, and his influence on the life of the city was immense; the writers Friedrich von Schiller and Johann Gottfried von Herder lived here; musical residents included Franz Liszt and Richard Strauss; the philosopher Nietzsche spent his final years here (his house contains a small museum, *Open* Apr–Oct Tue–Sun); and in the 20th century, Walter Gropius founded the Bauhaus movement here.

There are lots of sights, many associated with Weimar's famous residents. Despite the tourist crowds (particularly in summer), it can be a relaxing city, helped by its manageable size, neat squares, outdoor cafés and, above all, by the huge park that extends along the River Ilm almost to the heart of Weimar.

Goetheswohnhaus▶▶ on the Frauenplan (*Open* Tue–Sun) will be at the top of most people's lists. This combines Goethe's own family house—still complete with his study, books, furniture and collections of coins, minerals and art—with an imposing museum explaining the writer's life and influence (most explanations in

Weimar's Wittumspalais (top)
Goethe, Germany's most famous writer, lived in a simply furnished home in the middle of Weimar (above)

INFORMATION
Weimar: Markt 10,
tel: 03643/74 50;
www.weimar.de

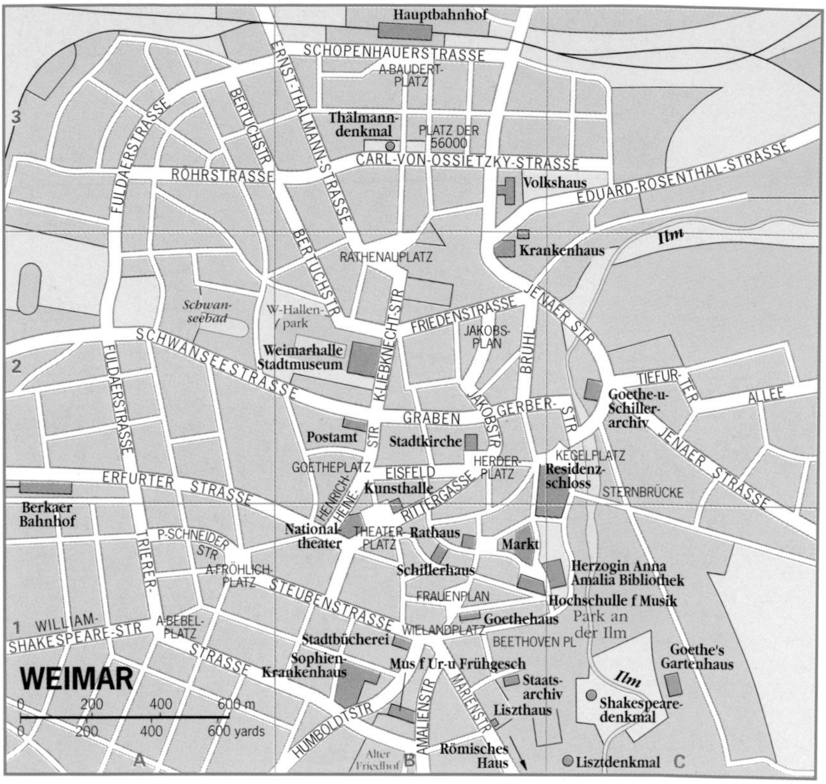

Map of Weimar with labels:

Hauptbahnhof

SCHOPENHAUERSTRASSE

A-BAUDERT-PLATZ

ERNST-THÄLMANN-STRASSE

BERTUCHSTR.

FULDAERSTRASSE

RÖHRSTRASSE

Thälmann-denkmal

PLATZ DER 56000

CARL-VON-OSSIETZKY-STRASSE

Volkshaus

EDUARD-ROSENTHAL-STRASSE

Ilm

Krankenhaus

RATHENAUPLATZ

BERTUCHSTR.

Schwan-seebad

W-Hallen-/park

FRIEDENSTRASSE

JAKOBS-PLAN

JENAER STR.

BRÜHL

FULDAERSTRASSE

SCHWANSEESTRASSE

Weimarhalle Stadtmuseum

KLEEBNECHTSTR.

JAKOBSTR.

GERBER-STR.

TIEFUR-TER ALLEE

Goethe-u-Schiller-archiv

GRABEN

Postamt Stadtkirche

HERDER-PLATZ

KEGELPLATZ

JENAER STRASSE

GOETHEPLATZ EISFELD

HEINRICH HEINE STR.

Kunsthalle

Residenz-schloss

STERNBRÜCKE

ERFURTER STRASSE

HEINRICH HEINE STR.

National-theater

THEATER-PLATZ

Rathaus

Markt

RITTERGASSE

Berkaer Bahnhof

P-SCHNEIDER STR

RIERER-STR.

A-FRÖHLICH-PLATZ

STEUBENSTRASSE

Schillerhaus

FRAUENPLAN

Herzogin Anna Amalia Bibliothek

Hochschule f Musik

WILLIAM-SHAKESPEARE-STR

A-BEBEL-PLATZ

STRASSE

Goethehaus

WIELANDPLATZ

BEETHOVEN PL

Park an der Ilm

WEIMAR

Stadtbücherei

Sophien-Krankenhaus

Mus f Ur-u Frühgesch

Goethe's Gartenhaus

0 200 400 600 m

0 200 400 600 yards

HUMBOLDTSTR.

AMALIENSTR.

MARIENSTR.

Staats-archiv

Lisztbaus

Ilm

Shakespeare-denkmal

A Alter Friedhof B Römisches Haus

Lisztdenkmal C

BUCHENWALD CAMP

On a hill near Weimar lies the largest Nazi concentration camp on German soil: 56,000 people died here, many from torture or starvation. A memorial and museum (*Open* Tue–Sun) give the details movingly. The No. 6 bus runs from Weimar to the camp site. The GDR regime firmly put the accent on the sufferings of the German Communist and Russian prisoners, and ignored Jewish people. This shocking bias has now been corrected, and there is a Jewish memorial—also a museum about the cruel Soviet prison camp on the site in 1945–49, where 7,000 died.

German only). There's a charming small garden at the back. A few hundred metres away, in the Ilm Park, you can also visit **Goethe's Gartenhaus▶** (*Open* daily), an idyllic rural retreat in which he lived for six years.

The renovated **Schillerhaus▶** (*Open* Wed–Mon), on Schillerstrasse, was lived in by Schiller for the last three years of his life and incorporates many of his and his family's possessions and a modern museum annex documents his work.

The **Lisztbaus▶** (*Open* Apr–Oct Wed–Mon), by the west entrance to the Ilm Park, was used by the composer as a summer residence for 17 years and sets out his living and working quarters with many of his possessions, documents, pictures and other mementoes.

The **Wittumspalais**, one of the city's many palaces and castles, stands on the Theaterplatz, immediately opposite the National Theatre, with its famous double statue of Goethe and Schiller. The small baroque palace (*Open* Tue–Sun) was built for Duchess Anna Amalia in the 1770s when the main city palace burned down. It has been furnished in baroque style and has the atmosphere of a typical prosperous town house of the period. One room, the Tafelrundenzimmer (round-table room), was a popular meeting point for artists who were friendly with the court. In one wing of the palace there's a museum commemorating another famous Weimar resident, the writer Christoph Martin Wieland. Beside the palace is a museum (*Open* daily) devoted to the Bauhaus movement.

The main **Weimar Castle** (*Open* Tue–Sun), rebuilt in 1803, is an inspiring neo-baroque structure overlooking the Sternbrücke (Star Bridge) and River Ilm. It contains a collection of local paintings and fine arts.

The nearby **Herzogin Anna Amalia Bibliothek** (*Open* Mon–Sat) was almost totally destroyed by fire in 2004. Before this, it housed the 900,000 volumes of the Library of the German Classics. The building is due to reopen in 2007, but about 30,000 books have been lost, as well as many of its original manuscripts and works of art.

Out of Town It is a very pleasant 20-minute walk along the River Ilm to the south of the town, passing through a large relaxed park, to the '**Roman House**' (*Open* Apr–Oct Tue–Sun). This classical pavilion, which was built in the 1790s, enjoys a beautiful setting overlooking the river and inside there's a collection of local works of art.

A further 5km (3 miles) out of town in the same direction brings you to **Schloss Belvedere** (*Open* Tue–Sun. *Closed* Nov–end Mar), a modest but charming country retreat and hunting lodge that was built in the 1730s. It is flanked by two delightful single-floor pavilions. The surrounding park was landscaped in the early 19th century, when it acquired a large exotic plant collection that is kept in the Orangery and nearby greenhouses.

About 5km (3 miles) northeast of the town of Weimar, **Schloss Tiefurt** (closed for renovation), built in 1760, became a major cultural focus in the late 18th century. The castle contains interesting displays of furniture, busts, porcelain and a collection of paintings and fine arts of the period, and stands in a handsome landscaped park stretching down towards the banks of the River Ilm.

GOETHE'S TOMB
In 1999 some reporters discovered that 30 years ago East Germany Communist Party officials and forensic experts secretly opened up Goethe's tomb in Weimar and had the remains 'cleaned up'. They went about the task with typical thoroughness, cleaning out the skull (in which they found just dust), reducing the remains to a clean skeleton and measuring the corpse. Goethe was not as large as some statues of him suggest—he was a mere 1.67m (5.5ft) tall. The results of the examination and post-mortem can be seen (on prior request) in the National Museum in Weimar.

169

The Duchess Anna Amalia lived in this small yellow baroque palace (above) after the death of her husband in 1767. Here she held intellectual salons that were attended by, among others, Goethe, Schiller, Herder and Wieland

►► Wernigerode

132A2

Wernigerode, strategically situated on the northern fringe of the Harz Mountains, is famed for its fine half-timbered houses and its elaborately carved, twin-spired, late Gothic town hall. The town was granted its charter in 1229 and in 1449 became the seat of the powerful counts of Stolberg, and a prosperous trading base. Its decline perhaps helped to keep its medieval character. Inevitably the town suffered a number of fires in earlier periods, but miraculously its town hall, most of its charming streets and part of its defensive walls (with impressive gates) were spared. In the 18th century some baroque buildings were added.

Overlooking the town, Wernigerode's castle, which was largely rebuilt in the mid-19th century, stands on the site of a much older fortress that dates from 1121. It is rapidly being rediscovered as a tourist base for the Harz, and there are several rebuilt and restored hotels. The town lies at the northern terminus of the Harzquerbahn narrow-gauge steam railway to Nordhausen, close to superb walking country.

It's worth going 50km (31 miles) east of Wernigerode to **Quedlinburg**►► (see also page 123), which has been designated a UNESCO World Heritage Site because of its astonishing wealth of half-timbered houses along narrow streets and courtyards, with groups dating from the late Gothic (15th century) period onwards. One example, in Wordgasse, dating from the first half of the 14th century, is the oldest house in central Germany. With its narrow windows and uneven floors, it has been beautifully restored as a museum (*Open* Fri–Wed).

The castle, built between the 16th and 17th centuries, also houses a museum (*Open* Apr–Oct daily; Nov–Mar Sat–Thu). The Renaissance Town Hall, with a statue of Roland dating from 1426 symbolizing citizens' rights, overlooks a handsome pedestrianized square fringed by old inns, cafés and attractive shops.

OLD AND NEW ALLIES
In 1346 a group of six towns from the Oberlausitz (Bautzen, Görlitz, Lobau, Laubau, Kamenz and Zittau), with imperial permission, banded together. Their aim was to further the development of cloth-making and linen-weaving and to protect each other against attacks from robber knights and their followers. In the 1990s, following German reunification, the towns reconstituted this union as an aid to economic survival, an interesting example of history partly repeating itself.

The countryside surrounding Wittenberg

INFORMATION
Wittenberg: Schlossplatz 2, tel: 03491/49 86 10; www.wittenberg.de

► Wittenberg

132B2

'Lutherstadt' Wittenberg is forever associated with Martin Luther, the great Protestant reformer, and his criticism of contemporary clergy and particularly of the sale of indulgences or pardons. As was then customary, in 1517 his 95 theses were nailed up on the town's church door. His ideas gained further prominence at Wittenberg's university, which was founded in 1502, then spread throughout the whole of Europe. Luther's house (Lutherhaus or Lutherhalle) is a museum with the world's largest collection of exhibited material devoted to the Reformation

The Stadtkirche of St. Mary in Wittenberg, where Martin Luther often preached

(*Open* Apr–Oct daily; Nov–Mar Tue–Sun). On the site of Luther's Oak, in front of which a Papal Bull condemning him was burned, a (later) oak tree stands. Local contemporaries of Luther included court painter Lucas Cranach the Elder and theologian Philipp Melanchthon, whose 16th-century home is also a museum (*Open* Apr–Oct daily; Nov–Mar Tue–Sun).

▶ Zittau   *132C1*

Zittau lies in the extreme southeast of Germany in the area known as Dreiländereck, where lakes and heather predominate. The town dates from the 13th century, when it became an important trade base under the protection of the Bohemian kings.

The town's former fortifications have now been replaced with green spaces and a flower clock, which in winter is decorated with moss, pine cones and branches instead of flowering plants. It has a market square with a Mars fountain dating from 1585 and an Italian-style town hall. The Marstall (stables) of 1511 dominates the Salzmarkt and the Dornsprachhaus is a lovely Renaissance building. The church of St. Petri and St. Pauli was originally an old Franciscan monastery church; the buildings now house the town's museum.

The 12km (7.5-mile) narrow-gauge steam railway was opened in 1890 to the spa towns of Oybin and Jonsdorf. It passes through beautiful rocky landscape in the Zittau Mountains, a paradise for walkers and climbers. Oybin has a medieval castle, churches and monastery ruins. Jonsdorf is a former weavers' village, and has fine examples of the Oberlausitz Umbindehaus, a characteristic style of vernacular architecture with wooden arches over the house front to support the weight of looms.

THE SACRED CLOTH
The citizens of Zittau were horrified to find that a centuries-old sacred cloth from their local church was being used by soldiers in a nearby Red Army garrison as a tent. The cloth, a *Fastentuch*, hung before the altar at Lent, had been missing for more that 200 years. Before the town could recover the cloth from the Red Army it disappeared again and was given up for lost when the Soviet Union disintegrated and pulled its troops out of East Germany. The cloth resurfaced in Switzerland and is now back in Zittau's Kreuz-kirche (Church of the Holy Cross), where it can be viewed daily from May to October. The cloth, dating from 1472, measures 8m by 7m (26ft by 22ft) and is decorated with 90 paintings of biblical scenes.

INFORMATION
Zittau: Rathaus, Markt 1, tel: 03583/75 21 37; www.zittau.de

Oppenheim Darmstadt Meßpelbrunn Eschau A3 Würzburg Dettelbach
A63 Höchst Zwingenberg Main Marktbreit
Meisenheim Lorsch Bensheim Michelstadt Miltenberg Wertheim Ochsenfurt
A61 Worms Heppenheim Erbach Amorbach Röttingen
Frankenthal A67 Weinheim Bad Mergentheim Creglingen
A6 MANNHEIM Eberbach Weikersheim Rothenburg
Kaiserslautern Ludwigshafen Heidelberg Zwingenberg A81 ob der Tauber
Deidesheim Schwetzingen Neckar Jagsthausen Jagst
Pfälzer Wald Speyer Mosbach Neudenau Langenburg
673m Kalmit Guttenberg Hohenloher Ebene
A62 A65 Landau Bad Wimpfen Öhringen A6
A8 A6 Neckarsulm
Pirmasens A5 Waldenburg Schwäbisch Hall
Neudorf Bruchsal Heilbronn Schloss Vellberg
Bad Bergzabern Comburg
Besigheim Marbach Murrhardt Ellwangen
Karlsruhe Maulbronn Kocher
A8 Ludwigsburg Aalen
Rastatt Pforzheim Schorndorf Schwäbisch Gmünd
Schloss STUTTGART Hohenstaufen
670m Solitude Esslingen Göppingen
Baden-Baden Merkur Hirsau Sindelfingen
1002m Böblingen Holzmaden Heidenheim
Badener Höhe Bebenhausen A8 Geislingen
Kehl 1163m Wildberg Tübingen Reutlingen Günzburg
Hornisgrinde Nagold Bad Urach
Baiersbronn Rottenburg Alb Blaubeuren Ulm
Offenburg Freudenstadt Haigerloch Marchtal Vöhringen
Gengenbach Alpirsbach Hohenzollern Donau Laupheim A7
A5 Wolfach A81 Schwäbische Zwiefalten
Ettenheim Schiltach Rottweil Sigmaringen Biberach
Schramberg an der Riss
Waldkirch Triberg 567m 1015m Schwenningen Steinhausen Memmingen
Burkheim Kaiserstuhl Stöcklewald Bad Schussenried
1242m Furtwangen Tuttlingen Messkirch Bad
Breisach Kandel Donaueschingen Bad Waldsee Würzach
Freiburg Titisee Überlingen Salem A96
1284m 1493m Engen Weingarten
Schauinsland Feldberg Wutach Mainau Birnau Ravensburg
1414m Häusern Singen Meersburg Argen
Belchen Reichenau A96 Isny
Müllheim Todtmoos Konstanz Friedrichshafen Oberstaufen
Rötteln Waldshut Bodensee Lindau
Lörrach
Bad Säckingen CH Rhein 0 20 40 60 km
A 0 10 B 20 30 miles C

172 F

The southwest is an appealing region for gentle rural exploration, with plenty of peace and quiet, charming countryside, deep forests, wooden farmhouses and smart spas. This is good walking country and sports facilities are plentiful. A wide range of accommodation is available, offering higher standards than in other regions.

The region incorporates **Baden-Württemberg**, one of the youngest of the German *Länder* (States); it was formed only in 1952 and still has two distinct sides to its character.

The people of Baden, predominantly Catholic, are known for their friendly and relaxed dispositions, as opposed to their neighbours in Württemberg (or Swabia), who take life more seriously and are reputed to be careful how and when they spend their money. Other Germans call them *Häuslebauer* (house builders), believing them to spend most of their time and money on bourgeois home-tied pursuits.

The southwest is dominated by several upland masses, principally the **Schwarzwald** (Black Forest), which rises to over 1,200m (3,937ft). The **Danube** rises in the Schwarzwald and follows a course east, forming a deep gorge as it approaches the **Schwäbische Alb** (Swabian Jura), a less elevated and far less well-known area of limestone ridges with cliff-top castles, half-timbered villages and many gushing waterfalls.

The Rhine defines the western border with France. Germany's largest lake, the **Bodensee**, shared with Austria and Switzerland (and also known by its other name, Lake Constance), is like an inland sea and has a string of pretty resorts on its shores.

Another river, the **Neckar**, is Swabia's main waterway. Flowing through a country of vineyards and fruit trees in its upper course, and through wooded valleys in its lower course, it passes through the lovely university towns of **Tübingen** and **Heidelberg**.

More commercial and industrial places, such as **Stuttgart**, **Mannheim** and **Karlsruhe**, constitute the modern face of Baden-Württemberg. The region's attractions are well known—Heidelberg and the main resorts of the Black Forest and Bodensee are the principal draws.

▶▶Baden-Baden   *172A3*

Stylish in its woodland setting on the edge of the Upper Rhine plain, Baden-Baden draws visitors from all over the world to its renowned spa and its casino, Germany's oldest. Its position in the lush valley of the River Oos, on the western slopes of the northern part of the Black Forest, adds much to its attraction. Though its heyday may be over, it remains a handsome place, with elegant 19th-century hotels, a Jugendstil (art-nouveau) Trinkhalle (pump room) where you can test the saline waters, a white neo-classical **Kurhaus▶** (spa building) and a long park that looks as expensively groomed as most of the visitors.

Baden-Baden's mild climate makes it a pleasant place to visit all year round, but it is best known for its thermal springs, among Europe's hottest, gushing out at 69°C (156°F). The Roman emperor Caracalla bathed here in AD213; you can view remains of the baths through a glass plate window in the basement of the 19th-century Friedrichsbad.

Spectacular views from above Baden-Baden

Baden-Baden, still a fashionable and popular spa town

INFORMATION
Baden-Baden: Trinkhalle,
Kaiserallee, tel:
07221/27 52 00;
www.baden-baden.de

174

The Lichtentaler Allee, Baden-Baden's lovely pedestrian *corso*, runs from the Kurgarten, site of both the Trinkhalle and the Kurhaus, to the old Cistercian monastery at Lichtental, passing the Theatre, the International Club, the Kunsthalle (art gallery) and the new contemporary art gallery, Museum Frieder Burda (*Open* Tue–Sun).

Baden-Baden suffered a calamitous fire in 1689, which destroyed most of the old town. The Stiftskirche fortunately survived. Inside is the tomb of Margrave Ludwig Wilhelm and a huge sandstone crucifix, a masterpiece carved in 1467 by Nikolaus von Leyden. The Neues Schloss was built in the 19th century in a combination of Renaissance and baroque styles on medieval foundations. The castle can't be visited, but there are views over Baden-Baden and the Black Forest from the grounds. The decorative former railway station has been transformed into a foyer for its 2,500-seat Festspielhaus (concert hall) recently built at its back.

Excursion Rastatt, north of Baden-Baden, was rebuilt on uniform lines in the 18th century by Margrave Ludwig Wilhelm of Baden (nicknamed Louis the Turk because of his role in the anti-Turkish wars). Its massive red sandstone Schloss is Germany's first example of a palace in the style of Louis XIV's Versailles. It houses the national Army Museum (with many of Ludwig Wilhelm's war trophies) and the Museum of Liberation with displays on the evolution of German Liberalism. *Open* Tue–Sun in summer; Fri–Sun in winter. FreiheitsMuseum: Tue–Sun) Ludwig's widow, Sibylla, was responsible for the Schloss Favorite, 5km (3 miles) outside town.

'BEAUTIFUL CASINO'
The casino at Baden-Baden can accommodate 2,500 gamblers at 35 tables. According to Marlene Dietrich, 'The most beautiful casino in the world is at Baden-Baden—and I have seen them all'. It was built in 1853 and in the decades that followed its portals welcomed many royal guests, including Kaiser Wilhelm I. The Russian novelist Dostoyevsky lost a fortune on its gaming tables.

▶ **The Bergstrasse (Mountain Road)** *172B4*
This long-established route (the Strata Montana of the Romans and today's B3) runs through the orchards at the foot of the forested Odenwald hills for 58km (36 miles).

The fruit trees and almonds between **Darmstadt** and **Heidelberg** come into blossom earlier than anywhere else in Germany, and are spectacular in late March/mid-April, while a string of picturesque little towns offers a welcome at all seasons.

South of Darmstadt is the half-timbered town of **Zwingenberg**, which is the oldest place along the route, with steep alleyways and a pretty little market square overlooked by the 13th-century church. Prettier still are the narrow streets of **Bensheim**, lined with half-timbered houses and leading to shady cobbled squares. For a magnificent view of the Rhine valley and the Odenwald forest, climb to the 13th-century **Schloss Auerbach**, one of several castles of this region captured by French armies in 17th century wars. Just east of Bensheim and Schloss Auerbach is the extraordinary **Felsenmeer (Stone Sea)**, a jumble of thousands of huge granite blocks, the site of a Roman quarry and weathered by time into an eerie landscape.

Fürstenlager Park was laid out in the 18th century with pavilions and garden monuments in the style of the time. There is a trail laid out among the exotic trees that flourish in the mild climate.

Heppenheim is dominated by the ruins of Schloss Starkenberg. Within the ruins is an observatory and a youth hostel. The place has the cheerful air of a focus of wine production, with fine timber-framed buildings in the market square, including an ancient apothecary's shop. The square is overlooked by the massive neo-Gothic church, the 'Cathedral of the Bergstrasse'.

Weinheim has picturesque streets, an old tanners' quarter and a marketplace. The town's attractive Schlosspark (castle park) has many rare trees and nearby, up in the valley of the Weschnitz, is the castle of Wachenburg, with a fine panorama towards Mannheim and the Rhine.

PIONEERING CASINO
Baden-Baden has long been a playground for the rich and famous—Brahms, Dostoevsky and Queen Victoria were among its many visitors. Following the construction of the Kurhaus in the 1820s, the French impresario Jacques Benazet opened a casino, the first in Germany. The famous Iffezheim races began here in 1858, enhancing the town's prestige. The Lichtentaler Allee is the most glamourous thoroughfare, scene of many historic events.

ANCIENT TORHALLE
A great Benedictine abbey once stood at Lorsch. What remains is the delightful little arched and brickwork-decorated markethall-like structure known as the Torhalle, Germany's oldest intact building, dating from the late 8th century and probably erected as a triumphal gateway for the Emperor Charlemagne.

175

Windeck Castle, on the Bergstrasse, Weinheim

INFORMATION
www.lake-constance.com

LAKE WINE
Seewein (lake wine) is a good reason for visiting the Bodensee. On the shores of the lake, Meersburg holds a wine festival every September, a very good introduction to the region's wines.

▶▶ **Bodensee (Lake Constance)**   172C1

Fed by the Rhine and shared with Austria and Switzerland, the Bodensee is the second largest (after Lake Geneva) of the great Alpine lakes. Sometimes called the 'Swabian Ocean' for its sheer size, roughly 65 by 12km (40 by 7.5 miles), it has the character of an inland sea, which, together with the distant backdrop of the Alps and a mild climate that allows exotic vegetation to thrive, has made it a popular place for German visitors, who flock to the chain of resorts along the north shore.

The historic town of **Konstanz▶** stands at the end of a peninsula astride the channel linking the main body of the lake—the Obersee—to the smaller Untersee, with its varied shoreline. The lakeside at Konstanz is attractive enough, with steamers tied up in the harbour, a verdant park (the Stadtgarten), old defensive towers and the venerable warehouse of 1388 known as the Konzil. In summer the traffic-free Altstadt (old town) has a bustling, almost Mediterranean atmosphere; there is a cathedral (the Münster) and a fine Renaissance Rathaus. The Rosgarten Museum, the former guildhall of the butchers (*Open* Tue–Sun), exhibits finds dating back to prehistoric times. Now an elegant lakeside hotel, the town's 13th-century Dominican monastery was also the birthplace of Graf Zeppelin, the airship pioneer.

Mainau▶, reached by road and footbridge or by lake steamer, is a paradise island of tropical plants with a fairy-tale castle. Laid out by Grand Duke Friedrich I of Baden in the mid-19th century, it is now owned by the flamboyant Swedish count Bernadotte.

Reichenau Island▶▶ is accessible along its causeway or by boat. Less crowded than Mainau, it is of exceptional interest because of its three Romanesque churches, testimony to an important monastic past. Look particularly for the 10th-century frescoes at Oberzell church. Mittelzell abbey dates from the 10th century and has Gothic reliquaries in its treasury. **Singen**, farther west, is dominated by Hohentwiel, the biggest castle ruin in Germany (*Open* daily). The castle was razed by the French in 1801, but the ruins still offer a terrific panorama of lake and Alps.

One-thousand-year-old **Meersburg▶**, easily reached by car ferry from Konstanz, is perhaps the prettiest place

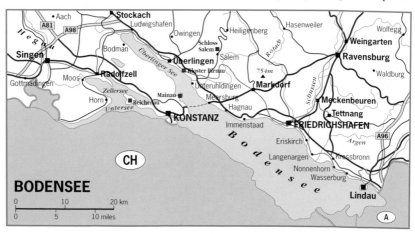

BODENSEE

0   10   20 km
0   5   10 miles

along the lake, with a formidable feudal castle, the Altes Schloss (*Open* daily), and a baroque palace, the Neues Schloss (*Open* Apr–Oct daily). Both castle and palace were built for the bishops of Konstanz, who fled here when that town turned Protestant. The cliff-like shoreline between the Oberstadt (upper town), with its delightful Marktplatz (market square) and the Unterstadt (lower town), with its busy lakeside promenade, provides excellent growing conditions for the vines that have made Meersburg the focus of the Bodensee wine trade.

North of Meersburg the shore of the Überlingersee, a northwest-reaching arm of the Bodensee, continues steep and rugged in places. At **Unteruhldingen** a prehistoric lake dwellers' village has been imaginatively reconstructed as Pfahlbaumuseum (*Open* Apr–Oct daily; Mar and Nov weekends only). A short distance inland lies Schloss Salem, its Gothic church complemented by baroque abbey buildings. Since 1922 this has been

Konstanz, the main town on the Bodensee (Lake Constance), is popular with visitors and has not been spoiled by high-rise construction

A street in Freiburg leading to the 13th-century Swabian gate, part of the old ramparts (opposite)

Germany's most famous boarding school. One of the most appealing of all Germany's baroque buildings, the pilgrimage church at **Birnau▶** stands in a romantic setting among the vineyards overlooking the lake. Inside you can see a famous little figurine, a honey-stealing cherub licking his fingers.

Medieval **Überlingen**, clinging to its steep lakeside site, retains most of its fortifications and is dominated by its richly furnished, five-aisled late Gothic Münster.

From Meersburg to Lindau Southeast of Immenstaad the lakeside becomes flatter and the main points of interest are the lakeside settlements such as **Friedrichshafen**, where Zeppelin based his great airships; **Wasserburg** on its peninsula; and, above all, **Lindau▶**. Built on the lake's largest island and connected to the mainland by two bridges, this ancient city is the southernmost in Germany, priding itself on its mild climate, its spectacular setting against the backdrop of the Alps and its high reputation as a summer resort. The harbour entrance is guarded by the Lion of Bavaria and a lighthouse, the quayside by another lighthouse, the 13th-century Mangturm. Behind its traffic-free promenades, the Altstadt is full of interest, not least because of its blend of architectural styles, medieval painted houses, 15th-century Rathaus, baroque Cavazzen House (with a local museum, *Open* Apr–Oct Tue–Sun, guided tours only) and Jugendstil train station.

178

Loved by yachtsmen, the big Bodensee is sometimes called 'the Swabian ocean'

▶ Donaueschingen   *172B1*
High up among the rich farmlands of the Baar plateau between the Black Forest and Swabian Jura, little Donaueschingen owes its name to its position at the source of the Danube, Europe's second largest river after the Volga. The river's starting point, 2,859km (1,776 miles) from the Black Sea, is marked by the monumental fountain standing in Donaueschingen's Schlosspark (castle park), though the name Danube really only applies downstream from the confluence of the Breg and Brigach, just outside the town. From 1723 Donaueschingen was the seat of the princes of Fürstenberg. Their Schloss (*Open* Easter–Sep daily) was rebuilt twice, first in 1772 and again in 1893. It houses a sumptuous collection of porcelain, gold and silver plate, as well as Brussels tapestries. The Fürstenberg princes' rich art collections can be viewed in the Karlsbau (*Open* Apr–Nov Tue–Sun). They include paintings by both Cranachs, as well as by a number of 15th- and 16th-century Swabian masters.

MUSIC FESTIVAL
Apart from brewing, Donaueschingen prides itself on its excellent annual music festival, the *Donaueschinger Musiktage*. It is held each year in October and features works by contemporary composers.

▶▶ Freiburg (Breisgau)   172A1

Known as the capital of the Black Forest, Freiburg has a lovely setting surrounded by green hills and vineyards, and a sunny climate. This is a city where foreigners love to live. It is famous for its cathedral, and for many Germans it also conjures up images of youth: Some 30,000 students are housed here, giving the town an unusually lively atmosphere all year round. The Albert Ludwig University was founded in 1457; the College of Education, State Music College, and seven research institutes are more recent additions.

What to see A walk through the squares and arcaded streets of the old town is delightful, but the real glory of Freiburg is its red sandstone **Münster**▶▶, with a soaring tower that dominates the city. Medieval and baroque-style houses (many of them post-war reconstructions) fringe the cathedral square.

Begun as a ducal burial place by Bertold V of Zähringen, whose family founded the city between 1118 and 1120, the Münster passed into the hands of the citizenry after the last of the Zähringens died in 1218. To the late Romanesque east end were added the Gothic nave and the incomparable west tower. The desire of rich families for their own burial chapels determined the form of the late Gothic choir, begun in 1354. Its consecration in 1513 marked the completion of the minster. Since 1827 the Münster has been the seat of an archbishop. The rich interior bears witness to the generosity and civic pride of local families: stained-glass windows with coats of arms of patricians and guilds; the magnificent high altar triptych by Hans Baldung Grien; and the splendid furnishings of the choir chapels with their 16th-century windows

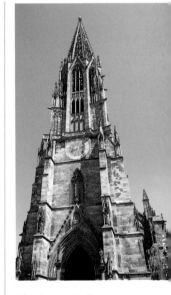

The glorious Freiburg Munster

INFORMATION
Freiburg: Rotteckring 14, tel: 0761/3 88 18 80; www.freiburg.de

and fine altars and monuments. The cathedral tower, with its splendid traceried spire, has been described as the most beautiful tower in Christendom (you can climb the tower).

Augustinermuseum▶ This owes its name to the former monastery of the Augustinian Hermits, going back to about 1300. Since 1923 the church and cloisters of the monastery buildings have housed the attractively displayed collections of the museum, which specializes in Upper Rhenish art from the Middle Ages to the baroque. Besides the medieval art treasures, there is a special section for southwest German baroque sculpture and a rich collection of objets d'art.

The Augustinermuseum also has a section holding a collection of clocks, local costumes and folk art of the Black Forest. In the 19th century, artists became aware of the beauty of the Freiburg area and the Black Forest, and some of their canvases can be seen in the section devoted to Baden painters (*Open* Tue–Sun).

Remnants of the medieval town walls can still be seen south of the Augustinermuseum, while the old fishermen's quarter, known as the Insel (Island), has sensitively restored old buildings.

Other sights The Münsterplatz (cathedral square) is graced by the Gothic/Renaissance Kaufhaus (merchants' hall), with an arcaded façade that contains statues of Habsburg rulers; the baroque Erzbischöfliches Palais (Archbishop's Palace); the 18th-century Wenzingerhaus; and the restored 15th-century Kornhaus (the original was destroyed during World War II).

A short distance away is Rathausplatz (town hall square), pleasantly shaded by chestnut trees. It contains the Neues Rathaus (the present town hall), once the university's main building.

Excursions
Some worthwhile side trips can be made to nearby places, such as the fortified town of **Breisach**, which towers immediately above the Rhine and the French frontier. Other interesting places to visit are the **Kaiserstuhl**, a volcanic, vine-clad hill standing isolated in the plain, and the wine town of **Burkheim**—all three are less than 24km (15 miles) west of Freiburg.

▶▶ Haigerloch   172B2
This is one of southwestern Germany's most delightful small towns, a perfect synthesis of buildings and landscape at a point where the River Eyach has carved a deep double loop in the limestone of the Swabian Jura. The best panoramas of the town in its setting are seen from the Kapf viewpoint, from the rococo St. Anne's pilgrimage church, and from the tower known as the Römerturm. The Schloss Haigerloch, now a privately owned hotel, dominates the place; its Gothic church has a resplendent rococo interior.

A curiosity in this remote place is the Atomkellermuseum, where scientists tinkered (unsuccessfully) with a nuclear reactor near the end of World War II (*Open* May–Sep daily; Mar–Apr, Oct–Nov Sat–Sun).

WINE FESTIVALS
A showcase for Baden wines, the Freiburger Weintage (Freiburg Wine Festival) is held in Münsterplatz in July. Another city celebration with wine associations is the Fastnet (carnival) in February, when masks traditionally ward off evil spirits from the vines.

SCHNAPPS
A sixth of all Germany's distilleries are in the Freiburg region, most of them on Black Forest farms. An ancient church edict gave Black Forest farmers the right to distil their own schnapps, and the ruling still applies. Farms with distillery rights are allowed to produce and sell locally 300 litres (66 gallons) a year. If a distillery falls into disuse it cannot be revived and no further concessions are given. The best Black Forest schnapps are made from cherries (the famous Kirsch), but you can also find excellent ones produced from damsons (Pflümli) and Williams pears (Williams).

►►► Heidelberg *172B4*

For people the world over, friendly Heidelberg is the very image of romantic Germany. The River Neckar flows through its deep wooded valley past ancient towers and bridges; the red sandstone castle ruin rises majestically over the roofs of the old town. This, and the sheer exuberance of the life led by the students of Germany's oldest and most tradition-bound university (immortalized in Sigmund Romberg's operetta *The Student Prince*), all combine to make the place quite irresistible to countless visitors. A big draw are the boisterous student pubs of the old town, former haunts of the exclusive *Verbindungen* (fraternities). Here giant mugs of beer, shaped like a boot or horn, are passed around the tables. There is also a vigorous cultural life, with more than 10 museums, several theatres and an annual theatre festival in August.

There are good views of Heidelberg from the graceful Alte Brücke (old bridge) spanning the fast-flowing waters. The bridge's gateway, its twin towers topped by spiky helmets, has long been one of the city's landmarks. It has been a popular inspiration for poets and painters, among them the English artist J. M. W. Turner, who came in 1836 and left many oils and watercolours of the city in its changing moods. If time permits, there are breathtaking views from the **Philosophenweg**► above the quayside, the 'philosophers' path' trod by many wishing to contemplate the incomparable panorama to the south.

SCIENTIFIC POWERS
Despite the romantic image of the city, Heidelberg is a major exporter of scientific know-how to countries throughout the world. Today 'Made in Heidelberg' is proof of excellent quality for a number of famous products. Research institutes include the European Molecular Biology Laboratory, the German Cancer Research Centre and some of the Max Planck Institutes.

INFORMATION
Heidelberg: Willy-Brandt Platz 1, tel: 06221/1 94 33;
www.cvb-heidelberg.de

181

Heidelberg's great 17th-century castle above the River Neckar

GIANT WINE VAT

The Grosses Fass (great vat) in the Fassbau in Heidelberg's castle is a wine barrel, with a capacity of 2,200 hectolitres (48,400 gallons), built in the 18th century to hold the tithe of Palatinate wines. On top of it is a platform that is used as a dance floor.
'Fill me the beaker!
Now, Rhine and Nekkar,
Health to ye both, ye
noble streams!
Yours is a power,
To bring the hour
High above Wisdom's
heavy dreams'. – Walter Savage Landor, 'Gardens at Heidelberg'.

STUDENT DUELS

A generation or two ago, the caricature of a German male would show a reddened, almost bald head with perhaps a few bristles adorning the roll of fat overlapping the collar, a monocle framing a glaring eye, and a scar or two adorning a cheek. Worn with pride, and known as a *Schmiss*, such a facial scar would have been acquired in the course of the fencing bouts that were a feature of upper-class student life in the more tradition-bound universities. The contestants, wearing goggles and padding to protect their vital parts, would face each other in the company of their supporters and attendant medics. The liberal-minded students of the post-war generation were eager to put such behaviour, with all its associations of fanaticism and militarism, behind them. But the tradition persisted among certain student associations and has come into prominence again.

The Schloss►►► High above the city's alleyways are the majestic ruins of the castle (guided tours daily), graced with fine terraced gardens, the creation of Friedrich V between 1616 and 1619. The princes of Pfalz (the Palatinate) lived here for 500 years, and included Friedrich V, who married the English princess Elizabeth Stuart, daughter of James I. It was for her that he built the Englischer Bau (English Building), near the Dicker Turm (Fat Tower), and the Elisabethentor (Elizabeth Gate), in the form of a classical triumphal arch.

It was as a 17-year-old bride that Elizabeth came to the court over which she presided for five years before she was forced to flee to Prague when Friedrich V, who was a Protestant, failed in an attempt to oust the Catholic Habsburgs from their supreme position. He was eventually stripped of his titles, and his machinations contributed to the outbreak of the Thirty Years' War. Later, the Schloss, and the city itself, suffered badly when Louis XIV attacked the Palatinate, to which he laid claim, in 1689 (four years later, a disastrous fire destroyed the old town). The castle fabric was much restored in the 19th century by Count de Graimberg, but numerous earlier features survive.

The Well House contains Roman pillars brought from Charlemagne's palace at Ingelheim. Look, too, for the 16th-century Dicker Turm and the Glockenturm (bell tower), built for defence but with six subsequent residential floors added. The Deutsches Apotheken-Museum (German apothecary museum; *Open* daily) within the castle complex provides a fascinating look into baroque and rococo workshops of German pharmacists from the early 17th century.

The University Heidelberg's is the oldest university in Germany, founded by Elector Ruprecht I von der Pfalz in 1386. It was badly neglected during the 18th century, but in 1803 Grand Duke Karl Friedrich declared it the first state university of Baden. One part of Universitätsplatz, dating back to the 18th century, is devoted to the Alte Universität (old university) while the rest of the square is taken up by university buildings of the 1930s.

The Studentenkarzer (students' jail; *Open* Apr–Oct Mon–Sun, Nov–Mar Tue–Sat), in use from 1778 to 1914, was built for unruly students, whose graffiti are still in evidence. In the library (*Open* Mon–Sat), the **Codex Manesse►**, a 14th-century collection of Middle High German poetry, is illuminated with 137 exquisite miniatures. Here, too, is *Des Knaben Wunderhorn* (*The Boy's Magic Horn*), a collection of folk poetry that inspired the German Romantic poets and composer Gustav Mahler.

Excursion

About 13km (8 miles) west, **Schwetzingen** is known for its **Schlossgarten►**, a wonderfully fanciful 18th-century dreamland of romantic follies and eye-catching sites. Beyond the formal French garden lie a Temple of Apollo, a statue of Pan playing the flute in a grotto, mock ruins, tricks of perspective and more. Mozart conducted an orchestral concert of his own works in the theatre here. (Garden *open* daily; castle *open* Apr–Oct Tue–Sun; Nov–Mar Fri–Sun.)

►► Karlsruhe   *172B3*

Karlsruhe is the youngest of German cities. In 1715, tired of living in a medieval castle, in nearby Durlach, that had seen better days, Margrave Karl Wilhelm of Baden Durlach began building a new residence deep in the hunting forests of the Rhine plain. A city soon grew up, laid out in the shape of a fan, with the palace at its heart. This unusual pattern persists today, enhanced by the sober civic buildings in neo-classical style by Friedrich Weinbrenner. On his Marktplatz stands the famous pyramid where the town's founder is buried.

What to see Standing neatly in its formal gardens facing the middle of the city, the Schloss is now the home of the **Badisches Landesmuseum►** (*Open* Tue–Sun), where the rich and beautifully presented collections include the unique Türkenbeute, the booty won by Louis the Turk (see page 174) from his Ottoman opponents. Nearby are the excellent galleries of the **Kunsthalle►** (superb old masters, including Grünewald's intensely moving *Crucifixion*, together with fine examples of German 19th-century painting) and the Orangery (*Open* Tue–Sun). The latter has works by the 19th-century German artist Hans Thoma, who died in Karlsruhe, as well as German and French Impressionists (Monet, Cézanne) and Cubist-inspired pictures by Delaunay and Léger.

Excursions
There are superb views of the surrounding area from the **Turmberg**, high above the margrave's old castle at Durlach. Karlsruhe's sleek tramway system will whisk you out beyond the city to delightful half-timbered **Ettlingen**, also with a Schloss, or even farther into the Black Forest itself, to the upland resort of **Bad Herrenalb**.

HERTZ AND BENZ
Students of Karlsruhe's School of Technology (founded in 1825) have included such illustrious names as Heinrich Hertz, the discoverer of electromagnetic waves; Carl Benz, inventor of the car; and Karl von Drais, said to have invented the bicycle.

183

CONSTITUTIONAL COURT
Karlsruhe is no longer the capital of Baden, but its importance was confirmed by the siting here of Germany's Federal Constitutional Court, the country's supreme judicial authority.

The Schloss (ducal palace) in Karlsruhe built by the Margrave Karl Wilhelm

Intellectuals enjoy high status in Germany, and many universities boast hundreds of years of tradition. Before World War II they tended to be élitist, conservative bastions—many German students and professors supported Hitler's rise to power.

Students performing for passersby in Tübingen, an ancient university town with a lively cultural scene

184

The student movement and after Following the subdued period of the *Wirtschaftswunder* (economic miracle) in the 1950s, a generation of post-war German youth began questioning the establishment—and the university system—in the student movement that exploded in 1968. Student self-governing committees were formed and curricula opened to all qualified high-school graduates. Universities became vastly overcrowded, and the quality of teaching fell. In addition, students extend their studies well into their 30s, supported by generous government grants, although some universities are showing signs of growing impatience with their 'middle-aged undergraduates'. Munich University refused to admit 9,000 of them to the 1999 summer semester. Of the University's postgraduates studying for doctorates in 1999, 8,000 had exceeded the permitted three-year time limit for submitting their final theses.

In Germany students rarely live on campus as they do in Britain or the United States, although they eat together in a student *Mensa*, or cafeteria. Attendance is not compulsory, and many students are accused of not taking their studies very seriously. However, this may be changing—proposals for more rigorous, 'élite' universities are gaining ground, and a new generation of competitive Germans has appeared.

STASI SUSPECT
Involvement by the West since unification has had some negative consequences. For example, in Berlin, Western authorities dismissed the popular head of Humboldt University, the theologian Heinrich Fink, because of suspicions of secret police (Stasi) contacts under the Communist regime. This unleashed a storm of student protest, particularly since it was suspected that many Western academics were after positions in the better-known universities of East Germany.

In the East Under the Communists, East German universities established their own traditions, with student admissions based on political criteria. The peaceful revolution in 1989 threw the universities into chaos, with large-scale firings of professors and restructuring of departments according to Western standards.

▶ Mannheim 172B4

The second-largest river port in Europe and an important industrial base, Mannheim is at the meeting point of the Rhine and the Neckar. Like Karlsruhe, it is an 18th-century planned town focused on its Schloss, a huge edifice that is now the seat of Mannheim's university. (Guided tours of the Schloss, Tue–Sat). Laid out on a grid pattern, the streets define 144 city blocks, each of which is designated by a letter and a number, a logical system without parallel in Germany.

Mannheim is proud of its former eminence in the world of music and theatre, but little of its original 18th-century architectural elegance survives. The most striking part of the town is the Jugendstil Friedrichsplatz, laid out around a huge water tower. Here is the **Kunsthalle▶** (*Open* Tue–Sun), with one of Germany's leading displays of 19th- and 20th-century art. In the Zeughaus (arsenal) is the Reiss EngelhornMuseum (*Open* Tue–Sun), where the local collections evoke the look of the city before its industrialization.

INFORMATION
Mannheim: Willi-Brandt-Platz 3, tel: 0621/10 10 11; www.mannheim.de

FRENCH ART
Mannheim's Städtische Kunsthalle has an excellent collection of 19th-century French art, including Manet's *Execution of the Emperor Maximilian of Mexico*, a work exemplifying the artist's realism and the influence of Spanish painting on his style.

▶ Maulbronn 172B3

Maulbronn has one of the earliest Cistercian monasteries (founded in 1147) to survive, a superb and almost untouched example (*Open* Mar–Oct daily; Nov–Feb Tue–Sun). As the locals tell it, a group of monks stopped by here to let their mules drink (the name originally meant 'mule well'), and they stayed on forever. This story is depicted in sketches for a fresco on a wall of the Brunnenkapelle (well chapel)—Romanesque with later Gothic additions. You can also see the cloisters with refectory and chapterhouse, early 15th-century chapels and a crucifix of 1473.

185

INFORMATION
Maulbronn: Klosterhof 31, tel: 07043/10 30; www.maulbronn.de

▶▶ Neckartal (Neckar Valley) and Odenwald 172B4

The Neckar rises in the Black Forest and runs for 400km (248 miles) before entering the Rhine at Mannheim. Downstream from **Bad Wimpfen** it flows through charming countryside of orchards and vineyards before cutting

The lovely Neckar River flows past numerous old castles and fortified medieval towns

Picturesque Bad Wimpfen (right) is not a spa town, but gets its name from the big local saltworks. Odenwald natural park (below) is gently pastoral in some parts, forested in others

SIEGFRIED'S SPRING
Siegfried, hero of the medieval German *Nibelungenlied* and immortalized in Wagner's music, was treacherously killed by the evil Hagen while drinking from a spring in the Odenwald. Several springs in the forest bear the name *Siegfriedquelle* (Siegfried Spring).

its way through the Odenwald uplands in a deep, narrow wooded valley. The best way of enjoying the Neckar's varied landscapes, attractive towns and castles is from a steamer (the river has been 'improved' for shipping as far as Stuttgart), but the road (the signposted touring route called the Burgenstrasse) and railway closely follow its winding course.

To the east of Heidelberg the road passes beneath the 658m (2,159ft) **Königstuhl** (King's Seat), crowned by a TV tower offering a panorama of the Neckar Valley and the Rhine Plain beyond. Equally dramatic views can be enjoyed from the castle ruins of **Dilsberg**, while Neckarsteinach is overlooked by no fewer than four castles. **Eberbach** has several quaint inns and pubs, including the Wirtshaus Krabbenstein, as well as Germany's oldest bathhouse (the 13th-century Altes Badhaus). The little resort of **Zwingenberg** has a splendid medieval castle, and the Wolfsschlucht ravine provided the inspiration for Weber's opera *Der Freischütz*.

Just off the main valley, **Mosbach** is well known for its fine collection of half-timbered buildings. Back on the Neckar again, **Burg Hornberg** (*Open* daily) dates back to 1148, while **Burg Guttenberg** (*Open* Apr–Oct daily) is famous today for its birds of prey, which are flown in public demonstrations.

Bad Wimpfen▶▶ is the highlight of the valley. This fortified medieval town was once the imperial residence of the Hohenstaufens and retains an appealing mixture of half-timbering, narrow streets and stepped gables. The tall tower known as the Blauer Turm stands squarely among the steep-pitched roofs and gives the best views over town and river.

Odenwald Stretching northwards from the Neckar, this wooded upland of beech and spruce contrasts strongly with the fertile landscapes of the Bergstrasse, running along its western rim. It is traversed from west to east by the Nibelungenstrasse on its way from Worms to Würzburg, an attractive touring route that passes through delightful **Michelstadt**. The little town's Rathaus, with its stout oak columns and its corner turrets, is almost too picturesque to be true.

Michelstadt makes a good base for visiting several of the Odenwald's other attractions: **Eulbach Park**, which has ornamental hunting grounds dating from the 18th century; Renaissance **Schloss Fürstenau**, in an attractive countryside setting; and **Erbach**, also with a Schloss, plus a unique museum of ivory carving (*Open* Mar–Oct daily; Nov–Feb Tue–Sun). The nearby Einhardsbasilika—like the Torhalle at Lorsch, a striking example of Carolingian architecture—was completed in the year 827.

187

▶ **Ravensburg**   *172C1*

This old town thrived in the Middle Ages, with its position on a great trade route that connected northern Europe to Italy. Before the rise of the Fuggers of Augsburg, the Ravensburger Handelsgesellschaft was southern Germany's most important trading company.

Ravensburg grew up at the foot of the Veitsburg, the fortified hill where Henry the Lion was born. The town walls are mostly intact, with several gates and towers, including the Mehlsack (flour-sack tower), originally erected so the citizens could keep an eye on the Veitsburg. The Marienplatz is full of character, with another tall tower, the Blaserturm; a 15th-century Rathaus; and the Waaghaus, the focus of trading. Its hall once rang with the cries of foreign merchants promoting their wares, while weights and measures were checked on the main floor.

▶ **Rottweil**   *172B2*

Rottweil enjoys a dramatic setting on a spur overlooking a bend in the upper Neckar. Its streets are a delightful collection of fine old houses, mostly Renaissance and baroque, with such features as elaborate oriel windows and exuberant carving. A further contribution to the townscape is made by four Renaissance fountains, of which the Marktbrunnen is the most splendid. The town's churches include the Kapellenkirche, which has been baroquified inside but has a richly decorated Gothic tower, and the Heiligkreuz Minster, which has a *Crucifixion* above its high altar attributed to Veit Stoss. The Lorenzkapelle houses a fine array of medieval sculpture.

The local museum recalls the Roman presence here with a 2nd-century mosaic of Orpheus, and displays some of the weird and wonderful wooden masks worn at carnival time. *Fasnet* (carnival) spans six days; the climax is the *Narrensprung* (Fools' Dance) on the Monday before Shrove Tuesday and on Shrove Tuesday.

Ravensburg, once a bastion of the Guelph political dynasty (13th–17th centuries) is a fine old town of towers and painted gateways

SCHWÄBISCHE ALB

▶ Schwäbische Alb (Swabian Jura)   *172B2*

The Schwäbische Alb is a range of limestone hills on the east side of the Black Forest. They are about 55km (34 miles) wide and 150km (93 miles) long. The young River Danube flows through part of the region in a landscape of wooded limestone cliffs, crag-top castles and lush green meadows. The southwest part of the Schwäbische Alb has been designated the Naturpark Obere Donau (Upper Danube Nature Park).

The name of Hohenzollern is closely associated with this part of Germany, forged by the marriage of the Zollerns, originally Swabian overlords, to the Burgraves of Nuremberg. From the early 1700s, the family, as rulers of Brandenburg and Prussia, fought to establish a German empire and finally achieved this in 1871 under Wilhelm I after his victory over France in the Franco-Prussian War of 1870–71. In 1918, after defeat in World War I, Wilhelm II abdicated and went into exile in the Netherlands, but the family name and tradition continue.

In **Sigmaringen**, at the mouth of the Upper Danube gap, the Swabian Catholic branch of the family managed to hold on to its huge **Schloss (castle)** ▶, which today is the product of several periods, most prominently of 19th-century Romanticism. During the height of the tourist season there are vast crowds, but it is well worth the wait. For those with an avid interest in European royalty this is a treasure trove, and there is perhaps the largest collection of armour and weapons in Europe, with more than 3,000 items in one hoard. In the neo-Gothic hall a splendid collection of south German art of the 15th and 16th centuries includes works by the Master of Sigmaringen—actually two brothers, Hans and Jacob Strüb (*Open* Feb–Nov daily). The Johanniskirche, on the castle rock, is decorated with elaborate rococo stucco work and houses the shrine of St. Fidelio, who was a local martyr.

BEURON MONASTERY
The village of Beuron, west of Sigmaringen, clusters around its huge abbey. Founded by the Augustinians in the 9th century, Kloster Beuron now belongs to the Benedictines. It is celebrated for the monks' singing of the Gregorian chant (which can be heard by visitors at High Mass and vespers) and for the Nazarenes, an early 19th-century group of artists who came here and adopted an early Christian art style (later known as the Beuron School). Male visitors might find accommodation in the abbey.

Between Sigmaringen and Tuttlingen the Danube flows through a superb gorge dominated by crags and lofty castles, including Burg Wildenstein (now a youth hostel), giving a spectacular view of the river, and the Knopfmacherfelsen, a magnificent viewpoint from a chaos of cliffs.

In a valley at the edge of the Schwäbische Alb lies **Zwiefalten**. The great Münster here rivals its Bavarian counterparts in splendour. The abbey church is largely the work of the south German 18th-century architect J. M. Fischer. Its spacious interior is lavishly decorated in a whirl of white and gold, with stucco masquerading as marble; the sculptures and large figures on the altar, set between pink and white columns, are by J. J. Christian. Among the many caves hollowed out in the soft limestone of the Alb, the **Wimsener Höhle** is perhaps the finest. It can be entered by boat.

The church at **Obermachtal**, built in 1686, displays stucco decoration and is an early example of wall-pillar construction, where a wall of internal buttresses represents a refinement to the medieval approach of using external flying buttresses.

Burg Hohenzollern ▶, the original seat of the Hohenzollern family, presents a spectacular outline, sited on a peak 850m (2,789ft) above sea level near the town of

CHERRY SPIRIT
Dettingen in the Schwäbisch Alb is famous for its *Kirschgeist* (cherry spirit). Selected cherries are cropped to make this strong, clear pick-me-up, which is drunk from thimble-size glasses.

189

BROOM PUBS
Amid the vine-clad hills east of Stuttgart, you'll find delightful wine pubs in the cosy villages— Stetten and Kernen, Uhlbach with its wine museum, and Strumpfelbach with its tiny quaint Rathaus. One old tradition in this area is that of the *Besenwirtschaft* (broom pub): From November to March, many wine growers put a broom outside their houses to show that their new wine is ready, and they run an impromptu pub. You can sit among the locals in a friendly atmosphere, drinking the semifermented wine at below pub prices.

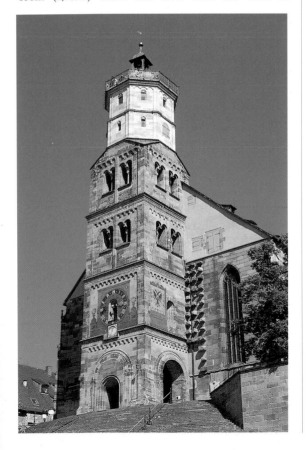

In Schwäbish Hall, St. Michael's church is noted for its high vaulted ceiling and fine 16th-century altarpiece

Southwest Germany

JURASSIC FOSSILS

At Holzmaden, near Kirchheim, the remarkable Hauff Urwelt-Museum displays fossilized skeletons of Ichthyosaurs 160 to 180 million years old. The Hauff family have long owned stone quarries here in the Swabian Jura, and they unearthed these crocodile-like Jurassic relics buried in the layered rock. Their museum has fossilized sea lilies looking like sea urchins, and a saurian mother with five embryos in her womb (*Open* Tue–Sun).

HOHENSTAUFEN

Schwäbisch Gmünd was once the possession of the Hohenstaufen family, which ruled the Holy Roman Empire from 1138–1254. When they fell from power, Schwäbisch Gmünd became a Free Imperial City.

INFORMATION

Schwäbisch Hall: Am Markt 9, tel: 0791/ 75 12 46; www.schwaebischhall.de

Hechingen. There are daily guided tours and the castle is open all year round. The castle was largely rebuilt in neo-Gothic style in the mid-19th century, but the 12th-century Catholic chapel of St. Michael, with beautiful stained glass, the oldest in Germany, remains. The Protestant chapel held the tomb of Frederick the Great until the mighty monarch's mortal remains were reburied at Potsdam in 1991 (see panel page 45). Many of his possessions, such as his uniforms and military decorations, can still be seen here.

Schloss Lichtenstein (*Open* Apr–Oct daily; Nov, Feb and Mar weekends only), a formidable 19th-century fortress, caps a craggy peak. Close by are several worthwhile caves, including the Nebelhöhle and the Bärenhöhle. Farther west, Rossberg (869m/2,851ft) gives a vast panorama of the region from its viewing tower.

Bad Urach is a pleasant small resort in a narrow valley and endowed with a pleasing half-timbered square. Out of town to the west, **Urach Waterfall** is found only a short walk away from the main road.

▶ Schwäbisch Gmünd   *172C3*

This attractive town set in good walking country, just north of the Schwäbische Alb, is famous for its jewellery and silver tableware. The 14th-century master builder Peter Parler was born here. One of the main works of the Parler family is the Heilig-Kreuz-Münster (Cathedral of the Holy Cross). The decorative exterior includes fine tracery, pinnacles and a depiction of the Last Judgement in the south portal. The interior conforms to the Cistercian hall plan. Notice the magnificent vaulting, the Tree of Jesse altar in the Baptistery and the carved choir stalls. The local museum (Johannisplatz 3) concentrates on late Gothic and baroque sculpture. The town maintains its craft traditions with its well-known college of gold- and silversmiths.

A short distance south of Schwäbisch Gmünd are the **Kaiserberge**, three wooded hills once topped by castles. One of these, Hohenstaufen, was the original seat of the great imperial family. There are wide-ranging views from ruined **Hohenrechberg**, where there is a baroque pilgrimage church.

▶▶ Schwäbisch Hall   *172C3*

One of the treasures of southwest Germany, this medieval town nestles in the heart of the Swabian forests, on the banks of the River Kocher, a tributary of the Neckar. Many of the houses and buildings are neatly arranged in tiers that overlook the ancient wooden bridges over the river. The site was already known for its saltwater springs in the 3rd century BC, and these encouraged a permanent Celtic settlement. During the Middle Ages, Schwäbisch Hall began to mint silver coins, first known as the *Häller* and then later renamed *Heller* (the name derives from *Hall*, meaning 'place of salt'). In the 13th century the town became a Free Imperial City.

Its charming, sloping **Marktplatz▶** is often reckoned to be among the most stunning in Germany. It is used for theatrical performances (Jun–Aug). The baroque **Rathaus▶**, built between 1730 and 1735, has a palatial appearance and is architecturally one of the most

important buildings of its time. It was rebuilt after war damage. The roof proudly displays a decorative clock and imperial eagle. The central part of the square is dominated by the Marktbrunnen, a 16th-century fountain adorned with statues of St. Michael with St. George and Samson. The old pillory forms part of the fountain's structure. The Pfarrkirche (St. Michael's) adjoins the Marktplatz; you can reach it by mounting a wide flight

Timbered buildings above the River Kocher in Schwäbisch Hall

HELLER UND PFENNIG

The word *Heller* in the German language means a very small monetary unit. If a German says he hasn't a *Heller*, he is flat broke. If he watches every *Heller und Pfennig*, then he is very careful with his money. This is a characteristic ascribed to the people of Schwäbisch Hall and other Württemberg towns. Significantly, Schwäbisch Hall—not exactly a financial metropolis—is the seat of one of the country's largest building societies.

of stairs. The church has hardly been touched since 1573, and besides the tombs in the chapels, there are interesting furnishings in the choir stalls, tabernacle and altars.

The Keckenburg, once an aristocratic mansion, houses the Hällisch-Fränkisches Museum (*Open* Tue–Sun), explaining the town's history.

About 30km (18 miles) north, the countryside between the Swabian Forest and the Tauber Valley is known as the Hohenloher Ebene, after the princely German family, the House of Hohenlohe; here the most common language is the Schwäbisch (Swabian) dialect, which even other Germans often find difficult to understand.

At **Jagsthausen** is the much restored Götzenburg castle (now a hotel), and the birthplace in 1480 of the knight Götz von Berlichingen—the Knight with the Iron Hand. Goethe wrote a drama about him, and every summer a drama festival including Goethe's play is held in the courtyard of the castle.

About 6km (4 miles) on from Jagsthausen is the Cistercian abbey of **Schöntal** in the Jagst Valley (guided tours daily). The church is famed for its 17th-century alabaster altarpieces.

At **Öhringen** the late Gothic Stiftskirche (dedicated to St. Peter and St. Paul), on the Marktplatz, contains tombs of members of the house of Hohenlohe. Note the monument to Philip of Hohenlohe, son-in-law of William the Silent, with detailed reliefs of battles from the Netherlands' War of Independence. Foremost among the furnishings is the high altar from around 1500.

The Schloss at **Neuenstein** (with an interesting collection of weapons) has been Hohenlohe family property since the 13th century and displays a variety of styles, including Renaissance, Romanesque and Gothic.

Waldenburg was once a fortified town, from which the princely family overlooked the plain and protected their empire against approaching enemies. Nowadays, the region offers a peaceful retreat, popular for quiet family holidays. Hiking, cycling and fishing are typical leisure-time pursuits.

SALT HEROES
Schwäbisch Hall's annual pentecostal festival recalls an occasion when salt workers saved the town's mill from fire. They were rewarded by the miller with a giant cake. The festival is thus called the *Kuchen-und Brunnenfest der Haller Salzsieder* (the Cake and Fountain Festival of the Salt Miners of Hall).

At Schwäbisch Hall in summer, a drama festival is held in the sloping Marktplatz

►►► Schwarzwald (Black Forest)   *172A2*

The highest land in southwest Germany, the Black Forest is a rewarding area for gentle exploration. Only in the gloom of its most inaccessible stands of spruce does the term 'black' seem appropriate, and by no means all of it is woodland. Picturesque wooden farmhouses and pleasantly unassuming villages nestling in green valleys are distinctive elements of the landscape; the terrain gets more open as you travel south into the orchards and farmlands of the Markgräfler Land. The western slopes are dominated by vineyards; the **Badische Weinstrasse** (Baden Wine Road) winds through the Black Forest foothills. Development across the region is mostly low-key and small-scale, with few big resorts.

Beneath all this is a thriving and well-organized tourist industry, mostly catering for the Germans themselves, who come for short breaks and nonmedical 'cures'. Newish hotels in traditional style are found on the edges of many villages and are scattered around the country areas. Sports facilities (particularly tennis and squash) have been developed to an impressive degree, even in

The Schwarzwald is noted for its special rural architecture, as well as traditional industries and local costumes, still occasionally worn for Sunday church and festivals

SCHWARZWALD

CH

| 0 | 10 | 20 | 30 km |
| 0 | | 10 | 20 miles |

A8

A5

A81

A65

A81

A5

6

5

4

3

2

1

A

B

C

F

Bad Bergzabern

Wörth

KARLSRUHE

Lauter

Rhein

Pfinztal

Bretten

LUDWIGSBURG

Ettlingen

Karlsbad

Malsch

Neuenbürg

PFORZHEIM

Leonberg

Pfarrkirche

STUTTGART

Schloss Solitude

Rastatt

Murg

Favorite

Gaggenau

Gernsbach

BADEN-BADEN

Bad Herrenalb

Calmbach

Wildbad

Bad Liebenzell

Hirsau

Calw

Weil der Stadt

Würm

Neckar

SINDELFINGEN

Bad Teinach

Wildberg

A81

Forbach

Bühl

Bühlertal

Badener Höhe
▲ 1002m

Hornisgrinde
▲ 1163m

Sasbachwalden

Achern

Ottenhöfen

Allerheiligen

Kehl

Oberkirch

Lautenbach

Oppenau

OFFENBURG

Kinzig

Elzklösterle

Berneck

Altensteig

Schönmünzach

Pfalzgrafenweiler

Baiersbronn

Murg

Herrenberg

TÜBINGEN

Nagold

Rottenburg

Neckar

Horb

Bad Imnau

Hechingen

Haigerloch

Hohenzollern

Freudenstadt

Lossburg

Griesbach

Bad Peterstal

Alpirsbach

Schömberg

Sulz

Geislingen

Balingen

Gengenbach

Berghaupten

Biberach

Zell

Steinach

Wolfach

Schenkenzell

Schiltach

Oberndorf

Schömberg

Grosser Heuberg

Lahr

Seelbach

Haslach

Hornberg

Vogtsbauernhof

Gutach

Lautenbach

Schramberg

Rottweil

Spaichingen

Mühlheim

Ettenheim

Elzach

Schonach

Triberg

Königsfeld

A81

Schwenningen

Tuttlingen

Kenzingen

Schönwald

Stöcklewald
1067m

St.Georgen

VILLINGEN

Bad Dürrheim

Endingen

Emmendingen

Donauquelle

Mönchenbach

Burkheim

Waldkirch

Brend
1149m

Furtwangen

Donau

Geisingen

March

Kandel
1242m

St.Peter

Gütenbach

Hexenloch

St.Märgen

Donaueschingen

Kaiserstuhl

A5

FREIBURG

Neustadt

Engen

Breisach

Hinterzarten

Schauinsland
1284m

Feldberg
1493m

Titisee

Löffingen

Lenzkirch

Blumberg

Tengen

Neuenburg

Mülheim

Bad Krozingen

Staufen

Münstertal

Sulzburg

Belchen
▲ 1414m

Neuenweg

Todtnau

Feldberg

Schluchsee

Schönau

Bernau

St.Blasien

Häusern

Bonndorf

Stühlingen

Singen

Breisgau

Bad Bellingen

Schloss Bürgeln

Zell

Kandern

Gerstbach

Herrischried

Todtmoos

Höchenschwand

Alb

Waldshut

Tiengen

Küssaburg

Wutach

Jestetten

Rhein

Schopfheim

Schloss Rötteln

Efringen-Kirchen

Wiese

Wehr

Rickenbach

Lauffenburg

Weil

Lörrach

Rheinfelden

Bad Säckingen

Huge ornamental clocks are typical of the Schwarzwald. One cuckoo clock at Schönach forms the entire side of a chalet

195

many smaller villages. The region excels as an area for outdoor pursuits, above all for walking. Marked paths of varying degrees of difficulty (including many very easy ones) abound and the signposting and tourist information are excellent. A useful tourist-board scheme is *Wandern ohne Gepäck* (walking without luggage), where you can walk from village to village, to prebooked guesthouses, and have your luggage transported by car. In winter, there is skiing on moderately challenging runs and a network of specially prepared cross-country ski trails.

There are many Black Forest specialities. Most famous are undoubtedly the *Schwarzwälder Kirschtorte* (of which the ubiquitous factory-made Black Forest cake is a bland imitation), and the cuckoo clocks on sale in every souvenir shop. *Zwiebelkuchen* (onion cake) is often served accompanied by a young white wine. Black Forest smoked ham is best eaten sliced thinly on locally baked bread. In season, white asparagus, plums and cherries appear on the menu. Local drinks include the Baden wines and Kirschwasser, Schnapps made from cherries (see panel page 180).

The heart of Black Forest clock making is based around the industrial town and spa of **Triberg** (see pages 196–197). **Furtwangen** is the home of the Deutsches Uhrenmuseum (German clock museum), a must even for non-enthusiasts (*Open* daily). There are also factories and workshops in the area, which will be only too pleased to give you a first-hand glimpse of local clock production in this region.

Southern Schwarzwald You will find this region one of the sunniest in Germany. The cherry trees display their blossoms in the early spring, while the mountains are still topped with snow from the previous winter. Four of the region's tallest hills lie close to **Freiburg**—the **Feldberg**, **Schauinsland**, **Kandel** and the **Belchen**. All are easily reached from the road, but the Belchen has the best views; and just north of it is **Münstertal▶**, a deep and especially pretty valley, steep-sided and graced with the baroque church of St. Trudpert. East of the Feldberg is one of the

CLOCK MAKING
The tradition of Black Forest clock making goes back to 1667, when the wooden clock with foliot (weighted arm) was made for the first time in Waldau. Metal for the mechanisms was imported until 1787, when Leopold Hofmayer set up his brass foundry in Neustadt. Since then numerous variations have been produced, among them musical clocks with trumpeters or flutes, clocks with painted or lacquered shields, clocks to control watchmen and regulators, alarm clocks, even modern quartz-crystal clocks and radio clocks. As early as 1840, subsidiaries of the Black Forest clock traders existed in four continents and 23 countries. In 1845, about 600,000 clocks were produced in the Black Fores; today the figure stands at 60 million a year.

main resort areas. Many visitors come for the two lakes, the **Titisee** and the **Schluchsee**. Of these, the Titisee, which is set among gentle woodlands, is the prettier, but the modern village on its northern side partly spoils the effect; the Schluchsee attracts older people and is less commercialized. More peaceful is **Hinterzarten**, which is a fashionable family resort.

The views are breathtaking in this area, whichever way you decide to travel. If it fits in with your plans, you might want to take a train ride from Freiburg to **Feldberg Bärental**, following a steep and winding route through the Höllental (Hell Valley) Gorge. The station at Feldberg Bärental is proud of its special location, which at 976m (3,202ft) is the highest train station in Germany. If you prefer to put on your hiking boots, the nearby **Feldbergsee** lies at the end of an unspoiled romantic road that is available only to walkers.

Farther south, the terrain is lower and less spectacular, but the country is more open, typically consisting of orchards, meadows and rounded hills of small-scale charm. There is less tourist development, and plenty of old-fashioned farmhouses have survived. Of the resorts, **Todtmoos** is especially pleasant, prettily placed amid gentle hills.

Not far from the Swiss border, halfway between Freiburg and Basel, is **Badenweiler▶**, a popular tourist attraction not only because of its spa, but also because of its fine views over the Rhine plain. The thermal springs here, which have been well preserved since their rediscovery in 1784, have been flowing since Roman times. Today's inhabitants are intent on keeping things as clean and intact as possible, and you have to leave your car on the edge of town and walk in. There are open-air pavilions where numerous musical events are held throughout the summer months.

About 8km (5 miles) to the south of Badenweiler is **Schloss Bürgeln**, built in 1764 on the orders of the abbot of the Benedictine abbey of St. Blasien. From here you can obtain a spectacular view of the surroundings as far as the Swiss Alps.

Gutach and Kinzig valleys: the central Schwarzwald A journey north through some fine towns and villages will bring you into the Gutach and Kinzig valleys. Here you will see examples of the distinctive Black Forest farmhouses with their low-hanging roofs, deep eaves and animal quarters under the roof, usually approached by an earth ramp. This is the heartland of Black Forest folk costume, such as the wide-brimmed hats with red pom-poms worn on special occasions by local girls. The **Schwarzwaldbahn** (Black Forest railway), with its 45 tunnels, crosses this landscape.

The highest waterfall in Germany (163m/535ft) is at **Triberg▶** (the Gutach falls). Cuckoo clock sceptics may be surprised that the business launched by Josef Weisser in 1824 in Triberg, called the 'Haus der 1000 Uhren' (House of 1,000 Clocks), is still thriving. Triberg is not just clocks, however. It is a year-round spa, a winter-sports resort and a relaxed sort of town. The forest at Triberg acts as a dust filter, and visitors to the spa and health resort often remark on the purity of the air. In Triberg's **Schwarzwald**

FRUIT CAKES
As well as *Schwarzwälder Kirschtorte* (cherry cake), Black Foresters have other delicacies to tempt the sweet tooth at coffee time.
Zwetschenkuchen (blue plums on a pastry base), *Käsesahnekuchen* (a rich cheesecake) and *Johannisbeerenkuchen* (a sponge cake with red currants) are just a few.

Museum▶ (*Open* daily) you'll find a wide array of local costumes on display, as well as wood carvings, ceramics and, of course, clock-making memorabilia, which will give you an idea of the rural culture.

Gutach is known for the Vogtsbauernhof, an imaginatively arranged open-air museum with an absorbing collection of reconstructed and traditionally furnished thatched farmhouses, complete with farm implements; in its pretty country setting, the whole place has the feel of a real village.

Freudenstadt▶ was badly damaged in World War II and has little ancient character, but it has been carefully reconstructed and is now second only to Baden-Baden as a health resort. The town sits high on a plateau at the meeting point of all the main routes in the northern Schwarzwald. The arcaded market square, which is Germany's largest, has neatly laid out streets and lawns. The unusual 17th-century Stadtkirche has aisles set at right-angles, each with its own green-domed tower, and a glorious 12th-century carved lectern.

To the south, **Schiltach** and **Wolfach**, both close to main roads, are among the prettiest Black Forest villages and boast half-timbered market squares.

The northern Schwarzwald The B500 Schwarzwald Hochstrasse linking Freudenstadt with Baden-Baden is a popular road. It runs along almost the entire spine of the

Dark green trees, reflected in dark water, give the 'Black' forest its name

DYING TREES
Dying and diseased trees with yellowing needles and peeling bark are widespread in the forests. Acid rain is thought to be the main culprit, and government pollution controls have been increased to curb the *Waldsterben* (Dying Forest Syndrome).

Black Forest. There are numerous roadside stopping places that will enable you to picnic alfresco—if the weather allows—and to admire the view. Alternatively, there are plenty of villages or hamlets for a meal or perhaps an overnight stay. At romantic **Allerheiligen▶**, the ruins of a 13th-century church stand next to three 18th-century ornamental fishponds.

The drive along the Nagold Valley from Freudenstadt (part of the Schwarzwald Bäderstrasse) brings you to **Pforzheim**, at the northern extremity of the Schwarzwald, some 30km (18.5 miles) north of Calw, with its half-timbered houses. At Pforzheim, the River Nagold joins the River Enz. As a focus of the jewellery trade, the town likes to think of itself as wealthy and has christened itself 'Goldstadt' (town of gold). The Schmuckmuseum (jewellery museum) has a collection of valuable pieces spanning 17 centuries in the Reuchlinhaus in Jahnstrasse (*Open* Tue–Sun). Pforzheim is also the starting point for hikes into the northern tip of the Schwarzwald (see **Walks**, below, for possible walking routes).

Walks

Black Forest footpaths

The Black Forest offers excellent long-distance walks, with viewpoints, unspoiled farmland, villages and wetlands. Signposting (look for diamond-shaped signs) and path maintenance are of a high standard;

there is plenty of good-quality accommodation on the way, and there's no shortage of refreshment facilities.

Long tracks divide into *Höhenwege* (hill paths), which take north–south courses along the footpaths, and *Querwege* (linking paths), which lead west–east. Of the four *Höhenwege*, the longest is the 350km (217 miles) Pforzheim-to-Basel Westweg. The *Querwege* range from the 164km (102 miles) Freiburg-to-Bodensee Querweg to short expeditions such as the 48km (30 miles) Rheinfelden-to-Albbruck path.

Boats at Titisee

►► Speyer

The **cathedral**►► in the Rhine town of Speyer is one of Europe's great Romanesque churches. Founded in 1030, it was remodelled at the end of the 11th century with four towers and two domes. Located in front is the Domnapf (cathedral bowl) of 1490, where wine is traditionally poured at the induction of a new bishop or for other special occasions, such as the 2,000th anniversary of the city in 1990. At the entrance to the vault of the emperors, or **Kaisergruft**►, the name given to the huge 11th-century crypt► (the largest of its period in Germany) where eight rulers were buried, is the 13th-century tomb of Rudolph of Habsburg.

From the cathedral's west front the broad Maximilianstrasse leads to the massive 13th-century Altpörtel, the only city gateway to have survived.

At the Historisches Museum der Pfalz (Palatinate Museum; *Open* Tue–Sun) the Bronze Age 'Golden Hat' of Schifferstadt is the highlight of the collection, that includes paintings and porcelain from ancient through to modern times. The Weinmuseum (Wine Museum; *Open* Tue–Sun) in the same building houses wine-making equipment with, amazingly, a 3rd-century bottle of wine (complete with its contents).

The synagogue that once existed in Speyer has been destroyed, but 10m (33ft) below ground level in Judenbadgasse is the Judenbad, a fine example of the ritual baths used by Jews for cleansing on important religious holidays and by brides prior to their wedding.

HEAVY DIET
Speyer hosted 50 imperial diets (assemblies) in the course of the Holy Roman Empire's history. As well as the emperor and the six electors, the diet was made up of 30 lay princes, 140 counts and lords, 120 bishops and archbishops and the representatives of 200 cities.

Of the baroque churches of upper Swabia, one of the finest is the Wallfahrtskirche in the village of Steinhausen, near Biberach

► Steinhausen

Steinhausen's Wallfahrtskirche (pilgrimage church), built between 1728 and 1733, is the work of Dominikus and Johann Baptist Zimmermann, who perfected the baroque style in their work. Dominikus designed the building and Johann was the painter; both were involved in the stucco work. The airy oval nave with an encircling gallery above has been left as the brothers decorated it. Stucco flowers, insects, birds and squirrels form part of the composition. Not all the work originally intended was completed, as the building cost four times as much as was estimated in 1727. Work ceased in 1733. The church is popularly described as the world's most beautiful parish church.

Southwest Germany

DAIMLER AND BENZ

Stuttgart's prosperity is built on the work of Gottlieb Daimler, who developed the gasoline engine and produced one of the world's first automobiles in the city in the 1880s. In 1926 the Daimler company merged with that of Carl Benz (another automobile pioneer) to form Daimler-Benz and in 1998 merged with the American automobile company Chrysler, to form one of the world's largest auto groups.

INFORMATION

Stuttgart: Königstrasse 1a, tel: 0711/2 22 82 40

Looking out across the elegant Schlossplatz

►► Stuttgart 172B3

Capital of the *Land* of Baden-Württemberg, Stuttgart has an enviable valley setting among green hills. Home of charismatic names like Mercedes, Porsche, Bosch and Zeiss, the city is one of the most glittering jewels in the crown of industrial Germany, its standard of living one of the highest in the country. Cultural and environmental standards are high, too, with splendid galleries and a park system that is a model of its kind.

Stuttgart's evolution was closely tied to the fortunes of the House of Württemberg, who made the city their seat in the 14th century. Under Napoleon, who made Württemberg a kingdom, the city became a royal capital, and though this lasted only a century, something of the feeling of royal splendour has persisted to the present.

Stuttgart takes its name from a stud farm (*Stutengarten*) established in the 10th century by the Duke of Swabia, and a horse features in the city's coat of arms. In spite of being the focus of a metropolitan region of some 2 million people, the city has a relaxed air about it, possibly something to do with the abundance of vineyards within the municipal boundary; grapes grow within spitting distance of the central station.

CAR MUSEUMS

The Porsche Museum and the splendid new Mercedes-Benz Museum are outside central Stuttgart, but easily accessible by S-Bahn. Porsche (*Open* daily) features racing cars, Mercedes-Benz (*Open* Tue–Sun) all kinds of stars from the Mercedes stable to the first 'Popemobile'.

A good way of starting your tour of Stuttgart is to ascend the 217m (712ft) TV Tower (Fernsehturm), completed in 1956 and the first of its kind in Germany. It rises above the woods in the south of the city. The viewing platform offers a magnificent panorama.

What to see The traffic-free main street, Königstrasse, runs south from the monumental train station to the vast Schlossplatz. Here are some of Stuttgart's great civic buildings, such as the baroque Neues Schloss, last home of the Württemberg kings and now used for government purposes and the shop-lined neo-classical Königsbau.

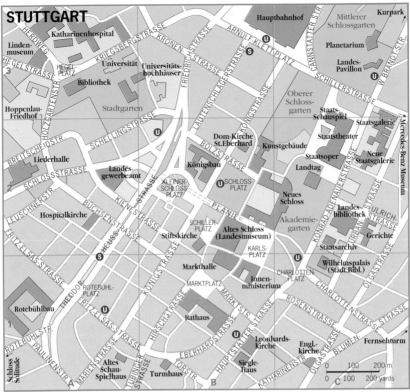

STUTTGART

Katharinenhospital
Linden museum
HERDWEG
HEGELSTRASSE
HEGEL-PLATZ
KRIEGSBERGSTRASSE
Universität
Universitäts-hochhäuser
Bibliothek
Hoppenlau-Friedhof
Stadtgarten
HOLZGARTENSTR.
FRIEDRICHSTRASSE
LAUTENSCHLAGERSTRASSE
KRONENSTRASSE
ARNULF-KLETT-PLATZ
Hauptbahnhof
CANNSTATTER STR.
Mittlerer Schlossgarten
Kurpark
Planetarium
Landes-Pavillon
W. BRANDT STR.
SCHILLERSTRASSE
Oberer Schloss-garten
Staats-Schauspiel
Staatsgalerie
Mercedes-Benz Museum
Staatstheater
Neue Staatsgalerie
SCHELLINGSTRASSE
BREITSCHEIDSTR.
Liederhalle
SCHLOSSSTRASSE
Landes-gewerbeamt
KIENESTRASSE
Dom-Kirche St.Eberhard
BOLZSTRASSE
Königsbau
KLEINER SCHLOSS-PLATZ
SCHLOSS-PLATZ
Kunstgebäude
Staatsoper
Landtag
KONRAD-ADENAUER-STRASSE
URBANSTRASSE
ULRICH-STRASSE
LEUSCHNERSTR.
Hospitalkirche
BUCHSENSTRASSE
HEUSSSTRASSE
PLANIE
Neues Schloss
Akademie-garten
Landes-bibliothek
FRITZ-ELSAS-STRASSE
SCHILLER-PLATZ
Stiftskirche
Altes Schloss (Landesmuseum)
KARLS-PLATZ
Staatsarchiv
Gerichte
Rotebühlbau
ROTEBÜHL-STR.
PAULINENSTR.
THEODOR-HEUSS-STRASSE
ROTEBÜHL-PLATZ
KÖNIGSTRASSE
Markthalle
MARKTPLATZ
Innen-ministerium
Wilhelmspalais (Stadt.Bibl.)
CHARLOTTEN-PLATZ
CHARLOTTENSTRASSE
GASTSTRASSE
ROSENSTRASSE
MARIENSTRASSE
TÜBINGERSTRASSE
Altes Schau-Spielhaus
Turmhaus
HIRSCHSTRASSE
TORSTR.
Rathaus
MARKTSTR.
EBERHARDSTRASSE
HAUPTSTÄTTER STRASSE
Leonhards-kirche
Siegle-Haus
KATHARINENSTR.
Engl.-kirche
OLGASTRASSE
BLUMENSTR.
Fernsehturm

Schloss Solitude

0   100   200 m
0   100   200 yards

A   B   C

The new Kunstmuseum (*Open* Tue–Sun) dominates Kleiner Schlossplatz—a striking glass cube full of artworks from the 18th century to the present, including canvases by local Swabian Impressionists, the world's largest Otto Dix collection and an impressive display of abstract and modern figurative art. Linking the much more atmospheric Schillerplatz is the **Altes Schloss►**, part medieval castle, part Renaissance palace, home of the Landesmuseum (*Open* Tue–Sun) with its memorabilia of the House of Württemberg as well as an excellent collection of Swabian religious sculpture.

It is possible to walk from central Stuttgart via parks and gardens to the far bank of the Neckar and Bad Cannstatt.

A good 15km (9 miles) from Stuttgart is **Schloss Solitude►**, a fine example of 18th-century rococo and a glimpse of life under the Württemberg rulers, who used it as a summer residence (*Open* Tue–Sun, guided tours only).

Several places of interest lie close to the Neckar and other rivers. To the north are **Ludwigsburg**, with one of Germany's largest baroque **palaces►►** former residence of the Württemberg rulers (guided tours daily), where mechanical figures act out fairy-tales in the Märchengarten (Fairytale Garden); **Marbach**, where Friedrich Schiller was born in 1759—his house (*Open* daily) contains a few personal mementoes—and where today the impressive **Schiller National Museum►** (*Open* Tue–Sun) and the new Museum of Modern Literature attracts literary pilgrims; and **Besigheim**, with its walls and towers.

The Duke of Württemberg still inhabits Ludwigsburg's vast castle

The Staatsgalerie was founded by Wilhelm I of Württemberg in 1843. Its famous extension, inaugurated in March 1984, was designed by a British architect, the late James Stirling. This new building put Stuttgart on the map in the world of art and architecture. Its varied forms and bold use of different materials have made it one of the landmarks of postmodernism, and it is surprisingly popular with the public. Some 25 per cent of the DM 70 million for its construction came from lottery funds collected since 1958.

202

Modern collection Without doubt the art is worthy of the building, with important works by Henri Matisse and Oskar Schlemmer, Joseph Beuys and Alberto Giacometti, Paul Klee, Piet Mondrian, Franz Marc and Giorgio de Chirico. Modern German art is particularly well represented. The gallery also houses the largest Picasso collection in Germany. Sculptures are displayed in the interior courtyard.

The old gallery The mainstream collection provides an overview of the history of western European painting, with works from medieval times to the 19th century, from early altarpieces to French Impressionists. There is a particularly fine collection of works from the local 15th-century Swabian school; other German works include Cranach's *Judith with the Head of Holofernes* and Hans Baldung Grien's *Man of Sorrows*. One of the most important works is the Herrenberg Altar, with vivid scenes of Christ's Passion painted by Jörg Ratgeb (1518–19) for the Herrenberg collegiate church; it was brought to Stuttgart in 1892. Almost every major 19th-century French painter is represented, including Manet, Monet and Cézanne. One of the best-known works of German Romantic painting, Caspar David Friedrich's *The Cross in the Woods*, is in the Staatsgalerie.

If you prefer Romantic art, don't miss the eight scenes from *The Legend of Perseus* by English Pre-Raphaelite Edward Burne-Jones. The Dutch masters—Memling, Hals, Rubens and Rembrandt—are prominent, too. Some of the best treasures are displayed in the basement of the building; this is for security reasons *and* also to preserve the collection from environmental damage.

The gallery is at Konrad-Adenauer-Strasse 30–32; *open* Tue–Sun.

Outside Tübingen's old Rathaus, the farmers mix with students on market days

►► Tübingen 172B2

Situated on the tranquil upper reaches of the Neckar River, Tübingen is one of Germany's oldest and most atmospheric university towns. Less plagued than Heidelberg by tourism, though quite its equal in charm, it has a castle, Hohentübingen, high above the houses, their gables turned to the river. The university, founded in 1477, has always been strong on philosophy, theology and medicine. The philosopher Hegel (1770–1831) was a student here.

The best view of the town is from the Eberhardsbrücke over the Neckar. The bridge gives access to a long island between two arms of the river. The Platanenallee promenade, so called because it is lined with plane trees, is a popular place for an evening stroll.

Schloss Hohentübingen, built on 11th-century foundations, dates from the Renaissance. Its entrance gateway bears the coat of arms of the house of Württemberg, together with the Order of the Garter awarded to one of the dukes by Queen Elizabeth I of England.

The Marktplatz, with its Neptune fountain, seems to be the hub of all the narrow winding streets and is still the focus of attention, particularly on market days (Monday, Wednesday and Friday). On one side of the square is the 15th-century (but much restored) **Rathaus►**; a short distance east (in Münzgasse) is the Protestant collegiate church of St. Georg, which contains late Gothic features, notably the rood screen, vaulting and tracery.

Excursion

Reutlingen, 10km (6 miles) east of Tübingen, retains town walls and numerous fine buildings, despite war damage. In particular see the Marienkirche, a strikingly unified Gothic church of the 13th and 14th centuries. The Cistercian monastery at **Bebenhausen►**, north of Tübingen, was founded 1185 and is encompassed by a double wall and focused on a late Gothic cloister (completed in 1496).

INFORMATION
Tübingen: An der Neckarbrücke 1, tel: 07071/91 36 0; www.tuebingen-info.de

FAMOUS WRITERS
After the establishment of the Cotta publishing house, which published works by Goethe and Schiller, many distinguished writers and poets came to make their home in Tübingen. These included Friedrich Hölderlin, and the tower where he lived, insane, for 36 years is on the riverbank (it can be visited Tue–Sun). The poets Eduard Mörike and Ludwig Uhland, as well as the philosophers Hegel and Schelling, also came to Tübingen.

*Ulm Münster (right)
boasts a set of
15th-century carved
choir stalls (below)*

204

►► Ulm 172C2

Ulm's location at a significant crossing point of the Danube made it an important trading base in the late Middle Ages. The city suffered severe damage in a bombing raid in 1944, which virtually destroyed the old heart, but many of the ancient edifices have now been restored. Ulm's famous son was Albert Einstein, born here in 1879.

The best general view is from the Tahn Ufer, on the far side of the Danube. Look for the leaning gateway known as the Metzgerturm (butchers' tower). The **Münster►►** is one of the largest and most important religious buildings in Europe, and it was fortunately little damaged by the 1944 bombs. Construction began in 1377, and was completed, with the tower and steeple, in 1890. The latter, the tallest in the world, soars 161m (528ft) above the rest of the city. You can climb almost to the top (768 steps) for a small charge and take in a view stretching from the Danube across the Black Forest to the Swiss Alps, if the weather is on your side.

Details of the Book of Genesis are carved above the doorway under the tower, as well as figures of Mary and the Apostles. There is much to be seen in the massive interior, including a magnificent set of 15th-century carved choir stalls and a display of architectural plans by the various designers of the cathedral. The huge Ulmer Museum has 50 exhibition rooms, with a heavy accent on Gothic art in Upper Swabia, plus works by 20th-century artists (*Open* Tue–Sun). The baroque monastery at Ulm-Wiblingen is famous for its rococo library (*Open* Apr–Oct Tue–Sun; Nov–Mar weekend afternoons only).

West of Ulm, the former abbey church at **Blaubeuren►** (*Open* Easter–Oct daily; Nov–Easter Mon–Fri afternoons only; Sat–Sun 11–4) is charmingly reflected in a deep blue pool. The building contains an exceptional 15th-century late Gothic altarpiece, the work of a group of local craftsmen.

▶ Wertheim   *172C4*

At the meeting point of the Main and Tauber rivers, Wertheim is a town of delightful half-timbered houses neatly erected along narrow streets amid a setting of wooded hills. The ruined Altes Schloss, towering over the town, was built by the counts of Wertheim in the 12th century. There are wonderful views from here. A glass museum in Mühlenstrasse has collections of historic glass, while the 16th-century Rathaus contains an historical museum. The impressive Stiftskirche was built in the 14th century, and the Kilianscapelle (St. Kilian's chapel) in the 15th: Its basement served as an ossuary. In the Marktplatz you will see half-timbered houses and the Engelsbrunnen (Angels' Well), dating from 1574, named for the stone angels bearing the Wertheim coat of arms. From the left bank of the Tauber there is a spectacular view.

▶ Worms   *172B4*

This cathedral city on the banks of the Rhine, one of the oldest in Germany, has a particularly eventful past. There was a Celtic settlement here, then a Roman garrison. A Burgundian tribe, the Nibelungen, established itself in Worms in the 5th century and provided the material which gave rise to the famous legend which bore its name and so inspired the composer Richard Wagner. Worms has a Nibelungen bridge, built near the spot in the river Rhine where the evil Hagen, the treacherous slayer of Siegfried, is said to have thrown treasure he captured from the defeated Burgundians. In medieval times over 100 imperial diets, or assemblies, were held in Worms, the most noted being the Reichstag of 1521 (Diet of Worms), which summoned Luther to stand before it. He refused to retract his doctrines and was banned from the empire.

Besides industry, Worms has a flourishing wine trade. The famous Liebfraumilch comes from here, taking its name from the Liebfrauenkirche (Church of Our Lady), standing in the middle of a vineyard to the north of the city. It contains a 15th-century Madonna and tabernacle.

One of the best examples of Romanesque architecture in Germany is **Worms' cathedral▶▶**, the Kaiserdom, with two domes and four corner towers. St. Martins Kirche, also Romanesque, has the same design as the cathedral.

JEWISH CEMETERY
The synagogue of Worms, the oldest in Germany, and the Jewish cemetery date back to the 11th century. There was a large Jewish community here up until the 1930s. The Alte Synagoge was rebuilt in 1961, and the cemetery contains over 1,000 gravestones and pillars carved in Hebrew, amazingly untouched by the Nazis. After Prague, this is the second-largest Jewish cemetery in Europe.

205

Worms' superb cathedral is Catholic, although the city itself is two-thirds Protestant

Northern Bavaria

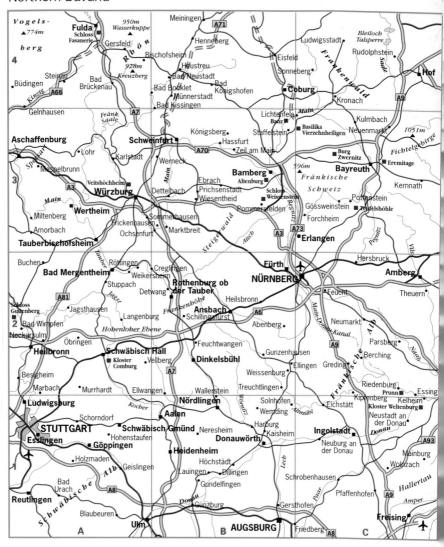

Stretching from Aschaffenburg in the northwest to Passau on the Austrian border far to the southeast, this region offers some of Germany's most fascinating historical cities, including **Nürnberg**, **Regensburg** and **Würzburg**, and stretches of unspoiled countryside. The world-famous **Romantische Strasse** (Romantic Road) links medieval towns, while backwaters of the Bavarian Forest are explored by the **Bayerische Ostmarkstrasse**.

The region's cultural riches are unsurpassed. In the late Middle Ages and early Renaissance, some of the most characteristically German contributions to the arts were made by painters (Altdorfer, Cranach and Dürer) or by master craftsmen (Veit Stoss and Tilman Riemenschneider). Their work can be seen in museums such as the outstanding Germanisches Nationalmuseum at Nürnberg, or sometimes in the original settings, such as

Tilman Riemenschneider's *Madonna in a Rose Garland* in the little church at Volkach. Architecture particularly worth noting includes a number of sumptuous 18th-century baroque and rococo edifices.

National parks offer unparallelled opportunities for exploring, on foot, bicycle or by canoe along the rivers. Rural scenery ranges from the romantic **Altmühl Valley** to the mysterious depths of Europe's last remaining fragments of virgin forest in the **Bayerischer Wald**.

Enjoy the region for its food and drink. Hearty game dishes and spicy sausages from Nürnberg are complemented by famous beers (the world's oldest brewery is at **Freising**, near Munich) or wines from Franconia, where Main Valley vineyards rival those of the Rhine and Mosel. This is a popular holiday area, with bargains to be had in remoter places along the border with the Czech Republic.

CONTROVERSIAL CANAL
The lower reaches of the Altmühl have become part of the new Main–Danube Canal. Completed in 1992, this gigantic and controversial project connects the waterways of western and central Europe, allowing large vessels to ply between the Rhine and the Black Sea. Nowhere else has a river landscape been so transformed nor so carefully restored, a process best seen at Essing, just down-stream from Prunn. Here the idyllic riverside scene of village, barbican and ancient timber bridge seems untouched by time.

The Befreiungshalle (Liberation hall) above Kelheim on the Danube, built to celebrate 'liberation' from Napoleon's rule

▶▶ Altmühltal (Altmühl Valley)   *206C1*

This is one of Germany's most attractive river valleys, with unspoiled towns and villages, dramatic crags topped by castles, and one of the nation's largest nature park, **Altmühltal**. The river rises in the Frankenhöhe (Franconian Heights), near Rothenburg-ob-der-Tauber; crosses gently rolling countryside to the small spa town of Treuchtlingen; then twists deeply through the limestone of the Fränkische Alb (Franconian Jura), joining the Danube at Kelheim.

The meadowlands, rock pinnacles and juniper-studded slopes are enjoyed by walkers and by cyclists on the riverside bicycle path.

Downstream is **Eichstätt▶**, a superior little episcopal city of classic elegance, an architectural showpiece. Its 14th-century cathedral, a mix of Romanesque, Gothic and baroque, contains the famous Pappenheim Altar, an arresting late medieval depiction of the Crucifixion. Rococo mansions, neatly painted pale blue or yellow, line the Residenzplatz, crowned by a gilded statue of the Virgin. All is aesthetically impressive, but almost too much like a stage set, with the Willibald fortress looming on a hill above. The town has a small private Catholic university. There are fine views from the Frauenberg pilgrimage chapel crowning a hilltop or from the chunky, chalk-white Willibaldsburg overlooking the river.

The valley's most extraordinary castle is 11th-century Prunn, perched precariously over the river.

▶ Amberg
206C2

Untouched by wars and heavy industry, Amberg has within its medieval walls a variety of buildings from its prosperous past, including four fine gateways and the ancient bridge—the Stadtbrille (City Spectacles); note the reflection of its twin arches in the waters of the River Vils.

The gabled and arcaded Gothic Rathaus, one of the finest town halls in Germany, dominates the market square. The churches include the stately St. Martin's (1421), St. George's, given a baroque interior in the late 17th century, and the Deutsche Schulkirche, a rococo gem. Stations of the Cross lead uphill to the late Renaissance pilgrimage church of Mariahilf, with its fine views over the town and the countryside of the Oberpfalz (Upper Palatinate).

Amberg holds its Altstadtfest in June and its Bergfest in July, though the products of its nine breweries can be sampled at any time.

▶ Ansbach
206B2

Administrative and cultural heart of central Franconia, Ansbach is one of Germany's finest 'Residenz towns', its history and townscape fashioned by its role as the seat of its rulers, the margraves of Brandenburg-Ansbach. Streets and squares feature many attractive buildings, from high-gabled medieval burghers' houses to the three-towered church of St. Gumbertus, redesigned in the 18th century to become an ideal 'preaching church', dominated by the pulpit rather than the altar.

The **Residenz▶** (*Open* Tue–Sun) itself is a splendid Renaissance structure, incorporating parts of the original medieval moated stronghold. Its rococo interior contains the Bavarian state collection of Ansbach ceramics. Beyond is the palace's park, the Hofgarten, with stately avenues of lime trees and an impressive orangery. There is also a memorial to the enigmatic foundling Kaspar Hauser, mysteriously murdered here in 1833 and the subject of fascinated speculation ever since and of various books and films.

▶ Aschaffenburg
206A3

The first Bavarian town for visitors coming from the Frankfurt direction, Aschaffenburg is dominated by the huge red sandstone **Schloss▶** standing foursquare on a bluff overlooking the River Main. Known as the Johannisburg, it was erected at the start of the 17th century by the bishop of Mainz, Aschaffenburg's overlord. The interior includes state apartments, fine paintings (including pictures by Cranach), and a range of glass and ceramics (*Open* Tue–Sun). Other master works including another fine Cranach and a Grünewald can be found in the town's Stiftskirche, a church incorporating a variety of architectural styles from the Romanesque onwards.

The town's two parks, Schöntal (in central Aschaffenburg) and Schönbusch (on the far bank of the Main), are excellent examples of German landscapers' attempts to imitate the 'English Style' in garden design.

Schonsbusch Park was one of the nation's earliest examples, completed in 1790 by architect Friedrich Ludwig Sckell, with artificial lakes and hills and even an observation tower and a Temple of Friendship.

INFORMATION
Ansbach: Hallplatz, tel: 09621/10-239; www.amberg.de

209

A golden baroque statue-fountain adorns Ansbach

INFORMATION
Aschaffenburg: Schlossplatz 1, tel: 06021/39 58 00; www.aschaffenburg.de

Aschaffenburg's Schloss above the River Main. Next door is a quiet quarter of old Fachwerk *(half-timbered) houses down narrow alleys*

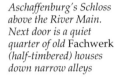

AUGSBURG'S ALMSHOUSES
One of Bavaria's unusual landmarks is the Fuggerei in Augsburg, a collection of neat almshouses built in 1521 by Jakob Fugger 'the Rich', a philanthropic banker. Here he housed some of the city's poor families, virtually for free. The snug kitchens must have seemed ultramodern then. More than 150 poorer people live there now in the 140 apartments, and the Fugger family still runs the place (*Open* daily).

HOLBEIN AND LUTHER
Augsburg's position meant that it was subject to the northwards-moving influences of the Italian Renaissance. Churches, patrician houses and public buildings were built or rebuilt, great artists including Holbein the Elder gave their best and metalworkers created masterpieces in gold and silver. Luther's visits reflected the hold that Protestantism had here.

Excursions

The Spessart East of Aschaffenburg the River Main swings south then north again in a great bend, forming the southern boundary of the Spessart, one of Germany's finest areas of unspoiled uplands. Here are some of the country's most extensive woodlands, magnificent stands of beech and oak stretching away to distant horizons, an awesome prospect even when viewed from the great scenic highway, the Frankfurt–Nuremberg autobahn.

In the romantic setting of a deep forest valley lies **Schloss Mespelbrunn** (*Open* mid–Mar to mid-Nov daily), its picturesque silhouette reflected in the calm surface of its moat. Still inhabited, the castle's furnished interior is pleasingly evocative of the life of the provincial nobility.

The stretch of the Main upstream from Aschaffenburg forms part of the Franconian wine-growing area (see page 236). It is a landscape of orchards, south-facing vineyards and pleasant little towns and villages, among them half-timbered **Miltenberg**, which has been described as 'the very essence of medieval Germany'.

►► Augsburg 206B1

With a population of 262,000, Augsburg is Bavaria's third-largest city, as well as its oldest, founded in Roman times and named after Emperor Augustus. Commanding the Alpine trade routes linking northern Europe to Italy, Augsburg enjoyed its heyday in the 15th and 16th centuries. Second then only to London as a banking centre, it became the base of great financial dynasties, such as the immensely rich Fuggers. The former family home, the **Fuggerhaus**, sits majestically on busy Maximilianstrasse, busts of two Fugger patrons adorn the entrance to the 16th-century building, and a restaurant, crowded with today's local businessmen, is in the cellar. The social welfare settlement founded by the Fuggers, the **Fuggerei**, a picturesque quarter of tiny houses, is still home to more than 150 local Catholic elderly people, who have to pray daily for the Fugger family in return for a peppercorn rent. Later names associated with Augsburg include Mozart's father Leopold, whose birthplace, Frauentorstrasse 30, is now a Mozart museum (*Open* Tue–Sun); Rudolf Diesel (who invented his engine at the MAN engineering works); Willy Messerschmitt (famous for his fighter planes); and the playwright Bertolt Brecht (who was born here).

What to see Augsburg has a big central area, focused on Ludwigplatz. Here the imposing Renaissance Rathaus (1620) has a glorious Goldener Saal (golden hall), once Germany's largest city hall (*Open* daily). The landmark tower, the Perlachturm, offers good city views from its top (*Open* May to mid-Oct daily). To the north stands Augsburg's Cathedral, the Domkirche St. Maria Heimsuchung, originally Romanesque but much altered and added to. The Augustusbrunnen (1594), with its majestic figures of the emperor and river gods, stands in Ludwigplatz, the Herkulesbrunnen (1596–1602) in the broad Maximilianstrasse to the south. This stately city artery is lined with many splendid residences, including the Fuggerhaus and the rococo Schaezlerpalais, which has art collections and a Festsaal (banqueting hall; *Open*

INFORMATION
Augsburg:
Schiessgrabenstrasse 14,
tel: 0821/5 02 070;
www.augsburg-tourismus.de

211

Wed–Sun). Ancient historical finds are on display in the Römisches Museum, while more recent developments are shown at the Maximilian-Museum (both *open* Wed–Sun).

Excursion

Just east of Augsburg is the small town of **Friedberg**. Its notable features include a castle dating from 1150, a Renaissance Rathaus, and above all Herrgottsruh, a pilgrimage church with an exuberant rococo interior.

The Rathaus and Perlachturm in the Ludwigplatz at Augsburg

Northern Bavaria

BISMARCK'S VISIT
Kissingen's saline waters and equable climate have attracted visitors since the 18th century, though the town's origins go back to the early Middle Ages and something of the atmosphere of an old Franconian town remains, especially around the Old Rathaus of 1577. The town's heyday came in the 19th century, under the patronage of the Bavarian royal family. Poets, painters and politicians (among them the Iron Chancellor, Bismarck, who visited 15 times) flocked to take the waters. Russian and English guests were numerous, necessitating the building of both an Orthodox and an Anglican church.

212

► **Bad Kissingen**   *206B4*

Located among parks and gardens along the banks of the River Saale, this is Bavaria's most popular spa.

The spa buildings include an 1856 arcade and the monumental 1911 Regentenbau, a complex of halls and public rooms linked to the Wandelhalle, a covered promenade. The Theatre, completed in 1904, has a fine Jugendstil interior. On the far bank of the Saale from the Wandelhalle is the immaculate Kurpark with buildings housing a spa and a casino.

Crowning a hilltop south of town are the ruins of Bodenlauben Castle, once the residence of the medieval poet and keen crusader Otto von der Bodenlauben, whose statue forms part of the fountain on the Rathausplatz.

The Rhön Bad Kissingen is one of the main 'gateways' to this area of varied upland scenery that stretches northwards to **Fulda**. Rising in places to over 900m (2,952ft), the rounded summits carry a covering of moorland and pasture rather than forest. This splendid walking country is also popular with gliding enthusiasts. The most extensive views, both involving a short hike of half an hour or so, are from the **Wasserkuppe** (950m/3,116ft) and the **Kreuzberg** (928m/3,044ft). In the valleys are attractive little towns such as **Gersfeld**, with its three castles, and

An elegant Kurpark and Kurgarten are features of Bad Kissingen

Bad Brückenau, a spa with classical buildings inspired by the ubiquitous King Ludwig. **Bad Neustadt** has kept intact its ring of medieval fortifications. Within the walls stands the former church of the Carmelites, dating from the 14th century but with an exceptionally fine baroque interior. On the far bank of the Saale are the spa facilities, including a Kurhotel comfortably installed within an 18th-century castle.

Münnerstadt, too, has retained its walls, but its greatest treasure is the high altar by the great Riemenschneider in the parish church.

A popular short excursion from Bad Kissingen is to **Bad Bocklet**, on the historic mail coach that plies between the two spas, passing the Renaissance castle at **Aschach**, its rooms filled with fine furniture and paintings and a collection of oriental art.

▶ Bad Mergentheim   206A2

Pleasantly situated in the picturesque valley of the River Tauber, this is an important stopping place along the Romantische Strasse, as well as a spa. In contrast to the newer spa district, the old town has a picturesque market square, churches, high-gabled Rathaus and an ancient fountain. The most prominent structure is the mid-16th-century Deutschordensschloss (*Open* Tue–Sun; see also Ellingen, page 222). The castle is a fascinating assembly of high walls, gables, towers and turrets. Inside there is a splendid Renaissance staircase. The baroque castle church has a light-filled interior with a magnificent ceiling painting; in the crypt are the tombs of long-dead grand masters.

Excursion

The parish church at **Stuppach** (*Open* Tue–Sun, except Dec–Feb), about 7km (4 miles) southwest, has a *Madonna and Child* by the great Grünewald, one of this tormented master's more spiritual paintings (see panel page 214).

▶▶▶ Bamberg   206B3

Bamberg is perhaps the most perfect of all Germany's ancient cities, a wonderful synthesis of architecture of all periods in a harmonious setting of river vale and gentle hills. Since 1994 it has been named as part of UNESCO's World Cultural Heritage.

Founded in AD973, the city was made a bishopric by King Henry II, and its division into two distinct districts is still apparent: the Bürgerstadt, or merchants' town, by the River Regnitz, and the Bischofsstadt, or ecclesiastical quarter, on the slopes above. Linking the two is the extraordinarily picturesque old **town hall▶**, an incongruous mixture of rustic half-timbering and rococo elegance perched on a tiny island in the Regnitz. Downstream is Bamburg's Little Venice, once the home of fishermen.

Higher up is the **Kaiserdom▶▶**, the city's great cathedral, with its four tall towers finding their echo in those of St. Michael's Church, crowning the hilltop in the middle distance. The cathedral is a triumph of the transitional period between late Romanesque and early Gothic. Its

Northern Bavaria

Bamberg's quaint old Rathaus was built on an island in the river, so it could serve the city's two rival parts

STUPPACHER MADONNA
The little parish church of Stuppach, 11km (7 miles) south of Bad Mergentheim on the B-19, found itself in possession of one of the greatest German Renaissance paintings in 1908 when a dark, grimy altar picture of the Virgin Mary was identified as the work of the early 16th-century master Matthias Grünewald. Later repainting of the picture had given it a flat and undistinguished surface. Now the restored Stuppacher Madonna can be seen in all its original glory. (The church is open Tue–Sun, and closed Dec–Feb)

CITY OF SCULPTURE
Bamberg is making a name for itself as a 'city of sculpture'. After a highly successful city-wide exhibition of 14 large sculptures by the South American artist Fernando Bottero, Bamberg citizens organized an initiative to keep at least one of the works. Bottero's sculptures command very high prices, but that did not daunt the good burgers of Bamberg, who raised more than £500,000 to buy a symbolic statue of a typical Bottero fat lady, riding a bull. It stands on one of the squares in Bamberg's pedestrian shopping zone.

interior is enlivened by some of the most remarkable sculpture to be found in Germany. The **Bamberger Reiter▶** (Bamberg Knight) on his stone steed has come to represent the essence of medieval chivalry, while the **tomb of Henry II▶** and his Queen Kunigunde is one of the masterpieces of the great Tilman Riemenschneider (*c* 1513). The royal pair appear again in the elaborately carved choir stalls, while the Marienaltar (1523) is by the Nürnberg wood-carver Veit Stoss.

The Domplatz (cathedral square) is overlooked on one side by the Neue Residenz, with its splendid baroque interior, and on the other by the Alte Hofhaltung. Beyond the Renaissance gateway the undulating cobbled courtyard is enclosed by a delightfully irregular sequence of late Gothic galleried buildings.

Bamberg offers much to the unhurried explorer, including churches (from St. Jakob to the rococo interior of St. Gangolf), splendid town residences (the richly decorated Böttingerhaus or the riverside Concordiahaus) and museums—the Diocesan Museum, off the cathedral cloister (*Open* Tue–Sun), or the local history museum, in the Alte Hofhaltung (*Open* May–Oct Tue–Sun). Live culture is provided by the well-regarded Bamberg Symphony Orchestra. A close-up of the city can be seen from the Vierkirchenblick (four-church view), south of the cathedral, a more distant prospect from the old Bishops' castle, the Altenburg, 3km (2 miles) southwest.

Excursions
In **Pommersfelden**, 20km (12.5 miles) south, is Schloss Weissenstein, one of Germany's most grandiose baroque palaces, built by Prince-Bishop Schönborn of Bamberg in 1711–18. There is a sumptuous interior and an English-style park beyond (Palace *open* Apr–Oct daily; guided tours only each hour, 10–4). The **River Main** joins the Regnitz downstream from Bamberg. Along its course lie a number of pretty little places: Zeil-am-Main, half-timbered Königsberg and Hassfurt, graced by a parish church and late Gothic Ritterkapelle (Knights' Chapel).

215

▶▶ Bayerischer Wald (Bavarian Forest) *207D2*

Between the Danube and the Czech border stretch 6,000 sq km (2,316sq miles) of upland country, forming, with the Sumava (Bohemian Forest) on the far side of the frontier, 'Europe's Green Roof'. Rising to 1,456m (4,777ft) at the Grosser Arber, the area contains traces of primeval forest and ancient stands of spruce carefully preserved as part of Germany's first national park. Woodland is continuous on the higher land, interspersed elsewhere with attractive farming countryside and meticulously modernized villages. Churches with onion domes pierce the skyline and little streams channel through steeply sloping meadows to tributaries of the Danube.

Though there are no large towns, impeccably engineered roads stitch the whole area together, and the occasional two-coach train still trundles the single tracks of the surviving branch lines. With an abundant variety of accommodation, this is one of the areas popular with Germans for their holidays. Attractions are plentiful, from relics of the metalworking industries that flourished until recently to castle ruins perched on rocks, or little medieval towns. Many places have their Heimatmuseum (local-history museum), and there are curiosities like the snuff museum at Grafenau.

Klein Venedig (Little Venice) is a charming area of Bamberg, on the Regnitz River

INFORMATION
Neuschönau: Hans-Eisenmann-Haus, Böhmstrasse 35, tel: 08558/9 61 50; www.nationalpark-bay-erischer-wald.de

WINTER SPORTS
Long winters provide the perfect conditions for winter sports in the Bayerischer Wald. As well as some provision for downhill skiing, there are altogether more than 2,000km (1,240 miles) of cross-country trails.

Drive

Passau to Cham

Climbing from the Danube, the B85
(Bayerische Ostmarkstrasse) is
a scenic highway linking Passau on
the Austrian border with Bayreuth.

Near **Tittling**, look around the
Museumsdorf Bayerischer Wald,
where old buildings have been renovated and filled with traditional
furniture, clothing, tools and farming
equipment (*Open* Apr–Oct daily).

Continue on the Ostmarkstrasse to
Cham via Regen, located on the
Schwarzer Regen, and Viechtach with
its 17th-century Rathaus, or detour
around the Grosser Arber. Just north of
Neuschönau, the Hans-Eisenmann-
Haus, the visitor centre run by the
Bavarian Forest National Park, has dis-
plays, leaflets (in English) and
self-guided trails that tell you all about
the origins of the forest and its wildlife
(*Open* daily 9am–5pm; closed
Nov–Dec).

The road northwest to the Arber
goes through towns where the glass
industry flourishes, though Spiegelau,
Frauenau and Zwiesel are more like
resorts than manufacturing centres.

Some glassworks can be visited,
while Frauenau has a superb new

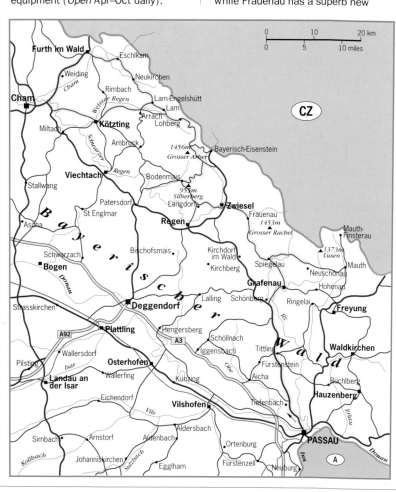

Open views across the Bayerischer Wald

Glasmuseum (*Open* daily).
Bodenmais, in the Bavarian Forest, deals in glass, but outside the town is the **Silberberg**, mined for its copper, tin and silver and now open to visitors (though no longer in production. *Open* Apr–Oct daily; variable times rest of year, tel: 09924/304).

To the north rises the Arber, with remnants of the inaccessible primeval forest. This is one of the most inhospitable areas in Germany. Frost occurs on 200 or more days a year, and deep snow lies well into spring. Solitude can be enjoyed here, though not around the chalets on the banks of the **Arbersee**.

An arduous ascent on foot (3.5 hours there and back) will take you to the summit of the **Grosser Arber**—more easily reached by the ski-lift on the highway to **Lam**. This ridge-top road gives views of the mountains (notably from the Hindenburg viewpoint) before descending into gentler countryside around Lam.

The Ostmarkstrasse is rejoined at **Cham**, with its fine market square, via either Kötzting, rebuilt after a great fire in 1867, or Furth im Wald. Kötzting has a flamboyant Whit Monday procession (*Pfingstritt*) and Furth has the *Drachenstich*, a pageant in which an 18m (60ft) animated dragon is slain, with much jollity. On the Regensburg–Plzen (Pilsen) road, Furth is a frontier town: The Skoda cars of Czech shoppers can be seen parked among the local cars on its little market square.

INFORMATION
Bayreuth: Luitpoldplatz 9,
tel: 0921/8 85 88;
www.bayreuth-
tourismus.de

WAGNER'S THEATRE
Wagner's real monument is the bulky Festspiel-haus, on rising ground north of central Bayreuth. Designed by Semper, but aesthetically no rival to the Markgräfliches Opern-haus, it provides the optimum setting for the master's works. At intermission time during the festival the grounds fill with up to 1,800 people recovering from the operatic onslaught. Admire the massive bust of Wagner by Arno Breker, one of the Third Reich's most successful sculptors, as well as the representations of Cosima and of Liszt, who died during the 1886 festival.

Modern Bayreuth, much rebuilt since Wagner's day

►► Bayreuth   *206C3*

Founded as long ago as the 11th century, Bayreuth first came into its own in the 18th century under the rule of Margrave Friedrich and his energetic and talented spouse, Wilhelmina, sister of Frederick the Great. A second flowering occurred in the late 19th century, when Richard Wagner made it the showcase for his innovative operas (see page 237). The operatic tradition persists, attracting fans in their thousands to the Bayreuth Festival, held annually in July and August.

Traces of Bayreuth's medieval past can still be seen, for example in narrow alleyways and the typically Bavarian elongated market square, as well as the Gothic Stadt-kirche (city church). The original residence of the margraves, the Altes Schloss (old palace; *Open* daily) goes back to the 14th century and its present appearance is due to 18th-century rebuilding.

The baroque age contributed most to Bayreuth's architectural character, again largely because of the energetic Wilhelmina. The Neues Schloss (new palace, 1753) has lighthearted rococo interiors, including grotto and garden rooms, and houses some of the town's museums (*Open* daily). The grounds of the Hofgarten are an early example of Romantic landscape design.

To the north is the 18th-century Markgräfliches Opernhaus. Undistinguished outside, it has a galleried interior that shows the baroque style at its most theatrical.

Connected to the Hofgarten by a gateway, erected in 1874 to celebrate the composer's 61st birthday, is Wagner's Bayreuth residence, the classical Haus Wahnfried, now the Richard-Wagner Museum (*Open* daily). In the gardens stands the grave of the great man. His wife Cosima, daughter of Franz Liszt, is buried beside him, his faithful hound Russ a short distance away.

Marking the eastern extremity of the great limestone outcrop that begins far away in the Jura Mountains, Bayreuth is one of Germany's most romantically picturesque regions. The porous rock has been eroded to form some two dozen deep and narrow valleys through which flow clear trout streams that once powered ancient mills. Medieval castles cap many crags; look for the one perched above the tiny town of Pottenstein. Nearby Tüchersfeld has an even more bizarre setting, with fairy-tale houses wedged among the rock pinnacles. Below ground, equally strange landscapes can be seen in the caves known as the Tcufclshöhle, where there are weirdly shaped concretions and the bones of prehistoric animals.

Excursions

The beautiful grounds of the **Eremitage** (Hermitage; *open* Apr to mid-Oct daily; garden open all year), 4km (2.5 miles) northeast of Bayreuth, go back to the 17th century, when the margraves would come here to escape court life in town. The original hermitage, the Altes Schloss, was built by the ruling margrave in 1715.

The **Fichtelgebirge** (Fichtel Mountains), ancient granite-littered uplands, form a horseshoe-shaped massif enclosing eastwards facing lowlands, and are named after the extensive forests of *Fichte* (spruce) that clad their slopes. The area's abundant rainfall feeds rivers flowing to all points of the compass, the Eger east to the Elbe in the Czech Republic, the Naab south to the Danube, the Weisser Main west to the Rhine.

The Ochsenkopf summit (1,024m/3,360ft), with its TV tower (chairlift from Bishofsgrün), gives majestic views. In contrast the tranquil scene by the banks of the little Fichtelsee, set deep among the dark conifers, or the Luisenberg labyrinth, a chaos of granite blocks eroded into strange shapes, were much admired by Goethe. Here is Germany's oldest open-air theatre, still the venue for summertime performances.

The towns in the sheltered lowland include the area's little capital, **Wunsiedel**, with the Fichtelgebirgsmuseum (*Open* Tue–Sun), and busy **Marktredwitz**, on the route leading to the northwestern Czech Republic.

The **Frankenwald** (Franconian Forest) is Germany's smallest upland, with peaceful valleys, remote hamlets,

Baroque sculptures (above) reflect the golden age of 18th-century Bayreuth under Princess Wilhelmina

SANSPAREIL GARDEN
The picturesque potential of rocky outcrop and eerie forest was appreciated by Margravine Wilhelmina. Around the crag-top ruin of Zwernitz Castle she laid out a romantic landscape to tickle the refined sensibilities of her contemporaries and called it Sanspareil, in the Francophile fashion. Beyond Morgenländischer Bau (an Asian hermitage), winding paths lead past strange rock formations to fanciful features like the theatre conceived as a ruin and set in a grotto. The castle itself forms part of the artful composition and from its keep you can see a wonderful panorama reaching far away to the Frankenwald and the Fichtelgebirge.

THE STRONGEST BEER
The picturesque little market town of Kulmbach lays claim to the largest per capita production of beer in Germany: 4,250 litres (935 gallons) per man, woman and child. More than a quarter of Kulmbach households earn a living directly or indirectly from the town's six breweries. One of them, the Erste Kulmbacher Union, produces the strongest beer in the world—the Doppelbock Kulminator 28. With an alcoholic content of more than 11 per cent, it has the kick of a mule. At the end of July and start of August, Kulmbach has a nine-day beer festival that rivals Munich's Oktoberfest; the beer, at any rate, is stronger.

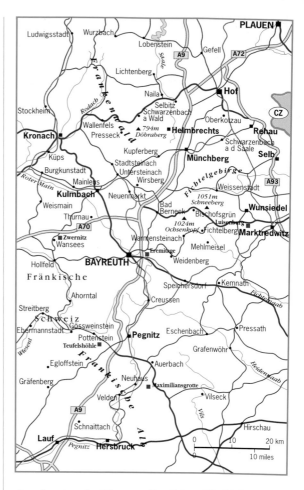

deep forest and wild areas of heath bog. The highest point is the Döbraberg (794m/2,605ft) with a tower giving panoramic views to the Fichtelgebirge to the south and the Thuringian heights on the other side. North from Bayreuth is **Kulmbach**, whose large breweries are known for their bitter dark beers and strong, sharp Pils (see panel). They lie below the **Plassenburg▶**, a splendid stronghold with a fine Renaissance courtyard.

The castle, which was once a prison, now houses the Zinnfigurenmuseum, the national collection of 300,000 tin figurines (*Open* daily). Kronach has beautifully preserved medieval houses, including the birthplace of Cranach (1472–1553), painter of rugged landscapes and courtly nudes. Above the town rises its great fortress, the Rosenberg. With its triple ring of walls pierced by a single entrance above ground, this is Germany's most extensive medieval stronghold to remain intact. Its picture gallery (*Open* Tue–Sun) includes works by Cranach.

The River Wiesent runs through one of the prettiest valleys in **Fränkische Schweiz** (Franconian Switzerland) and is best seen from viewpoints in the little market town of Gössweinstein, famous for its pilgrimage church.

▶▶ Coburg   *206B4*

During Germany's division, Coburg was on the edge of things, situated in a cul-de-sac ending at the East German border. Its name, which is linked to half the dynasties that once ruled Europe, never lost its fame, and the place, busier now with the disappearance of the frontier, is still dominated by its two, very different, ducal castles.

High above the town, and visible from far across Coburg's attractive rural surroundings, broods the majestic **Veste**▶ (fortress; *Open* Apr–Oct daily; Nov–Mar Tue–Sun), called 'the Crown of Franconia' because of its tower-studded outline. Founded in the 11th century and much rebuilt in Renaissance times by the vigorous Duke Johann Casimir, it ranks among the country's most splendid strongholds. Within its double ring of defensive walls there are many treasures, including the 300,000-plus items of its print collection, paintings by a number of German masters (among them Cranach), arms, armour, furniture and Johann Casimir's State Carriage (1560). Martin Luther stayed here in 1530, and his visit is commemorated by the room named after him.

Linking the Veste to town is the Hofgarten, its verdant slopes embracing a Natural History Museum (see panel). In the 16th century, the dukes moved down the hill into their new castle, the **Ehrenburg** (*Open* Tue–Sun). Remodelled externally to suit the 19th-century taste for the Gothic, it retains much of its original interior, including its chapel and the Riesensaal (Giants' Hall), so called because of the 28 plaster heavies holding up the painted ceiling. You can also see the bedroom where the British Queen Victoria stayed while visiting Ehrenburg.

While the burghers built their fine half-timbered and high-gabled town houses, the dukes gave the town a Renaissance touch. Johann Casimir was responsible for the academy known as the Casimirianum and for the Stadthaus, facing the rococo town hall across the cobbled market square. The ducal imprint can be seen, too, in the Gothic Church of St. Moriz, with its incredibly elaborate 13m-high (43ft) memorial to Duke Johann Friedrich (*d*1598).

THE SAXE-COBURGS
The influence of this aristocratic family was out of all proportion to its possessions or power. Comely rather than rich, its children were married off judiciously and, by the 19th century, were well established in many of the courts of Europe. Most famous of them was Albert—consort to the British Queen Victoria—born at Rosenau Castle, near Coburg, and brought up in the Ehrenburg. His statue stands in the market square. Coburg blood ran in Victoria's own veins and after Albert's death in 1861 she stayed here several times. One of her grandsons, Carl Eduard, ruled the duchy until its abolition in 1919. In the same year, Ferdinand von Coburg-Kohary returned here after his abdication as Czar of Bulgaria, devoting his life to ornithology. The birds he stuffed form the basis of the collection in the town's Natural History Museum (*Open* daily).

INFORMATION
Coburg: Herrengasse 4, tel: 09561/7 41 80; www.coburg-tourist.com

221

Coburg's massive Veste fortress above the town

CHILDREN'S APPEAL
Dinkelsbühl has escaped the ravages of wars, though there was a close shave in the course of the Thirty Years' War, when the fury of the besieging Swedes was mollified by an appeal made to their commander by the town's children. The event is marked by the *Kinder-zeche*, a lively 10-day festival held in July.

INFORMATION
Dinkelsbühl: Marktplatz, tel: 09851/9 02 40; www.dinkelsbuehl.de

Oxcarts for tourists keep the medieval touch alive in Dinkelsbühl, a town that still has watch-towers and ramparts

►►► Dinkelsbühl 206B2

More compact than Rothenburg-ob-der-Tauber, farther up the Romantische Strasse (Romantic Road; see page 230), Dinkelsbühl is one of Germany's most delightful medieval towns, perfectly preserved within its ring of walls, bastions and 16 towers.

The best approach is across the causeway leading to the late 14th-century gateway known as the Rothenburger Tor. From the gate the broad Martin Luther Strasse curves down to the market square with its splendid early Renaissance town houses, among them the Deutsches Haus, with seven projecting floors reaching up into its high gable. The nearby Hezelhof has tiered flowerladen balconies in its lovely inner courtyard. The church of St. George still has its Romanesque tower; it is one of the grandest hall churches in southern Germany, with fan vaulting spanning the lofty interior, carving and statuary.

Dinkelsbühl has many more delights that you can discover on your own by wandering the narrow streets, or take a polyglot tour on foot that starts at St. George's. An evening walk around the ramparts at night is an atmospheric experience, especially in the company of the town's nightwatchman as he does his rounds (Easter–Oct daily 9pm; Sat only in winter).

A BAROQUE GEM
Ellingen was rebuilt following its destruction in the Thirty Years' War and is a little gem of baroque town planning, with a pretty Rathaus and several churches.

► Ellingen 206B2

Ellingen was for many years the headquarters of the Deutscher Orden (the Order of Teutonic Knights), a militant brotherhood of priests and soldiers founded around 1190 during the First Crusade, but best remembered for their vigorous conversion to Christianity of the pagan population of the Baltic seaboard. Their dour castle, built between 1711 and 1721, rears clifflike over the town and is awkwardly approached from the side. It is enlivened by its main façade, a splendid staircase, rococo interiors and an elaborately decorated church. The corridors are hung with portraits of the Hoch- und Deutschmeister, the order's leaders.

▶ Freising   206C1

Easily reached from Munich by S-Bahn suburban train, Freising is a city in its own right, a bishopric from as early as 739. The dominant feature of the town is the Domberg, a bluff of higher land looking out over the interminable flatlands stretching southwards to Munich. The chalk-white cathedral rises over a cluster of churches and other ecclesiastical buildings, including the Prince-Bishop's Residenz, now a museum (*Open* Tue–Sun), and the Gothic Johannes-Kapelle, with its baroque interior. The cathedral interior exults in baroque splendour, but a more sombre era is evoked in the crypt, with its capitals and columns bearing strange figures of men and beasts.

▶ Ingolstadt   206C1

Strategically situated on the upper reaches of the Danube, Ingolstadt is one of Bavaria's great cities, with a long history and a thriving present (oil refineries, Audi works). First mentioned in AD806, Ingolstadt blossomed in the Middle Ages. Come into town via the brick Kreuztor gateway of 1385. Beyond is the minster, dedicated to Our Lady, its high west gable flanked by asymmetrical towers. There are fine old houses, including the Ickstatt-Haus of 1740, a rococo confection in yellow with white stucco icing. The interior of the church of Maria de Victoria is from the same period. Note its painted ceiling, which is a masterpiece of perspective effects.

Excursions

Weltenburg Abbey (45km/28 miles east via Neustadt) is on the Danube at the entrance to the Donaudurchbruch, a spectacular gorge cut by the river en route to its confluence with the Altmühl at Kelheim. 'The Danube in Flames', a floodlit lighting of the gorge, takes place on the first Saturday in July. A high point of German 18th-century baroque, the abbey church's oval interior verges on high kitsch, with a tableau of St. George smiting the dragon and cherubs flying around in chunky clouds. It certainly draws the crowds, whom you can join for beer (the abbey's own) in the courtyard.

WEIHENSTEPHAN
On a wooded bluff to the west of Freising is Weihenstephan, famous for its beer (from the world's oldest brewery; 1040) and dairy products. It also has an outpost of the Technical University of Munich, concerned with food, land use and environment.

MILITARY MUSEUM
Ingolstadt's importance as a fortress and garrison town was enhanced in the 19th century with the construction of massive fortifications. Most have been razed, but some severely classical gateways remain, including the Kavaller Heydeck. The Gothic Neues Schloss, a relic of earlier defences, is an appropriate setting for the Bavarian Army Museum (*Open* Tue–Sun).

NEUBURG AN DER DONAU
Neuburg an der Donau is an old Residenz town 16km (10 miles) up the Danube from Ingolstadt. The place is dominated by the Renaissance palace built by Protestant Prince Ottheinrich, whose hope of making the town's Hofkirche a beacon of Protestantism in Catholic Bavaria was frustrated by the Counter-Reformation.

223

The 14th-century Kreuztor gateway, hexagonal, with six pointed turrets, stands at the entrance to Ingolstadt's old town

LAVISH PAGEANT

In 1475, at the peak of its prosperity and prestige, Landshut marked the wedding of its Prince George to a Polish princess with lavish celebrations which became a byword all over Europe. These great days are recalled every four years by contemporary Germany's most extravagant pageant, the Landshuter Hochzeit, when revellers in period costume perform against the splendid stage set of Landshut's historic townscape. The next pageant is in 2005.

INFORMATION

Landshut: Altstadt 315, tel: 0871/92 20 50; www.landshut.de

'DANIEL' TOWER

Nördlingen's massive grey stone parish church of St. George has a lofty white interior and an 89m (292ft) tower nicknamed 'Daniel'. It is worth the climb for the view over the red roofs of the oval-shaped town. From here, an inner oval of streets can clearly be picked out, marking the course of an older ring of fortifications, long since demolished.

Nürnberg's huge Schöner Brunnen (beautiful fountain) contains 40 different figures arranged in a pyramid

▶ Landshut

207D1

On the banks of the River Isar at the foot of Trausnitz Castle, Landshut has kept much of the appearance and atmosphere of the provincial capital it once was. This old city is focused on two fine market streets lined with late medieval town houses, many with stepped gables and arcaded courtyards. The gently curving Altstadt (old town) dates to the founding of the city in 1204, and the Neustadt (new town) was laid out a century later.

The Altstadt is closed off by the church of St. Martin, a bold Gothic building. Its slender tower rises to 131m (428ft), higher than the castle behind it and the tallest brick structure of its kind in the world. Among the treasures of the light and airy interior is a huge Madonna and Child, carved in 1520 by a local man, Hans Leinberger.

In 1543, Duke Ludwig X moved from the castle into the Stadtresidenz, which has a splendidly decorated interior; part of it houses Landshut's museum (*Open* Tue–Sun). Not long afterwards, the castle itself (*Open* Tue–Sun) was refurbished as a base for the lavish court life of Prince William of Bavaria. He kept the 13th-century chapel, with its superb Romanesque statuary, adding a fine galleried courtyard in the Renaissance style, and had the famous Narrentreppe staircase painted with robust figures from the Italian comic theatre. The castle terrace gives a spectacular panorama over the town.

Excursion

A sixth of the world's hops are grown in the **Hallertau** area around Mainburg. This is pretty, hilly countryside, with hops standing out against dark woodlands. Pickers no longer camp in the fields, but the season is still celebrated by the election of a Hop Queen in the village of Wolnzach. Beer drinkers may be interested in the Hopfenmuseum (hop museum; *open* Tue–Sun) being assembled here.

225

▶ **Nördlingen**   *206B1*

Nordlingen's heyday came between the 14th and 16th centuries, when its great Whitsun Fair drew traders from all over Germany. Its subsequent stagnation has helped preserve its townscape, much to the delight of today's many visitors. It is now one of the principal stops along the Romantische Strasse. The ramparts, intact after 500 years, have 16 towers and five gateways, from which five main streets converge on the Marktplatz with its 13th-century Rathaus.

Excursions

Two fine churches are close to Nördlingen. In spite of its baroque furnishings, the former abbey church at **Kaisheim** (6km/4 miles northeast of Donauwörth) evokes the severe lives of its 14th-century Cistercian founders.

   Neresheim (19km/12 miles southwest) has a fine abbey church, too. The last work of Balthasar Neumann, it is a fitting conclusion to the career of this foremost architect of the South German baroque. Under its three domes, the interior is unusually light and spacious, with fine ceiling paintings by the Tirolean Martin Knoller.

▶▶▶ **Nürnberg (Nuremberg)**   *206C2*

Crowning the outcrop of warm red sandstone from which much of Nürnberg is built, the **Kaiserburg**▶ (*Open* daily), or imperial castle, goes back to the city's founding years in the 11th century. Kings and emperors resided here for 500 years, and the sprawling complex of buildings was added to, demolished and rebuilt throughout this time. Thus the tall five-sided tower dates from 1040, the two-tier Imperial Chapel from the 12th century and the stables (now the youth hostel) from the late 15th century.

   Directly below the castle timber-framed and gabled houses are crammed up against the ramparts. The painter

Nürnberg's Hauptmarkt, the site of Germany's biggest pre-Christmas market, the Christkindlsmarkt

MEDIEVAL HEYDAY
Before the devastation wrought by the air raids of 1945, Nürnberg was Germany's greatest surviving medieval city. The destruction was not total, and sensitive rebuilding has respected the ancient street pattern, enabling the visitor to recapture the atmosphere of the city's heyday, in the 15th and 16th centuries, when it was the principal focus of Germany's politics, culture, trade, science and technology.

INFORMATION
Nürnberg: Hauptmarkt 18, tel: 0911/2 33 61 35; www.nuernberg.de

TOY FAIR
In view of Nürnberg's long-standing role as the toy-manufacturing capital of Europe, it is fitting that the annual Toy Fair, the most important of its kind, is held here.

'THE NASTY GIRL'
Passau was confronted with an ugly chapter from its Nazi past in a film which achieved international success. It was based on research in the 1980s by a local girl, Anja Rosmum, who courageously examined the past of many respected burghers: She found that some had once been active Nazis, but had kept it hidden. For this she was victimized and physically attacked locally. But nationally she became a heroine. The film *The Nasty Girl* told her story.

These decorated steins (beer mugs) are typical of Passau, which is famous for its beer

NAZI RALLIES
The huge parade ground outside Nürnberg where Hitler held his biggest rallies (filmed by Leni Riefenstahl) is now a weed-covered expanse of crumbling concrete echoing with memories. The tribune from where Hitler harangued the Nazi hordes still stands. A historical exhibition about the Nazi dictatorship can be seen in the nearby Kongresshalle (styled on the Colosseum in Rome; *open* daily). The Palace of Justice where the Nürnberg war crimes trials were held is still the main law court (Fürtherstrasse 212).

and engraver Albrecht Dürer lived here from 1509 until his death in 1528. The Dürer-Haus (Albrecht-Dürer-Strasse 39. *Open* Tue–Sun) has good interiors and displays, though there are more copies than original works In the Burgstrasse is the 16th-century Fenbohaus, now the city museum (*Open* Tue–Sat). Beyond it is the Rathausplatz, with the Altes Rathaus and, opposite it, the twin towers of the early Gothic **St. Sebald's Church▶**, with outstanding artwork in the interior by Kraft (*Christ Carrying the Cross*), Vischer (*Shrine of St. Sebald*), and Stoss (*Passion and Crucifixion*).

South is the Hauptmarkt, a daily market and site of the pre-Christmas Christkindlesmarkt. The Schöner Brunnen fountain competes with the gabled façade of the Gothic Frauenkirche (Church of Our Lady) and its 16th-century mechanical clock with automata that perform at noon. Clock-making has a long tradition in the city.

Nürnberg's Altstadt is divided into roughly equal halves by the River Pegnitz. One arm of the river is bridged by the Heiliggeist-Spital, a 14th-century almshouse, now a restaurant; downstream is the Weinstadl, a venerable wine store that, together with an old water tower, covered bridge, and weeping willows, makes the most idyllic scene.

Although the southern half of the Altstadt has a more modern air, it contains much of interest. The Gothic church of St. Lawrence has a cathedral-like west front. Inside are splendid works: Stoss's carving of the Annunciation is suspended from the vaulting; the tall tabernacle is carried by the sculpted figures of Adam Kraft and his apprentices. The nearby Mauthalle of 1502

was built to store corn; its six-floor roof is pierced by sinister hooded dormers, so characteristic of the city.

Although Nürnberg has long lost its medieval dominance in German politics and culture, it retains a fine choice of museums. The Spielzeugmuseum (Toy Museum; *Open* Tue–Sun) holds the largest and most varied toy collection in the world and is great fun for children young and old. Highlights include the dolls' house collection, a mechanical Ferris wheel, 'Tin World' with its toy train sets and steam engines. At the outstanding **Germanisches Nationalmuseum▶▶** (*Open* Tue–Sun), founded in the 19th century, exhaustion is only avoided by concentrating on a fraction of the exhibits. Don't miss the works of the great painters who spanned the transition from Middle Ages to Renaissance (Dürer, Altdorfer, Cranach) or the carvings and sculptures of their contemporaries, including Kraft, Riemenschneider and Stoss.

226

►► Passau
207E1

On a long tongue of land at the confluence of the rivers Danube, Inn and Ilz, Passau has one of the most spectacular settings of any German city. Wooded heights hem in the rivers and provide splendid sites for the pilgrimage church of Maria Hilf to the south and for the Veste to the north, the great fortress built by the city's prince-bishops to keep unruly townsfolk firmly under control.

Passau is still one of Germany's main gateways to Austria; steamers sail from here to Vienna and beyond, to Budapest and the Black Sea. Inland, the web of narrow streets leads to the **cathedral►**, with its trio of helmeted towers. Founded in the 8th century, it owes much of its present appearance to a thoroughgoing baroque rebuilding (1680). Inside is the world's biggest church organ, installed in the 1920s and with a total of 17,774 pipes and 233 registers. It is played daily at noon and at 7.30pm on Thursday in summer. Reconstruction spared the flamboyant Gothic east end of the cathedral, best viewed from the Residenzplatz, an irregular square flanked by fine Renaissance mansions. Opposite the 14th-century Rathaus is a large museum of glass, in the Hotel Wilder Mann (*Open* daily).

The city's splendid roofscape is best appreciated from the lofty tower of the Veste. The bishops began building the fortress in 1219 and added to it over the centuries, creating an extraordinary mixture of Gothic, Renaissance, and baroque architecture. It now houses a medley of museums and galleries, including an interesting folk museum (*Open* daily).

INFORMATION
Passau: Rathausplatz 3, tel: 0851/9 55 980; www.passau.de

BAROQUE MONASTERIES
To the west of Passau are delightful landscapes between the rivers Vils, Rott and Inn. Visit the baroque monasteries (Vornbach, Aldersbach and Fürstenzell, the last with a particularly splendid library), castles (Neuburg, looming over the Inn; Ortenburg, with one of the finest carved ceilings in Germany) and attractive small towns (Vilshofen, Aidenbach and Rotthalmünster, with a fine parish church and pilgrimage chapel).

227

Passau, on the Danube, has a legacy of glorious buildings from its past as a Free Imperial City

ROMAN GATE
Regensburg's history
goes back further than
the Middle Ages. The
Celtic name, Radaspona,
survives in the French
name of Ratisbonne. As
Castra Regina, it
guarded the frontier of
the Roman Empire at the
northern point of the
Danube. The remains of
the Roman Praetorian
Gate still stand in the
strangely named street
Unter den Schwibbögen
(Under the Flying
Buttress).

INFORMATION
Regensburg: Altes
Rathausplatz 4, tel:
0941/5 07 44 10;
www.regensburg.de

HAPPY ANGEL
Regensburg cathedral's
rich sculptural decora-
tion includes the famous
*Angel of the
Annunciation*, positively
bursting with enthusiasm
at the good news he has
to tell, while another
note is struck by the figures popularly known as
*The Devil and His
Grandma*, housed in
niches in the main portal.

▶▶▶ **Regensburg**   207D2

The capital of eastern Bavaria, this historic cathedral city
on the Danube was one of the largest in Germany to
escape wartime destruction. Its narrow cobbled streets
and intimate squares evoke its medieval heyday, when its
merchants were among the most prosperous in Europe.

Near the remains of the Roman Praetorian Gate rise the
lacelike **cathedral**▶▶ spires, added as late as 1869 to the
great edifice begun in the 13th century. This is one of
Germany's finest Gothic churches and has lovely cloisters
and 14th-century stained glass (guided tours daily.) The
squares around the cathedral form the kernel of the city.

The cathedral's parish church, the Niedermünster-
kirche, is a mid-12th-century basilica built over the
remains of three previous churches. The oldest (AD700)
goes back to the Merovingian Age and was erected on top
of Roman remains. Across the Alter Kornmarkt is the
ancient Liebfraukirche (Church of Our Lady). Its interior
was remodelled in rococo style to suit 18th-century tastes.

Whole days could be spent wandering Regensburg's
labyrinth of streets and alleyways lined by venerable
houses in a style as much Italian as German. Like their
counterparts in various Italian towns, the city's leading
families built towers in competition with each other and in
the 13th century there were 60 such structures, of which 20
survive to give the city its unique skyline. Among them is
the Baumburger Turm, with its gallery, and the Goldener
Turm in the Wahlenstrasse, the city's oldest street.

The broad Danube makes a pleasing contrast to this
medieval inner city, best appreciated from the upper
arches of the Steinerne Brücke (Old Stone Bridge), built in
the 12th century and for 800 years the only river crossing
hereabouts. To the left of the towered gateway guarding
the bridgehead is the immense roof of the 17th-century
salt store and at its side, Regensburg's oldest restaurant,
the Historische Wurstküche.

The mostly 19th-century palace of the princes of Thurn
und Taxis presides over the far side of central
Regensburg. The palace incorporates the cloisters of the
church of St. Emmeram, famous for its tombs. Among
them is that of poor Queen Emma, who died in AD876 and
whose tomb bears a mournful expression. (Guided tours
of the palace and cloisters: Apr–Oct daily; Nov–Mar
Sat–Sun only.)

The aristocratic air of an earlier era is captured in the
Gothic Altes Rathaus, with splendid interiors redolent of
the Imperial Diet, which used to assemble here.

The Historisches Museum (*Open* Tue–Sun), in the buildings of an old monastery, displays a wonderful scale
model of the city as it used to be, and the works of members of the Danube School, including Albrecht Altdorfer.

Excursions

Kallmünz, about 27km (17 miles) northwest, is a self-con-
scious little place and a favourite subject for painters. The
old stone bridge near the confluence of the rivers Vils and
Naab is overlooked by the castle, ruined in the Thirty
Years' War but still a wonderful lookout point.

Walhalla▶, a gleaming copy of the Parthenon, sits in an
un-Grecian setting of wooded slopes running down to the
Danube. Inspired by Ludwig I of Bavaria and completed in

1842, it houses 126 busts of the great and good of Germanic history, such as Frederick the Great, Goethe and Schiller. The difficult choice of who should be celebrated, stretching over several centuries and countries, has not always been uncontroversial. Some of them are now totally forgotten, as earlier historical assessments are re-examined and modified over the years. River boats from Regensburg and Kelheim make the journey to Walhalla, but be warned— you have to climb 358 steps to the temple. The easiest way to reach it is by road. At the top is a view over the Danube and the ruins of Donaustauf castle (*Open* daily. Boat trips to Walhalla start from Regensburg Apr to mid-Oct at 2pm).

A view over the River Danube at Regensburg

THURN AND TAXIS
Schloss Emmeram, the Thurn and Taxis ancestral home, has seen many high dramas over the centuries, and in more recent times some wild parties thrown by its high-living young *maitresse*, Princess Gloria, until her husband, Prince Johannes, died in 1991. His death left crippling taxes to pay, and she was reduced to selling much of her jewels and family furniture before the Bavarian state relented and allowed her to keep the bulk of the palace's other treasures on condition she open her home to visitors. It was the final humiliation in the decline of a family whose fortune was built on Germany's early postal system.

ALBRECHT ALTDORFER
Altdorfer raised landscape painting to high emotional intensity, and found time to serve his native Regensburg as city architect.

The statues on the main doorway are typical of the elaborate decoration of St. Peter's cathedral

RIES VALLEY

Both Nördlingen and the little Residenz town of Wallerstein lie in the vast fertile depression known as the Ries. Its origin was long a subject of controversy, but it is now known to have been created by the impact of a meteorite some 15 million years ago. The Apollo 7 astronauts studied the region in preparation for their moon landing. The history of the Ries valley and its continuing significance for terrestrial and space research is described in Nördlingen's Rieskrater Museum (*Open* Tue–Sun).

230

Würzburg, on the Main, lies amid vineyards. The people are jovial and open-minded, as so often in wine-producing areas

►► Romantische Strasse   *206A3*

Germany's renowned Romantische Strasse is the most popular of all the named tourist highways spanning the country. Linking Würzburg in the wine country of Franconia with the Alps at Füssen, and some 350km (217 miles) long, it is less remarkable for the tranquil scenery it traverses than for the string of historic towns through which it passes. Between them they encapsulate the essence of the country's past, from medieval *Gemütlichkeit*, or cosiness (Rothenburg-ob-der-Tauber, Dinkelsbühl, Nördlingen), via the mercantile magnificence of the early Renaissance (Augsburg), to the wonders of the baroque (Würzburg). The major destinations on the way are described under their own headings, but others mentioned here should also be seen if possible.

The route strikes southwest from **Würzburg** (see pages 235–236) to join the pretty valley of the Tauber at **Tauberbischofsheim**, an unspoiled medieval town with timber-framed buildings and a good local history museum in the old princely palace. Beyond **Bad Mergentheim** (see page 213) is **Weikersheim**, the home of the Hohenlohe family (with a splendid Knights Hall and formal park).

At **Creglingen** and **Detwang** there are churches that feature fine altarpieces by Tilman Riemenschneider, while **Feuchtwangen** has Romanesque cloisters that serve as an open-air theatre in summer.

On the far side of the Ries (see panel), standing out boldly above the countryside, **Harburg Castle** no longer bars the way since the road tunnels straight under it.

On either side of **Augsburg** (see pages 210–211) the road runs across the broad Bavarian plain. To the south of the city is the **Lechfeld**; today it is a NATO base and it is redolent of military memories. In AD955 it was the site of one of the most decisive battles in European history, when Otto the Great finally put an end to the heathen Hungarians' incursions into western Europe and drove them back down the Danube.

Beyond the hillside town of **Landsberg** (see pages 251–252) lie the Alps, a spectacular barrier when seen from the town walls of **Schongau** on a clear day. Easily reached from the Romantische Strasse as it nears its end at **Füssen** (see page 245) are some of Bavaria's greatest architectural treasures, the rococo church at **Wies** (see page 265) and the royal castles at **Hohenschwangau** and **Neuschwanstein** (see page 246).

►►► Rothenburg-ob-der-Tauber 206B2

Rothenburg is among Germany's best-preserved and most picturesque medieval towns, but *very* touristy. At one time more important than Nürnberg, Rothenburg stagnated after the Thirty Years' War before being discovered by Romantic artists and writers in the 19th century as the 'epitome of Germanic medievalism'.

Completely ringed by ramparts, the town overlooks the winding valley of the Tauber. A succession of charming pictures unfolds as you stroll the cobbled streets or pace the sentry walk along the walls. A sea of red roofs rises above the half-timbered, high-gabled houses, no two quite alike, crowded together along the crooked streets. The highest roof is the Gothic St. Jakobs-Kirche. Its cool interior holds a meticulously carved 1505 altarpiece by the great Tilman Riemenschneider. The focal point of the town is the Marktplatz, dominated by the **Rathaus►**, half Gothic, half

BIBULOUS SAVIOUR
Rothenburg's perfect state of preservation is in part due to its having survived the Thirty Years' War intact. The threat by General Tilly to raze the town was averted when Mayor Nusch accepted, and won, a challenge to drain a six-pint-plus measure of wine in one go. This feat—the so-called *Meistertrunk*—is commemorated by the mechanical figures on the clock attached to the Ratstrinkstube and also by a lively pageant.

231

Renaissance, with a splendid Imperial Hall inside. Enjoy the view from the top of the 60m (197ft) bell tower.

Another excellent viewpoint is from the Burggarten, the little park on the promontory once occupied by the castle of the Hohenstaufens. Spanning the river below is the strange Doppelbrücke (Double Bridge), and not far away the even stranger Topplerschlösschen, a defensive tower on which an ordinary little house is perched.

Picturesque highlights of Rothenburg's townscape include the Plönlein, where changing street levels enhance the scene around the 1385 Siebersturm gateway; the patrician mansions along the Herrengasse; the Rodertor gateway, flanked by twin little tollhouses; and the Gerlach Schmiede (smithy) nearby, with its impossibly exaggerated gable.

Rothenburg-ob-der-Tauber retains its old-world quaintness

INFORMATION
Rothenburg: Marktplatz 2, tel: 09861/40 48 00; www.rothenburg.de

The French national anthem, the *Marseillaise*, rings out from a *Glockenspiel* (carillon) in the town hall tower of Cham, on the northwest edge of the Bavarian Forest, every day at five minutes past noon, in tribute to the little town's most famous son, Nikolaus Graf von Luckner. Luckner was a professional soldier who rose to the rank of Marshal in the French Army in 1791. The newly composed *Marseillaise* was dedicated to him in Strasbourg in 1792. Luckner's luck ran out during the French Revolution, however, and he died on the guillotine scaffold in 1794.

232

▶ Staffelstein 206B3

Staffelstein, with its fine Rathaus, is one of a number of half-timbered small towns and villages on the fertile floor of the broad and tranquil valley of the Main, north of Bamberg. Lichtenfels, the country's basket-making base, is just upstream. Attractive enough in themselves, these places are visited less for their own sake than for their proximity to two great works of baroque architecture facing each other across the tranquil vale.

Crowning the wooded height to the west is the massive **Kloster Banz▶** (*Open* daily), a monastery founded by Benedictine monks in 1069 and rebuilt between 1695 and 1768. The domestic buildings (with collections that include an ichthyosaurus) are dominated by the twin spires of the church, the work of Johann Dientzenhofer. The interior is outstanding, with splendid stuccoes, bright frescoes and vigourous altarpieces. From the terrace are sweeping views across the valley towards the pilgrimage church of Vierzehnheiligen.

Vierzehnheiligen Pilgrimage Church▶▶ (*Open* daily) is one of the key buildings of the 18th century in Germany. The basilica is a place of pilgrimage not only for the faithful but for anyone prepared to be persuaded that the German spirit is capable of the most sublime flights of fancy.

The Benedictine monastery of Kloster Banz, not far from Staffelstein

A stiff uphill walk from the large parking area leads to a bevy of booths selling every kind of souvenir. The church's conventional exterior, in rough-looking sandstone, is grand enough, with two tall towers, but gives little hint of the delights that lie beyond. Inside, the mood changes; all semblance of convention disappears in the abundant light that illuminates an extravagant interior in a froth of pink, gold and white decoration.

The focal point is less the main altar at the east end than the central confection, 'half coral reef, half fairy sedan chair' (Nikolaus Pevsner), adorned with figures of the 14 saints who gave the church its name. This ecstatic creation is the work of the great Balthasar Neumann. His patron was the ambitious prince-bishop of Bamberg, Friedrich Carl von Schönborn.

▶ Straubing   207D1

Once one of Bavaria's most important cities, Straubing is still the focus for the rich arable region known as the Gäuboden and has kept much of the air of a prosperous provincial city of the late Middle Ages.

The Romans built a fort here to guard their Danube frontier; spectacular evidence of their presence is provided by the rich hoard of gold masks and other objects that is the pride of the Gäuboden Museum (*Open Tue–Sun*). The wealth of a later age is expressed in a heritage of fine buildings, including such churches as St. Peter's, with its atmospheric walled graveyard; the tall-towered Jakobskirche; and the little baroque jewel of the Ursuline church. Straubing's main landmark is its 14th-century tower dividing the elongated market square into two parts; its corner turrets enabled an all-around watch to be kept for intruders or for the fires that could easily devastate the timber-built towns of the time.

Straubing's main festival, the biggest in Bavaria after Munich's Oktoberfest, is the Gäuboden Fair, which is held annually in August.

Excursions

Deggendorf, some 34km (21 miles) southeast, resembles Straubing on a smaller scale, with a fine market square dominated by the town tower.

Nearby are two splendid baroque monasteries: **Metten**, with a particularly fine library (tours daily), and **Niederalteich**, the first foundation of its kind in Bavaria. Built as a Gothic hall church, it was remodelled in baroque style. The unusual lantern windows in the galleries offer a good view of the vaulting.

The rich agricultural land around Straubing was settled at an early date and is well endowed with old churches, including the picturesquely sited Romanesque church at **Rankam**. Of later date are the Benedictine buildings of the monastery at **Oberalteich**, completed in 1630, though the interior had to wait another 100 years before being decorated with its spectacular frescoes.

AGNES BERNAUER

Straubing's most famous figure was Agnes Bernauer, a barber's daughter whose beauty so impressed Duke Ernst's son that he married her in spite of her humble origins. This so enraged the duke that in 1435 he had Agnes tried on a trumped-up charge of witchcraft, then executed by drowning in the Danube. The tragic tale is re-enacted in the courtyard of the ducal castle every four years.

233

Straubing, always lively, is at its most boisterous during the Gäuboden festival in August

▶▶ Waldsassen

In the Middle Ages, many monasteries were established in the densely wooded uplands along the ancient border between Bavaria and Bohemia. Monks toiled to convert the forest to farmland and bring Christianity to the few inhabitants. Waldsassen (1133) is one of the greatest of these bases of medieval civilization. It stood alone for centuries until the little town to which it gave its name began to develop in the early 17th century.

The monastery buildings date from 1681 to 1704. The long, narrow church is one of the masterpieces of the great Bavarian baroque architect Georg Dientzenhofer, who worked with a cosmopolitan team including the Italian Carleone, who embellished the interior with 200 stucco angels. Attracting special reverence is a battered figure of Christ, found hanging on the border barrier with Czechoslovakia in 1951 at the height of the cold war.

In the monastery itself is the library. Karl Stopl, the master carver responsible for this extraordinary interior, took as his theme everything that goes into the production of a book; the sequence of 10 figures supporting the upper level includes the humble rag collector (gathering raw materials for paper), the author, the critic (his bound hands symbolizing his unproductive vocation), and the reader (a portrait of the artist).

Excursions

The gentle hills and vales of Waldsassen have always attracted admirers, including Goethe. **Tirschenreuth**, to the south, is the area's market centre. The Renaissance Rathaus survived a great fire in 1814. All around are pools and ponds, breeding carp and trout.

On a hill to the northwest of Waldsassen stands one of the most unusual buildings in Bavaria, the pilgrimage church of **Kappel**. Commissioned by the abbot of Waldsassen, Dientzenhofer designed a church to celebrate the Holy Trinity, linking together three rounded apses, each topped with a bulbous tower. Seen across the fields, the church's exotic outline is more reminiscent of Orthodox Russia than Catholic Bavaria.

THE SUDETENLAND
On the Czechs' side of their frontier with northern Bavaria and Saxony is the much-contested Sudetenland. Because of its large German minority, Hitler seized it in 1938: then the Czechs won it back in 1945, and in reprisal expelled most of the Germans. Many of them settled in Bavaria, and during the Communist era felt deeply bitter. Even with today's open borders, hard feelings linger.

Waldsassen dates from the early 17th century

▶▶▶ **Würzburg**   *206A3*

This university city, the ancient seat of powerful prince-bishops, stands among vineyards on the steep banks of the River Main. Celtic tribesmen first fortified the strategic height occupied by the massive Marienberg fortress, but Würzburg's history really begins with the martyrdom here in AD689 of an Irish missionary, St. Kilian, whose mission was to convert the locals to Christianity. His gravestone is in the cathedral named after him, in the middle of the old city on the eastern bank of the river.

Würzburg is notable for its many churches. One of the oldest is the round, thick-walled Marienkirche, in the courtyard of the **Marienberg fortress▶**. The fortress was rebuilt and extended over the years to become a most formidable stronghold. Occupied for nearly 500 years by the prince-bishops, it now houses the splendid collections of the regional **museum▶** (Mainfränkisches Museum; *Open* Tue–Sun); its greatest treasures are the tenderly sculpted sandstone figures of Adam and Eve by the great Tilman Riemenschneider (1460–1531), who was both artist and mayor.

By the 18th century, the Marienberg had become too cramped for the bishops' lifestyle, and the bishop's quarters moved to purpose-built accommodation on the far side of the city. Their new address, the **Würzburg Residenz▶▶**, designed by Balthasar Neumann, is the greatest baroque building of its kind in Germany, dominating the vast cobbled square linking it to the town. Its interior spaces are staggering, in both sheer size and lavishness of decoration. They include the grand staircase, covered by the largest ceiling painting in the world (by

The Marienberg fortress overlooks the River Main at Würzburg

INFORMATION
Würzburg: Falkenhaus, Am Markt, tel: 0931/37 23 35; www.wurzburg.de

the Venetian Tiepolo), the oval Kaisersaal (with *trompe-l'oeil* painting, also by Tiepolo) and the sumptuous Gartensaal, the great ground-floor room linking the palace to the gardens beyond. These form a perfect example of rococo garden art and make an ideal backdrop for the summer Mozart Festival that is held here. Neumann's palace chapel, the gorgeous Hofkirche (Residenz; *Open* daily), is a popular place for weddings.

The city suffered almost as grievously as Dresden in World War II, when an air raid left most of central Würzburg in ruins. Bravely rebuilt, it is a cheerful and lively place, with plenty of wine taverns and a buzz of student life. Its restored churches include the splendidly severe Romanesque **Cathedral▶**, with the gravestones of the prince-bishops; among them are two wonderful examples by Riemenschneider.

Opposite the cathedral is the Neumünster, built over St. Kilian's grave and given a fine baroque façade in the early 18th century. It also has a garden with the grave of Germany's medieval troubadour Walter von der Vogelweide. In the market square stands the Gothic Marienkapelle, with Neumann's tombstone at its portal. Nearby is the fine rococo façade of the Haus zum Falken, meticulously restored after the bombing (and now the city tourist office). Spared destruction were the two great charitable institutions founded to house the city's senior citizens, the Bürgerspital of 1319 and the Juliusspital of 1576. Both derive part of their income from their vineyards; their produce is dispensed in their atmospheric wine taverns.

Würzburg's only church to survive the war unscathed was the Käppele pilgrimage chapel. Owing its good fortune to its isolated position above the wooded ravine separating it from the Marienberg, it is yet another dazzling display of baroque virtuosity by Neumann.

Excursions On either side of Würzburg, the deep valley of the Main forms one of Germany's most distinctive wine-growing regions. Its excellent wines are relatively dry and come in bulbous flasks, Bocksbeutel, quite different from the elegant bottles of Rhine and Mosel vintages.

Upstream from the city, one delightful little place succeeds another: **Sommerhausen**, popular with artists; half-timbered **Ochsenfurt** ('Oxford') within its ramparts; **Frickenhausen**, accessible only through one of its four gateways; **Marktbreit**; **Sulzfeld**... Walled **Volkach** has many picturesque houses, a 16th-century Rathaus, and a local museum in the baroque Schelfenhaus. Crowning the hilly vineyards outside the town is Maria im Weingarten (Our Lady of the Vineyard), a late Gothic pilgrimage church, housing one of Riemenschneider's most delicate works, *Madonna in a Rose Garland*.

The summer palace of the prince-bishops of Würzburg, **Veitshöchheim**, 7km (4.5 miles) northwest (*Open* Apr–Oct Tue–Sun), has an exquisite rococo garden, a delight of hedged enclosures, playful statuary, and the Grosser See, an artificial lake with an even more artificial Mount Parnassus rising from it. This jewel of landscape architecture was rescued from neglect by the indefatigable King Ludwig I of Bavaria, who restored it to its former glory.

236

Würzburg's splendid Residenz was intended to symbolize the wealth and power of the ruling prince-bishops

Revolutionary, exile, focus of scandal, writer and composer—Richard Wagner led a life that at times matched the more dramatic passages of his titanic operas. Certainly, in works such as Tristan und Isolde, *the themes of his own eventful career found their most eloquent musical expression.*

In 1834, at the age of 21, Wagner was appointed director of the Magdeburg opera. Here he wrote his first operas, and married a singer, Minna Plater, with whom he lived for 25 years in a largely unhappy marriage. To escape his private life he composed increasingly, including *Rienzi* (1840) and *Der fliegende Holländer* (*The Flying Dutchman*, 1842). In the latter, the romantic idea of redemption through love—a theme recurring in Wagner's operas but absent from his marriage—is first expressed. Mixed receptions of his next, less conventional, works, including *Tannhäuser*, reinforced his belief in his own ability; this period of musical innovation even saw him as a political revolutionary, manning barricades during the Dresden uprising.

New rules Wagner abandoned the traditional 'rules' of recitative and aria for a continuous musical dialogue, and used the leitmotiv, a representation of symbols and characters in musical terms, to perfection. With the help of his friend Franz Liszt, *Lohengrin* (1850) was triumphantly performed in Weimar, despite Wagner's enforced exile in Zürich due to the failure of the uprising. In Zürich he began a passionate affair with the wife of a Swiss benefactor and conceived the idea for *Tristan und Isolde*, while also working on his masterwork, *Der Ring des Nibelungen*, a cycle of four epic operas based on German mythology.

Scandal erupted again when Cosima, Liszt's daughter and the wife of composer Hans von Bülow, bore Wagner a child. She obtained a divorce and, after Minna's death in 1866, Cosima married Wagner in 1870.

In his later years, Richard Wagner turned his attention to the foundation of the ideal opera house. In 1876 the Bayreuth Festspielhaus was opened with a complete performance of Wagner's *Ring* cycle. (The opera house is now the venue for the annual Bayreuth Festival.)

After a very full life, which among other things saw him writing on a variety of subjects, including vegetarianism and hygiene, Wagner died in 1883. He is buried at Wahnfried, his Bayreuth villa.

237

Richard Wagner (1813–1883, above) Detail from a tapestry inspired by the music of Wagner (top)

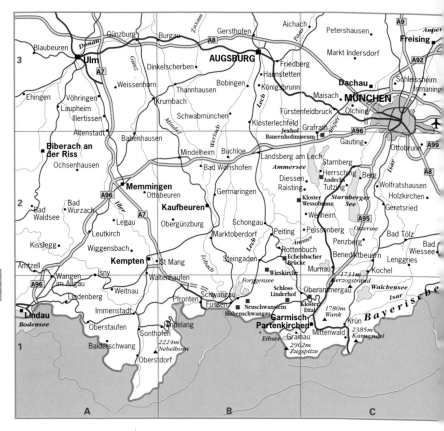

The panorama from Munich's Olympic tower makes this region appear remarkably compact. The easygoing, cosmopolitan Bavarian capital lies on a fertile plain that extends southwards towards the snowy peaks of the Alps, Germany's highest and most dramatic mountains. In between are neat, clustered villages, pine forests, sparkling lakes and gently rolling pastures.

This is a rewarding area for exploration, with a host of entertainment and cultural offerings in Munich, magnificent scenic variety and (particularly away from the Alps) a number of historic small towns. All over the area are examples of Bavarian baroque churches and castles, many of them spectacular compositions with ornate stuccowork and frescoed ceilings.

While the German Alps comprise only a thin strip (the bulk of the great range lies in Italy, Austria, Switzerland and France), the mountains form a backdrop that is the key to much of the charm of the low-lying hinterland. The scenery immediately around Munich is rather flat, but farther south are several lakes, popular for walks, boat trips and sailing. The Alps themselves can be enjoyed by driving along the **Deutsche Alpenstrasse** (German Alpine Road), a scenic road threading its way from **Lindau** to **Berchtesgaden** and passing close to the four remarkable 19th-century castles of Ludwig II, Bavaria's mad king, whose extravagant fantasies now provide the region with

Moosburg · Vilsbiburg · Massing · Pfarrkirchen
Eggenfelden · Triftern
Isar
Velden · Neumarkt-St.Veit · Simbach
Taufkirchen · Vils · Rott
·Erding
·Altenerding · Isen · Ampfing Neuötting · *Stausee*
Dorfen Mühldorf · Altötting
Wald Kraiburg · Burghausen
Markt · Kraiburg
· Schwaben · Haag · *Inn* · Garching · *Alz*
Hohenlinden
A94
Ebersberg · Tittmoning
·Grafing Wasserburg Obing · Trostberg · *Salzach*
am Inn · Altenmarkt · Stein Fridolfing·
Glonn· Rott· · Traunreut
Seebruck· Waging· Laufen
Chiemsee
Bruckmühl Bad Endorf· ■ Fraueninsel Traunstein Freilassing
· Aibling Prien· ■ Herreninsel Ainring·
Rosenheim · Bernau A8
leisbach Bad Feilnbach Aschau · Grassau Ruhpolding
laubham A93 1640m ▲ Marquartstein Bad Reichenhall
·Schliersee Kampenwand Unterwössen
Tegernsee 1838m *Chiemgauer Berge*
·Rottach- Wendelstein ·Sachrang Reit im Berchtesgaden
Egern Winkl ▲ 1834m
reuth Bayrischzell Kehlstein
Alpen *Königssee*
2713m
Watzmann

A

0 10 20 30 40 50 km
0   10   20   30 miles

D   E

its top tourist attractions. Tourism is big business, with
numerous resorts geared to winter sports and medical and
nonmedical 'cures'.

For most of the year, many Alpine summits can be
reached by cable cars and chairlifts; at the top there's often
a strategically placed restaurant. Walking is by no means
confined to arduous mountain ascents; easy paths, meticulously signposted, give gentle strolls through woods, along
gorges, around lakes and up to viewpoints. However the
mountain resort towns are not especially interesting.

Southern Bavaria, with the notable exception of liberal
Munich, is staunchly conservative, both politically and in
general outlook. You will see men wearing Bavarian hats
and *Lederhosen* (leather trousers), and women in embroi-
dered dirndl dresses. Festivals are celebrated with gusto,
particularly May Day, when huge maypoles are erected
and decorated. The tradition of painting murals (and the
family name in old Gothic lettering) on house exteriors is
widespread. Food is hearty and traditional—pork,
dumplings, potatoes and sauerkraut are *de rigueur* in country areas. The region is strongly Catholic: *'Grüss Gott'*
(God's greeting) is the standard greeting (never *'Guten
Tag'*—good day), and churches have a prosperous look.
Much of the region is accessible within a day trip from
Munich, but beware of crowds and traffic jams at peak
times at the main sights and resorts.

▶ Ammersee and Andechs 238C2

Ammersee, a 35km (22-mile) lake west of Munich, is a popular weekend retreat, with small, quiet resorts, reedy shores and pleasant, low hills. Boat trips and yacht rentals are offered, and swimming is quite feasible in the warmer months. The west side is more congested, but Herrsching, the main resort, is on the east shore, a starting point for gentle lakeside walks.

The pilgrimage church of the Benedictine monastery of **Andechs▶**, close to Herrsching, is one of the rococo masterpieces of Bavaria, with frescoes and stuccowork by J. B. Zimmermann. Carl Orff (1895–1982), the composer best known for his *Carmina Burana*, is buried here. The tower offers a good view of the lake.

Next door, the monastery Bräustüberl (beer hall) does a roaring trade in the excellent beer produced by the monks and dispensed straight from the barrel. The monastery shop sells a Klosterlikör (monastery liqueur) and its own bottled beer.

Hohen Peissenberg, southwest of the lake and accessible by road from Hohenpeissenberg village, has been a place of pilgrimage since the 16th century, when peasants erected a chapel on this lofty site, with its magnificent panorama of the German Alps (on a clear day you can even discern the restaurant on top of the Zugspitze). The church has been expanded and given the ubiquitous rococo treatment; note in particular the organ loft's elaborate parquetry.

Railings on the roof of the adjacent house mark the site of the world's first weather station (1781). Observations were made first by Augustinian monks and then by priests and teachers; in 1937 an official weather station was set up here.

The 15 huge satellite dishes at **Raisting**, just south of the Ammersee, that dominate the area constitute one of the world's largest telecommunications bases. They link Germany's domestic telephone network to international connections.

WESSOBRUNN ABBEY
Wessobrunn Abbey, west of the Ammersee, is famous for the *Wessobrunner Gebet* (Wessobrunn Prayer), a poetic fragment of nine lines that dates from the early 9th century. Although written in a Bavarian dialect, the Wessobrunn Prayer is often considered the oldest-known text written in the German language.

Ammersee is popular with weekenders

▶▶ **Berchtesgadener Land** *239E2*

Jutting into Austria, Germany's southeastern corner offers glorious Alpine scenery; **Salzburg** is within close reach just across the border. The vicinity of **Schonau** and **Berchtesgaden** is ideal as a base for exploration.

Berchtesgaden▶▶ is a comfortable medium-sized resort with an active central area; turn-of-the-20th-century villas full of character perch on the hillside. The menacing form of the Watzmann (2,713m/8,901ft) looms high to the south; not surprisingly, the mountain inspired many artists and is the subject of local legends.

The town is the place to visit on bad-weather days. Particularly interesting are the still-functioning **Salt Mines**▶ (*Open* daily), where visitors don miners' clothes and travel on the mine wagons. You can even slide down a slope (heavy-duty trousers are issued for the purpose) and raft across a subterranean lake. The guides are very knowledgeable and will explain the salt-extraction process.

In the middle of town are the Heimatmuseum (*Open* Tue–Sun. *Closed* Nov), which has a display of local wood crafts, and the Schloss (*Open* Whitsun–Oct), which was formerly an Augustinian priory, then from 1810 a Wittelsbach palace. Today it is a museum housing a collection of weapons and paintings.

For details of guided walks (May–Oct) visit the national park offices in Berchtesgaden or Königssee.

As with much of Bavaria, the area has many baroque churches. The most photographed are probably **Ramsau** and the idyllically sited **Maria Gern**.

Berchtesgaden won additional fame during the Third Reich because of its popularity as a retreat for top Nazi

Tables with a view at a Berchtesgaden mountaintop café

▶▶▶ REGION HIGHLIGHTS

Berchtesgaden (including Salt Mines, Königssee) *page 241*

Chiemsee *page 244*

Dachau *pages 244–245*

Füssen and royal castles *pages 245–246*

Garmisch (and Zugspitze) *pages 249–250*

Mittenwald *page 252*

Munich (and museums) *pages 253–259*

Ottobeuren *pages 262–263*

Wieskirche *page 265*

INFORMATION
Berchtesgaden:
Königsseer Strasse 2,
tel: 08652/96 70;
www.berchtesgaden.com

Berchtesgaden, an active resort set on the hillside, and an ideal base for exploring the Berchtesgadener Land mountains

leaders, most notably Hitler and his deputy Martin Bormann. They built villas on a slice of mountaintop, the Obersalzberg, and a guesthouse, the Kehlsteinhaus, at the summit (see page 244). Hitler built a road from the valley that climbs 740m (2,428ft) in just over 6km (4 miles).

From May to October special buses make the journey from Berchtesgaden to a parking area 150m (490ft) below the summit. From there a lift built inside the mountain takes visitors to the Kehlsteinhaus, where there is a restaurant and a staggering view that led one diplomat guest of Hitler's to give the building its abiding nickname, the 'Eagle's Nest' (or 'Adlerhorst', as Hitler himself knew it).

Often likened to a Norwegian fiord, the much-visited **Königssee►►** stretches over 8km (5 miles) below the mighty slopes of the Watzmann, its depths plummeting over 190m (620ft). At the lake's northern end, from the village of Königssee (a tourist trap of kitschy souvenir shops, fortunately invisible from the lake itself), boat trips are available over the length of the water, with breathtaking vistas all the way. The round-trip takes an hour and three quarters and operates all year, weather permitting. Attractions near the far end include short walks to the chapels of St. Johann and St. Paul, and a more ambitious ascent to an ice 'chapel', which even the summer heat fails to melt (allow an hour each way).

A pleasant 75-minute circular walk, the Malerwinkel Rundweg, starts to the left of the main boat pier (at the lake's north end), taking an easily managed gravel track up into the trees. The crowds disappear and you are soon rewarded with views over the lake.

Also from Königssee you can take the cable lift up the **Jenner** (1,874m/6,148ft), where the mountaintop restaurant gives views of the lake on one side and of nearby Austria on the other.

The Almbachklamm, a gloomy chasm with dramatic rock overhangs and swirling waterfalls, can be explored between May and October by a gently rising path (admission charge), which can be followed for an hour and a half to the Theresienklause Dam; the best of the gorge is seen at the beginning. The parking area is signposted from highway 305, northeast of Berchtesgaden at the 5.5km post.

Bad Reichenhall is a spa that is reputed to have the most powerful saline springs in Europe. Look for the Quellenbau: King Ludwig I gave it his royal seal of patronage in the early 19th century, commissioning an elaborate salt works and ornate spa pavilion, the Alte Saline and Quellenhaus. They now house a museum (Salzmuseum) with displays describing the history of the salt trade and a glass foundry (*Open* May–Oct daily; Nov–Apr Tue). You can sample the saline waters in the attractive spa gardens. A short excursion from Bad Reichenhall across the Austrian border will take you to Salzburg, where Mozart was born. Its name, meaning 'salt castle' points to the former importance of the local salt trade.

The Hintersee

This small lake nestles beneath the wooded lower slopes of the Schottmalhorn (2,045m/6,709ft) and the Hochkalter (2,607m/8,553ft). The walk around takes about 45 minutes, with an optional climb of the Wartstein (15 minutes). Start at the Seeklause parking area at the 25km post on the Ramsau–Weissbach road, west of Berchtesgaden. Turn left out

of the parking area and walk along the road, which soon crosses a stream; immediately turn right along a broad path bordered with wooden railings. Ignore turns to the right, and walk through the **Zauberwald** (magic wood). After following the shore, reach an intersection and turn left, signposted Fussweg am See. After 30m (100ft) or so, detour right to the **Wartstein** (signposted), keeping right at subsequent intersections until the summit, with its fine view and tiny cave shrine. Return the same way to the bottom, turn right and continue the signposted Fussweg am See, which passes in front of the hotels and branches off left. The final section leads left along the path by the road.

The Wimbachtal

The **Wimbachklamm**, west of Berchtesgaden on highway 305 at the 19km post, is a pretty gorge and a good starting point for walks

along the Wimbachtal (the Wimbach River valley).

Start at the parking area, and take the rising road (closed to cars) called Wimbachweg. After the road becomes unsurfaced, fork left into the gorge. A gentle 2.5-hour ascent leads you to the Wimbachgrieshütte, sited in a postglacial valley below the Watzmann and the Hochkalter. There is a restaurant (Wimbach Schloss) midway along. Return the same way.

FRAUENINSEL

On the intimate little Fraueninsel (Women's Island on the Chiemsee), Benedictines have had a monastery since AD780, and nuns still live there (hence the name). They run a girls' boarding school, and still brew their *Klostergeist* liqueur ('convent spirit'), which can be tasted in their Klostercafé. Behind the altar of the tiny 13th-century church are charmingly naive ex-votos, some done by local fishermen giving thanks to the island's saint.

INFORMATION

Bernau-am-Chiemsee: Felden 10, tel: 08051/ 96 55 50; www.chiemsee.de

The landing stage of Fraueninsel, a lushly fertile little island, full of apple trees, birdsong and religious peace

HITLER'S EYRIE

On the Obersalzberg heights above Berchtesgaden (see page 242) Hitler built a grandiose mountain retreat, where he welcomed many top-rank visitors. It was razed to the ground in 1945 (only some stone slabs now remain); and it is not signposted, so as to deter neo-Nazi pilgrims from using it as a shrine. A museum documenting the area's Nazi past and the history of the Third Reich opened there in 1999 (*Open* May–Oct daily; Nov–Mar Tue–Sun).

▶▶ **Chiemsee**   *239D2*

Bavaria's largest lake looks best from the northern side, particularly from the little resort of Gstadt; the Alpine foothills form part of a distinguished backdrop. It makes a good base for hiking, with easy routes in the vicinity of the lake itself and more energetic rambles in the hills to the south.

Boating is the other main attraction, with yachts for rent in many of the resorts, and a passenger boat service making stops around the lake. Try to see both of the principal islands.

On **Herreninsel**, the larger, stands Herrenchiemsee, an unfinished palace of Ludwig II (*Open* daily). The King decided to make a replica of Versailles, but only built the central portion before funds ran out. What exists is impressive, with formal French gardens, a hall of mirrors, and a state room where classical concerts are held by candlelight. This would have been Ludwig's largest castle.

Nearby is lovely **Fraueninsel** (see left). From Prien, on the west side of the lake, a steam train pulls 19th-century

wooden carriages 2km (1.2 miles) to the pier for boats to the islands. The old village of Breitbrunn is a haunt of writers and artists from Munich. Local tourist offices stock booklets detailing the annual classical music festival held in several venues in the area between May and July. A stage on the lake (Seebühne Chiemsee) has been built near Prien, where the audience can enjoy live entertainment as well as the view of Herrenchiemsee and the distant Alps in the background.

To the south lie the Alpine foothills, which are an excellent area for medium to energetic walks without the daunting scale of the Alps proper. The **Kampenwand** (1,640m/5,380ft) is a popular objective and has cable lifts to get you up to the high ground. **Reit im Winkl** is an Alpine resort of much charm.

▶▶ **Dachau**   *238C3*

There are a few places in the world that cause a frisson at the mention of their very names. Dachau, a small commuter town near Munich, is one of them. It was the site of the Third Reich's notorious first concentration camp, established in 1933 in a former munitions factory. The camp has become a memorial museum (*Open* Tue–Sun).

Although Dachau was not an extermination camp, torture, disease and death were commonplace. The barracks have gone, but accurate reconstructions give an idea of the cramped conditions prisoners had to endure. Around the perimeter fence, watchtowers still stand. The Jourhaus (guardhouse), formerly the camp entrance, still displays the chillingly inappropriate legend *Arbeit macht frei* (work makes freedom). The gas chambers, which were disguised as shower rooms, were never used for extermination, but hanging by the stake, a common punishment, was carried out within them; adjacent are the cremation ovens, which were kept burning day and night. A museum now occupies one side of the site, which has a disturbing account of the camp and a half-hour film (in English at 11.30am and 3.30pm).

As an antidote to the bleakness of the visit to the camp, walk into **Dachau town**, perched above the River Amper. Despite its proximity to Munich, its heart has an unspoiled small-town atmosphere, with a pretty Hofgarten (castle garden), a nicely laid out local museum and a Gemäldegalerie (picture gallery) of works by a colony of artists who were attracted to the area because of the unique light of the Dachauer Moos, an area of heathland. Both the museum and the gallery are closed Monday and Tuesday.

Dachau camp is easily visited from Munich; take the S-Bahn 2 (direction Petershausen) to Dachau, from where, outside the station, bus 726 takes you to the Konzentrationslager (KZ) Gedenkstatte (concentration camp memorial).

▶▶▶ Füssen, Neuschwanstein and Hohenschwangau   *238B1*

Füssen abuts the Forggensee, a popular sailing area, and has its back to the Alps. Among several scenes of picturesque charm is the cobbled main street, the Reichenstrasse, with a trio of the town's most distinguished buildings at its far end—church, abbey, and towering above it, the castle, the Hohes Schloss. Close by, an archway gives onto a riverside park by the Lech, a tributary of the Danube.

The Benedictine abbey of St. Mang now operates as a local museum (*Open* Tue–Sun), and there is a violin maker's workshop included among the displays. Above all, the abbey is an enjoyable place just to wander around and appreciate the host of well-preserved baroque rooms, including a very attractive oval library. Within the Hohes Schloss (*Open* Tue–Sun) there is an exhibition of medieval religious art from the Allgäu and Swabia.

Königschlösser (royal castles) Despite unavoidable tourist crowds for most of the year, the wonderfully spectacular castles of Ludwig II—Linderhof (see page 261), Herrenchiemsee (see page 244), Hohenschwangau and Neuschwanstein (see page 246)—are very seldom disappointing. Fair-weather timing assists an appreciation of the mountain setting, but may also bring out the crowds. There is quite a lot of walking involved, particularly a fairly steep haul up from the parking area by Hohenschwangau to Neuschwanstein; alternatively, you may prefer to make use of the horse-and-carriage service. It is probably best to make Hohenschwangau your first stop in order to avoid a sense of anticlimax (see also **Walk** on page 248).

DACHAU: GRIM SNAPSHOTS

- Over 206,000 prisoners were registered between 1933 and 1945; numerous other internees were never registered. Jews, religious and political dissenters and other 'undesirables' were all brought here.

- More than 65,000 prisoners died, although the exact number will never be established. Thousands were summarily executed.

- In addition to camp work, many prisoners were victims of human experimentation, which included infection with malaria and experiments on tolerance of high pressure.

- Punishment, including hanging from the stake and lashing, was dispensed for the most trivial offence, such as not making beds correctly.

- SS men during 1940–41 executed many Jews by removing the prisoners' caps and hurling them into the neutral zone, ordering the Jews to retrieve them, then they were shot 'for trying to escape'.

- Roll call often lasted hours when not all the prisoners could be found. They would stand absolutely still, even in freezing conditions, as the slightest movement would be severely punished. Many of the sick simply collapsed on the spot.

245

246

Linderhof, one of Ludwig II's castles, was built in a mix of baroque and Renaissance styles. The gardens include a Moorish pavilion with bronze peacocks

VISITING THE CASTLES
The castles can only be visited by guided tours (in English). Advance booking is required in summer (www.ticket-center-hohenschwangau.de; tel: 08362/93 08 30).

Hohenschwangau► (*Open* daily), on a forested hill, is the older of the two castles, built in the 12th century, but destroyed by Napoleon and restored by Crown Prince Maximilian (later Maximilian II), who made it his summer residence in the 1830s. Ludwig spent his early years here. The décor is troubadour style, with wall paintings of Bavarian knights and folk heroes; Ludwig's bedroom is decorated with stars that were illuminated in the evening. The music room evokes his love of Wagner.

Neuschwanstein►► (*Open* daily) stands high and mighty, bristling with turrets and mock-medievalism, its interior styles ranging from Byzantine through Romanesque to Gothic. This fairy-tale fantasy come true was built between 1869 and 1886 for Ludwig II but the King spent less than six months here before being certified insane and drowning mysteriously in the Starnberger See. Only about a third of the building was actually completed and the unfinished feeling is manifest everywhere—the second floor is a mere shell, doorways open to nothing but suicidal drops, and steps in the throne room lead to a throneless stage. The 15 rooms you do see on the tour show astonishing craftsmanship and richness of detail, which extend to the lamp fittings and elaborate central heating system. The wood carving in Ludwig's bedroom took 14 carpenters four and a half years to complete. Wagner's operas are referred to everywhere, in murals and even in a mini-grotto recalling the Venusberg in *Tannhäuser*. Nowadays the castle serves as an exclusive setting for a series of classical concerts given each September by top artists, perhaps an appropriate tribute to a king who preferred music and theatre to the demands of government.

The best view of the castle is from the **Marienbrücke** (Mary's Bridge), which spans a deep gorge. On the path between here and the castle is a vista of Hohenschwangau and the Alpsee lake. A recommended extra is the cable-car up the **Tegelberg** (1,720m/5,643ft), signposted between Hohenschwangau and Schwangau. It operates all year and there is a summit restaurant.

Map labels:
Bernbeuren, Böbing, Penzberg, Lechbruck, Rottenbuch, Uffing, A95, Benediktbeuern, Steingaden, Wildsteig, Staffelsee, Riegsee, Lech, Ach, Wieskirche, Bayersoien, Saulgrub, Murnau, Grossweil, Rosshaupten, Bad Kohlgrub, Schlehdorf, Glentleiten Freilichtmuseum, Kochel, Halblech-Trauchgau 1638m, Kochelsee, Forggensee, Ammer, Ohlstadt, Bannwaldsee, Unterammergau, Herzogstand 1731m, Walchensee, Ammergebirge, Oberammergau, Füssen, Schwangau, Schloss Linderhof, Graswang, Kochel-Walchensee, Bayerische Alpen, Neuschwanstein, Hohenschwangau, Deutsche Alpenstrasse, Ettal, Oberau, Estergebirge, Isar, Loisach, Kreuzspitze 2185m, Wallgau, Reutte, Garmisch-Partenkirchen, Klais, Krün, Soiernspitze 2257m, Plansee, Grainau, Elmau, Lech, Eibsee, Mittenwald, 2385m, A, Zugspitze 2962m, 0 5 10 km, 0 5 miles

Drive

The Deutsche Alpenstrasse

A tour around the German Alps, using the Alpine Road for much of the way. Remember your passport!

From pretty Füssen, the road heads northeast past the Hohenschwangau and Neuschwanstein turning for the fairy-tale castles built by Ludwig II, and skirts the Bannwaldsee before reaching Steingaden. At Steingaden head east.

Detour south at the signpost for the sumptuous baroque **Wieskirche**. Between the low-lying lakes, the **Staffelsee** and **Kochelsee**, is the turnoff for the **Glentleiten Freilichtmuseum** (open-air museum), which is worth a visit.

From Kochel, the road climbs into the Alps, passing the prettily set Walchensee, best seen by taking the cable car up the Wendelstein.

Detour to the village of **Mittenwald** before continuing to **Ettal Abbey** and past **Linderhof**, a Ludwig II castle.

Cross the Austrian border to reach Reutte and continue on to arrive back at Füssen.

The deep-blue Walchensee, one of the loveliest Bavarian lakes

Walk

Hohenschwangau and Neuschwanstein

A good way of seeing castles and the Marienbrücke, and avoiding the crowds. Allow one hour for walking and at least two for sightseeing.

Park at either of the first two parking areas (on the left) for the castles. Cross the road and take the steps to the left of the information office to **Hohenschwangau**. After seeing the castle, retrace your steps, then, just after the end of the castle building, take the right fork, to drop down to hotels and restaurants. Cross the road and take steps to the left of the Schloss Hotel, and carry on up to reach the road. Cross over and take the stony path opposite, which ascends steadily. At the top, there is a surfaced track near a wooden shelter. Here detour right and then immediately left to the **Marienbrücke** then return to the shelter and turn right to **Neuschwanstein** (don't miss the viewpoint over Hohenschwangau on the left). After leaving the castle, follow the main driveway down, forking right after 500m (1,640ft) down steps (signposted Cafe Kainz) to reach the parking areas.

Schwangau, the village close to Hohenschwangau, is famed for its Colomansfest, on the second Sunday of October, when the blessing of horses takes place. The festivities include a grand procession of horse-drawn carriages, in which usually more than 200 horses take part.

248

Hohenschwangau, set high among the mountain crags

FORGGENSEE THEATRE
In 2000 a theatre opened on the shores of the Forggensee, just outside Füssen, with a world-première performance of a musical based on the life and times of King Ludwig II of Bavaria. In 2005 it was succeeded by a new show—Ludwig2—now features year-round with daily performances (except Mon). The music blends together folk themes, traditional musical harmonies and Wagnerian elements (www.ludwig-musical.com).

As well as ski resort, Garmisch is a centre of Bavarian folklore, with a major Heimatmuseum

249

▶▶ **Garmisch-Partenkirchen**   *238C1*

Garmisch-Partenkirchen is really two towns, joined together but quite different in character. Garmisch has village origins and retains some old-world rusticity in Frühlingstrasse (in the northern outskirts) and surroundings, with quaint whitewashed, gabled houses and the village fountain. Partenkirchen has been a town for much longer, and has lively, narrow main streets. Both towns have expanded for tourism, above all for the winter-sports industry, together becoming the largest German Alpine resort. As the site of the 1936 Winter Olympics and the 1978 alpine skiing world championships, the town is endowed with an Olympic ice stadium and ski jump. It is not a very good place to get away from the crowds, but nearby villages make good bases.

The **Zugspitze**▶▶▶ (2,962m/9,718ft), Germany's highest mountain, dominates the area and can be reached effortlessly by rack railway from Garmisch; clear-weather views justify the substantial fee, and there is a restaurant at the top. A quicker but less exciting way up is to take the

Germany's leading ski resort lies beneath the nation's highest mountain, the Zugspitze

INFORMATION
Garmisch-Partenkirchen:
Richard Strauss Platz 2,
tel: 08821/18 07 00;
www.garmisch-
partenkirchen.de

Zugspitze, towering over Garmisch-Partenkirchen

BADERSEE
Near the peaceful village of Grainau, west of Garmisch, the tiny Badersee is sited secretively among the trees. For a few euros you can rent a boat and view an endearingly ludicrous statue of Nixe, a nymph, placed at the bottom of the lake by Ludwig II.

cable-car from the **Eibsee**, itself a lovely lake encircled by a 7km (4-mile) footpath. Other mountains where you can ascend by chairlift from town and walk down gently graded paths include the **Wank** (1,780m/5,840ft) and the **Eckbauer** (1,238m/4,062ft); both have summit restaurants.

Whatever the weather, be sure to visit the famous **Partnachklamm▶▶**. From the Olympic ski stadium, walk or take a horse and carriage along a traffic-free road to the entrance to the gorge.

The path is one of the wonders of the Alps, snaking near the bottom of the very deep chasm past spraying water and remarkable rock formations. A cable car runs from the gorge entrance to the Hotel Forsthaus Graseck. From here follow the track up the valley, enter the gorge at its far end and walk back down.

Less crowded, owing to its relative inaccessibility, is the **Höllentalklamm**, sandwiched between the bases of the Alpspitze and the Waxenstein; allow at least 2 hours to travel each way, starting from Hammersbach, southwest of Garmisch.

Walk

Eckbauer and the Partnachklamm

This route takes the chairlift up the Eckbauer, where there is a viewing platform, with close-ups of Alpspitze.

An easy ascent zigzags into a valley of Alpine meadows before the finale along the Partnachklamm, a magnificent gorge. The Gasthof on the summit serves excellent buttermilk.

Take the Eckbauerbahn (chairlift) from the ski stadium in **Garmisch**. At the top, walk past the Berg Gasthof Eckbauer and follow signs for the Partnachklamm, down through woods, later forking right to reach a track near Forsthaus Graseck.

Turn left (a detour is possible to Hohe Brücke, a high bridge over the gorge), return to the main route to reach the top entrance to the gorge, and follow it downstream. If this is closed, follow the track the other way, past the Graseck to the bottom entrance.

From there, you either walk along the traffic-free road or take a horse and carriage.

▶ Kaufbeuren 238B2

The unspoiled middle of town, with its twisting, cobbled streets, merits exploration; the tourist information office (in the Rathaus) publishes a walk about town in English. A walk along the town walls to Kaufbeuren's northwest corner leads past the Fünfknopfturm (five-spired tower) to the 15th-century church of St. Blasius. The church's greatly treasured high altar by the master Bavarian woodcarver Jörg Lederer (1518) features golden-robed figures of the Virgin and Child, St. John the Baptist, and St. Anne. The Stadtmuseum in Kaisergässchen (*Closed* for restoration) has an impressive collection of crucifixes. In Ludwigstrasse, the Puppentheater-museum (*Open* Tue–Sun) has puppets from Europe and the Far East.

The town's big annual event is in July, when the Tänzelfest takes place. This medieval-style pageant is played out by as many as 1,600 children and is accompanied by processions and re-enactments of scenes from the town's history.

The suburb of Neugablonz was built after World War II for Germans expelled from the Gablonz district in Bohemia, Czechoslovakia. They brought with them their glass-blowing and jewellery-making skills, set up new factories and gradually recovered their international markets. The Isergebirgs-Museum tells their success story (*Open* Tue–Sun).

▶ Kempten 238A2

A busy commercial base rather than a tourist destination, Kempten nevertheless has some good museums (*Open* Tue–Sun). These include the Alpenländische Galerie (Alpine arts gallery), Alpinmuseum (museum of the people and mountains of the Alps), the new Allgäu-Museum für Kunst und Kulturgeschichte (local history) and the Römisches Museum (Roman museum).

East of the middle of town, across the River Iller, a tributary of the Danube, the Archäologischer Park (*Closed* Mon and mid-Dec to Feb) occupies the former site of the Roman town of Cambodunum. The complex includes a partial reconstruction of a Roman-Celtic temple as well as many archaeological finds from the vicinity.

▶ Landsberg-am-Lech 238B2

On the Romantische Strasse (Romantic Road, see page 230) and quickly reached by train from Munich, the hillside town of Landsberg has retained an authentic old-world atmosphere without losing its workaday spirit. The signposted Stadtrundgang (circular town walk) takes in the best of Landsberg, weaving down crooked alleys and beneath arches, and climbing onto the largely intact town ramparts, with its series of gateways and views of red roofs huddled by the River Lech. Since the route is complicated, collect a free town map showing the walk from the tourist office in the Rathaus, whose rich stucco exterior by Dominikus Zimmermann graces the Hauptplatz. Zimmermann was also responsible for the Johanniskirche, which he designed using the plans for the more famous Wieskirche (see page 265).

Of the town's towers and gateways, the Bayertor is the most renowned and is one of the largest Gothic fortifications in southern Germany.

HITLER IN PRISON
Chosen by Henry the Lion as a castle site in the 12th century, Landsberg became a regional base in the Middle Ages and gained prosperity, particularly as a trading town for salt mined in southeast Bavaria and sold to Swabian merchants. In the last century, Adolf Hitler was imprisoned here following his unsuccessful *putsch* of 1923. He wrote *Mein Kampf* during the time he was incarcerated.

Kaufbeuren is an old-world town of narrow streets and tall churches

251

High rocky peaks, the Karwendel and Wetterstein rise high above Mittenwald

The Neues Stadtmuseum has a fair miscellany, including medieval religious art (*Closed* Mon).

►► Mittenwald   238C1

In a beautiful Alpine setting close to the Austrian border, the village has expanded as a tourist resort but retains much of its charm and numerous corners of old-world rusticity, with a photogenic array of houses with white-washed walls, wooden balconies, and green or brown shutters. The best houses are in the Obermarkt and the Gries quarter.

The baroque church has fine frescoes. Outside stands a statue of violin-maker Matthias Klotz (see panel). The craft continues to be carried out here by such veteran masters as Anton Maller at his workshop in Stainergasse 14, and souvenir spin-offs include miniature violins and liqueurs sold in violin-shaped bottles. The Geigenbau Museum close by (*Open* Tue–Sun) has a collection of old violins and other string instruments, and exhibits detailing their history and manufacture.

Excursions

Cable-car and chairlift excursions are available to the **Karwendel** (2,384m/7,821ft) by Mittenwald and, farther north, the **Herzogstand** (1,731m/5,679ft), majestically placed above the attractive **Walchensee**. Mittenwald is surrounded by more than 100km (62 miles) of marked hiking paths. A short journey into Austria will take you to the famous resort of Seefeld.

KLOTZ'S VIOLINS
Matthias Klotz (1653–1743) brought the violin-making tradition to Mittenwald. He is thought to have been a pupil of the great Amati of Cremona. This industry may have saved Mittenwald from economic oblivion after Venetian merchants, who brought prosperity to the village, returned to Italy. Mittenwald violins are highly regarded by musicians and fetch good prices.

Monument to a music maker: the statue of violin maker Matthias Klotz, in Mittenwald

▶▶▶ **München (Munich)**   *238C3*

Germany's third-largest city contrasts sharply with the cosy conformism of much of the rest of southern Bavaria. With its exuberant atmosphere and vitality, it is one of the great cultural hearts of Europe. Despite wartime devastation the city has a seductive atmosphere, with blue-and-cream trams, tree-lined boulevards, fountains, parks, outdoor cafés, beer halls and beer gardens. Its array of museums is only surpassed by Berlin.

Central Munich is easy to see on foot. From the main railway station, you literally enter the city through one of its historic gateways, **Karlstor**. Ahead of you are busy pedestrianized shopping streets, leading to the **Marienplatz▶** at the heart of Munich; the square is dominated by the neo-Gothic Neues Rathaus, its exterior jollified by the famous carillon whose mechanical musicians, jousting knights and dancing coopers perform at 11am, noon, 5pm and 9pm. Close by are the **Frauenkirche▶**, the symbol of Munich, with huge onion-domed towers that dominate views from all around, and the Renaissance **St. Michael's Church**, with Wittelsbach tombs (see page 258) in the crypt. Immediately south of the Marienplatz, the **Viktualienmarkt▶** is a cheerful food market, excellent for regional cheeses and prepared hams in particular; the high quality is matched by the high prices.

A short distance southwest are two of the finest churches, the **Damenstiftskirche**, high baroque and thick with incense, and the astonishing **Asamkirche**, the ultimate statement in rococo, with no square inch unadorned in its dark, compact interior.

In the north-central area lie some of Munich's most impressive streetscapes. **Max-Joseph-Platz** is presided over by the massive Corinthian columns of the National

The tower of the neo-Gothic Neues Rathaus (1867–1908) offers a good view over the town

INFORMATION
München: Hauptbahnhof, Bahnhofsplatz 2, tel: 089/23 39 65 00; www.mw-muenchen.de

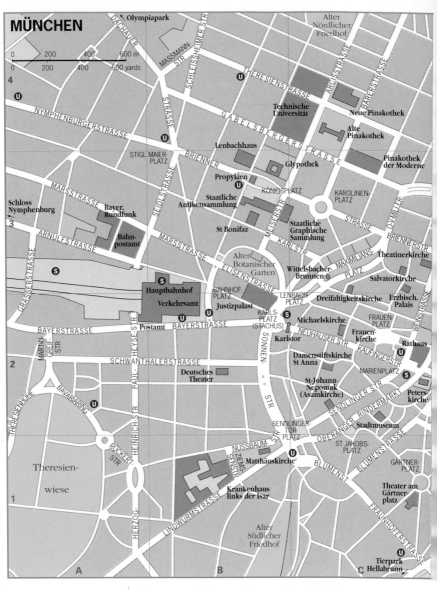

MÜNCHEN

Theatre and the southern end of the huge Residenz, which marks the western end of **Maximilianstrasse▶**. This is a tree-lined thoroughfare known for its expensive boutiques and galleries and dominated at its far end by the towering Maximilianeum (1874), the Bavarian parliament and senate.

Odeonsplatz▶, full of students on bicycles, has a reconstructed look, but the regularity of the composition is pleasing. Adjacent is the massive dome of the baroque Theatinerkirche, whose bright yellow façade contrasts with an intricate grey stone interior. Across the road, the former royal garden, the Hofgarten, offers a peaceful retreat from the city bustle.

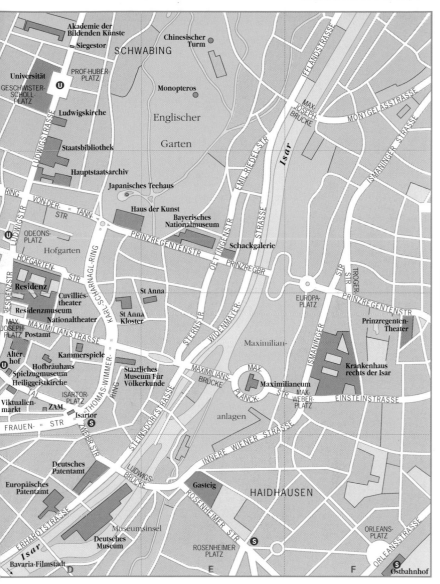

The Odeonsplatz looks northwards to the Siegestor, a triumphal gateway close to the university; beyond it lies Leopoldstrasse, which is the main axis of the district of **Schwabing▶**, with numerous bars, outdoor cafés, theatres, cabarets and other entertainment venues. Around Münchener Freiheit, at the junction of Leopoldstrasse and Ungererstrasse, is good territory for browsing in secondhand shops.

Northwest of the centre are two adjacent squares, Lenbachplatz and Maximiliansplatz, with pricey antiques shops, and the main **museum quarter**.

The **Englischer Garten▶▶** (English Garden) extends along the banks of the River Isar, a tributary of the

Danube, for roughly 7km (4 miles) and is one of the largest city parks in the world. The 'garden' resembles parkland landscaped in the English manner, with informal areas of grass and mature woodlands and is the haunt of strollers, cyclists, joggers, picnickers, sunbathers and the occasional nudist. The Chinesischer Turm (Chinese Tower), with its beer garden, is a popular rendezvous. Japanese tea ceremonies are conducted by an expert at the Japanisches Teehaus.

Less countrified in character, but equally popular, is the **Olympia Park►**, north of the centre, the site of the ill-fated 1972 Olympic games, when Israeli athletes were taken hostage and died in a tragic shoot-out. Today people come for walking, jogging and boating, and for the range of sports facilities, which include the Olympic swimming pool. You can walk into the strange tentlike structure of the Olympic stadium and also take part in 'virtual reality' reconstructions of Olympic sports in the newly opened 'Olympic Spirit' exhibition centre and fun park (*Open* daily). On clear days thousands take the lift up to the top of the Olympic Tower for a panorama of Munich and the Alps. The tower is open daily until midnight.

Museums and galleries

Alte Pinakothek►►► (Barerstrasse 27; *Open* Tue–Sun). This great art museum specializes in paintings up to the 18th century and is famed for works by Dürer (*Self Portrait, The Four Apostles, The Baumgärtner Altar*) and for its Spanish, Dutch and Italian collections. Its assembly of works by Rubens, Van Dyck and Jordaens is considered unique. Among other Old Masters represented here are Titian, Tintoretto, Rembrandt, Hals, Murillo and Velázquez. Altogether the museum houses more than 800 European paintings, one of the most significant collections in the world.

Antikensammlungen (Königsplatz 1; *Open* Tue–Sun) Next to the Glyptothek (see pages 257–258), this state collection

Street musicians are a familiar sight in this cosmopolitan, university city

of classical art owes its origins to the collecting endeavours of Ludwig I. Among the exhibits, it boasts some superb Etruscan gold jewellery and a renowned set of Greek decorated vases.

Bavaria Filmstadt▶ (Bavariafilmplatz 7; *Open* Mar–Oct daily) Guided tours (lasting 1½ hours) of the one of the largest film studios in Europe.

Bayerisches Nationalmuseum▶ (Prinzregentenstrasse 3; *Open* Tue–Sun) Three floors of Bavarian arts and crafts, with about 18,000 items covering nine centuries. Highlights include wooden sculptures by Tilman Riemenschneider and a wonderful collection (the world's largest) of nativity tableaux, as well as an assembly of old musical instruments.

Deutsches Museum▶▶▶ (Museumsinsel 1; *Open* daily) Rated the world's foremost museum of science and technology, this has everything from do-it-yourself chemistry experiments and complicated models of hydraulics and bridges, to areas of more mainstream appeal, such as historic cars, locomotives, computers, telecommunications, space travel and aircraft.

Glyptothek (Königsplatz 3; *Open* Tue–Sun) Greek and Roman statuary, nearly all collected by Ludwig I, housed

The Olympic Park remains a popular sports venue

TRAINS AND BUSES
Munich's public transport system works admirably well but can confuse the newcomer. You can buy tickets individually or in blue strips (which works out cheaper); if choosing the latter, you need to use one strip for short journeys (five bus or tram stops, or three train or subway stops) or two strips for longer journeys. You are allowed to transfer among different modes of transport as long as you don't double back on your direction of travel. If you are doing a lot of touring or are in a group, buy a *Tageskarte* (day pass).

PLAYS AND MUSIC

Munich is well endowed with theatres and concert halls. The Münchener Kammerspiel is one of the most famous theatrical companies; the Cuvilliés-Theatre makes an evening out just for the architecture. The Nationaltheater in Max-Joseph Platz is a venue for opera and ballet. Munich's resident orchestras, include the Bayerisches Rundfunk Sinfonie Orchester and the Münchener Philharmonie. For details contact the tourist offices at the train station or in the Rathaus.

in an aptly classical building designed by Leo von Klenze. **Lenbachhaus▶** (Luisenstrasse 33; *Open* Tue–Sun) Of interest for the Italianate villa, complete with 19th-century furnishings, and for its collection of works by the Blauer Reiter group of expressionist painters, including Kandinsky, Macke, Marc and Münter.

Neue Pinakothek (Barerstrasse 29; *Open* Wed–Mon) Munich's 'new' art gallery has a very fine collection of late 18th- and 19th-century work, from German Romantics such as Caspar David Friedrich to the French Impressionists (Manet, Degas and Monet are particularly well represented). Major works by van Gogh, Gauguin and Cezanne are also on display, as are such German Impressionists as Liebermann and Corinth. Sculptures from this period include marble pieces by Canova and Thorwaldsen, and bronze figures by Rodin and Maillol. **Nymphenburg▶▶** (*Open* daily) In the western suburbs stands this great summer residence of the Wittelsbachs, former rulers of Bavaria. Ludwig II was born here. Although built and added to over many centuries, the

Some beer houses take pride in their collection of decorated beer mugs

palace has a strikingly unified symmetry. The best-known feature of its splendid baroque interior is the Schönheitengalerie, 36 beauties of the day painted between 1827 and 1850 for the pleasure of Ludwig I. Adjacent to the house is the Marstallmuseum, with a grand array of royal carriages and sleighs, and rooms of Nymphenburg porcelain.

Behind the palace lies perhaps its chief glory: a park with canals, a lake and a series of whimsical hunting lodges and pavilions. Of these, the Amalienburg steals the show, a neat essay in rococo, with a hall of shimmering mirrors: From the centre you see yourself reflected in all 10 of these. The Magdalenenklause was built as a mock-hermitage, complete with a bizarre grotto chamber.

Next door, the fine Botanical Garden (Menziger Strasse 65; *Open* daily) has an alpinum, rhododendrons and greenhouses.

Pinakothek der Moderne (Barerstrasse 40; *Open* Tue–Wed, Sun 10–5, Thu–Fri 10–8) This latest addition to Munich's museum scene brings together five important collections that were once distributed in various galleries and storage cellars: modern, 20th-century art and sculpture, graphic art and design, objets d'art, as well as the Technical University's architectural exhibits.

Residenzmuseum▶ (Max-Joseph Platz 3; *Open* daily) The vast baroque palace of the Wittelsbachs has been painstakingly restored after extensive wartime damage. Different parts of the building are open in the morning and evening, because there is far too much to see at once. In addition to the state rooms, do not miss the magnificent vaulted Antiquarium (begun in 1568), housing statues collected from the classical world, a dazzling treasury of pristine jewel-encrusted riches dating from the 11th century onwards, and the enchanting Cuvilliés-Theater (separate admission), a rococo creation by François de Cuvilliés, still used for performances.

Within the same complex, but requiring separate admission, are museums of coins (Münzsammlung) and Egyptian art. With 300,000 items the Münzsammlung (*Open* Tue–Sun) is one of the largest numismatic collections in the world.

Spielzeug Museum (Marienplatz; *Open* daily) In the tower of the old town hall is this most appealing (and nostalgic) treasure trove of toys, including retired dolls, vintage model cars and some pre-war teddy bears. There are also toys from as long ago as the second century.

Stadtmuseum (St-Jakobs-Platz 1; *Open* Tue–Sun) In a former arsenal, this is more than just the local history museum, with floors devoted to brewing, the early days of photography, a film museum, a worldwide collection of musical instruments and a splendidly entertaining puppet and fairground museum. Some of the 2,000 musical instruments are played in regular concerts and recitals there. A new section is devoted to interior design and furniture.

BMW Museum (Spiridion-Louis-Ring; *Open* daily; www.bmwmobiletradition.de) A fascinating display of transport technology over the past five generations, together with a splendid display of rare automobiles and motorcycles.

Munich is famed for its beer and beer halls

THE PASSION PLAY AT OBERAMMERGAU

The Passion play was first performed in 1633, after villagers had been spared the ravages of the plague; the play now takes place every 10 years, the next occasion being in 2010. Some 100 daylong performances are given to aggregate audiences of over 500,000 by a cast of 1,700. Tickets are difficult to obtain unless you book through a tour operator. Competition among the locals for the major parts is keen. Men grow long hair and beards for the event.

INFORMATION

Oberammergau: Eugen-Papst-Strasse 9a; tel: 08822/9 23 10; www.oberammergau.de

Painted buildings at Oberammergau, internationally known for its Passion play

▶ Oberammergau and area   *238C1*

Known the world over for its Passion play (see panel), Oberammergau is physically dominated by a rock pinnacle known as the Ettaler Mandl. The village has a number of painted houses and a baroque church, but gets completely overridden with visitors at peak times. Its main streets cater for the mass tourist trade, notably with its plethora of shops selling locally produced wood carvings (mostly on religious themes). The Heimatmuseum has a display of antique wooden artefacts (*Closed* Mon, also Nov and Feb). The Passion Play theatre offers guided tours (German and English) daily in summer and at times throughout the year (tel: 0822/945 88 33).

Ettal, the next village to the south, has two claims to fame. One is *Ettaler*, a sweet herbal liqueur originally made by monks. The other is the great Benedictine **abbey church▶**, with an unusual 12-sided nave beneath a huge dome, modelled on the Church of the Holy Sepulchre in Jerusalem. Though the foundation is 14th century, the church interior is high baroque, with a painted ceiling by Johann-Jakob Zeiller.

The road west from Ettal is a very pretty route, leading deep into the fir-clad mountains, hugging a rushing stream and crossing the Ammergebirge range, over the 1,200m-high (3,937ft) Ammer pass into Austria and the Austrian border town of Reutte. Except for cross-country skiers, it is not to be recommended in winter, when this corner of Germany can be snowed in for weeks on end, but throughout the year the road is kept open as far as

Born in 1845 in Nymphenburg Castle, near Munich, Ludwig II was a member of the Wittelsbach dynasty and became king of Bavaria at the age of 18. Within two years of his accession to the throne he became involved in a war with Prince Otto von Bismarck of Prussia; Bavaria was defeated, and the Prussians took over the Bavarian army.

In 1870, under Bismarck's influence, Bavaria was drawn into the war between Prussia and France that was to be the catalyst in the formation of the German Empire, of which Bavaria became a part. Bismarck now had Ludwig under his thumb and ordered the Bavarian king to send a letter naming Wilhelm I of Prussia as the Emperor of Germany. Disillusioned, Ludwig lost interest in politics and became increasingly eccentric. He built the castles—Neuschwanstein, Linderhof and Herrenchiemsee—at huge expense. A stage-set designer drew the first sketches for Neuschwanstein, the most theatrical of the three; Ludwig watched the progress of building through his telescope from Hohenschwangau. Linderhof, the only one of Ludwig's royal castles to be completed, was his favourite. Louis XIV became Ludwig's inspiration: His dream was

261

of absolute rule. He gave financial aid to Richard Wagner, whose operas fired his imagination. But the funds ran out; Ludwig's extravagance, homosexuality and near or actual insanity worried the Bavarian government, which colluded with Luitpold (his uncle and successor) to depose him. Ludwig was certified insane in his bedroom at Neuschwanstein; a few days later, on 13 June, 1886, he and his physician were found drowned in the Starnberger See. It has never been ascertained whether this was an accident or an assassination.

Linderhof, which is the site of perhaps the most appealing of King Ludwig's castles, **Schloss Linderhof▶** (*Open* daily; guided tours in English). Its isolated site is surrounded by forest, with the Alps towering in the distance to the south. A royal hunting lodge had previously occupied the site.

Schloss Linderhof was completed in 1878 for Ludwig II and modelled on the Petit Trianon at Versailles. Its interior, though nothing as spectacularly bizarre as Neuschwanstein (see page 246), is characteristically lavish, full of mirrors, painted ceilings and gilded cherubs, in a mixture of Renaissance and baroque styles.

The grounds have some wonderfully offbeat features, including a grand cascade, a water jet that shoots higher than the Schloss itself, a grotto modelled on the Venusberg of Wagner's opera *Tannhäuser*, and a Moorish kiosk resplendent with a 'peacock throne'.

Local wood carvings

OBERSTDORF

0   5   10 km
0   5 miles

(Map labels: Stiefenhofen, Simmerberg, Iller, Kranzegg, Wertach, Pfronten, Falkenstein 1268m, Alpsee, Rettenberg, Grünten ▲1738m, Vils, Deutsche Alpenstrasse, Oberstaufen, Immenstadt, Blaichach, Burgberg, Steibis, Weissach, Sonthofen, Hindelang, Jochstrasse, Oberjochpass, Hochgrat ▲1832m, Ofterschwang, Deutsche Alpenstrasse, Oberjoch, Bad Oberdorf, Balderschwang, Riedbergborn 1786m▲, Altstädten, Hinterstein, Bolgenach, Obermaiselstein, Fischen, Ostrach, Oberstdorf, Nebelborn ▲2224m, Breitachklamm ■, Freibergsee, Himmelschrofen ▲1790m, Hochvogel ▲2593m, Allgäuer, Spielmannsau, Alpen, Einödsbach, Stillach, Mädelegabel 2645m▲, A)

There's good walking and challenging rock climbing in the Oberstdorf valley

---

► Oberstdorf and area   *238A1*

Oberstdorf is a busy valley resort, excellently placed for exploring the Allgäuer Alps; it flourishes as a winter-sports (top-class skiing and skating facilities), climbing and hiking base. More peaceful bases include **Fischen**, on the valley floor but bypassed by the road; remote **Balderschwang**, high up a lonely side valley; **Oberstaufen**, large and neatly tended; **Altstädten**, with its characteristic wooden Allgäuer houses; and **Hindelang**, nestling in green countryside.

From Oberstdorf, horse-drawn carriages leave every day for the **Stillachtal**, the southernmost valley in Germany, with Einödsbach as its southernmost village. The road is closed to motor traffic and offers magnificent mountain views.

Southwest of Oberstdorf, the **Kleines Walsertal►**, an enclave of Austria, can only be reached from Germany and has typical wooden farms and modest family hotels within a dramatic Alpine setting. The walk along the **Breitachklamm**, west of Oberstdorf, squeezes through a magnificent gorge and beneath unlikely looking overhangs (closed during the spring thaw). Cable cars from the east side of town whisk you up to the **Nebelhorn** upper station for a chairlift to the summit (2,224m/ 7,296ft), which is graced with a summit restaurant and a superb panoramic view.

►► Ottobeuren   *238A2*

The Benedictine abbey church of Ottobeuren (*Open* daily 9–sunset) dwarfs the adjacent town. Founded in AD764, it prospered under the patronage of Charlemagne, and the complex was rebuilt in the 18th century by Johann Michael Fischer. It is Germany's largest baroque church, and the proportions are quite cathedral-like, with a nave 90m (295ft) long and a transept 60m (197ft) across. Its interior is wonderfully light, and adorned with frescoes by

Zimmermann, Amigoni and J. J. Zeiller, and stuccowork by J. M. Feichtmayr. The Trinity organ, built by K. J. Riepp, is one of the most splendid in Europe.

▶ Starnberger See 238C2

The largest lake close to Munich is served by a suburban train service (S-Bahn), which makes it a good out-of-town base for the Bavarian capital. It is well suited for yachting (boat rental available), strolls and relaxation; the scenery is undramatic but pleasant.

A boat sails around the lakes; stops include the Votive Chapel at Berg, erected in memory of Ludwig II, who drowned here in 1886. The best views are from the Bismarckturm (Bismarck tower), south of Berg, and from Ilkahöhe, a modest hill southwest of Tutzing, the main resort.

Just to the south is the peaceful and unspoiled **Ostersee**, part of a complex of over 20 small lakes, with reedy shores and wooded isles. The 8km (5-mile) Rundweg Ostersee, a circular path, is an easy 2-hour walk; the parking area is between Seeshaupt and Penzburg.

At **Kochel**, the **Franz Marc Museum▶** (*Open* Mar to mid-Jan Tue–Sun 2–6pm; tours in English by arrangement, tel: 08851/71 14) has masterpieces by the great 20th-century Bavarian artist and his contemporaries.

MEMMINGEN

Northwest of Ottobeuren, Memmingen has an attractive central area of arcaded buildings and patrician houses, with the irregular Marktplatz dominated by the Gothic tower of the Nikolaikirche (fine murals and stalls within). Parishaus, a pink-and-white building north of the Rathaus, houses the tourist office, which issues a leaflet detailing a walk around town. The Hermannsbau (1766) is the town's finest house, and now contains the local museum (*Open* May–Oct Tue–Fri and Sun), worth a look for its oak staircase and stucco ceilings; exhibits include porcelain, doll's houses, clocks, medieval religious art and an 1825 model of Memmingen itself.

263

Walk

The Heini-Klopfer Ski Jump and the Freibergsee

A varied walk (1–2 hours) that begins with a gentle riverside path. You can either ascend on foot or take the ski lift. The routes conjoin at the Eibersee, a small lake circled by wooded slopes, before you reach the final descent.

Start at the parking area northeast of the Freibergsee, in the Stillachtal.

From the west side of Oberstdorf, drive south (signposted Fellhornbarn and Schiflugschanze). The parking area can be seen in the trees after 4km (2.5 miles). Walk to the rear of the parking area and cross the footbridge; turn left, and follow the river 1.5km (1 mile) to reach the ski jump. Take the ski lift to the top and turn right at the path above the lift, or continue forwards, on a rising traffic-free road, forking right at the top and following signs to Freibergsee, past Gasthof Schwand, then forking right just before the ski jump. At the next major fork bear right downhill, then right again (signposted Parkplatz) to the river. Turn right to cross the footbridge into the parking area.

The Schliersee (above) is one of the loveliest Alpine lakes

Wangen's Rathaus rules over a town of painted gateways and modern sculptures

► **Tegernsee, Schliersee and Spitzingsee**   *239D2*

These three mountain-ringed lakes are an hour's train ride or drive southeast of Munich and at weekends are crowded with winter-sports enthusiasts, walkers and (in summer) with picnicking families. Tegernsee is the most popular and interesting of the three. A Benedictine monastery was founded here in the 8th century. The Bavarian King Ludwig I used it as a summer retreat following secularization in the early 19th century. A very fine beer is brewed within its ancient walls and it's served up in one of Bavaria's most original beerhalls, the **Bräustüberl**, directly adjoining the monastery church in lakeside Tegernsee town. Pleasure boats ply the lake, linking Tegernsee with three other resorts—fashionable Rottach-Egern, the expensive spa Bad Wiessee and ancient Gmund. Schliersee is quieter and less showy, while tiny Spitzingsee is tucked in the mountains between the two other lakes, at the end of a serpentine drive from the valley floor. There are moderately challenging ski slopes above Spitzingsee, and very fine hikes in the mountains which rise to around 1,884m (6,181ft).

► **Wangen im Allgäu**   *238A1*

An appealing town with a wealth of painted houses. Its old town is a crossroads, focused on the Marktplatz and entered by two frescoed gateways, the Frauentor (Ravensburg Gate) of 1608, the symbol of Wangen, and the St. Martin Tor (Lindau Gate), with its pyramidal roof and an array of gargoyles. A museum in a half-timbered building devotes itself to cheese-making and folk art in the Allgäu (*Open* daily; cheese-making Wed and Sun).

Isny, to the east, is another unspoiled old town, with 13th-century ramparts, a pretty corner by the church of St. Jakob and St. Georg, and 17th-century monastery buildings (now a hospital).

▶ Wasserburg am Inn   239D2

Wasserburg occupies a naturally fortified site all but surrounded by a tight meander of the turbulent Inn River, itself lined with white cliffs. This was one of the most prosperous towns in Bavaria during the Middle Ages, when it became a river port for Munich on a salt trading route and was allowed to levy tax on the salt that passed through town. Wasserburg's fortunes slumped after 1504, when the salt trade route was moved, and later suffered the ravages of war and plague. Its heyday gone, Wasserburg nevertheless retains a legacy of old merchants' houses and characterful winding streets.

Opposite the Rathaus, the façade of the Kernhaus displays outstanding 18th-century stucco work by J. B. Zimmermann. Behind the Rathaus, the local museum (*Closed* Mon and mid–Dec to Jan) has a fine collection of ancient farm furniture, implements and carriages.

The main town gateway dates from 1374 and displays wall paintings of two warriors bearing the banners of Wasserburg and Bavaria; within it, the Erstes Imaginäres Museum houses a collection of old masters from all over the world, with a difference: All of them are fakes (*Closed* Mon; also mid-Dec to Jan). Through the gateway, continue over the bridge over the Inn River, then turn left into Kellerstrasse for a path up to a fine view over the town.

At Wasserburg even some of the modern buildings by the Inn River have stepped gable façades

265

▶▶ Wieskirche   238B2

Set amid quiet, green meadows, the famous Wieskirche stands almost by itself. It was built as a pilgrimage church to house a figure of the Scourging of Christ, which had allegedly shed miraculous tears. The architect Dominikus Zimmermann gave it a wonderfully light, frothy interior, with an outstanding frescoed dome depicting the Gate to Paradise. His composition was a personal masterpiece (so much so that he spent the rest of his life in a house close by) and is one of the great rococo buildings of Europe.

Arriving and departing

To enter Germany you need a valid passport, or an identity card in the case of EU and some other countries. Visitors from 40 other countries, including Australia, Canada, New Zealand and the USA, do not need a visa for business or tourist visits of up to three months, provided they are not looking for work in Germany.

It is advisable to check entry regulations with the appropriate German Embassy before departure (see addresses under Embassies).

Channel Tunnel Eurotunnel operates frequent drive-on car and passenger carrying train services between Folkestone and Calais. Booking is advisable to avoid delays and to benefit from lower fares. For information telephone 0870 535 3535 or visit www.eurotunnel.com.

By air The main international airports are Frankfurt, Düsseldorf, Hamburg, Stuttgart, Munich and Berlin. Internal air services connect these and other airports within Germany. Lufthansa (German Airlines) will arrange train connections between main cities for its passengers (see Public transportation). There is a regular airport bus transfer between Berlin's Tegel and Schönefeld airports.

All German airports connect efficiently with the local urban transport network. In some cases there is a connecting coach service; other airports tie in with the metro system. Frankfurt airport is also served by some long-distance intercity rail links.

By boat
To Denmark: DFDS Seaways (tel: 0870 533 3000; www.dfds.co.uk) operates the only direct sailings to Esbjerg from the UK, out of Harwich, Essex, to Cuxhaven (three departures per week throughout the year). The crossing takes about 19 hours.

To Holland: Crossing to Holland from the UK means a shorter sea journey and unless you specifically want to visit the north of Germany, it is an alternative jumping-off point. Stena Line (tel: 0870 570 7070;

www.stenaline.co.uk) operates from Harwich to the Hook of Holland, taking about 4 to 6 hours depending on the vessel. P&O North Sea Ferries (tel: 0870 598 0333; www.poferries.com) offers crossings from Hull to Rotterdam (about 13 hours). DFDS sails from Newcastle to Amsterdam daily (about 16 hours).

To Belgium: Another option is to arrive at a Belgian port.
P&O North Sea Ferries sails from Hull to Zeebrugge; the crossing takes 14.5 hours.

To France: It could be that if you're heading for central and southern Germany a quick sea crossing to Dunkerque, Boulogne or Calais works out best for you. Driving times from Channel ports to German destinations vary from 4 hours to Cologne, to 10 hours down to Munich.

Ferry companies serving these ports from the UK are: P&O Stena Line (tel: 0870 520 2020), SeaFrance (tel: 0870 571 1711; www.seafrance.com) and Norfolkline (tel: 0870 870 1020; www.norfolkline.com), all linking Dover and Calais.

All ferry companies offer special deals of one sort or another, for instance concessions for family groups, senior citizens, special sailings and so on. It's advisable to read their brochures very carefully or to ask what kind of offers are available before booking.

By coach Eurolines (tel: 0870 514 3219) have frequent coach departures from London Victoria to Frankfurt, Hamburg, Munich, Berlin, Leipzig, Dresden and other destinations. Sample travel times are 14 hours to Cologne, 23 hours to Berlin and 25 hours to Dresden. Special children's fares operate on all routes.

By rail Eurostar trains go via the Channel Tunnel from London Waterloo (some stopping at Ashford in Kent) to Brussels Midi (2.75 hours), with connections to Cologne (a further 3 hours) and other German cities. Ring Eurostar telesales (0870 518 6186). There are also services from London,

Travel Facts

Liverpool Street, to Harwich via Manningtree for ferries to Hook of Holland.

Travel times vary, depending on which route is taken. Holders of rail tickets to the German border can purchase Euro Domino tickets for 3–8 days unlimited travel on German Rail, and also a variety of Regional Rail Passes; all are valid on days of the user's choosing within the period of validity, and offer unrestricted travel on rail and certain bus and boat services within Germany.

Also available are Rail Europe Senior Citizen Rail Cards for holders of UK Senior Citizen Railcards offering a third off rail ticket prices, and the Inter-Rail Pass (www.raileurope.co.uk/inter-rail) for under 26-year-olds and over 26-year-olds, valid for 16 days or one month on most northern European rail networks.

Camping
Germany abounds in campsites; there are about 2,500 sprinkled liberally around the country. The standard is high: even the most basic have toilet and washing facilities plus on-site shop. Top class campsites feature swimming pools, supermarkets, discos and all the trimmings.

Campsites are located by a blue sign carrying the international camping symbol: a black tent on a white background. Most are open from Easter to October, with around 400 staying open all year. June to September is the busiest season and as reservations are usually made on site, you must get there early to avoid disappointment, especially in popular places; better still, book in advance.

A list of campsites can be obtained free from the German National Tourist Office (address under Tourist offices). The German Camping Club publishes a complete guide, available from Mandlstrasse 28, D-80802 Munich, while the German motoring organisation ADAC (Am Westpark 8, D-81373 Munich) also publishes a guide to over 1,000 sites.

If you prefer to pitch your tent outside official campsites, you must first ask the permission of the landowner or local police.

Most of the major car rental firms will also rent out a camper van.

Children
If you're in need of a babysitter, enquire first at your hotel reception; they may well offer this service. Tourist offices in most towns and cities keep updated lists of recommended babysitters and details of local crèche facilities.

Under-fours travel free on public transport and children aged four to 11 go half price. Reduced rates are usually offered in hotels and guest houses for children, and it is the norm for attractions such as museums and historic buildings to offer discounts for younger visitors.

German theme parks tend to take the form of fairy-tale tableaux lands, such as the Märchenwald (www.maerchenwald-isartal.de), with its adventure playground, at Wolfratshausen near Bad Tölz in the Bavarian Alps, the Grimm 'fairy-tale park' (www.blueba.de) at Ludwigsburg, near Stuttgart, and the Taunus Wonderland (www.taunus-wunderland.de) at Wiesbaden. Attractions at Phantasialand (www.phantasialand.de; see page 89) at Brühl (halfway between Bonn and Cologne) include re-creations of the Wild West, ancient China and pre-war Berlin, a massive roller coaster and overhead monorail. Zoos and puppet theatres are popular features throughout the country.

Climate
Generally speaking the weather in Germany is rather similar to that in Britain: changeable, neither extremely hot nor cold and sprinkled with rain. The climate does not get dramatically warmer the farther south you go. Berlin has an average July temperature of between 15° and 24°C (59° and 75°F), more southerly Munich of between 13° and 24°C (55° and 75°F). This city also has an above average summer rainfall. However, Hamburg in the north is consistently several degrees cooler than, for instance, Frankfurt in the centre. Berlin has long been famous for its bracing air—the *Berliner Luft*—while South Bavaria has its *Föhn*. This

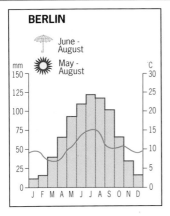

BERLIN

June - August

May - August

mm 150 125 100 75 50 25 0

°C 30 25 20 15 10 5 0

J F M A M J J A S O N D

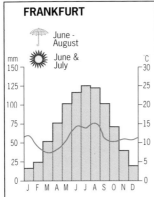

FRANKFURT

June - August

June & July

mm 150 125 100 75 50 25 0

°C 30 25 20 15 10 5 0

J F M A M J J A S O N D

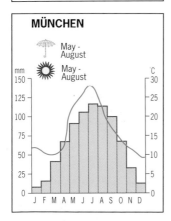

MÜNCHEN

May - August

May - August

mm 150 125 100 75 50 25 0

°C 30 25 20 15 10 5 0

J F M A M J J A S O N D

mountain wind can spring up at any season, causing a sudden change in temperature as it brings very warm conditions and a cloudless sky.

Summers are usually pleasantly hot and dry throughout the country. Towards the Alps they get shorter,

starting around May, and ending in warm autumns. May or October are good times to visit Germany; the popular haunts can get crowded in the peak tourist months of June to September. Later, snows start around November, and winter can be very cold: the January temperature in Berlin and Munich, for example, can hit a minimum of –5°C (23°F).

Crime

Crime figures have risen sharply since unification, but violent crime remains less common in Germany than in many countries. Trouble spots, as in any other nation, are large cities such as Hamburg, Frankfurt, and Berlin, where the usual car theft and house robberies are a hazard of urban life. Late at night in Eastern Berlin, visitors should be wary of empty areas or being alone in train carriages.

As a tourist, it makes sense to avoid attracting unwanted attention: Do not flaunt expensive jewellery or camera equipment, or leave baggage unattended, valuables on show in your car or your vehicle unlocked. Wear a shoulder bag on the side away from the street, or use a money belt for cash and travellers' cheques. It is a good idea to have photocopies of important documents, including passport, driving licence and travellers' cheques, and to remember to keep them in a safe, separate place from the originals.

If you are unlucky enough to fall foul of thieves, register the theft straight away with the police (*Polizei*). This is necessary if you wish to claim on your travel insurance. In an emergency, dial 110. When arriving at the police station, make sure you have some form of identification (one instance where your photocopies could be useful).

Do not inadvertently commit an offence yourself by, for instance, crossing the road before the green light for pedestrians shows. This may be acceptable behaviour at home, but is illegal in Germany. Far more serious is being caught in possession of drugs, of any sort—imprisonment or deportation is the penalty.

269

CONVERSION CHARTS

FROM	TO	MULTIPLY BY
Inches	Centimetres	2.54
Centimetres	Inches	0.3937
Feet	Metres	0.3048
Metres	Feet	3.2810
Yards	Metres	0.9144
Metres	Yards	1.0940
Miles	Kilometres	1.6090
Kilometres	Miles	0.6214
Acres	Hectares	0.4047
Hectares	Acres	2.4710
Gallons	Litres	4.5460
Litres	Gallons	0.2200
Ounces	Grams	28.35
Grams	Ounces	0.0353
Pounds	Grams	453.6
Grams	Pounds	0.0022
Pounds	Kilograms	0.4536
Kilograms	Pounds	2.205
Tons	Tonnes	1.0160
Tonnes	Tons	0.9842

MEN'S SUITS

UK	36	38	40	42	44	46	48
Rest of Europe	46	48	50	52	54	56	58
US	36	38	40	42	44	46	48

DRESS SIZES

UK	8	10	12	14	16	18
France	36	38	40	42	44	46
Italy	38	40	42	44	46	48
Rest of Europe	34	36	38	40	42	44
US	6	8	10	12	14	16

MEN'S SHIRTS

UK	14	14.5	15	15.5	16	16.5	17
Rest of Europe	36	37	38	39/40	41	42	43
US	14	14.5	15	15.5	16	16.5	17

MEN'S SHOES

UK	7	7.5	8.5	9.5	10.5	11
Rest of Europe	41	42	43	44	45	46
US	8	8.5	9.5	10.5	11.5	12

WOMEN'S SHOES

UK	4.5	5	5.5	6	6.5	7
Rest of Europe	38	38	39	39	40	41
US	6	6.5	7	7.5	8	8.5

Customs

There are currently no restrictions on the import or export of euros or any foreign currency.

Your private car is exempt from duty (subject to re-exportation) as are personal travel requisites.

People touring within the European Union are no longer entitled to import duty-free goods. However, visitors from outside the EU can bring in duty-free goods up to the current EU allowances:
Alcohol (over 22° vol): 1 litre or
Alcohol (not over 22° vol) 2 litres and
Still table wine: 2 litres
Cigarettes: 200 or
Cigars: 50 or
Tobacco: 250g
Perfume: 50ml
Toilet water: 250ml
If you are bringing expensive items such as computers, it may be worth carrying receipts.

Visitors with disabilities

The German government agency involved in assisting disabled people has details of hotels with special facilities to meet their requirements. Write to Nationale Koordinationsstelle Tourismus für alle e.v., Kirchfeldstrasse 149, D-40215 Düsseldorf (tel: 0221/336 80 01).

The wheelchair symbol (a wheelchair set in a box) indicates access for disabled tourists. Airports and rest stops on the autobahns are all equipped with toilet facilities, and at major railway stations staff are specially briefed to help passengers with disabilities.

Access guides produced in Germany by social services departments or groups of residents list hotels, restaurants, buses, accessible to disabled visitors. RADAR, 250 City Road, London EC1V 8AF, tel: 020-7250 3222; www.radarnetwork. org.uk) can give callers an idea which towns offer the best facilities. RADAR also publishes its own guide to holidays and travel which lists useful contact organizations.

Driving

The condition of autobahns, major and minor roads is excellent in the former West Germany, and has now

270

greatly improved in former East Germany. Autobahns are toll-free for cars.

Foreign motorists may drive a vehicle for up to one year in Germany with a national or international driving licence. Holders of Australian and US licences must carry an official translation. (Contact your Embassy or a German National Tourist Office.) Third-party insurance is compulsory. Check with your insurers and they will issue a Green Card to show that they have extended your cover to allow driving abroad.

Even if you come from outside the EU you do not need an international car registration document, though you should ensure that you always have your ordinary registration documents with you.

Germans drive on the right side of the road; traffic coming from the right normally has right of way.

Children under 12 are not allowed to travel in a front seat unless they are using special seats or safety belts suitable for children or unless the rear seats are occupied by other children. It is compulsory for driver and passengers to wear seat belts if fitted.

Some drivers go very fast on autobahns, even up to 200kph (125mph). Germany is one of the few countries in Europe without any official speed limit on its motorways, though 130kph (80mph) is a recommended maximum (100kph/62mph in some places. Certain stretches have separate, lower speed limits. Watch for the signs). There is a countrywide official limit on country roads of 100kph (62mph) and in built-up areas of 50kph (31mph).

On-the-spot fines are levied for speeding, and other road offences such as using abusive language, making offensive and derogatory signs and for running out of petrol on the motorway.

The rule for drinking and driving is that the level of alcohol in the bloodstream must be under 50mg/100ml, although it is, of course, wisest and safest not to drink and drive at all. Motorists are sometimes given breathalyzer tests if they seem to be driving incautiously, or after an accident, regardless of its cause.

Mozart's house, Augsburg

In the case of a breakdown, contact the ADAC (Allgemeiner Deutscher Automobil Club). On autobahns emergency orange telephones are sited at regular intervals (follow the yellow marker arrows). Ask for 'Strassenwachthilfe'. The ADAC breakdown number, country-wide, is 0180/222 2222. The ADAC do not charge you for their work, but only for materials (unless it's a serious problem, so check that your insurance covers this).

Filling stations are regularly sited along autobahns and in urban areas off the main roads. Lead-free petrol (*bleifrei*), is available everywhere, while leaded petrol has been phased out. Petrol prices vary, tending to be higher on autobahns, cheaper at self-service (SB-Tanken) stations.

Car rental: Pre-booking a rental car from home can save time and using a major company means you can pick up at one place and drop off at another for no extra charge. Most airports, railway stations and larger towns have offices if you prefer to arrange car rental (*Autovermietung*) in Germany. International firms include Hertz, Avis, Europcar and Sixt. Ask at the local tourist office for German car rental companies.

The minimum age at which you can rent a car is 21 and you need to have held a full driving licence for a year.

Electricity

The current in Germany is 220 volts, 50 cycles. Sockets are for the two-pin type of plug. You will find adaptors are widely available.

Embassies/Consulates

Of other countries in Germany:

Australia: Wallstrasse 76, D-10179 Berlin; tel: 030/88 08 80
Canada: Leipziger Platz 17, D-10117 Berlin; tel: 030/20 31 20
Eire: Friedrichstrasse 200, D-10117 Berlin; tel: 030/22 07 20
New Zealand: Friedrichstrasse 60, D-10117 Berlin; tel: 030/20 62 10
UK: Wilhelmstrasse 70–71, D-10117 Berlin; tel: 030/20 45 70
US: Neustädtische Kirchstrasse 4–5, D-10117, Berlin; tel: 030/23 85 174

Of Germany in other countries:

Australia: 119 Empire Circuit, Yarralumla, ACT, 2600; tel: 02/ 6270 1911
Canada: 1 Waverley Street, Ottawa, Ontario K2P 0T8; tel: 613 232 1101
Eire: 31 Trimelston Avenue, Booterstown, Blackrock, Co Dublin; tel: 01 2693011
New Zealand: 90-92 Hobson Street, Wellington; tel: (64) 4473 6063
UK: 23 Belgrave Square, London SW1X 8PZ; tel: 020 7824 1300
USA: 4645 Reservoir Road NW, Washington DC 20007–1998; tel: 202 298 4000

Emergency telephone numbers

Police: 110
Fire Department: 112
DZT (Deutsche Zentrale für Tourismus – German National Tourist Board) 069/97 46 40
ADAC – Allgemeiner Deutscher Automobil Club (Germany's leading motoring organization) – emergency breakdown number: 01802/22 22 22

Etiquette

In Germany, never call anyone by their first name unless you are invited to do so. Germans tend to be formal in business and in their private lives, too, though the younger generation takes a more relaxed attitude to this rule. Always use either Herr or Frau; it is considered an insult to address a woman as Fräulein, until you know for sure that she prefers to be called Miss. You should also say, 'Guten Morgen, meine Dame', as opposed to 'meine Frau'. When speaking to a professional person, such as a doctor, address him/her as Herr or Frau Doktor or with whatever other job title is appropriate. Holders of non-medical doctorates are also often addressed as Herr or Frau Doktor.

The distinction between 'Sie' and 'Du', both meaning you, is comparable to the difference between the French 'vous' and 'tu'. You must wait to be told to use the familiar 'Du', though it's always safe to use it with children and animals.

Germans shake hands when they meet, even if it's only a casual encounter between neighbours on the stairs.

Another German custom is to bring a gift when invited to someone's home. The safest and most welcome item to take is a bunch of flowers.

Health

Currently, no immunizations are required for entry into Germany. Health care is privatized, all Germans belonging to a health insurance scheme. EU citizens are entitled to free medical treatment in Germany, on production of a valid European Health Insurance Card (EHIC). Apply online for an EHIC (www.dh.gov.uk/travellers). Allow 2–3 weeks until you receive the card.

In addition you should take out travel insurance to cover expenses connected with illness, such as a special flight home or longer hotel stay, which are not covered by the (EHIC). And to be able to make a claim, remember to keep receipts of all medical treatment, prescriptions and other expenses to give your insurers once home. The number for emergency/weekend doctors and dentists can be found in local telephone directories for German cities. If you want to ensure that you will be treated by English-speaking medical staff, contact the local consulate, which should hold details.

Doctors' consulting hours are usually 7am–8pm in hospital outpatients' departments; doctors' surgeries about 10–noon, 4–6 (times vary); closed Wed pm. (Hospital outpatients' provide an emergency service outside these hours, too.) Dispensing chemists are open during normal shop hours; in larger towns they display a list of late night and Sunday opening pharmacies (see Pharmacies, page 277).

Hitch-hiking
Hitch-hiking is not illegal, except on the autobahns and their feeder roads, although it is not encouraged. However, since the recent increase in crime, motorists have generally become more suspicious and therefore they are more reluctant to pick people up.

Every major city has a Mitfahrerzentrale, which provides a useful alternative. Drivers inform this office when and where they are touring and those wanting a lift— and willing to share the cost of fuel —pay a fee to the office to get the driver's name and telephone number. This is by far the cheapest way of touring around the country by car, but again, not without hazards.

Lone visitors should always be aware of the inherent dangers of taking lifts with strangers. Some cities have women-only Frauenmitfahrerzentrale.

Insurance
Make sure you take out travel insurance. It should cover you for accident or illness in the areas of motoring and health, and also for the loss or theft of valuables while on holiday. This insurance is best taken out at home before departure. Speak to your insurers, travel agent or motoring organization, when planning your trip.

Internet
Internet cafés continue to sprout up in many towns. Information via the internet is readily available: Nearly all cities, towns and sights in this book have websites, some with English versions. Communication via email is widespread.

Language
There is one official standard German language, *Hochdeutsch* (High German), which all the children are taught in school and which everyone in the country should be able to understand. However, regional dialects, with strong local accents, are widely spoken in many areas. Some cities, notably Berlin and Cologne, retain their own dialects which a visitor from a village even 20km (12 miles) away may find hard to follow; and the *Plattdeutsch* (Low German) of northern Germany even has its own literature. Saxony, Bavaria and Swabia are regions with pronounced local dialects, which vary greatly. For example, 'We have seen it' is 'Wir haben es angesehen' in *Hochdeutsch*, 'Mir hens a guckt' in Bavarian, 'Mr hannet gesäh' in Swabian, and 'Wir haben's angekiekt' in Berlin.

Pronunciation guide
Vowels (in Hochdeutsch)
a (short) as in hat, eg, *Hand* (hand)
a (long) as in father, eg, *sagen* (say)
e (short) as in bet, eg, *Wetter* (weather)
e (long) as in day, eg, *geben* (give)
i as in fit, eg, *bitte* (please)
o (short) as in lost, eg, *voll* (full)
o (long) as in coach, eg, *Mond* (moon)
u as in boot, eg, *gut* (good)
ä (short) as in wet, eg, *Äpfel* (apple)
ä (long) as in wait, eg, *spät* (late)
ö as in fur, eg, *schön* (beautiful)
ü as in blue, eg, *über* (over)
ai as in spy, eg, the River *Main*

273

ei as in spy, eg, *ein* (one)
au as in how, eg, *Maus* (mouse)
ie as in tree, eg, *Lied* (song)
eu as in boy, eg, *treu* (true)
äu as in boy, eg, *Fräulein* (miss)

Consonants
Most are pronounced as written. The following are exceptions.
ch is either a throaty sound as in Scottish *loch*, eg, *Nacht* (night), or an unvoiced sh sound, eg, *nicht* (not)
j is as y in yacht, eg, *ja* (yes)
r is rolled
s is as z in zip, eg, *sein* (his)
sch is as sh in shut, eg, *scheinen* (to seem)
sp/st are pronounced shp/sht, eg, *sprechen* (speak), *Stadt* (town)
v is as f in fit, eg, *Vater* (father)
w is as v in very, eg, *Wand* (wall)
z is as ts in bits, eg, *Zeit* (time)

274

Words and phrases
Days of the week

Sunday	*Sonntag*
Monday	*Montag*
Tuesday	*Dienstag*
Wednesday	*Mittwoch*
Thursday	*Donnerstag*
Friday	*Freitag*
Saturday	*Samstag*
	or *Sonnabend*

Months of the year

Januar	*Juli*
Februar	*August*
März	*September*
April	*Oktober*
Mai	*November*
Juni	*Dezember*

Basics

yes/no	*ja/nein*
please	*bitte*
thank you	*danke*
	(can also mean 'no, thank you')
hello	*Guten Tag; Grüss Gott* (in the south)
goodbye	*Auf Wiedersehen*
Do you speak English?	*Sprechen Sie Englisch?*
I don't understand	*Ich verstehe nicht*
Help!	*Hilfe!*

Questions

| Where is/are | *Wo ist/sind* |

the bank?	*die Bank?*
the station?	*der Bahnhof?*
the airport?	*der Flughafen?*
the bus stop?	*die Bushaltestelle?*
the police station?	*das Polizeirevier?*
the nearest toilets?	*die nächsten Toiletten?*
right	*rechts*
left	*links*
straight ahead	*geradeaus*
How much is...	*Wieviel kostet...*
the fare?	*die Fahrkarte?*
the entrance fee?	*der Eintritt?*
When...	*Wann...*
does the museum open?	*wird das Museum geöffnet?*
does the train leave?	*fährt der Zug ab?*
at 10 o'clock	*um zehn Uhr*
at half past 10	*um halb elf*

Staying and eating

I'd like...	*Ich hätte gern...*
a single room	*ein Einzelzimmer*
a double room	*ein Doppelzimmer*
with bath	*mit Bad*
open	*Geöffnet*
closed	*Geschlossen*
Waiter!	*Herr Ober!*
May I see the menu, please?	*Die Speisekarte bitte?*
breakfast	*das Frühstück*
lunch	*das Mittagessen*
dinner	*das Abendessen*
bread	*das Brot*
butter	*die Butter*
egg	*das Ei*
cheese	*der Käse*
vegetables	*das Gemüse*
fruit	*das Obst*
coffee	*der Kaffee*
tea	*der Tee*
beer	*das Bier*
wine	*der Wein*

Numbers

0	*null*	18	*achtzehn*
1	*eins*	19	*neunzehn*
2	*zwei*	20	*zwanzig*
3	*drei*	21	*einundzwanzig*
4	*vier*		
5	*fünf*	30	*dreissig*
6	*sechs*	32	*zweiunddreissig*
7	*sieben*		
8	*acht*	40	*vierzig*
9	*neun*	50	*fünfzig*

10	*zehn*	60	*sechzig*
11	*elf*	70	*siebzig*
12	*zwölf*	80	*achtzig*
13	*dreizehn*	90	*neunzig*
14	*vierzehn*	100	*hundert*
15	*fünfzehn*	101	*hunderteins*
16	*sechzehn*	500	*fünfhundert*
17	*siebzehn*	1,000	*tausend*

Laundry

Most towns of any size in former West Germany have a launderette or *Waschsalon*. Campsites have their own washing facilities and many hotels offer a laundry service.

Lost property

All bus and railway stations have lost property offices; look in the telephone directory or enquire at the station for the *Fundbüro*.

It is very important to read carefully the instructions for loss issued with your travellers' cheques. Make a separate note of the serial numbers of all cheques (or take photocopies) and of the telephone number to call in case of emergencies. Major issuing companies will have refund facilities available. Contact their nearest office or, failing that, the nearest bank. Register loss of cheques with the police, and if you are stranded without money, contact the local consulate.

Lost passports should be reported to the police station and contact your consulate if you need emergency travel papers.

Maps

Road atlases: The *Grosse Shell Atlas* has good, detailed road maps of Germany (scale 1:400,000) with scenic routes, plus city plans, maps of the rest of Europe too, and a full index.

If you take the short ferry crossing the Automobile Association's 1:1,000,000 double-sided map of the whole of Germany could be useful as its coverage extends to the Channel ports from Dieppe.

Hallwag's three 1:500,000 maps of north, east and south Germany include plans showing approach and through roads in all big cities.

Hostelling: The Youth Hostels Map of Germany (Handbuch der Jugendherbergen) shows the location of 600 hostels plus a full list with addresses and phone numbers.

Walking: Special tourist maps showing footpaths and cycling routes in popular destinations are widely available (look for *Wanderkarte* or *Sonderkarte*). A list can be obtained from Stanford's, 12 Long Acre, London WC2E (tel: 020 7836 1321).

Media

The leading German quality daily papers are the conservative *Frankfurter Allgemeine Zeitung* and the more liberal *Süddeutsche Zeitung* (Munich). In addition, nearly every main city or area has its own daily, usually a morning paper. *Die Welt* and the mass-selling tabloid *Bild*, which tends to be sensational, are the two main dailies of the right-wing Springer group.

Some weeklies are very influential: the news magazines *Der Spiegel* and *Focus*, and women's weeklies such as *Brigitte*. In many towns, local publications will give you a run-down on what's on where: in Berlin, for instance, the best are *Tip* and *Zitty*.

The main national public broadcasting TV channels are ARD (first channel) and ZDF (second channel), supplemented by several regional third channels. There are also commercial satellite and cable channels, and many radio networks. In most hotels, TV sets can get CNN or Sky with news and other English-language shows.

Money matters

The unit of currency is the euro. Euro banknotes and coins are available in denominations of 5, 10, 20, 50, 100, 200 and 500; coins come in denominations of 1, 2, 5, 10, 20 and 50 cents and 1 and 2 euros. All euro coins have one side dedicated to their country of origin, while all euro notes (bills) are identical across the euro zone.

There are money exchanges (*Wechselstuben*) at airports, borders and major rail stations, that generally stay open from 6am–10pm daily. Otherwise, normal banking hours are Mon–Fri 8.30 or 9am to 12.30 or

275

1pm, then 2.30–4 (5.30 on Thu). Banks are closed Sat–Sun.

You can also change money at post offices, which are open Mon–Sat 8–6 (Sat until midday). Money exchange is usually available in larger branches in main towns only. The post office is closing down smaller branches and replacing them with agencies situated in supermarkets and other shops.

Travellers' cheques can be cashed in banks, currency exchanges and post offices, but used directly only in smarter shops in main cities.

Credit cards are less widely used in Germany than in some countries, so it is sensible to check that they are accepted before eating a meal or making a purchase.

National holidays

1 Jan: New Year's Day
6 Jan: Epiphany (only in Baden-Württemberg, Bavaria and Sachsen-Anhalt)
Good Friday
Easter Sunday/Easter Monday
1 May: Labour Day
Ascension Day (in May or June)
Whit Sunday and **Whit Monday** (May or June)
18 June: Corpus Christi (in June; celebrated only in certain areas)
15 August: Maria Himmelfahrt (Assumption of the Blessed Virgin Mary, only in Bavaria and Saarland)
3 October: Day of German Unity
1 November: All Saints' Day (celebrated only in certain areas)
25–26 December: Christmas

Opening hours

Legislation liberalizing Germany's traditionally strict shopping hours now permits shops to remain open until 8pm from Monday to Friday and until 4pm on Saturday. Very few shops open on Sundays.

Although most large department stores take advantage of the new hours, many smaller stores still close around 6pm. If you're really caught short of supplies at the weekend, head for a larger railway station, where bakeries and grocery shops can stay open especially for visitors. The expanding shopping facilities available at fuel stations also tend to stay open later and at weekends.

Time your arrival carefully at smaller out-of-the-way restaurants. They often serve meals only between noon and 2pm, then from 5 to 8pm.

Business people are usually at their desks by 9am, often as early as 7am, and government offices close punctually at 4pm, or 2pm on Fridays, and some are open to the public only in the morning.

For doctors' hours, see page 273 under Health.

Evening entertainments—theatre, concerts and so on—usually start at 8pm, and last about two hours.

Organized tours

Deutsche Touring (www.deutsche-touring.com) runs a variety of coach tours, such as the Romantic Road trip from Würzburg to Füssen, or vice versa. A variety of packages lasting from two to seven days is on offer; details from the company at Am Römerhof 17, 60486-Frankfurt am Main (tel: 01805/790 303).

See the German countryside afloat, on a river trip. The Köln–Düsseldorfer (KD) Line offers trips on the Rhine, Mosel, Elbe and Main. Trips last from five hours to five days and concessions for children and senior citizens are a regular feature. KD Lines is at Frankenwerft 35, 50667 Köln (tel: 0221/2 08 83 18; www.k-d.com).

Sächsische Dampfschifffahrt Gesellschaft Weisse Flotte boat company makes tourist trips on the Elbe in the Dresden area using nine historic paddle steamers. Contact them at Hertha-Lindner-Strasse 10, D-01067 Dresden; tel: 0351/86 60 90.

Hiking is very popular and the Jugendherbergswerk (German Youth Hostel Federation) publishes a list of guided walks, from two-day trips to cross-country treks. Contact them at Bismarckstrasse 8, D-32754 Detmold; tel: 05231/7 40 10.

In addition, the local tourist offices will be happy to suggest local opportunities for excursions.

Pharmacies

German chemists or their assistants can usually speak some English.

If you are taking a course of drugs and need to have a prescription filled while staying in Germany, get your doctor at home to write out a prescription using the generic rather than brand name. It's a good idea to have a letter from him or her to the effect that you need the drug for health purposes.

Check before leaving home that what you are taking with you is not illegal in Germany.

In larger towns, pharmacies—*Apotheken*—display late-night or 24-hour rota lists. Or ask at your hotel reception or local police station where to find one open.

Apotheken trade in pharmaceuticals only; cosmetics must be purchased at a *Drogerie*, although larger pharmacies are extending their product range.

Police
German police—*Polizei*—are well-mannered and expect members of the public to be equally correct. In emergencies call 110.

Post offices
The main post office—*Hauptpostamt*—in any large town is usually located near the railway station, but in major cities all mail is now handled in computerized distribution places (*Briefzentrum*) situated not too far from the *autobahn*. Mail reaches the UK in about three days.

To send a letter Poste Restante mark it Postlagernde Briefe/Sendungen and Bitte Halten. As it will be filed alphabetically, according to surname, write that first on the address. Mail is kept, free of charge, for two weeks. When collecting it, take along some ID.

Telegrams can be sent from post offices, or by telephone (see Telephones, page 278).

Public transportation
Domestic air services between major cities are frequent and fast. Within Germany, check with Lufthansa's central reservation service (tel: 0180/583 84 26; www.lufthansa.com) for advice on the many special ticket deals available.

A smaller German airline, LTU, also offers intercity services, as does Air Berlin and dba.

The Air Travel Advisory Bureau, 5 High Street, Royal Tunbridge Wells TN1 1UL (tel: 0870/737 0020) can give advice on agents who specialize in discount flights.

If you arrive at one airport and want to transfer to another, check with Lufthansa for onward train connections linking major cities.

German Railways (the Deutsche Bahn, or DB; www.db.de) operates a nationwide network that links even the smallest villages with the outside world. It achieves this with a flexible variety of services: the high-speed InterCity Express (ICE) trains linking Berlin, Hamburg, Munich, Frankfurt and many other important towns in between; the InterCity (IC) trains connecting all major towns and cities at hourly intervals (and, as EuroCity trains, with cities in neighbouring countries); the InterRegio (IR) trains concentrating on fast travel between the German regions; and long-distance trains running specifically to holiday destinations (mostly in the Alps). Completing the network are three types of metropolitan and short-distance trains: the RegionalExpress (RE), RegionalBahn (RB) and StadtExpress (SE).

If you think that's a complicated compilation, then the fare structure will really flummox you. It takes nearly 20 pages of a DB brochure to cover all the offers, most of which change yearly. Yet you can save enormously by taking advantage of the flexible fare structure. Never just buy a ticket from A to B but lay your travel plan in front of a (usually) helpful station counter clerk and ask for advice.

A BahnCard, for the frequent visitor to Germany, offers either 25, 50 or 100 per cent discount on standard fares for a year.

If you are under 26 you may be eligible for a Eurail Youthpass. This lasts for one, two or three months, and offers unlimited second-class travel in Europe.

Coaches
Coaches link rural areas that railways cannot reach. Many are owned by the DB and are timed and routed to complement the train ser-

277

vice. German towns operate their own local buses, and one ticket will often be transferable between these and other forms of city transportation, such as the S-Bahn, the Strassenbahn (trams), and the U-Bahn (underground). At the station or on entering the bus, train or tram, passengers insert their tickets into a machine that validates them for that trip. Inspectors make frequent rounds to check that tickets are valid, and they are tough on fare dodgers.

Long-distance buses are operated by Deutsche Touring, Am Römerhof 17, 60486 Frankfurt am Main (tel: 01805/79 03 03). Fares are much cheaper than rail, and buses are comfortable, many with hostess-service and on-board refreshments.

Taxis
It is possible to hail a taxi in the street or pick one up from the many ranks at train stations, hotels and so on.

They carry an illuminated roof sign, and fares are made up of a basic charge plus payment per kilometre. This varies from place to place, as do surcharges for carrying items of luggage.

Student and youth travel
There are over 600 youth hostels in Germany which accept members of all associations affiliated with Hostelling International, based at Gate Houe, Fretherne Road, Welwyn Garden City, Herts, AL8 6JH (www.hihostels.com).

Residents of the UK can obtain membership of the Youth Hostel Association from their office at Trevelyan House, Dimple Road, Matlock, Derbyshire DE4 3YH (tel: 0870 770 8868; www.yha.org.uk).

Deutsches Jugendherbergswerk Hauptverband (the German youth hostel association) publishes a complete list of hostels; it is on sale at tourist offices and hostels themselves.

It's wise, particularly in the high season, to pre-book accommodation in hostels; officially, there's a three-day limit to your stay, though if the hostel is not full you may be able to remain longer. The DJH is at Bismarckstrasse 8, D-32756 Detmold,

Germany (tel: 05231/7 40 10; www.jugendherberge.de).

If you are under 23, or a student under 27, enquire about the Tramper Monats Ticket, entitling holders to one month's unlimited travel on the DB system (except the ICE) and DB buses. Ask at railway stations for details (taking along some ID to prove your age).

Telephones
A few public call boxes still take coins, but most of them have been converted to phonecards (*Telefon Karte*), which you buy at the post or tourist office, kiosks and fuel stations.

You can make international calls except from booths marked 'National'. You can also go to a main post office where the connection will be made for you: you pay after the call.

Directory enquiries is on 11833 for domestic numbers, 11834 for foreign numbers and 11837 for English-language enquiries. The operator is on 0180-200 1033.

Call rates are lower after 6pm and at weekends. To dial Britain the country code is 0044; Eire, 00353; USA and Canada, 001; Australia 0061; New Zealand 0064.

Time
German time is 1 hour ahead of British time and normally 6 hours ahead of Toronto and New York time, 9 hours behind Eastern Australian time and 11 hours behind New Zealand.

Tourist offices
Staff are normally very helpful and will often provide free maps and literature on attractions in the area, plus a list of local hotels.

Deutsche Zentrale für Tourismus (German National Tourist Board) is responsible for international and national promotional activities, and has its head office at Beethovenstrasse 69, D-60325 Frankfurt-am-Main (tel: 069/97 46 40, fax: 069/75 19 03; www.deutschland-tourismus.de). In the **United States** the German National Tourist Office is at 122 East

279

42nd Street, New York, NY 10168-0072 (tel: 212/661 7200). The GNTO in **Canada** is at 480 University Avenue, Suite 1410, Toronto, Ontario M5G 1V2 (tel: 416/968 1685).

In the **UK** the GNTO can be contacted at PO Box 2695, London W1A 3TN (tel: 020 7317 0908). The London office also deals with enquiries from **Ireland**, which does not have its own GNTO branch.

In **Australia** the GNTO can be reached c/o the German-Australian Chamber of Industry and Commerce, PO Box 1461, Sydney NSW 2001 (tel: 02-8296-0488). For **New Zealand**, the nearest tourist office is based in Australia.

Tourist offices in major cities:
Berlin
Europa-Center Budapester Strasse, D-10787 Berlin (tel: 030/25 00 25)
Bonn
Windeckerstrasse 2, D-53103 Bonn (tel: 0228/77 50 00)
Hamburg
Steinstrasse 7, D-20095 Hamburg (tel: 040/30 05 13 00)
Köln
Verkehrsamt Am Dom, D-50667 Köln (tel: 0221/30 400)
Munich
Sendlinger Strasse 1, D-80331 München (tel: 089/2 33 03 00)

Taking in the fantastic view from Jenna Mountain, Berchtesgaden

Walking and hiking
There are more than 190,000km (117,990 miles) of walks in Germany. Detailed information can be obtained from the Verband Deutscher Gebirgs- und Wandervereine, Wilhelmshöher Allee 157–159, D-34121 Kassel (tel: 0561/9 38 730; www.wanderverband.de

The Deutscher Alpenverein, Von-Kahr-Strasse 2–4, D-80997 München (tel: 089/14 00 30; www.alpenverein.de), can advise on hiking in the Alps and organizes a number of mountaineering courses.

HOTELS

These recommended hotels are divided into three price brackets, for a double bedroom with breakfast for two:
(€) = budget: up to €80
(€€) = moderate: €80–€160
(€€€) = expensive: over €160

BERLIN

Adlon (€€€)
*Unter den Linden 77, D-10117 Berlin
tel: 030-22610; fax: 030-2261 2222;
www.hotel-adlon.de*
This hotel is extremely expensive, but even a brief stay at Berlin's historic Adlon is the kind of once-in-a-lifetime experience that can't be measured in terms of money. All-embracing luxury and comforts.

Charlottenburger Hof (€–€€)
*Stuttgarter Platz 14, D-10627 Berlin
tel: 030-329070; fax: 030-323 3723*
In a very convenient location (opposite the Charlottenburg S-Bahn station), basic but adequate facilities and the friendly staff make this an excellent budget hotel choice.

Residenz (€€)
*Meinekestrasse 9, D-10719 Berlin
tel: 030-884430; fax: 030-882 4726;
www.hotel-residenz.com*
The high-ceilinged rooms within this elegant turn-of-the-20th-century building give guests a sense of Berlin's pre-war beauty. Many art nouveau decorative features, particularly in the highly-regarded restaurant 'Grand Cru'.

NORTHWEST GERMANY

Benther Berg (€€)
*Vogelsangstrasse 18, D-30952 Ronnenberg-Benthe, Hannover tel: 05108-64060;
fax: 05108-64050; www.hotel-benker-berg.de*
Friendly, comfortable country-house hotel (with a modern extension). The extensive grounds spill over into woodland. Bus and S-Bahn bring you into central Hannover.

Kastens Luisenhof (€€–€€€)
*Luisenstrasse 1-3, D-30159 Hannover
tel: 0511-30440; fax: 0511-304 4807;
www.kastens-luisenhof.de*
Hannover's oldest hotel is also one of its best-managed and most stylish, furnished with antiques. Its restaurant is also one of Hannover's best.

Mittelweg (€€)
*Mittelweg 59, D-20149 Hamburg
tel: 040-414101-0; fax: 040-41410120
www.hotel-mittelweg.de*
An elegant turn-of-the-20th-century city mansion which has been tastefully converted into a charming hotel, with modern comforts and old-fashioned touches.

Ringhotel Jensen (€€)
*An der Obertrave 4-5, D-23552 Lübeck
tel: 0451-702490; fax: 0451-73386;
www.ringhotel-jensen.de*
One of Lübeck's old city mansions, a fine stepped-gable building directly overlooking the Trave River, has now been converted into a very comfortable hotel and restaurant. Most of the city's historic sights are a walk away.

Romantik-Hotel Altes Gymnasium (€€)
*Süderstrasse 2–10, 25813 Husum
tel: 04841-8330; fax: 04841-83312;
www.altes-gymnasium.de*
This former school is one of the most luxurious hotels on this stretch of Germany's North Sea coast. The red-brick exterior may be somewhat forbidding, but inside the building, discipline ends at the reception desk, and from then on it's all hedonism.

Strandhotel Blankenese (€€)
*Strandweg 13, D-22587 Hamburg
tel: 040-866230-0; fax: 040-864936;
www.strand-hotel.de*
A beautiful, fussily façaded art nouveau (Jugendstil) villa. Insist on a room overlooking the Elbe—if you can back your claim with a maritime connection it'll help.

24hours hotel (€€)
*Paul-Dessau-Strrasse 2, D-22761 Hamburg
tel: 040-855 07 0; fax: 040-855 07;
www.24hours-hotel.com*
Trendy boutique hotel appealing to the young-at-heart, with bright decor inspired by the 1960s and 1970s.

THE RHINELAND

Hotel Burg Reichenstein (€–€€)
*Burg Reichenstein, D-55413
Trechtingshausen tel: 06721-6101; fax:
06721-6198; www.hotel-burg-reichenstein.de*
This isn't the most luxurious of the castle hotels of the Rhine but it's unbeatable value, and includes a resident headless ghost if you're lucky. The rooms are large to immense in size, some with four-poster beds, and furnished in eccentric fashion. In good weather you can dine on a terrace above the Rhine.

Hotel im Wassterturm (€€€)
*Kaygasse 2, D-50676 Köln
tel: 0221-200 80; fax: 0221-200 8888;
www.hotel-im-wasserturm.de*
Cutting-edge accommodation in a circular 19th-century listed water tower with quiet, landscaped gardens and sumptuous ultramodern decor.

Rheinhotel Dreesen (€€–€€€)
*Rheinstrasse 45-49, Bad Godesberg, D-53179
Bonn tel: 0228-82020; fax: 0228-820 2153;
www.rheinhoteldreesen.de*
The gardens of this hotel extend down to the river and there's a delightful 'chestnut-tree garden' with sliding roof for all-weather summer dining. Insist on a room with Rhine views.

Ringhotel Central (€–€€)
*Kirchstrasse 6, D-65385 Rüdesheim am
Rhein tel: 06722-9120; fax: 06722-2807;
www.centralhotel.net*
An attractive house, with steep eaves, dormer and oriel windows. Within, modern comforts blend with traditional touches. The restaurant serves Rhineland specialities.

280

CENTRAL GERMANY

Residenz Domus (€€)
Erzbergerstrasse 1-5, D-34117 Kassel
tel: 0561-703330; fax: 0561-70333498;
email: info@hotel-domus-kassel.de
A stylish, comfortable hotel, retaining most of
its art nouveau features. It has a glass-domed
winter garden and a French-influenced
restaurant that are among the best in Kassel.

Dornröschenschloss Sababurg (€€)
Im Reinhardswald, D-34369 Hofgeismar
tel: 05671-8080; fax: 05671-808200;
www.domroeschenschloss-sababurg.de
This hotel is said to have inspired the Grimm
brothers' story of *Sleeping Beauty*. It's a little
self-consciously romantic, but comfortable.
The surrounding forest provides in-season
game for the (romantic, of course) restaurant.

Kaiserworth (€€)
Markt 3, D-38640 Goslar/Harz
tel: 05321-7090; fax: 05321-709345;
www.kaiserworth.de
A 15th-century guildhall that has been
converted into a hotel. Some rooms have four-
posters. In fine weather, you can dine on the
arcaded terrace.

Kempinski Hotel Gravenbruch (€€€)
D-63263 Neu Isenburg, Frankfurt-am-Main
tel: 069-38988-0; fax: 069-38988-900;
www.kempinski-frankfurt.dc
One of Germany's finest countryhouse hotels,
set in its own 14ha (36-acre) park. It also has
an extremely fine restaurant, wellness and
leisure centre, making it a popular weekend
break destination.

Mozart (€€–€€€)
Parkstrasse 17, D-60322 Frankfurt-am-Main
tel: 069-1568060; fax: 069-1568061;
www.hotelmozart.de
Mozart and his music are the motif of this
suitably harmonious city hotel. Rooms are
decorated and furnished throughout in
exquisite taste.

Zur Krone (€–€€)
Osterstrasse 30, D-31785 Hameln
tel: 05151 9070; fax: 05151-907217;
www.hotelzurkrone.de
Request a room in the main building of this
fine old half-timbered Hameln hotel. Central
location and a very good restaurant.

EASTERN GERMANY

Balance Hotel Leipzig Alte Messe (€–€€)
Breslauerstrasse 33, D-04299 Leipzig
tel: 0341-86790; fax: 0341-867 9444;
www.balance.de
A smart, functional city hotel. It offers special
rates at the weekend which places this
otherwise middle bracket hotel in the 'budget' category. All rates include LVB-Ticket for
free public transportation.

Bülow Residenz (€€€)
Rähnitzgasse 19, D-01097 Dresden
tel: 0351-800 30; fax: 0351-800 3100;
www.beulow-residenz.de
Small palatial hotel in a beautiful baroque

house at the heart of old Dresden. Facilities
include a beautiful courtyard, a cosy cellar-
bar and an intimate restaurant serving
regional specialties.

Haus Hainstein (€)
Am Hainstein 16, D-99817 Eisenach
tel: 03691-2420; fax: 03691-242109;
www.hainstein.de
Magnificent views of the Wartburg castle and
the surrounding countryside can be enjoyed
from many of the rooms and the garden-ter-
race of this turn-of-the-20th-century mansion.

Mercure Grand Hotel (€€)
Hafenstrasse 27–31, D-01662 Meissen
tel: 03521-72250; fax: 03521-722904;
email: H1699@accor-hotels.com;
www.mercure.com
Just a short walk from the town is one of
Meissen's few elegant villas, converted into a
stylish, luxury hotel in 1993, with a superb
restaurant. Porcelain tiles smother the fussy
façade, and elegant Jugendstil touches are in
evidence everywhere. There is a shuttle service from the hotel to Dresden airport.

Parkhotel Juliushof (€)
D-14806 Gross-Briesen
tel: 033846-40 245: 033846-40 245
www.hotel-juliushof.de
Simple log-cabln-style accommodation,south
of Brandenburg in the heart of pine forests.
Ideal for outdoor types and nature lovers.

Russischer Hof (€€)
Goetheplatz 2, D-99423 Weimar
tel: 03643-7740; fax: 03643-774840;
www.russischerhof.com
Now nearly 200 years old, this central luxury
hotel was once an early focus of cultural life in
Weimar. It was here that the composer Franz
Liszt founded his 'Neu-Weimar Verein' in 1854.
Heinrich Heine, Clara and Robert Schumann,
Hector Berlioz, Ivan Turgenev and Richard
Wagner have all stayed here.

Kempinski Hotel Taschenbergpalais (€€€)
Taschenberg 3, D-01067 Dresden
tel: 0351-49120; fax: 0351-4912812;
www.kempinski-dresden.de
This is one of Eastern Germany's finest
hotels. It is in a reconstructed city palace
that once housed members of the Saxon royal
family. Everything at the Kempinski is palatial, from the extensive rooms and suites to
the two restaurants.

SOUTHWEST GERMANY

Burg Hornberg (€€)
D-74865 Neckarzimmern am Neckar
tel: 06261-92460; fax: 06261-924644;
email: info@burg-hotel-hornberg.de
Ask for a room with a view overlooking the
river and book a window table in the
restaurant, where wines from the castle's
own vineyard are served.

Die Hirschgasse (€€–€€€)
Hirschgasse 3, D-69120 Heidelberg
tel: 06221 454-0 ; fax: 06221 454-11;
www.hirschgasse.de
Cosy, romantic hotel in one of Heidelberg's

oldest houses. Past guests include Mark Twain and Count Bismarck, who carved his name into a 200-year-old table in the hotel's historic Mensurstube restaurant.

Der Kleine Prinz (€€€)
Lichtentalerstrasse 36, D-76530 Baden-Baden
tel: 07221-346600; fax: 07221-346 6059;
www.derkleineprinz.de
The city's most original and friendliest hotel. Each room is decorated in an individual style, ranging from baroque and Biedermeier to American modern.

Romantik Hotel Zum Ritter St. Georg (€€€)
Hauptstrasse 178, D-69117 Heidelberg
tel: 06221-1350; fax: 06221-135230;
email: info@ritter-heidelberg.de
This is Heidelberg's most famous hotel. The Renaissance façade sets the style for the snug interior, which qualifies this hotel in every sense for that description 'Romantik'.

Zum roten Bären (€€)
Oberlinden 12, D-79098 Freiburg
tel: 0761-387870; fax: 0761-387 8717;
www.rote-baeren.de
Germany's oldest hostelry (dating from 1311), the 'Red Bear' is now an impressive baroque-style luxury hotel, although a beer tavern still nestles within its ancient walls.

NORTHERN BAVARIA

Bischofshof (€€)
Krauterermarkt 3, D-93047 Regensburg
tel: 0941-58460; fax: 0941-584 6146;
www.hotel-bischofshof.de
This hotel is a former bishop's palace with spacious rooms and a central cobbled courtyard. One of the suites incorporates part of a Roman gateway.

Eisenhut (€€€)
Herrngasse 3-7, D-91541 Rothenburg ob der Tauber tel: 09861-7050;
fax: 09861-70545;
www.eisenhut.de
This central hotel has a restaurant of note, a piano bar and a leafy beer-garden. A luxurious retreat from the crowds of tourists.

Goldener Anker (££)
Opernstrasse 6, D-95444 Bayreuth
tel: 0921-65051; fax: 0921-65500;
www.anker-bayreuth.de
Throughout the opera season you will have difficulty booking a room. The central location and a very good restaurant are strong recommendations.

Hotel-Weinhaus Steichele (€–€€)
Knorrstrasse 2–8, D-90402 Nürnberg
tel: 0911-202280; fax: 0911-221914;
www.steichele.de
A 19th-century wine merchant's warehouse transformed into a simple but comfortable hotel. The hotel restaurant and wine tavern serve authentic Franconian fare, including Nürnberg sausages.

Wilder Mann (€–€€)
Am Rathausplatz, D-94032 Passau
tel: 0851-35071; fax: 0851-31712;
www.wilder-mann.com

The guests' register of this historic hotel reads like an historical *Who's Who*. The rooms range from 'comfortable' to unashamedly luxurious.

MUNICH AND THE ALPS

Munich

Cortiina (€€–€€€)
Ledererstrasse 8, D-80331 München
tel: 089-24 22 49-0; fax: 089-24 22 49-100;
www.cortiina.com
This chic, minimalist hotel draws the smart set to its elegant rooms and sophisticated but relaxed cocktail bar, and business clientele to its conference suites. It is also well placed for the opera, theatres, restaurants and the fashionable boutiques of the city centre.

Gästehaus Englischer Garten (€)
Liebergesellstrasse 8, D-80802 München
tel: 089-383 94 10; fax: 089-383 94 133;
www.hotelenglischergarten.de
This simple, characterful guest house, with just 12 rooms, is a veritable oasis in the city centre—housed in an old windmill on the edge of the English Garden.

Kempinski Hotel Vier Jahreszeiten (€€€)
Maximilianstrasse 17, D-80539 München
tel: 089-21 25-0; fax: 089-21 25-2000;
www.kempinski-vierjahreszeiten.de
Munich's top hotel the 'Four Seasons' was established as a guest house for royalty visiting King Maximilian II and is still used to accommodate visiting dignitaries. It is on the city's most exclusive shopping street and prides itself on its quality of service and traditional elegance.

The Alps

Altes Fährhaus (€–€€)
An der Isarlust 1, Bad Tölz
tel: 08041-240 94; fax: 08041-722 70;
www.altesfaehrhaus-toelz.de
The old ferry boathouse enjoys a Beautiful location on the bank of the River Isar. It has a top-notch restaurant and five traditional-style bedrooms, all with balconies over the river.

Bayern (€€–€€€)
Neureuthstrasse 23, D-83684 Tegernsee
tel: 08022-1820; fax: 08022-182100;
www.hotel-bayern.de
Spectacular views of the mountain-ringed water from the terrace, pretty pink-toned restaurant and bedrooms in the main house.

Wittelsbacher Hof (€€)
Von-Brug-Strasse 24, D-82467 Garmisch-Partenkirchen tel: 08821-53096;
fax: 08821-57312;
www.wittelsbacher-hof.com
There are fine views of the Zugspitze from this hotel. The restaurant serves cuisine with a Bavarian touch.

Zur Linde (€€)
D-83256 Fraueninsel im Chiemsee 1
tel: 08054-90366; fax: 08054-7299;
email: hotel.linde.fraueninsel@t-online.de;

www.inselhotel-zurlinde.de
You have to catch a boat to this delightful
hotel, on a tiny island. Just the place to be
marooned in.

RESTAURANTS

BERLIN

Pan Asia (€€)
*Rosenthalter Strasse 38 tel: 030-27 90 88
11*
Tired of hearty German fare? The join the chic
set for sensational Thai, Vietnamese and
Japanese cuisine in the über-trendy minimalist
place in the hip Hackeesches Markt district.
Zur Nolle (€)
*Georgenstrasse –S-Bahnbogen 203
tel: 030-208-2645*
Many features still survive from Berlin's
swinging 1920s, one of which is a backlit
ceiling.

Bars/cafés

Eierschale (€)
All-Treptow 14–17 tel: 030-533 7370
The Eierschale café-restaurant has live music
and a Sunday jazz-brunch.
Friedrichstadtpalast (€€)
Friedrichstrasse 107 tel: 030-2326 2326
A historic Berlin variety and revue theatre; it
is the biggest in Europe, and has world-class
acts performing here.

NORTHWEST GERMANY

Fischereihafen-Restaurant Hamburg (€€)
*Grosse Elbstrasse 143, Hamburg
tel: 040-381-816*
The morning's catch lands on the lunchtime
menu. The experience is not cheap (try the
Fischerhaus at the Fish Market, Fischmarkt
14, if budget-dining) but it's memorable. The
menu offers traditional as well as
international dishes, including grilled zander
(perch-pike).
Georgenhof Sterns Restaurant (€€)
*Herrenhäuser Kirchweg 20, Hannover
tel: 0511-702244*
In fine weather, tables are laid on the shady
terrace, overlooking a pool and fountains.
The excellent menu is urbane and
international.
Landhaus Ammann (€€€)
*Hildesheimer Strasse 185, Hannover
tel: 0511-830818*
Hannover's best restaurant is in the skilful
hands of one of Germany's finest chefs,
Helmut Amman. He insists on the freshest
produce and grows his own herbs.
Landhaus Scherrer (€€€)
*Elbchaussee 130, Hamburg
tel: 040-8801325; www.landhausscherrer.de*
A select restaurant, where you'll dine with the
city's élite (publishers, mostly).

THE RHINELAND

Hotellerie Hubertus (€€)
Metzer Strasse 1, Tholey tel: 06853-91030
The imaginative dishes (Franco-German with
an international touch) are served either in a
splendid, vaulted dining room or in the rustic
Marktstube (Market tavern).
Das Kleine Stapelhäuschen (€)
Fischmarkt 1-3, Köln tel: 0211-257-7862
The Stapelhäuschen is a quaint, traditional
tavern-restaurant. The cooking is no-frills
Rhineland; try the Sauerbraten with bread
dumplings.
Schlosshotel Kommende Ramersdorf (€€)
*Oberkasseler Strasse 10, Bonn
tel: 0228-440734*
The menu is French but the setting is noble
German: The restaurant is in a converted wing
of a half-timbered, turreted Schloss.
Zum Schiffchen (€)
Hafenstrasse 5, Düsseldorf tel: 0211-132421
The tavern, which has been in business since
1628, still brews its own beer, served with
solid home-cooked Rhineland fare such as
grilled marinated beef.

CENTRAL GERMANY

Brückenkeller (€€€)
*Schützenstrasse 6, Frankfurt-am-Main
tel: 069-298-0070*
This is Frankfurt's best restaurant, and can be
found in a 17th-century vaulted cellar. The
menu is German-international, and the wine list
is cosmic.
Die Worth (€€)
Markt 3, D-38640 Goslar tel: 05321-709-0
This rustic restaurant, part of Hotel
Kaiserworth, serves delicious regional dishes
on trestle tables in an atmospheric stone
crypt with vaulted ceiling and stained-glass
windows. Try the local specialty *Harzer
Blaubeer Schmandschnitzel*—pork escalope
with blueberry-cream sauce.
Goldener Karpfen (€€)
Simpliziusbrunnen 1, Fulda tel: 0661-86800
This elegant and inviting restaurant is fitted
out with snugly comfortable furnishings and
discreet lighting.
Hotel Gude (€€)
*Frankfurterstrasse 299, Kassel
tel: 0561-48050*
The Hotel Gude's Pfeffermühle (Pepper Pot)
restaurant serves a range of international and
traditional German dishes.
Zum Gemalten Haus (€)
*Schweizerstrasse 67, Frankfurt-am-Main
tel: 069-614-559*
This is the most attractive of the countless
cider taverns of Frankfurt's Sachsenhausen
district. It is noisy and friendly and excellent
value for money.

EASTERN GERMANY

Auerbachs Keller (€€)
Mädlerpassage, Leipzig tel: 0341-216-100

283

Famous as the setting for part of Goethe's *Faust*. The cuisine, solidly Saxon (lots of roast meat, rich sauces and dumplings), is excellent value and they serve interesting East German wines.

Caroussel (€€–€€€)
Rähnitzgasse 19, Dresden tel: 0351-80030
You will need to reserve well in advance for this excellent restaurant in the Hotel Bülow Residenz, one of Dresden's more sophisticated small hotels, with baroque-style furnishings and a delightful interior courtyard. The menu offers dishes blending German and Mediterranean cuisine.

Glockenhof (€€)
Grimmelgasse 4, 99817 Eisenach tel: 03691-2340; www.glockenhof.de
The Glockenhof is among Germany's leading 500 restaurants. The imaginative menu is basically Thuringian, with international flourishes. The venison stew with dumplings is a classic.

Italienisches Dörfchen (€–€€)
Theaterplatz 3, Dresden tel: 0351-498-160
An attractive, historic complex of restaurant, tavern, café and beer garden, on the banks of the Elbe, with something of a Mediterranean feel about it.

Weinhaus Uhle (€€)
Schusterstrasse 13–15, Schwerin tel: 0385-562956
Dine in style below a beautifully frescoed, chandelier-hung vaulted ceiling. The excellent menu includes a variety of memorable duck dishes.

SOUTHWEST GERMANY

Bareiss (€€€)
Gärtenbühlweg 14, Baiersbronn-Mitteltal tel: 07442-470; www.bareiss.com
One of Germany's best gourmet restaurants with Franco-German cuisine. It is a rare (and expensive) dining experience.

Grimm's Märchen (€€)
G7, 17, Mannheim tel: 0621-103636
Grimm's Märchen is one of Mannheim's most affordable and interesting restaurants. On chilly evenings a welcoming fire blazes in the hearth.

Rappen (€)
Münsterplatz 13, Freiburg im Breisgau tel: 0761-31353
This restaurant has a wood-panelled dining room and also a small terrace which looks out onto Freiburg's market square and famous Münster. The wine list includes some interesting Black Forest wines.

Roter Ochsen (€)
Hauptstrasse 217, Heidelberg tel: 06221-20977
Of all Heidelberg's celebrated student taverns this is one of the best, a judgment confirmed by the parade of world dignitaries who have left their names on autographed photos or in the visitors' book.

Stuttgarter Stäffele (€–€€)
Buschlestrasse 2A/B (corner of

Augustenstrasse), Stuttgart tel: 0711-617276
You won't find better Swabian cooking than at this two-restaurant address. Take your pick from the large or the small restaurant, or opt for the wine-cellar, where more than 250 Württemberg varieties of wine are stored.

NORTHERN BAVARIA

Säumerhof (€€–€€€)
Steinberg 32, Grafenau tel: 08552-408-990; www.saeumerhof.de
An excellent gourmet restaurant; book well ahead, particularly if your visit is during the hunting season, when venison and game-birds feature prominently on the menu.

Schlenkerla (€–€€)
Beim Tiergärtnertor 3, Nürnberg tel: 0911-225-474
A good place to eat delicious Nürnberg sausages, made daily on the premises. The Franconian smoked beer (*Rauchbier*), straight from the barrel, is home-brewed, and it comes with a home-made cheese.

MUNICH AND THE ALPS

Munich

Nürnberger Bratwurst Glöckl am Dom (€)
Frauenplatz 9, Munich tel: 089-291945-0
The sausages served at this historic old restaurant are absolutely delicious 'Nürnberger Bratwurst', but otherwise it is quintessential Munich.

Tantris (€€€)
Johann-Fichter-Strasse 7, Munich tel: 089-361 9590; www.tantris.de
The Tantris is considered to be Munich's top restaurant. The décor is smart international, the food good enough to attract the admiration of French and American critics.

Weinhaus Neuner (€€)
Herzogspitalstrasse 8, Munich tel: 089-2603954; www.weinhaus-neuner.de
Munich's oldest wine tavern is panelled in dark oak and lit by slightly tipsy chandeliers. Venison is always an excellent bet and the steak, with Swiss-style rösti potatoes, is unbeatable.

The Alps

Reindl's Partenkirchner Hof (€€–€€€)
Bahnhofstrasse 15, Garmisch-Partenkirchen tel: 08821-943870
Chef Marianne Holzinger's menu combines Bavarian traditional excellence (particularly the sauces) with international flair. Just beneath the Zugspitze.

Residenz Heinz Winkler (€€€)
Kirchplatz 1, 83229 Aschau tel: 08052-17990; www.residenz-heinz-winkler.de
Winkler, one of Germany's top chefs, runs this superb country restaurant in part of a 300-year-old coaching inn.

Index

286

Index/Acknowledgements

288

Acknowledgements

The Automobile Association would like to thank the following photographers, libraries and associations for their assistance in the preparation of this book.

ALLSPORT UK LTD 17 JÖRG REICHARDT/BERLINER PHILHARMONIKER 15 MARY EVANS PICTURE LIBRARY 14 Beethoven, 24/5 French royalty, 25 French ruler, 26 German patricians, 27 Peasants co–opt leader, 27 Paul Rieth, 33 Friedrich Wilhelm Nietzsche, Hansel and Gretel, 75c Danzig, Ships – Hanseatic League, 120 Grimm's Red Riding Hood, 121 The Valiant Tailor, The Goose Girl, 147 Händel, 261 Ludwig II ILN 28b, 29, 237b SPECTRUM COLOUR LIBRARY LTD 14 Munich Oktoberfest, 20 Smoking chimneys, 21 BMW Black Forest, Car scrapyard, 47 Kurfürstendamm café, 167 Goethehaus, 259 Munich Oktoberfest THE BRIDGEMAN ART LIBRARY 35 People by the Pool, The Garden Café (Kirchner) TOPHAM PICTURE SOURCE 30 Breaking down the Berlin Wall WORLD PICTURES 18 Reichstag, 112 Frankfurt skyline. All remaining pictures are held in the AA's own photo library (© AA Photolibrary) with contributions from:
A BAKER 3, 4, 6,8, 9, 12, 16a, 20/1, 27c, 34, 38, 39, 42, 43, 44, 46, 50, 79, 80, 81, 82, 84, 88, 89, 90, 91, 92, 93, 95, 96, 98, 99, 100, 101, 106, 107, 113, 114, 131, 133, 166, 173, 174, 175, 177, 178, 179, 181, 183, 184b, 185, 186, 187, 189, 191, 192, 193, 195, 196/7, 198, 199, 200, 201, 202, 203, 204, 205, 208, 209, 210, 211, 212, 213, 214, 215, 217, 218, 219, 221, 222, 223, 224, 225, 226, 227, 228, 229a, 229b, 230, 231, 232, 233, 234, 235, 236, 240, 241, 242, 244, 246, 247, 248, 249a, 250, 251, 252, 253, 257, 258, 260, 261, 262, 263, 264, 265, 267, 271, 279 GETTY IMAGES/AFP 23a GETTY IMAGES/BONGARTS 23b GETTY IMAGES 23c GETTY IMAGES/SEAN GALLUP 23d P BENNETT 32t, 135c P ENTICKNAP 13a, 83 M JOURDAN 17t, 32b S McBRIDE 19tr, 43t C SAWYER 5, 7a, 7b, 31, 256 J SMITH 22b, 28t, 40t A SOUTER 22t, 49, 237t R STRANGE 240b D TRAVERSO 10, 13b, 15b, 31a, 35c, 40, 48, 51, 54, 55, 56, 57, 60, 61, 62, 63, 64, 65, 67, 68, 69, 70, 71, 73, 74, 75, 77, 105, 109, 110, 111, 117, 118, 119, 122, 123, 124, 125, 126, 127, 128, 129, 130, 134, 136, 138, 139, 140, 141, 142, 143, 144, 145, 146, 147, 148, 149, 150, 151, 152, 155, 156, 157, 158, 159, 160, 161, 162/3, 164, 165, 169, 170, 171, 184a, 270, 272

Contributors

Revision verifier: Teresa Fisher. Original copy editor: Joan Miller
Revision edit and design: Bookwork Creative Associates Limited